FAIRY TAIL

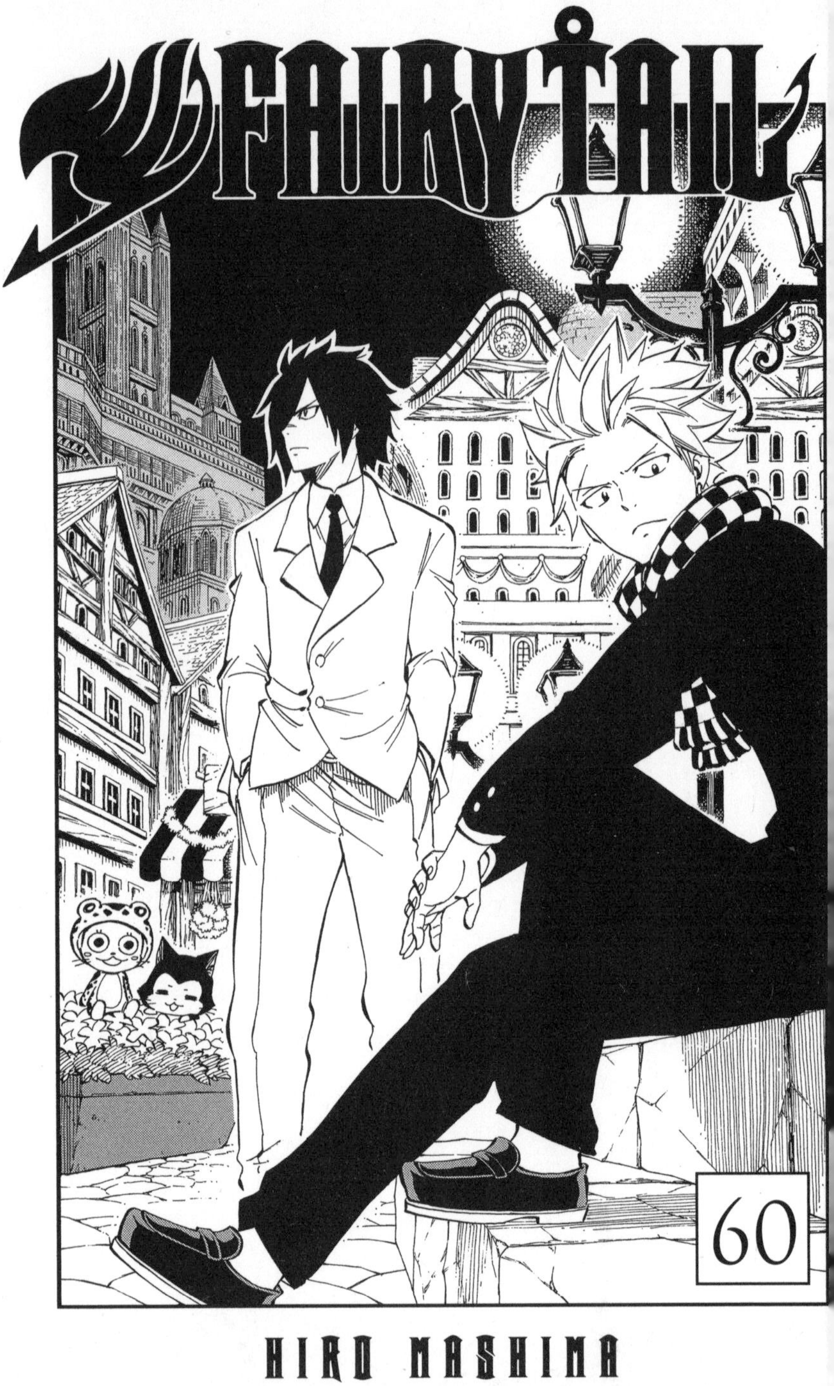
60

HIRO MASHIMA

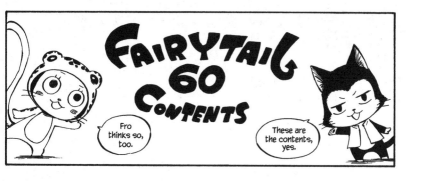

FAIRY TAIL
60
CONTENTS
These are the contents, yes.
Fro thinks so, too.

FAIRY TAIL
フェアリーテイル

Chapter 510: The Heart of Natsu

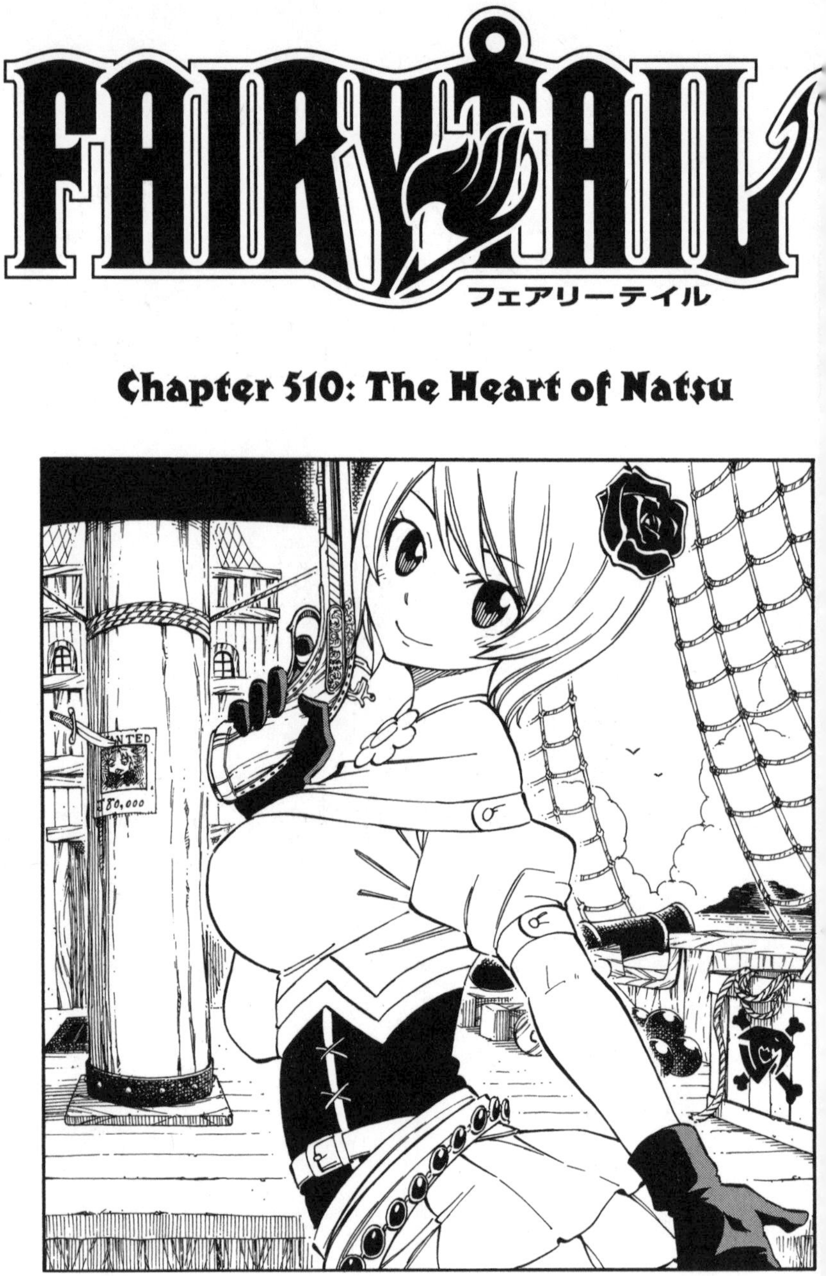

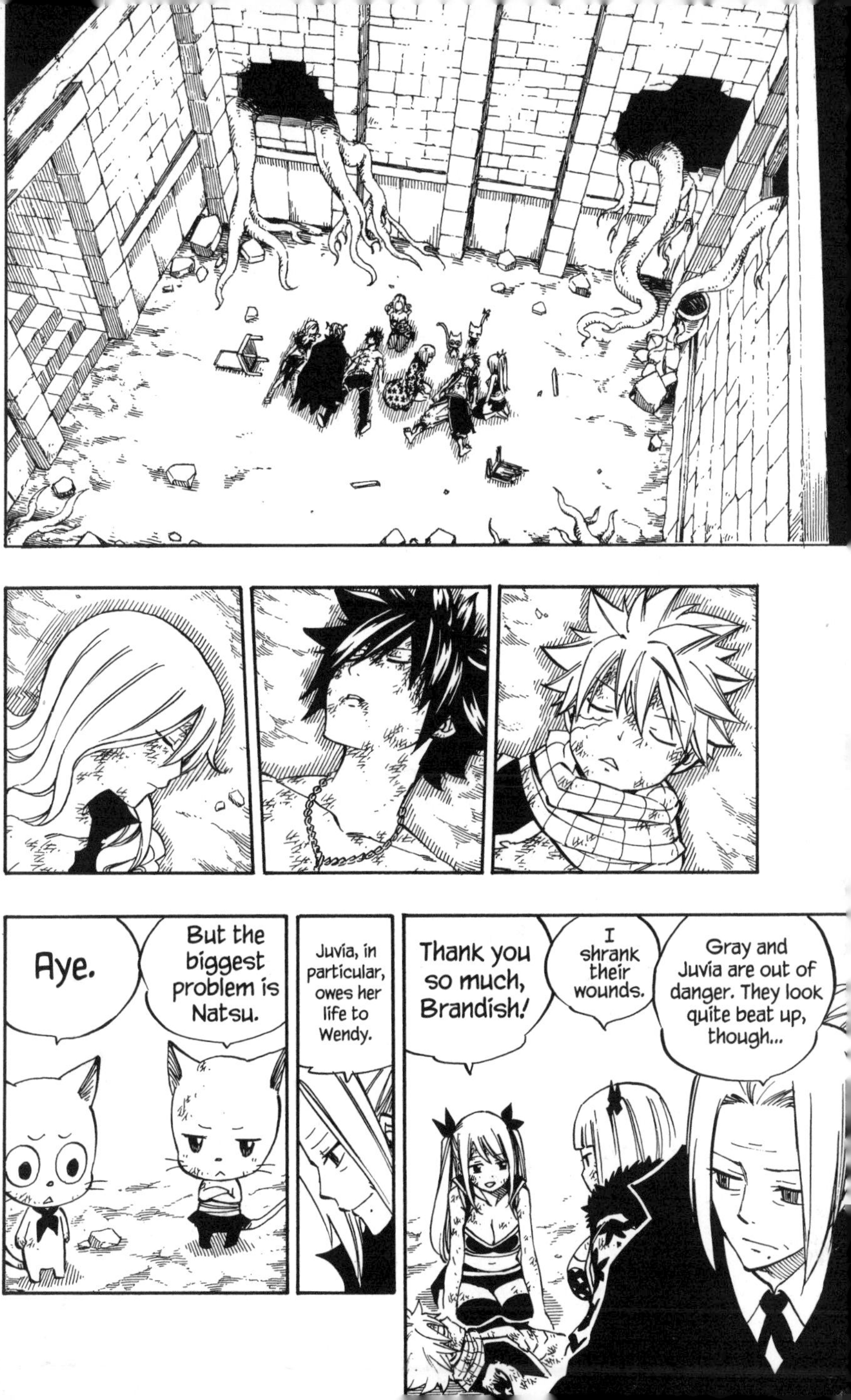
Gray and Juvia are out of danger. They look quite beat up, though...
I shrank their wounds.
Thank you so much, Brandish!
Juvia, in particular, owes her life to Wendy.
But the biggest problem is Natsu.
Aye.

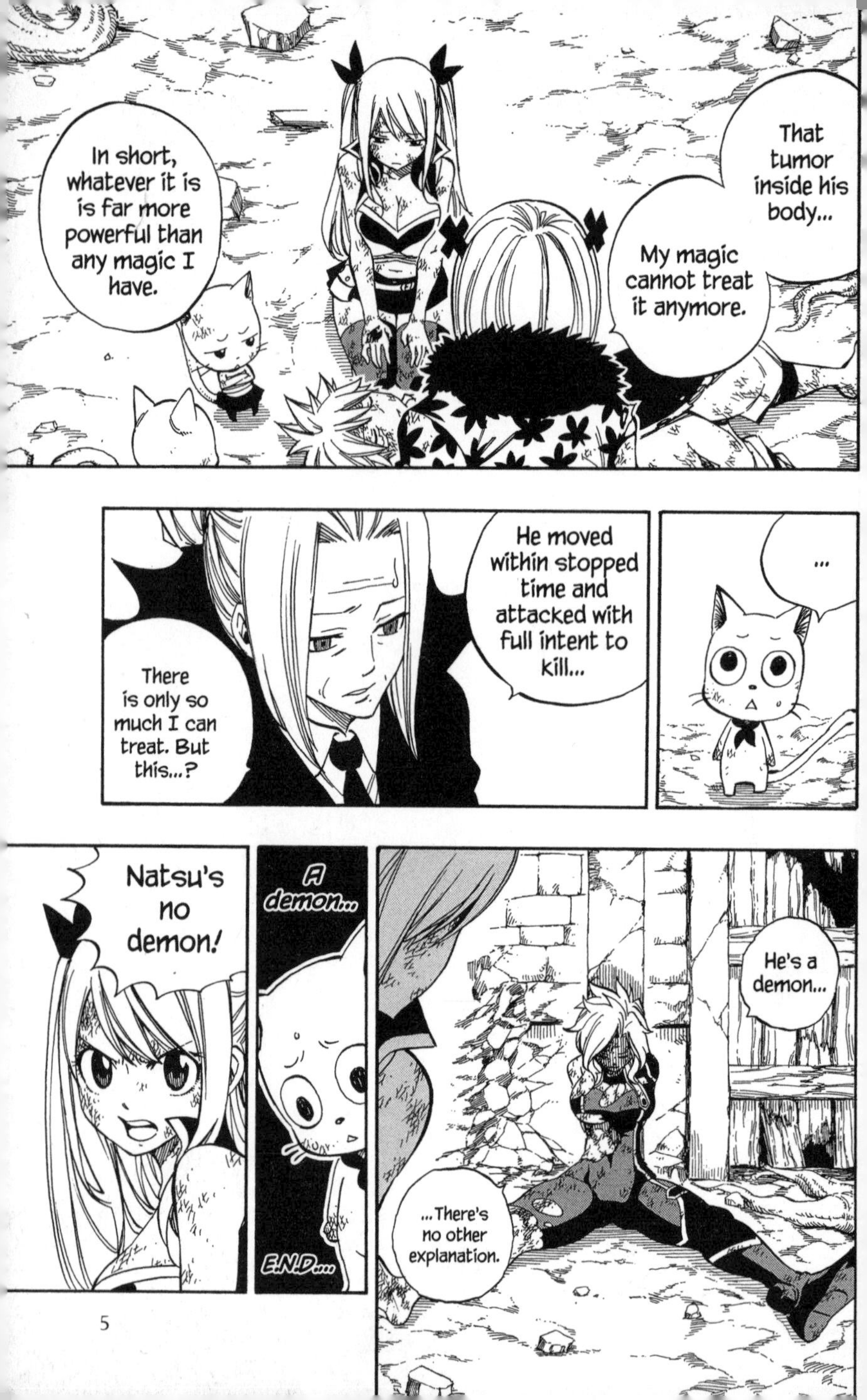
That tumor inside his body...
My magic cannot treat it anymore.
In short, whatever it is is far more powerful than any magic I have.
...
He moved within stopped time and attacked with full intent to kill...
There is only so much I can treat. But this...?
He's a demon...
...There's no other explanation.
A demon...
E.N.D....
Natsu's no demon!

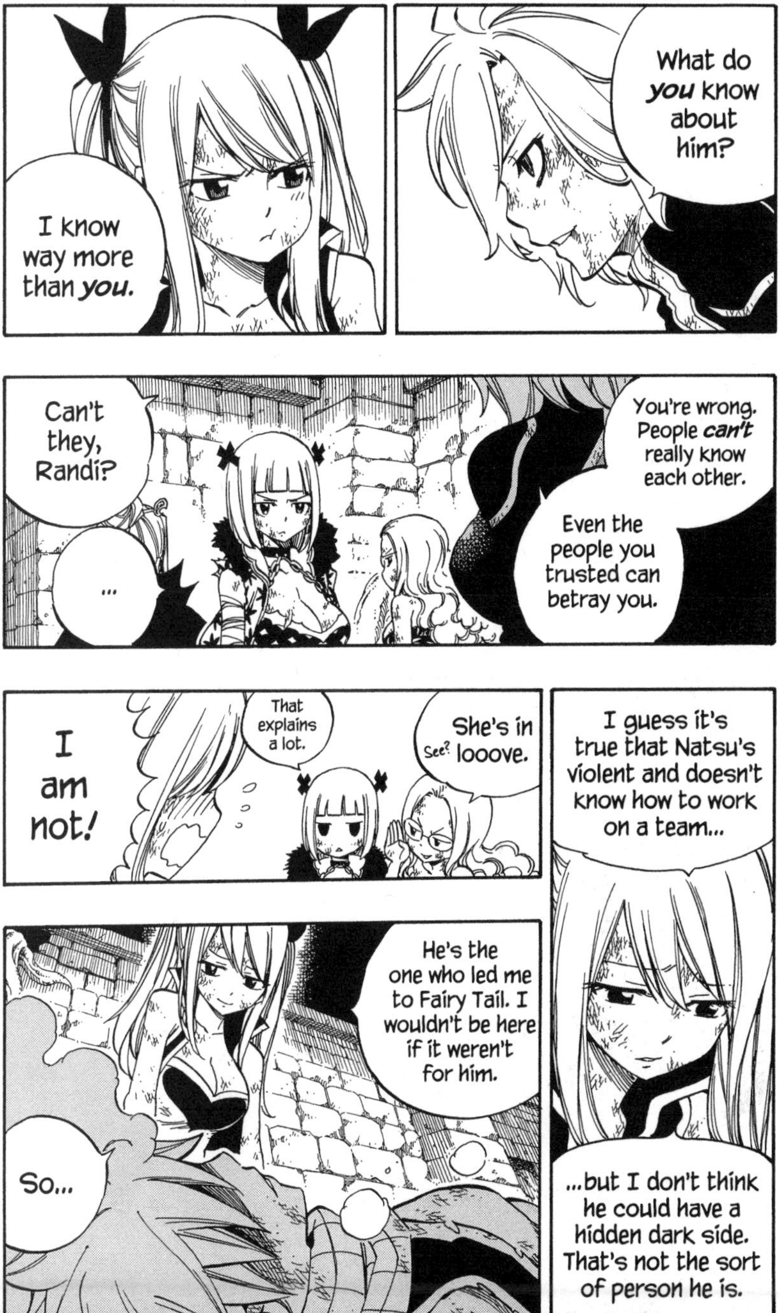

What do *you* know about him?
I know way more than *you*.
You're wrong. People *can't* really know each other.
Even the people you trusted can betray you.
Can't they, Randi?
...
I guess it's true that Natsu's violent and doesn't know how to work on a team...
...but I don't think he could have a hidden dark side. That's not the sort of person he is.
She's in looove.
See?
That explains a lot.
I am not!
He's the one who led me to Fairy Tail. I wouldn't be here if it weren't for him.
So...

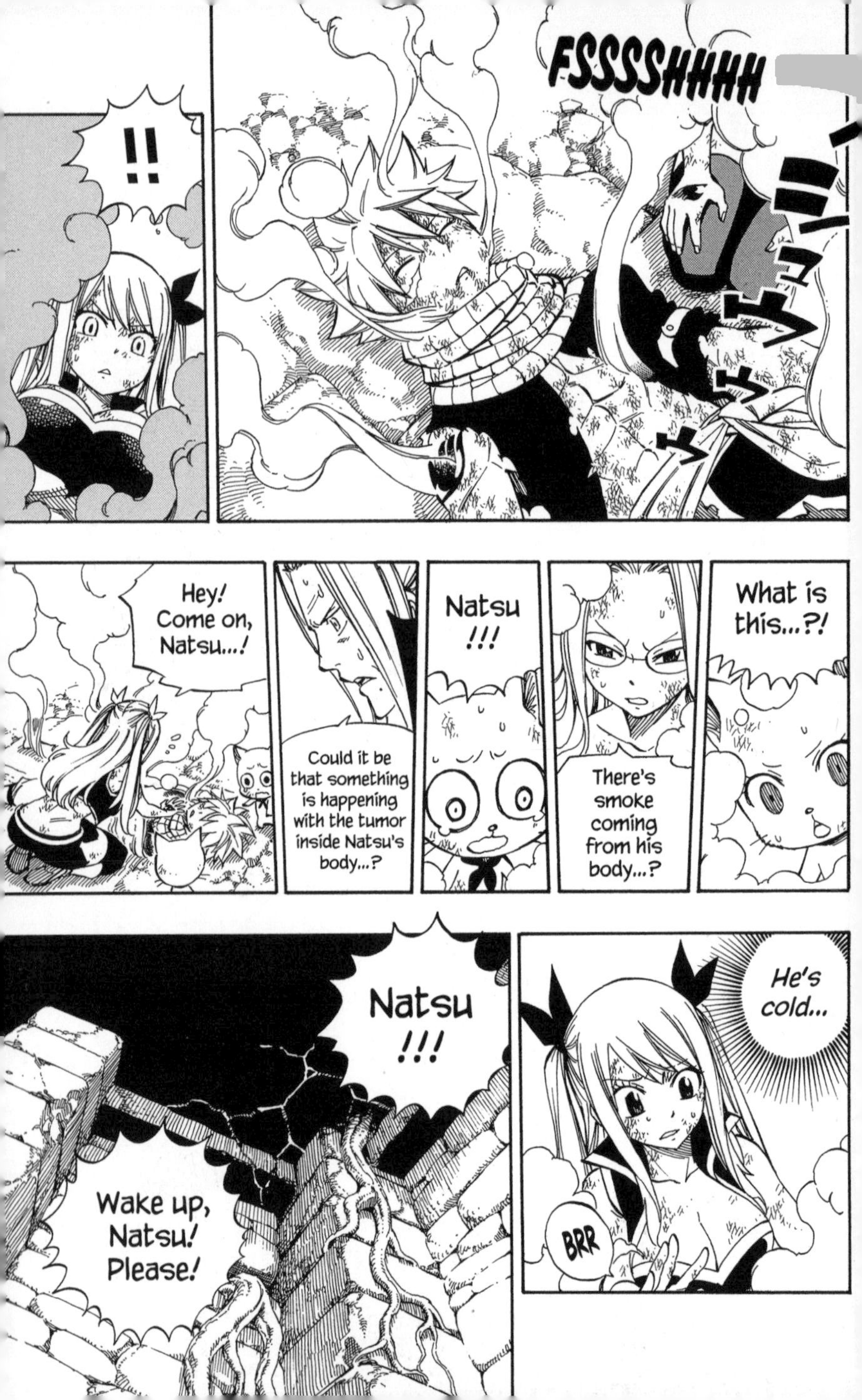
FSSSSHHHH
!!
What is this...?!
There's smoke coming from his body...?
Natsu !!!
Could it be that something is happening with the tumor inside Natsu's body...?
Hey! Come on, Natsu...!
He's cold...
BRR
Natsu !!!
Wake up, Natsu! Please!

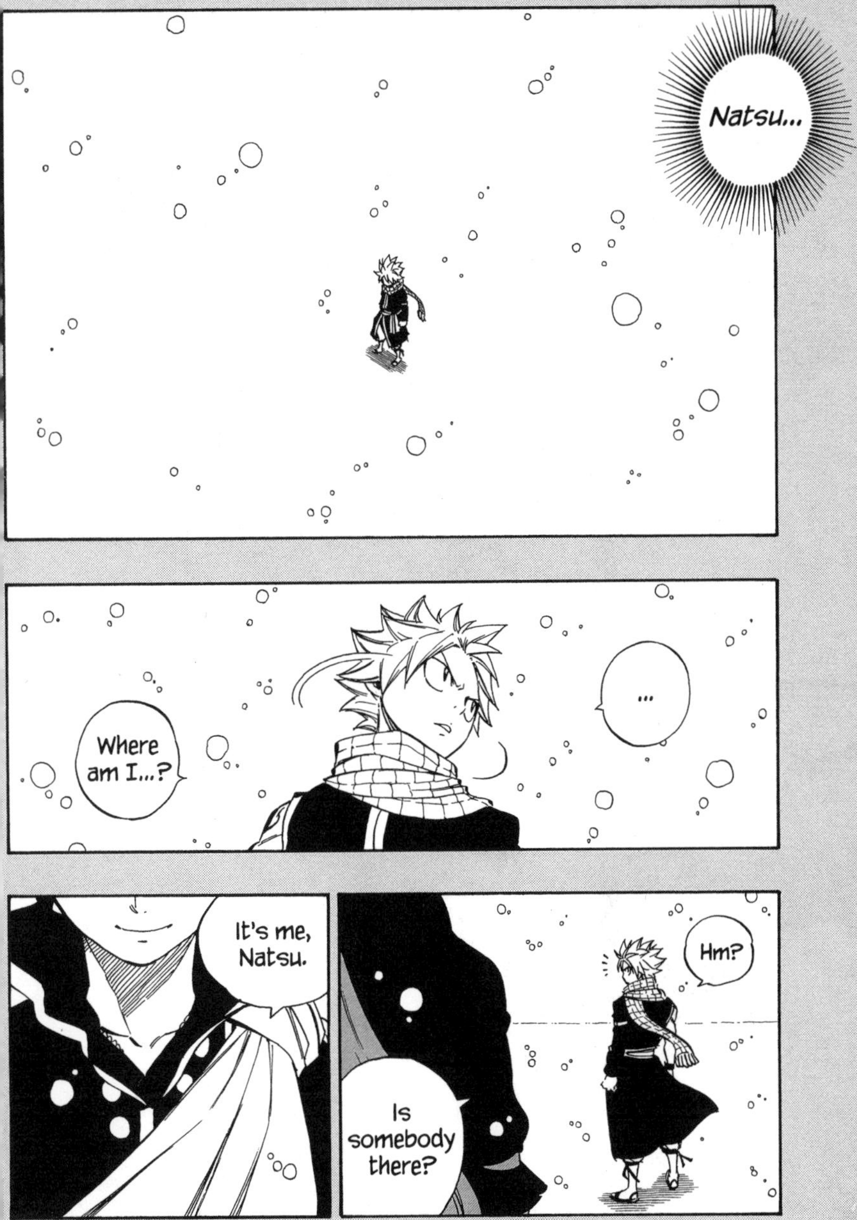

Natsu...
...
Where am I...?
Hm?
Is somebody there?
It's me, Natsu.

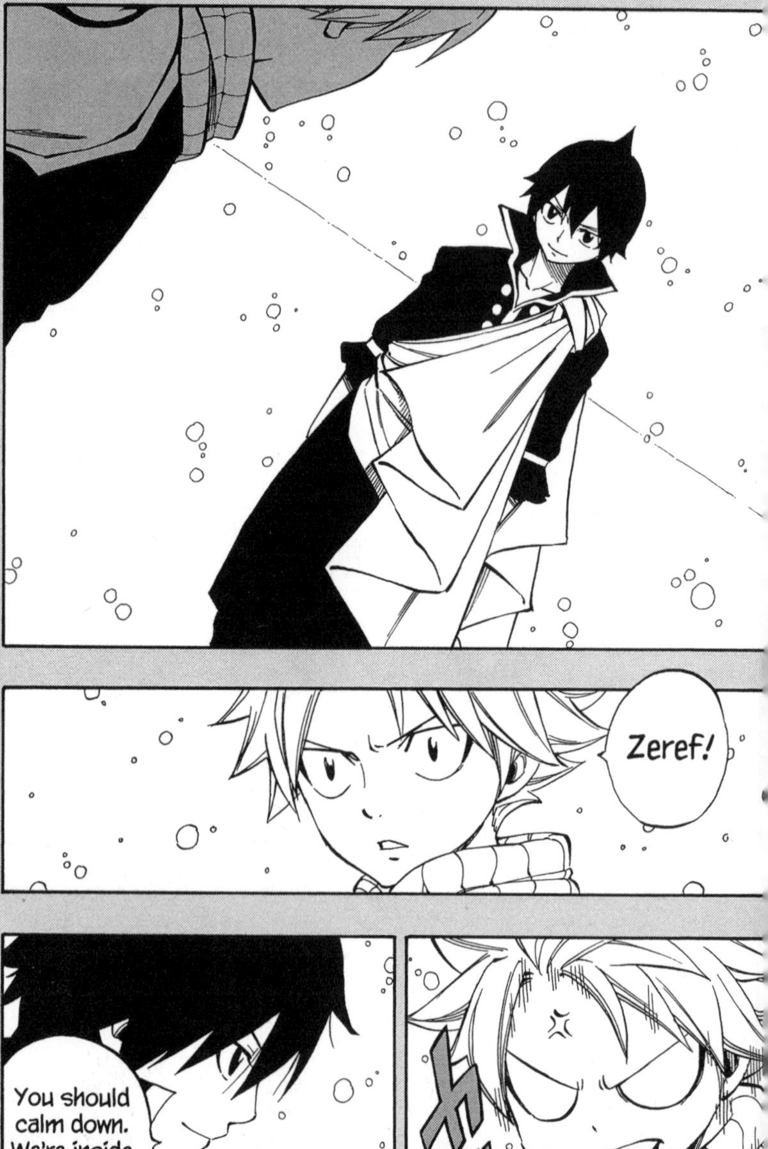
Zeref!
GRR! 14
You should calm down. We're inside your heart.

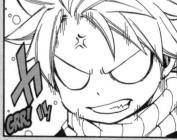

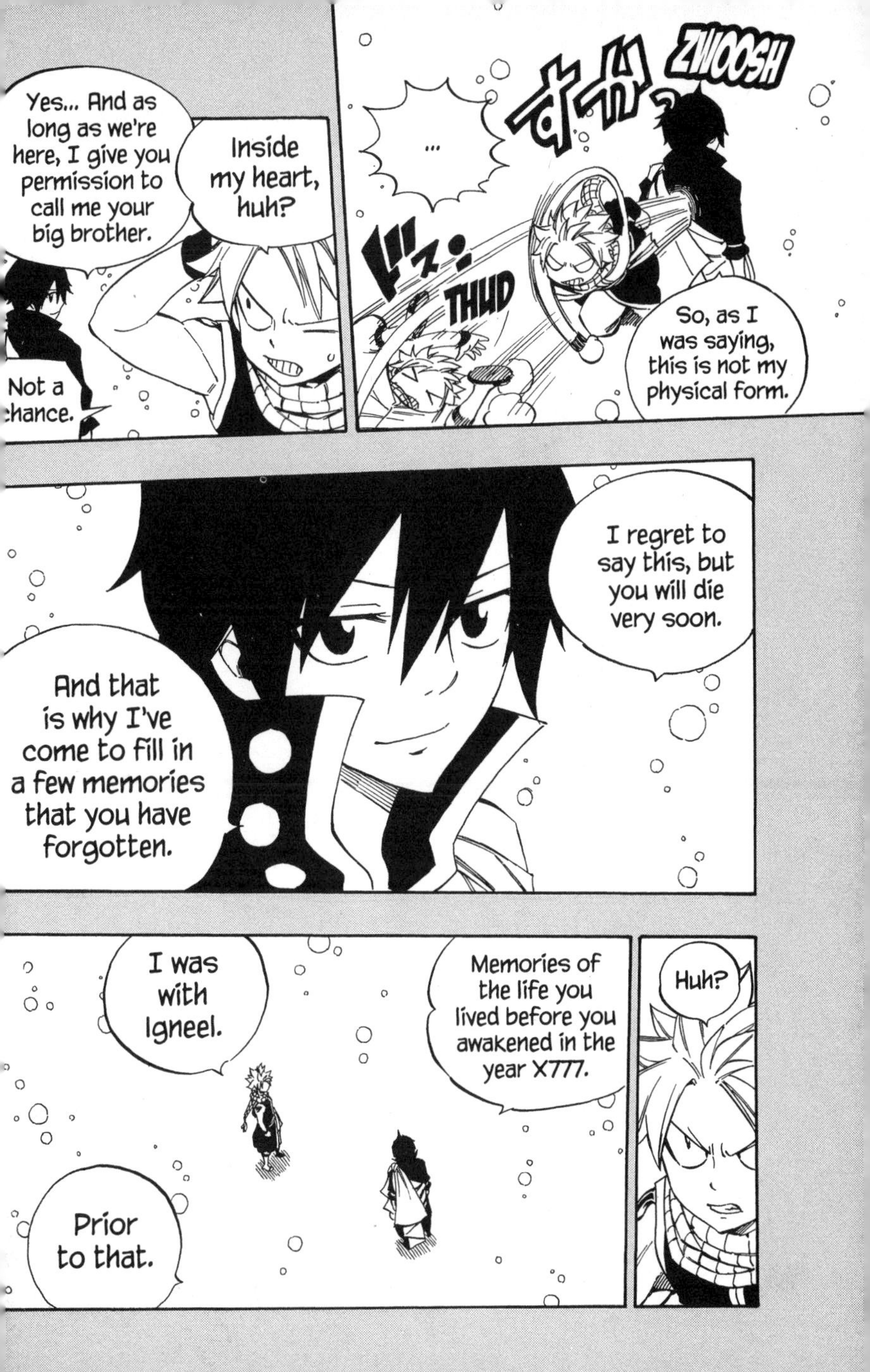

...
ZWOOSH
THUD
So, as I was saying, this is not my physical form.
Inside my heart, huh?
Yes... And as long as we're here, I give you permission to call me your big brother.
Not a chance.
I regret to say this, but you will die very soon.
And that is why I've come to fill in a few memories that you have forgotten.
Huh?
Memories of the life you lived before you awakened in the year X777.
I was with Igneel.
Prior to that.

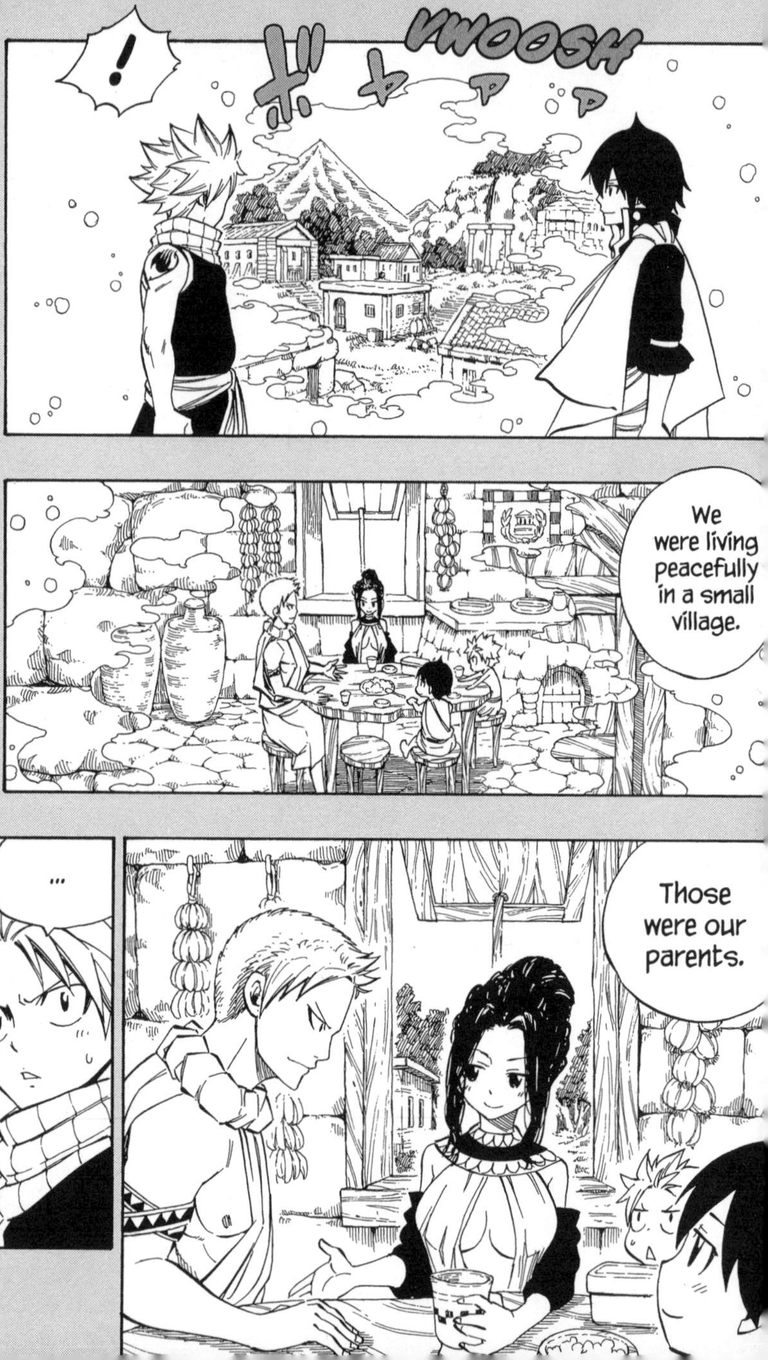
VWOOSH
!
We were living peacefully in a small village.
Those were our parents.
...

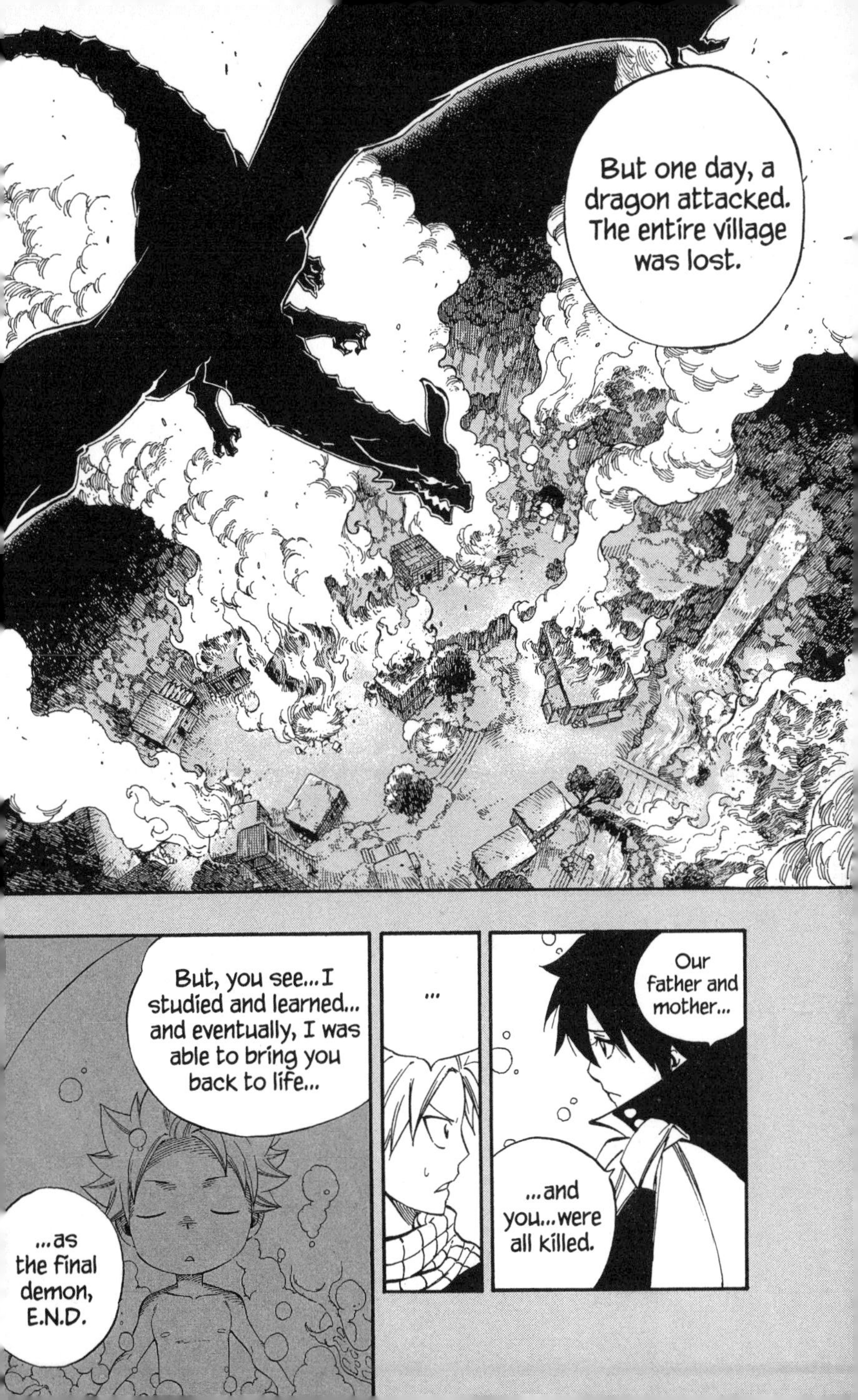
But one day, a dragon attacked. The entire village was lost.
Our father and mother...
...and you...were all killed.
...
But, you see...I studied and learned... and eventually, I was able to bring you back to life...
...as the final demon, E.N.D.

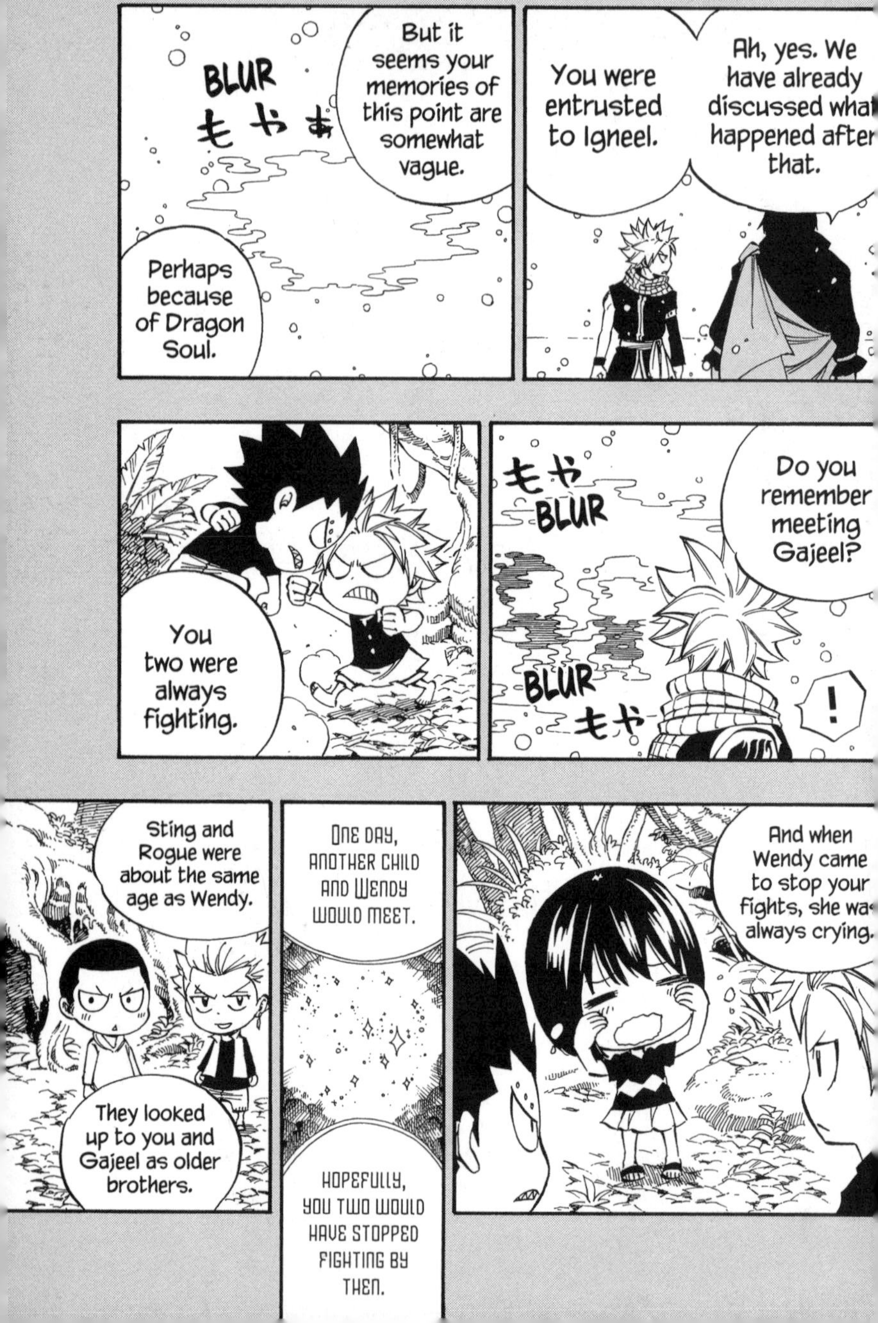
Ah, yes. We have already discussed wha happened afte that.
You were entrusted to Igneel.
But it seems your memories of this point are somewhat vague.
BLUR
もやぁ
Perhaps because of Dragon Soul.
Do you remember meeting Gajeel?
もや
BLUR
BLUR
もや
!
You two were always fighting.
And when Wendy came to stop your fights, she wa always crying.
ONE DAY, ANOTHER CHILD AND WENDY WOULD MEET.
HOPEFULLY, YOU TWO WOULD HAVE STOPPED FIGHTING BY THEN.
Sting and Rogue were about the same age as Wendy.
They looked up to you and Gajeel as older brothers.

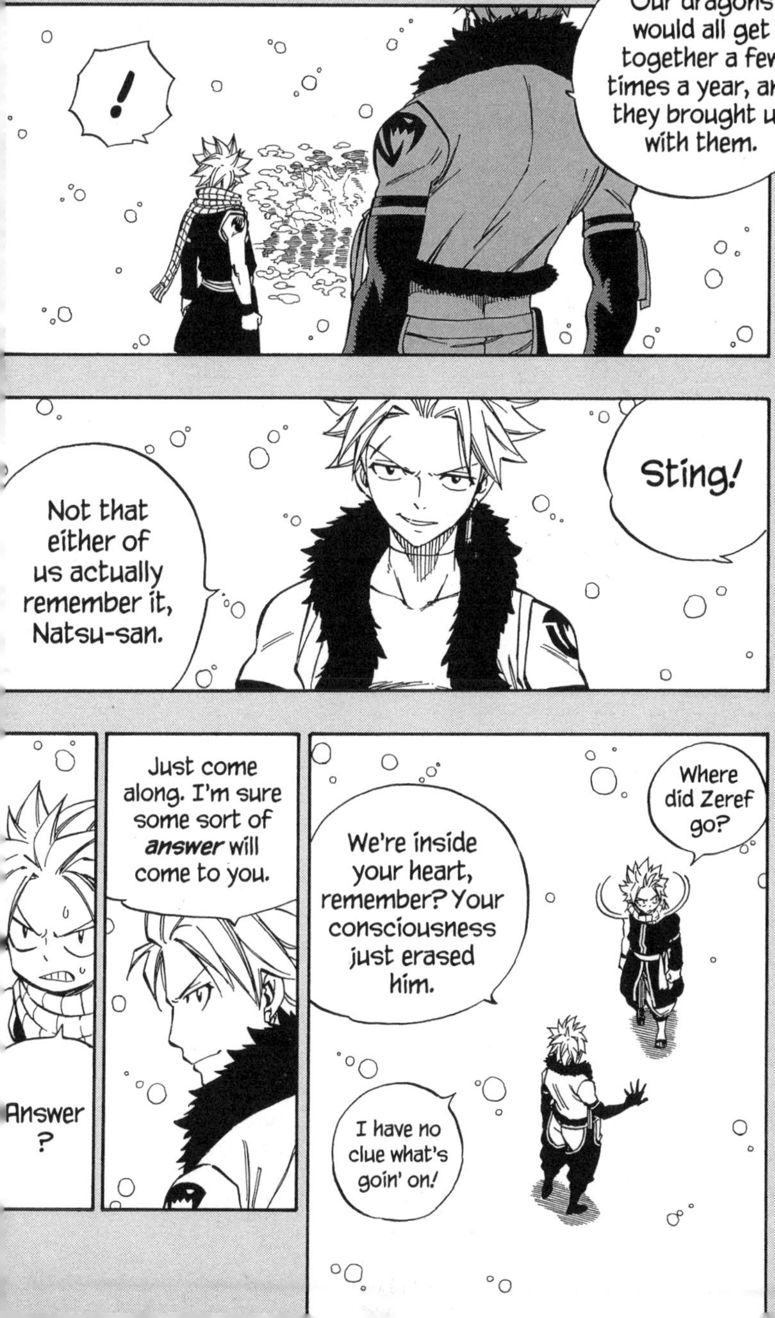
Our dragons would all get together a few times a year, and they brought us with them.
!
Sting!
Not that either of us actually remember it, Natsu-san.
Where did Zeref go?
We're inside your heart, remember? Your consciousness just erased him.
I have no clue what's goin' on!
Just come along. I'm sure some sort of *answer* will come to you.
Answer?

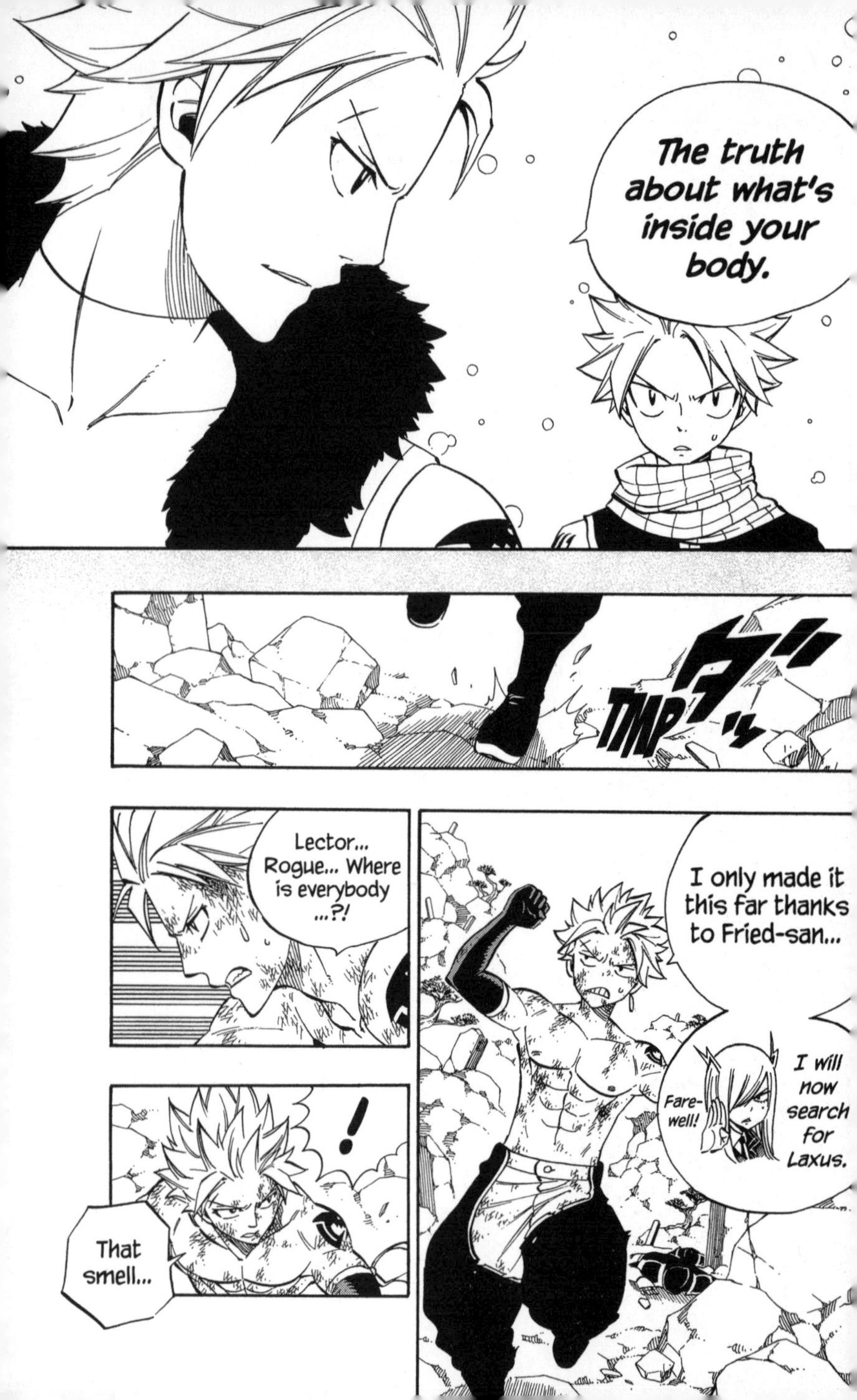
The truth about what's inside your body.
TMP
I only made it this far thanks to Fried-san...
I will now search for Laxus.
Fare-well!
Lector... Rogue... Where is everybody ...?!
!
That smell...

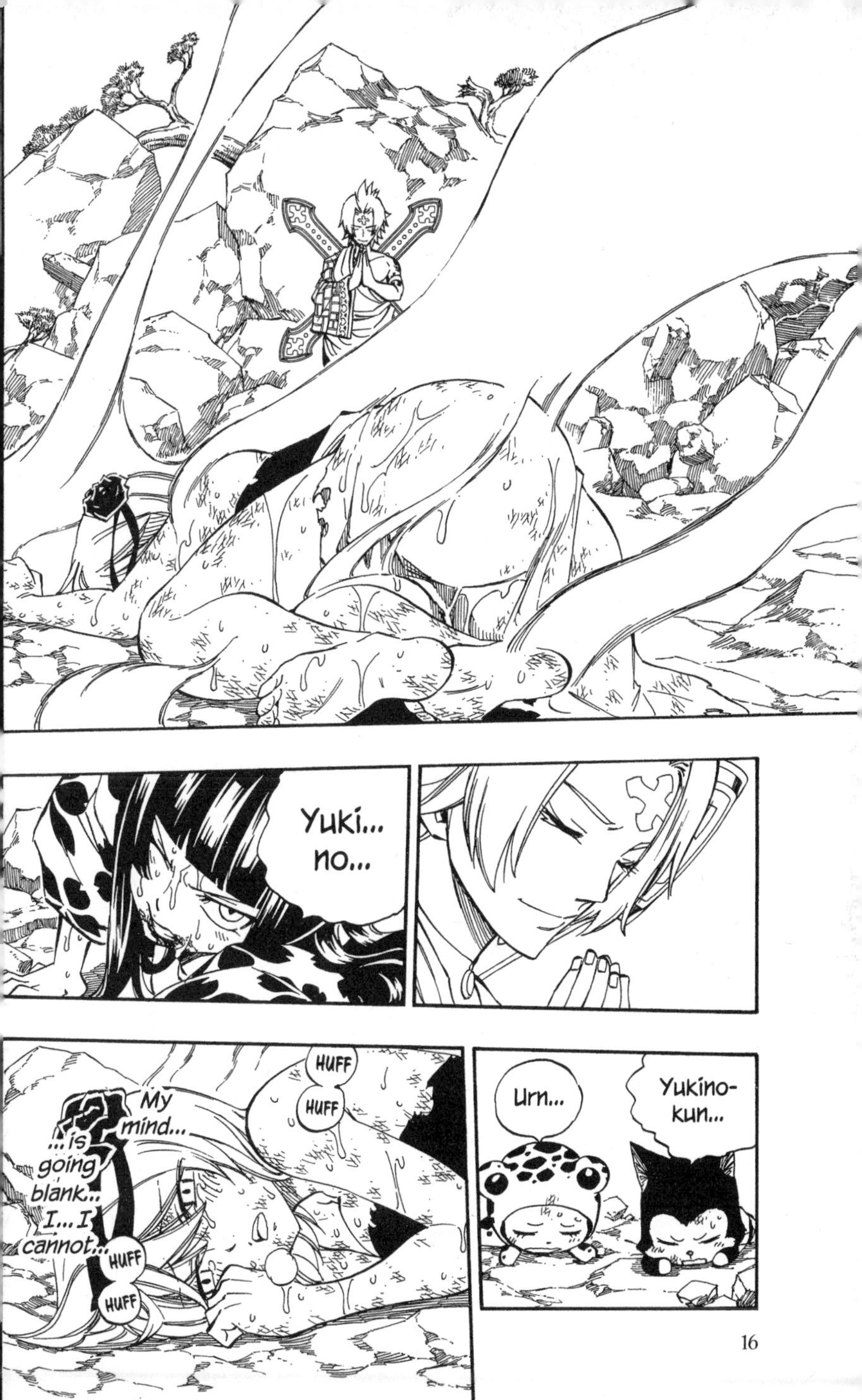
Yuki... no...
Yukino-kun...
Urn...
HUFF
HUFF
My mind...
...is going blank... I...I cannot...
HUFF
HUFF

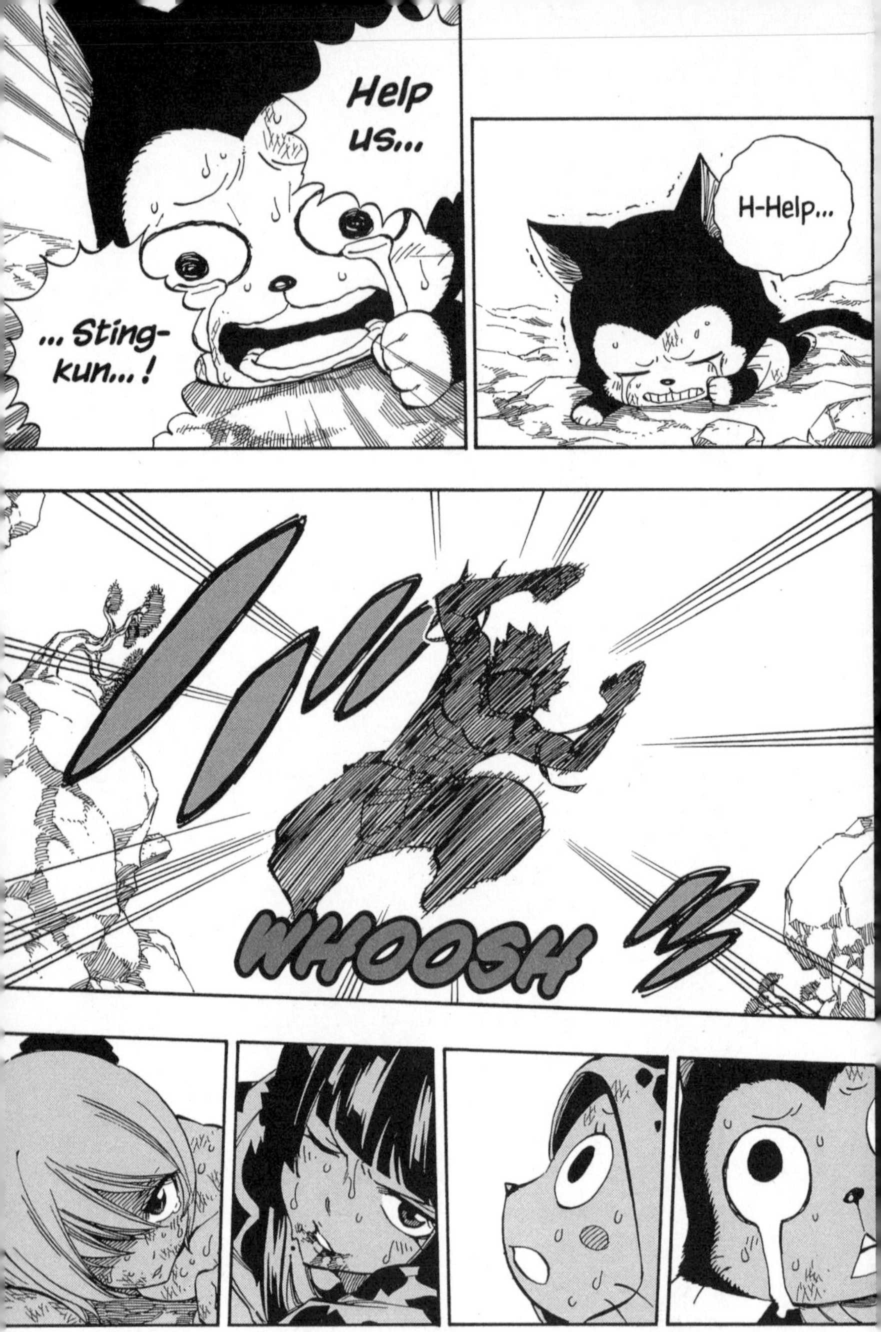
H-Help...
Help us...
... Sting-kun...!
WHOOSH

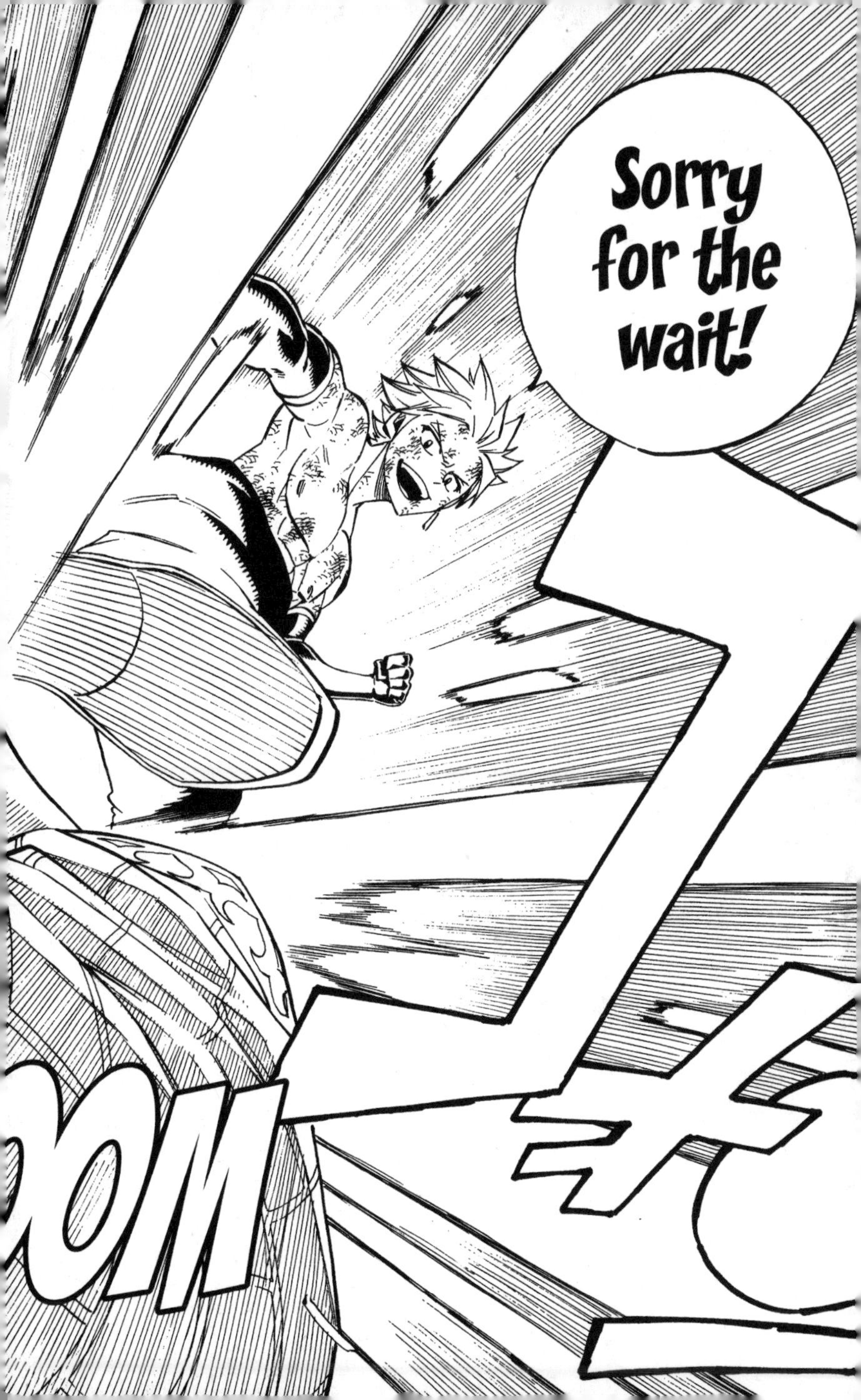
Sorry for the wait!

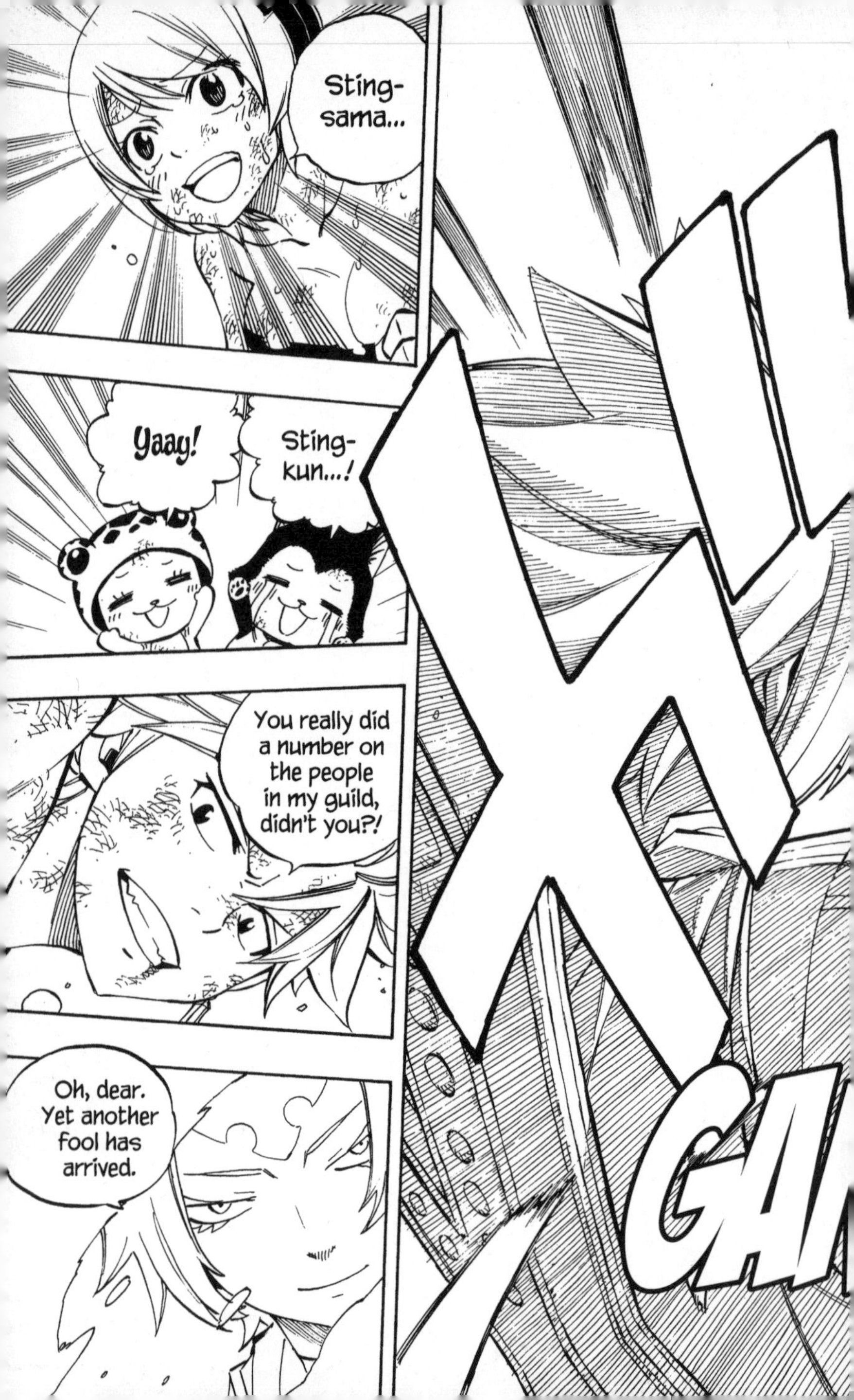

Sting-sama...
Sting-kun...!
Yaay!
You really did a number on the people in my guild, didn't you?!
Oh, dear. Yet another fool has arrived.

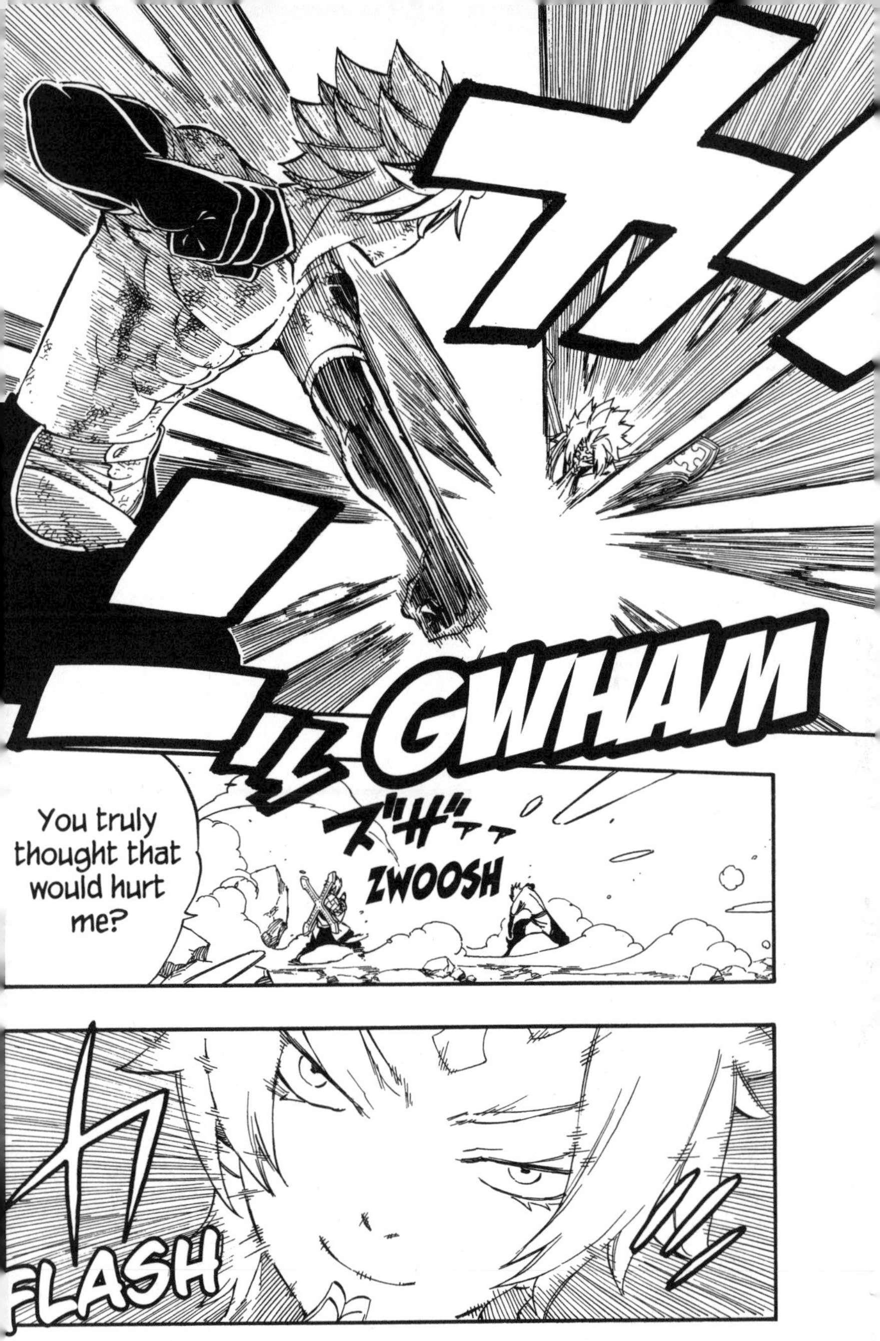
GWHAM
ズザァァ
ZWOOSH
You truly thought that would hurt me?
FLASH

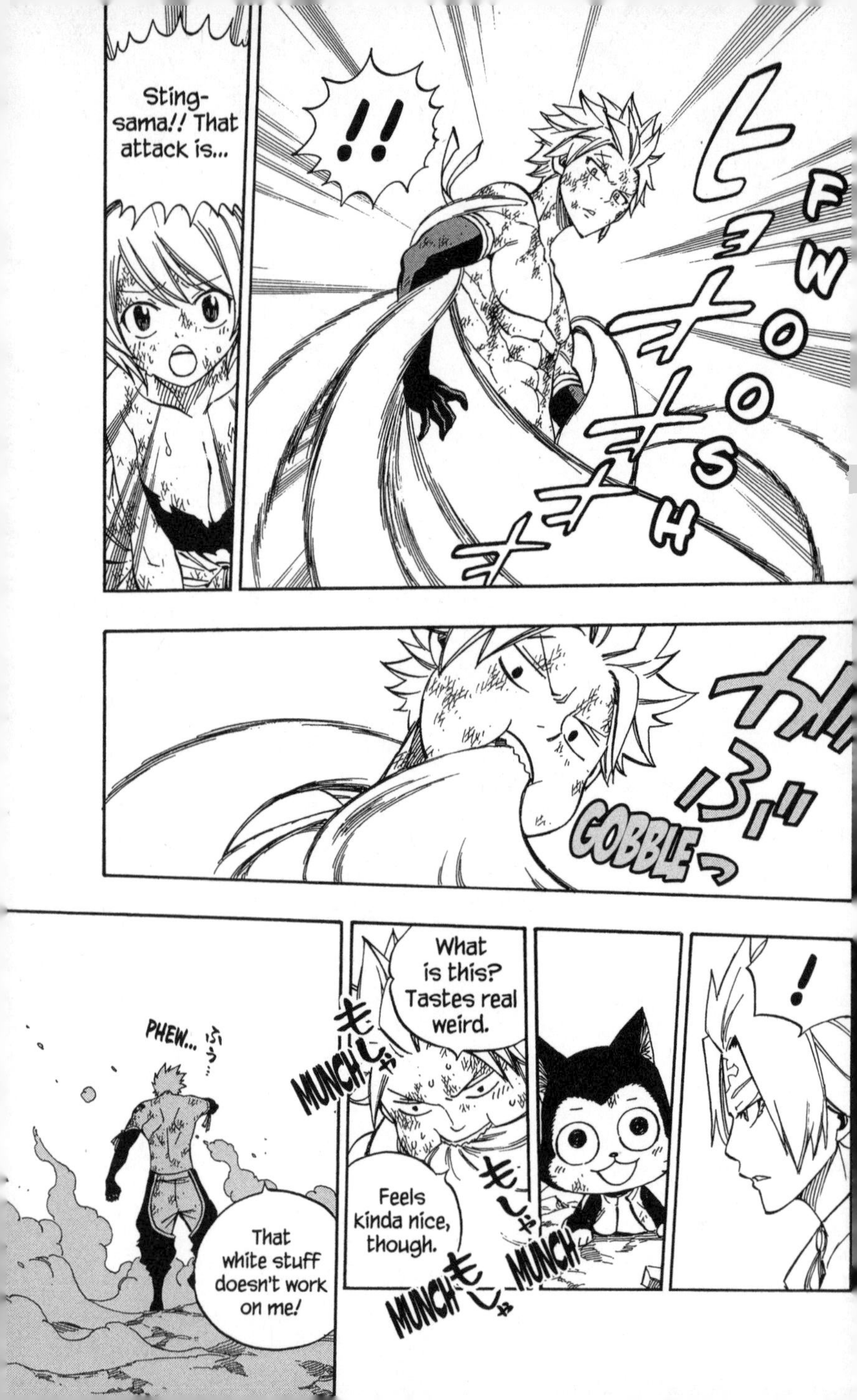

FWOOSH
!!
Sting-sama!! That attack is...
GOBBLE
!
MUNCH
MUNCH
What is this? Tastes real weird.
MUNCH
Feels kinda nice, though.
PHEW...
That white stuff doesn't work on me!

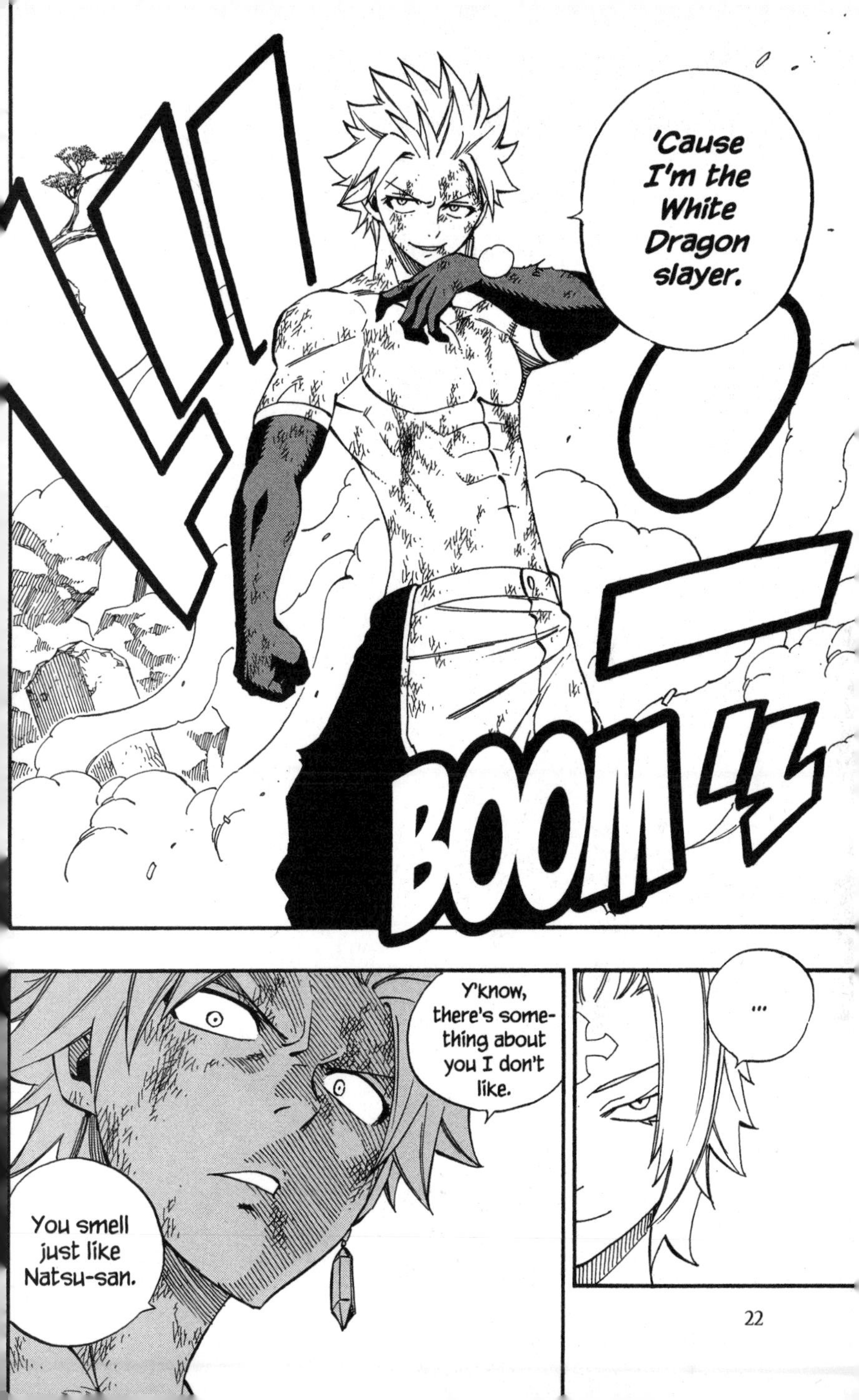
'Cause I'm the White Dragon slayer.
BOOM
...
Y'know, there's something about you I don't like.
You smell just like Natsu-san.

FAIRY TAIL

フェアリーテイル

Chapter 511: The Hell of Hunger

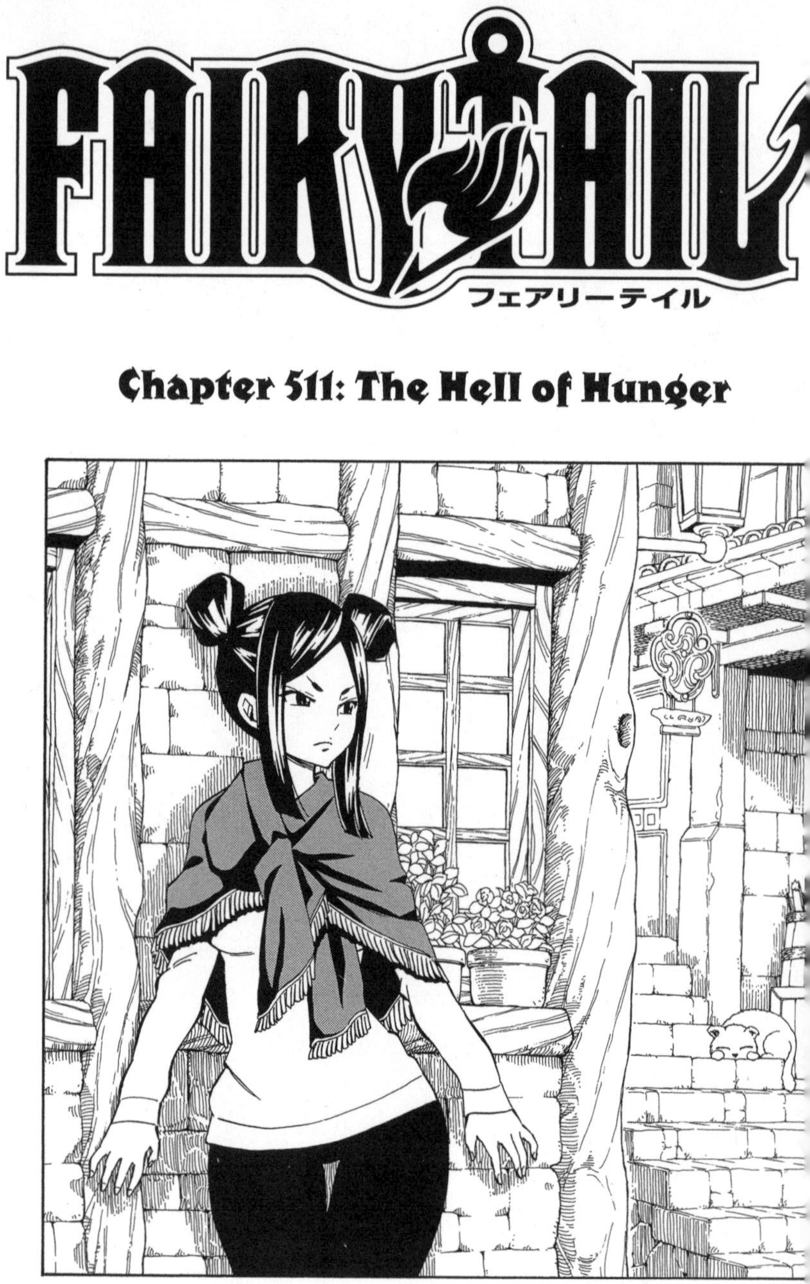

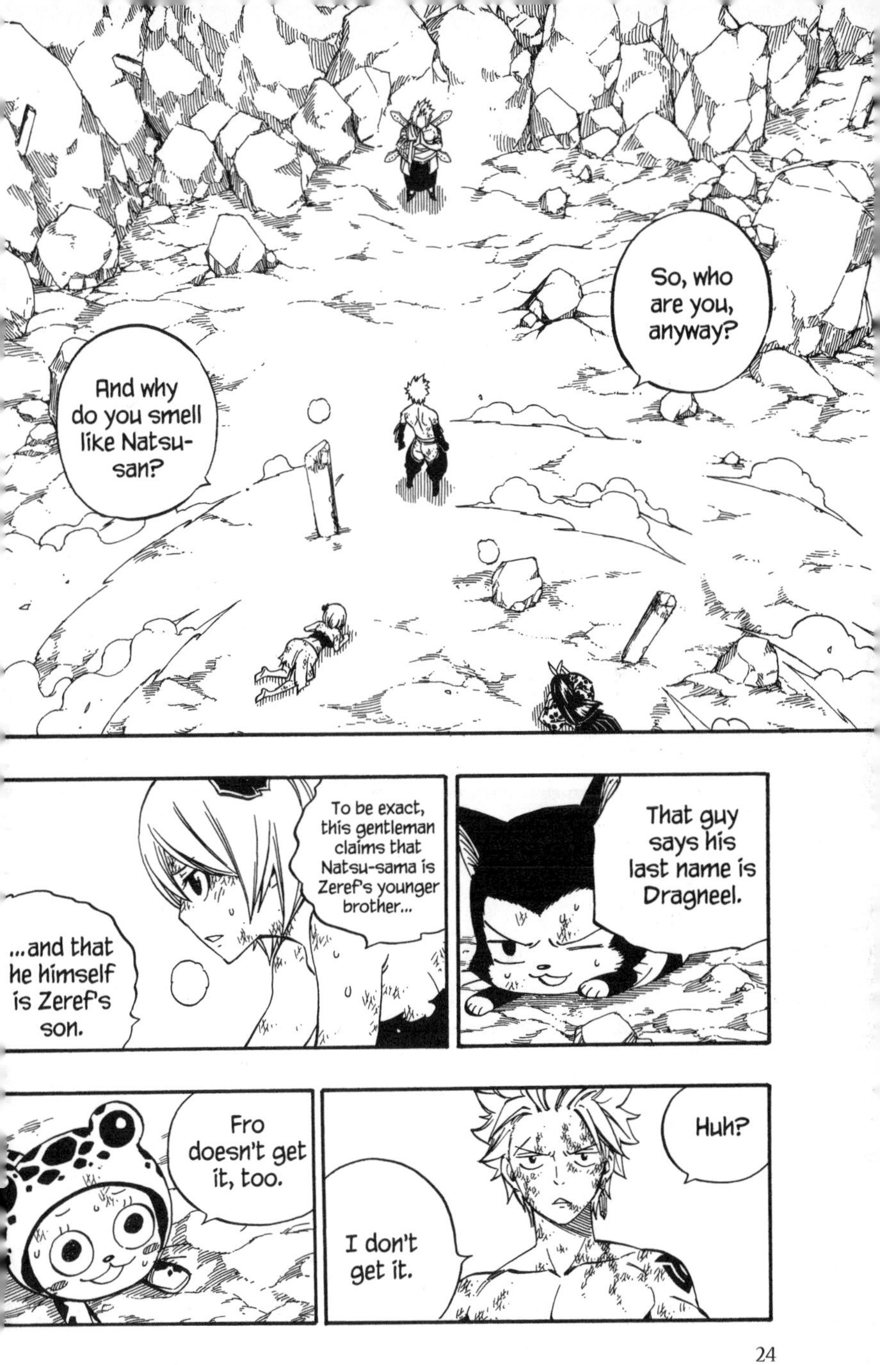
So, who are you, anyway?
And why do you smell like Natsu-san?
That guy says his last name is Dragneel.
To be exact, this gentleman claims that Natsu-sama is Zeref's younger brother...
...and that he himself is Zeref's son.
Huh?
I don't get it.
Fro doesn't get it, too.

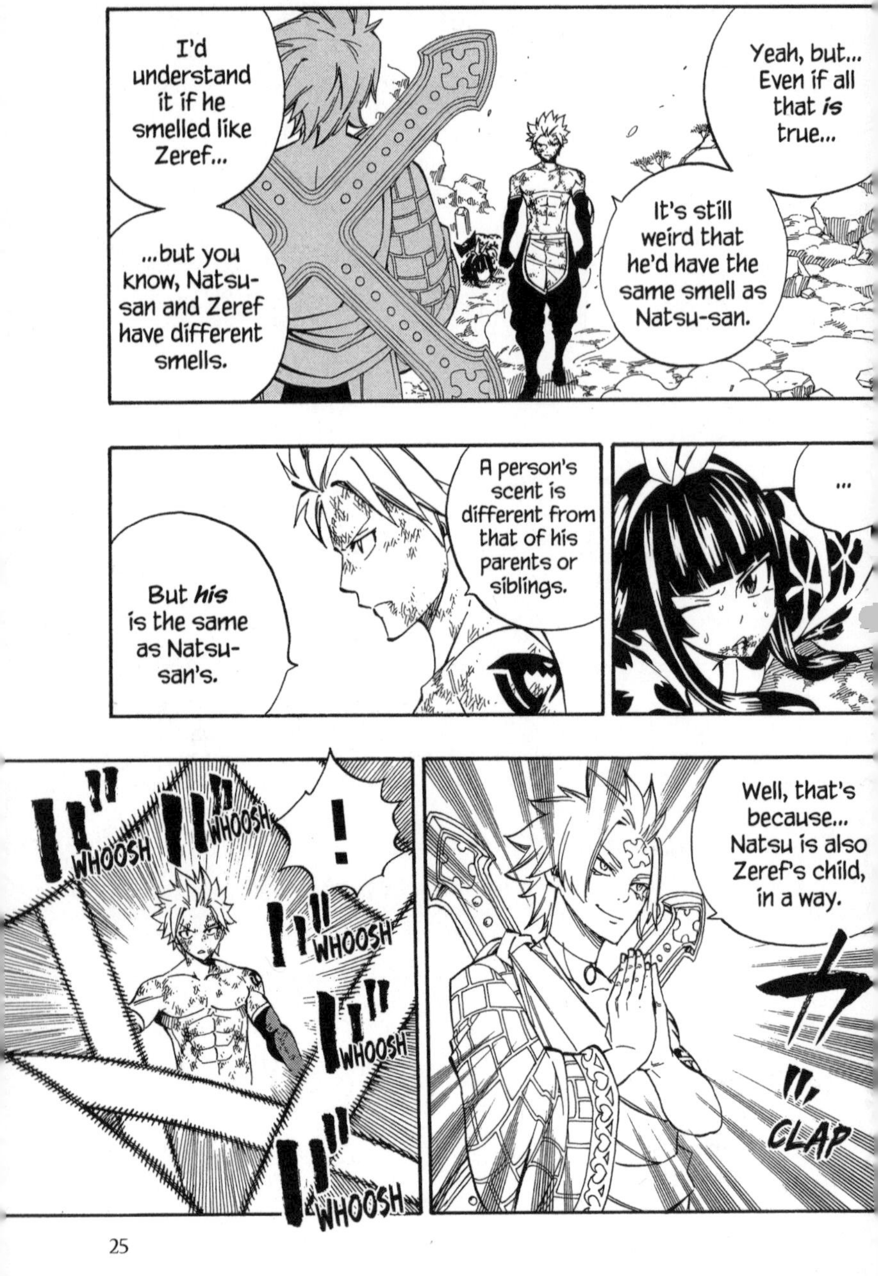
Yeah, but... Even if all that *is* true...
It's still weird that he'd have the same smell as Natsu-san.
I'd understand it if he smelled like Zeref...
...but you know, Natsu-san and Zeref have different smells.
...
A person's scent is different from that of his parents or siblings.
But *his* is the same as Natsu-san's.
Well, that's because... Natsu is also Zeref's child, in a way.
CLAP
!
WHOOSH
WHOOSH
WHOOSH
WHOOSH
WHOOSH

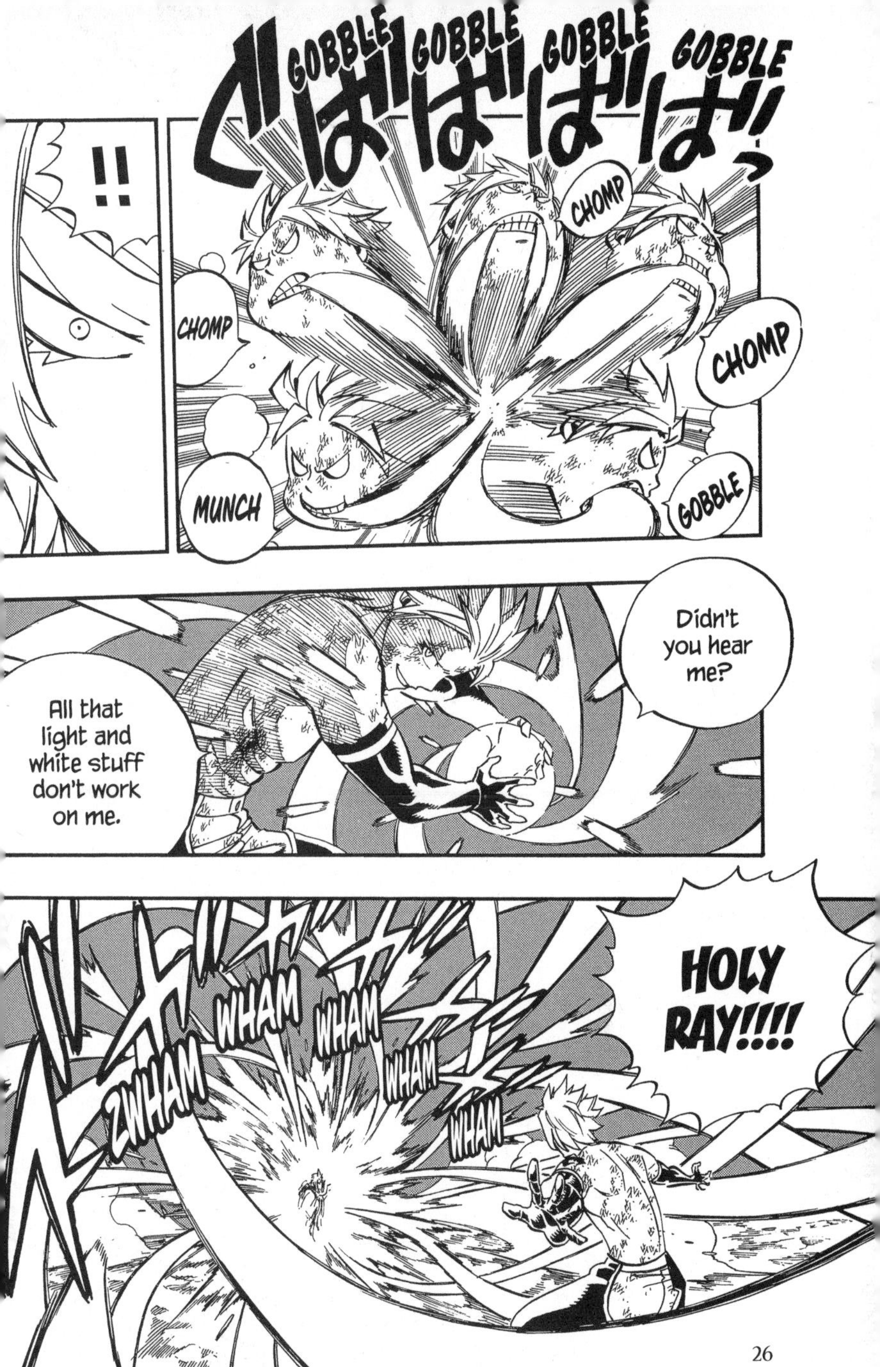

GOBBLE GOBBLE GOBBLE GOBBLE
ぐばばばばっ
CHOMP
CHOMP
CHOMP
GOBBLE
MUNCH
!!
Didn't you hear me?
All that light and white stuff don't work on me.
HOLY RAY!!!!
WHAM
WHAM
WHAM
WHAM
ZWHAM

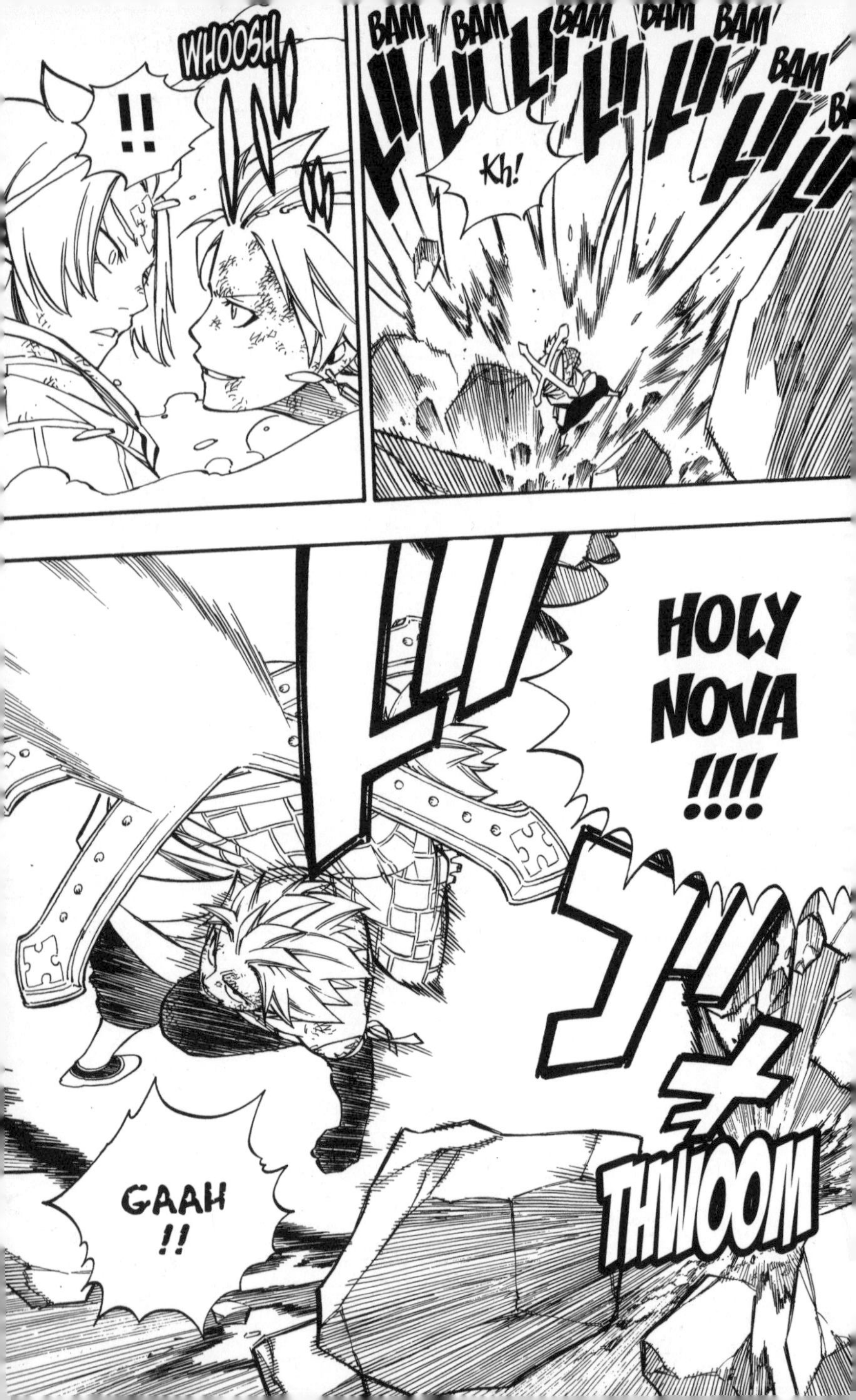
BAM BAM BAM BAM BAM BAM
Kh!
WHOOSH
!!
HOLY NOVA !!!!
THWOOM
GAAH !!

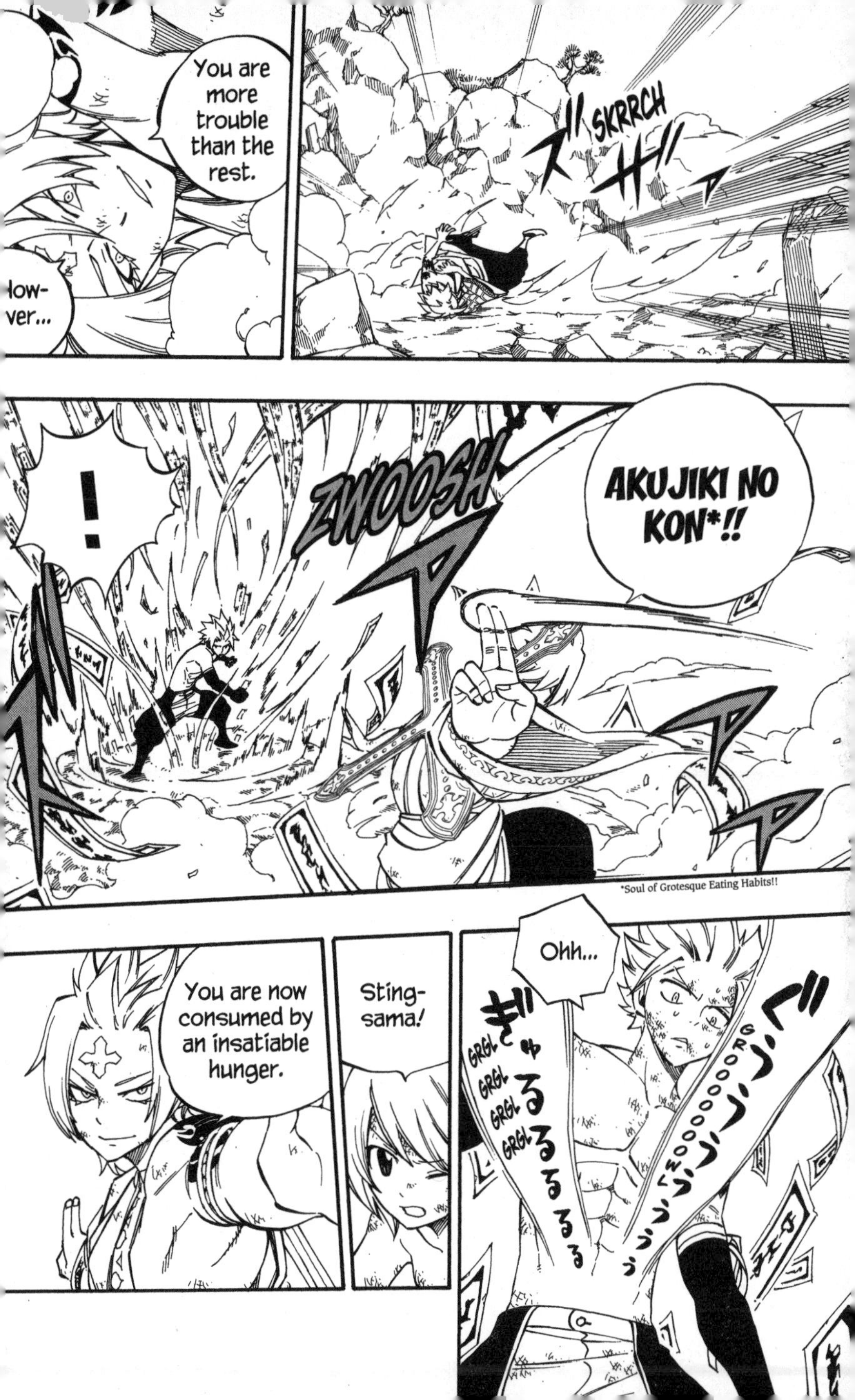
SKRRCH
You are more trouble than the rest.
low-ver...
AKUJIKI NO KON*!!
ZWOOSH
!!
*Soul of Grotesque Eating Habits!!
Ohh...
GRGL
GRGL
GRGL
GRGL
GROOOOOOOORG
Sting-sama!
You are now consumed by an insatiable hunger.

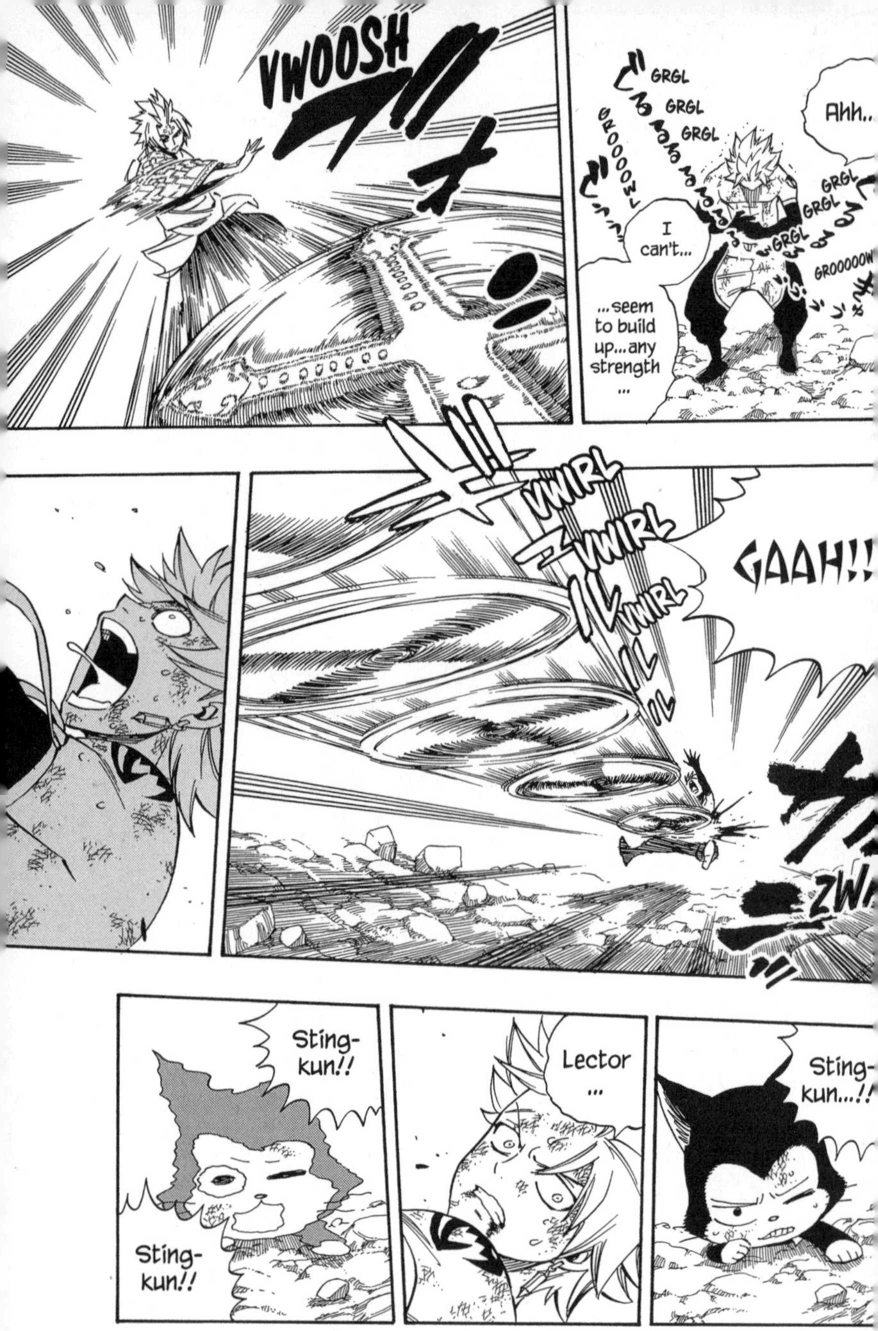
Ahh...
GRGL GRGL GRGL
GROOOOOWL
GRGL GRGL GRGL
GROOOOOW
I can't...
...seem to build up...any strength ...
VWOOSH
VWIRL VWIRL VWIRL
GAAH!!
Sting-kun...!!
Lector ...
Sting-kun!!
Sting-kun!!

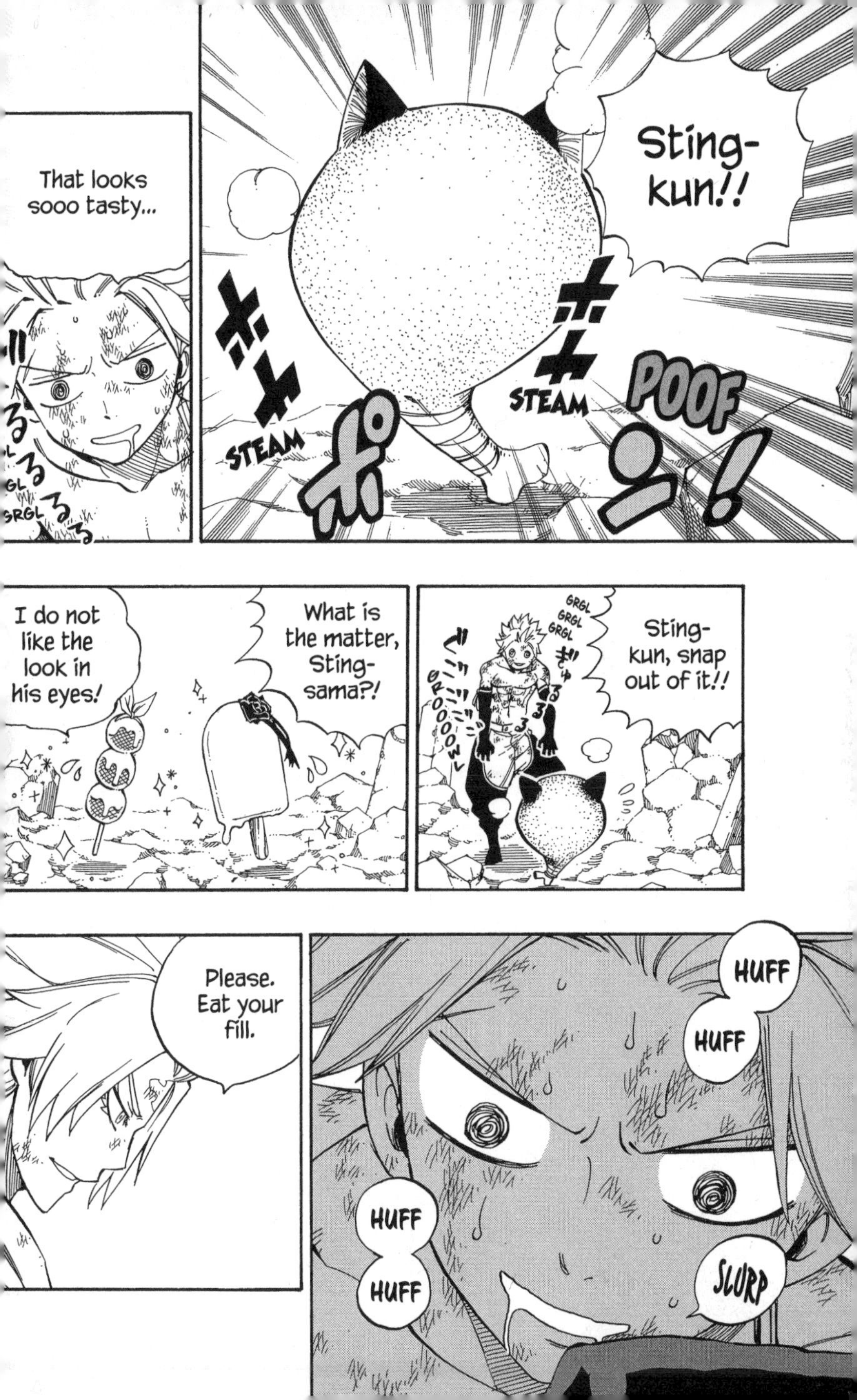
Sting-kun!!
STEAM
STEAM
POOF
That looks sooo tasty...
GRGL
GRGL
Sting-kun, snap out of it!!
GRGL
GRGL
GRGL
GROOOOOWL
What is the matter, Sting-sama?!
I do not like the look in his eyes!
HUFF
HUFF
SLURP
HUFF
HUFF
Please. Eat your fill.

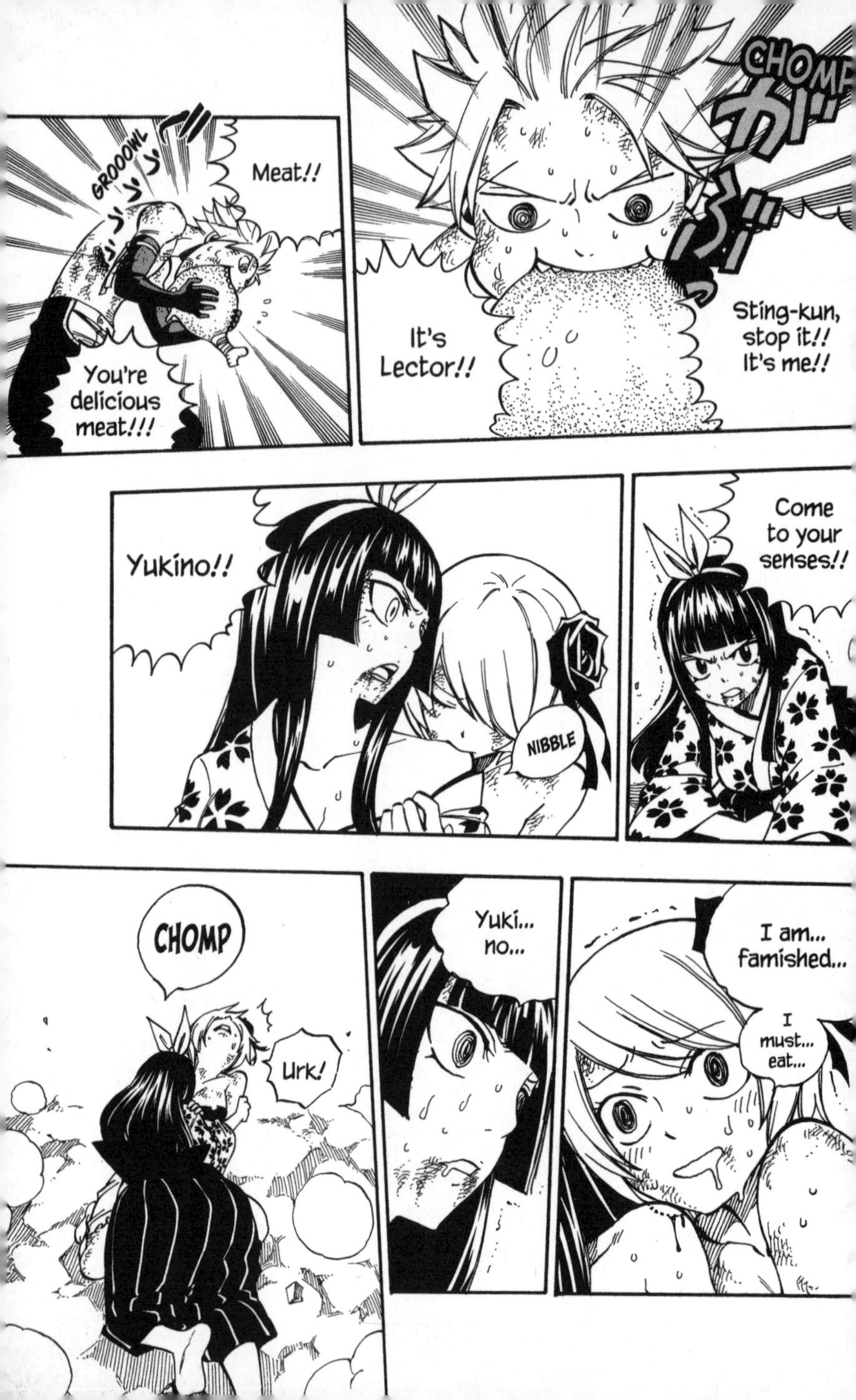
CHOMP
Sting-kun, stop it!! It's me!!
It's Lector!!
Meat!!
GROOOWL
You're delicious meat!!!
Come to your senses!!
Yukino!!
NIBBLE
I am... famished...
I must... eat...
Yuki... no...
CHOMP
Urk!

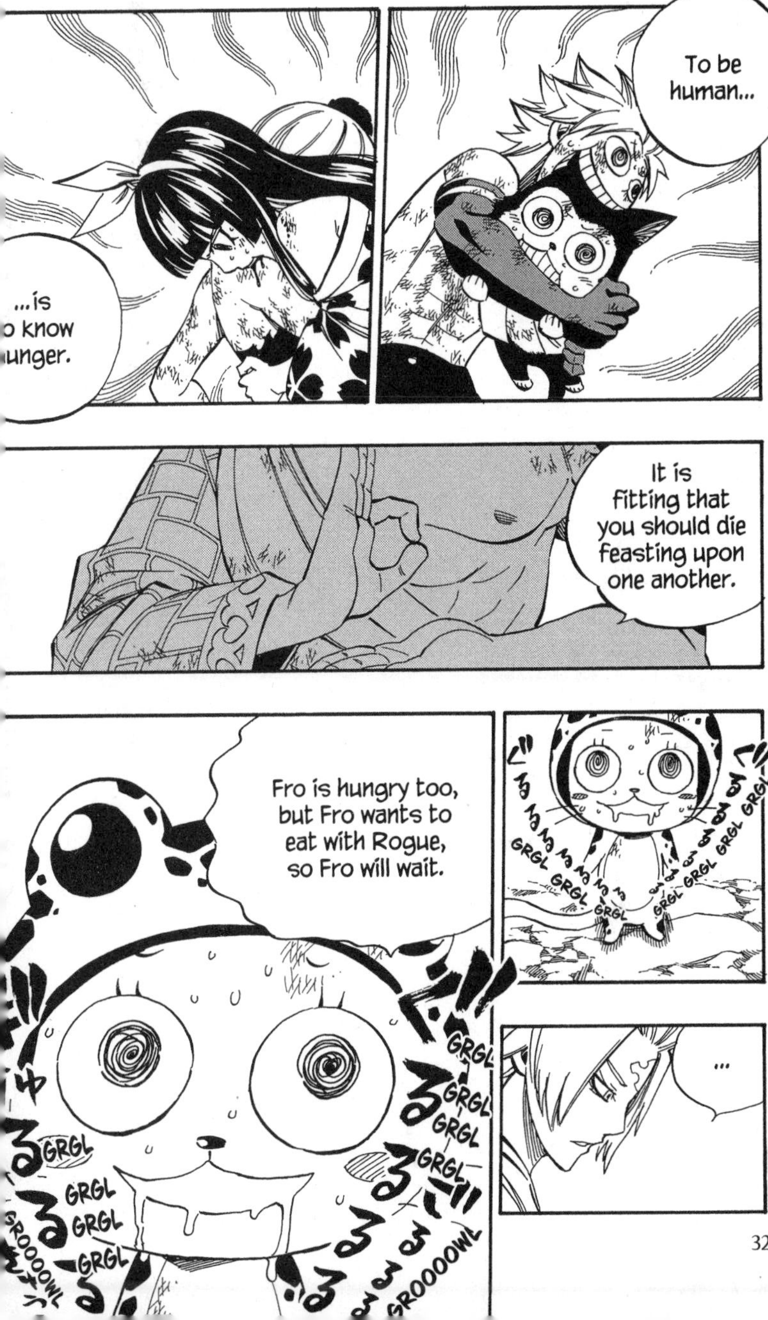
To be human...
...is
o know
unger.
It is fitting that you should die feasting upon one another.
GRGL GRGL GRGL GRGL GRGL GRGL GRGL GRGL
...
Fro is hungry too, but Fro wants to eat with Rogue, so Fro will wait.
GRGL GRGL GRGL GRGL GRGL GRGL GRGL GRGL
GROOOOWL GROOOOWL

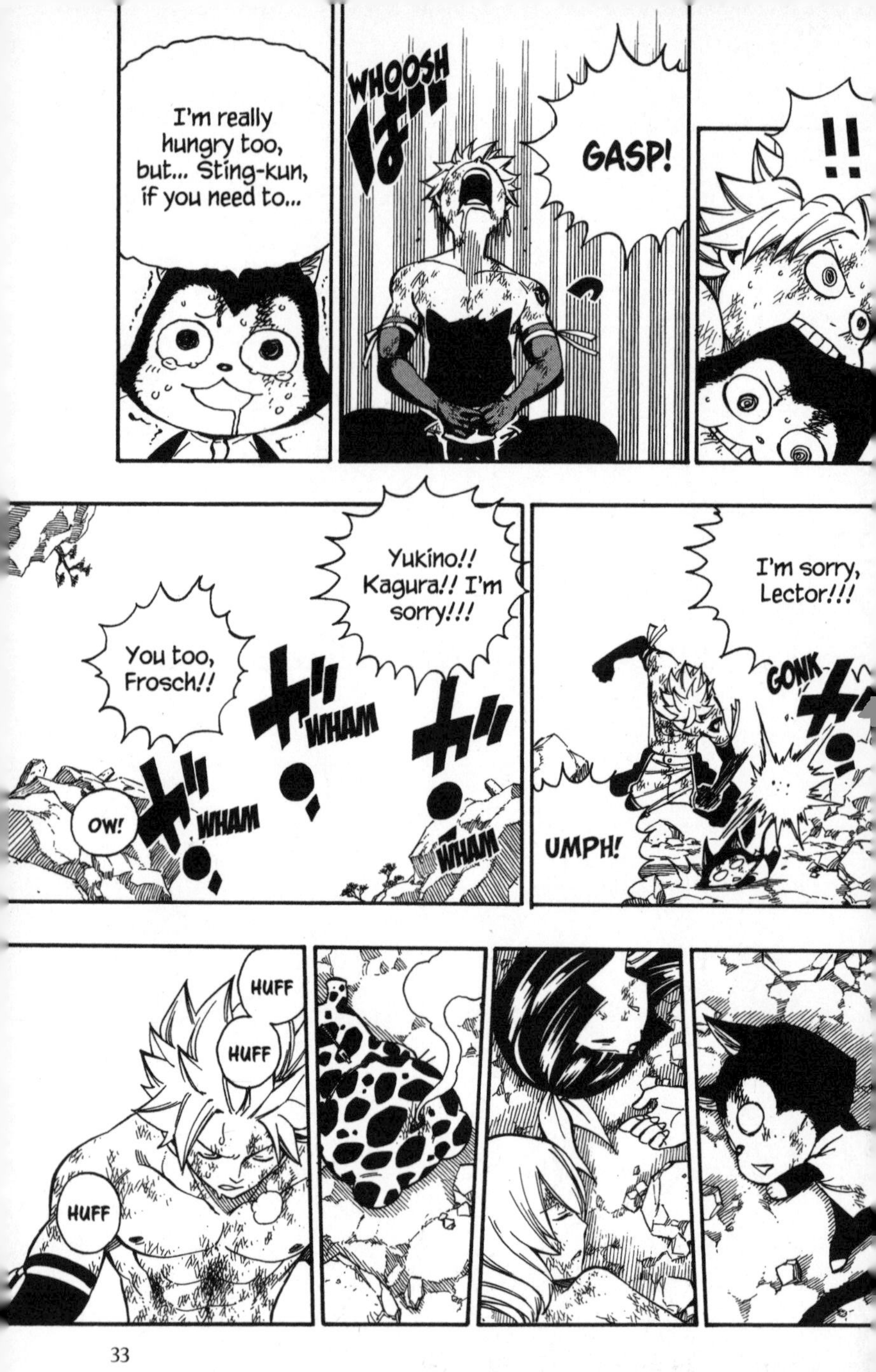
!!
WHOOSH
GASP!
I'm really hungry too, but... Sting-kun, if you need to...
I'm sorry, Lector!!!
GONK
UMPH!
Yukino!! Kagura!! I'm sorry!!!
WHAM
WHAM
You too, Frosch!!
OW!
WHAM
HUFF
HUFF
HUFF

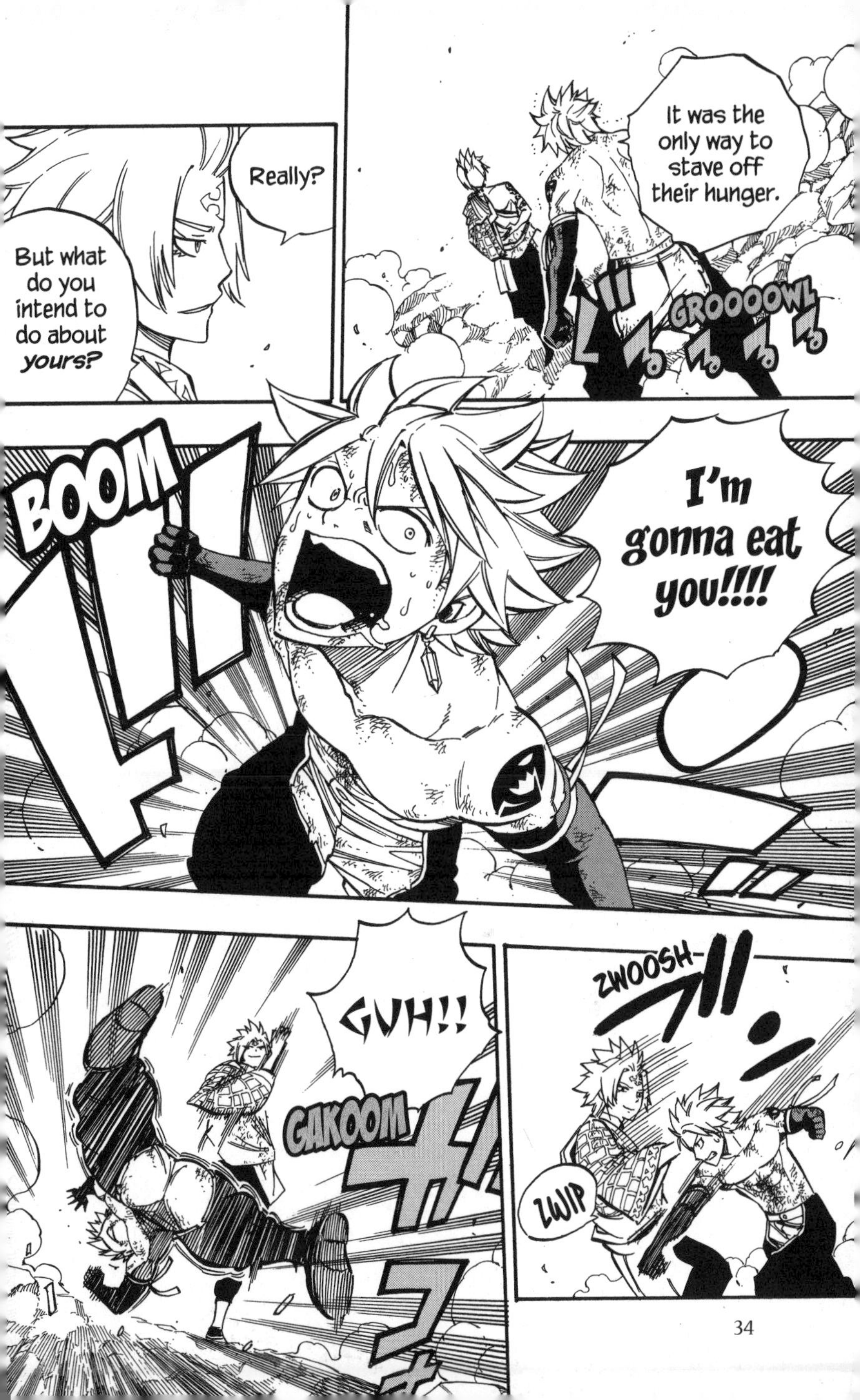
It was the only way to stave off their hunger.
GROOOOWL
Really?
But what do you intend to do about *yours?*
I'm gonna eat you!!!!
BOOM
ZWOOSH-
ZWIP
GUH!!
GAKOOM

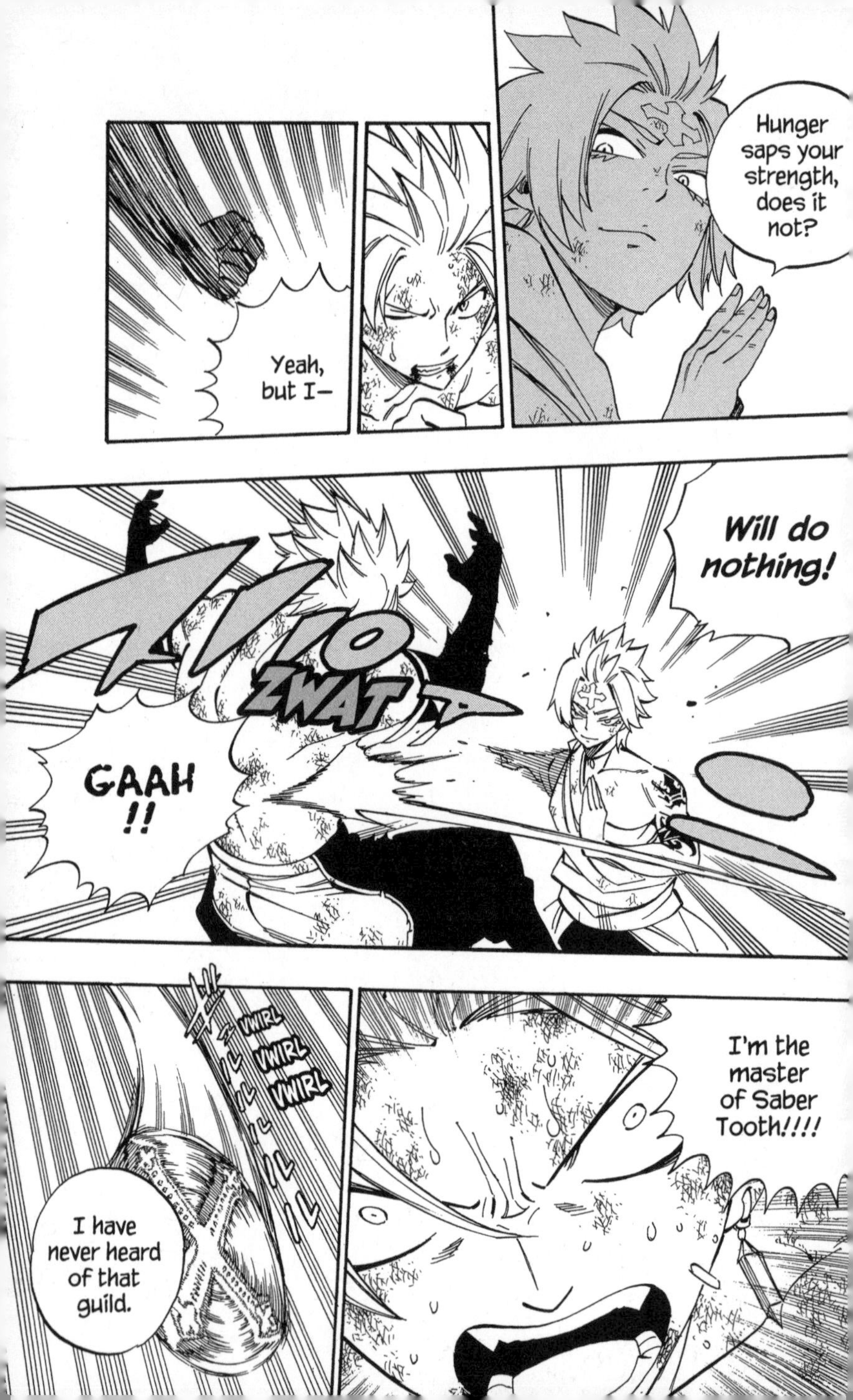
Hunger saps your strength, does it not?
Yeah, but I—
Will do nothing!
ZWAT
GAAH!!
I'm the master of Saber Tooth!!!!
VWIRL
VWIRL
VWIRL
I have never heard of that guild.

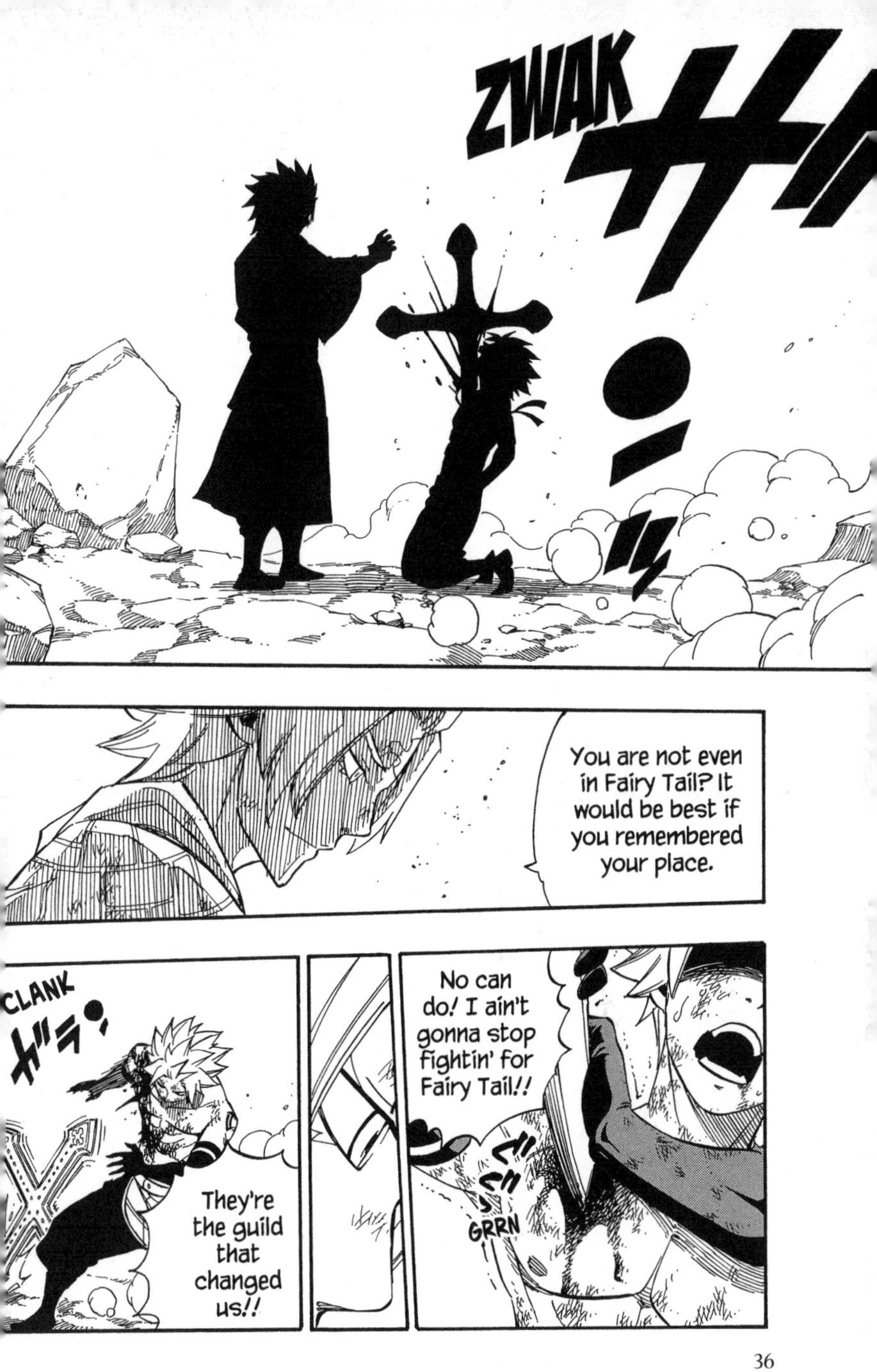
ZWAK
You are not even in Fairy Tail? It would be best if you remembered your place.
No can do! I ain't gonna stop fightin' for Fairy Tail!!
GRRN
CLANK
They're the guild that changed us!!

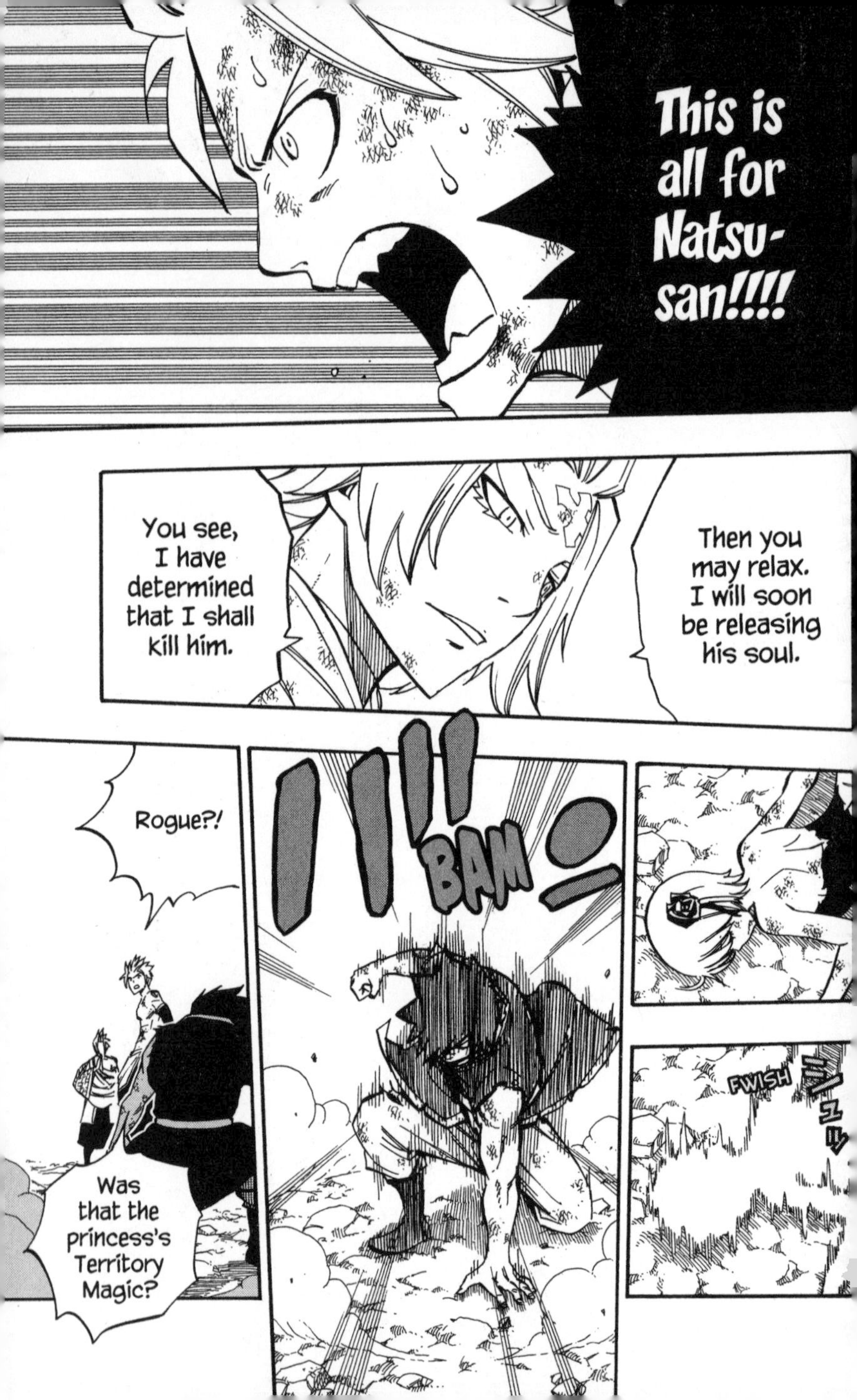
This is all for Natsu-san!!!!
Then you may relax. I will soon be releasing his soul.
You see, I have determined that I shall kill him.
FWISH
BAM
Rogue?!
Was that the princess's Territory Magic?

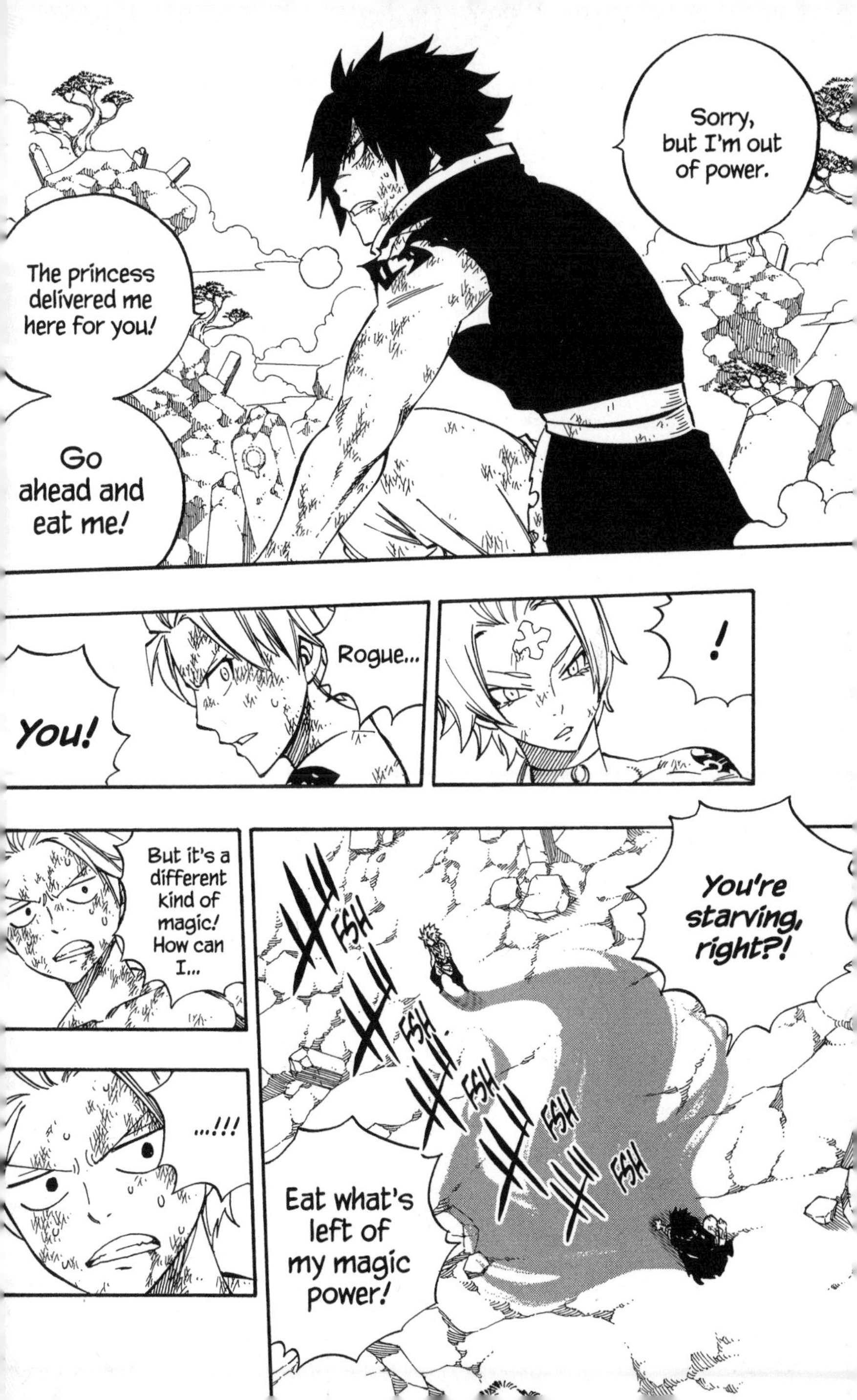

Sorry, but I'm out of power.
The princess delivered me here for you!
Go ahead and eat me!
!
Rogue...
You!
You're starving, right?!
FSH
FSH
FSH
FSH
FSH
Eat what's left of my magic power!
But it's a different kind of magic! How can I...
...!!!

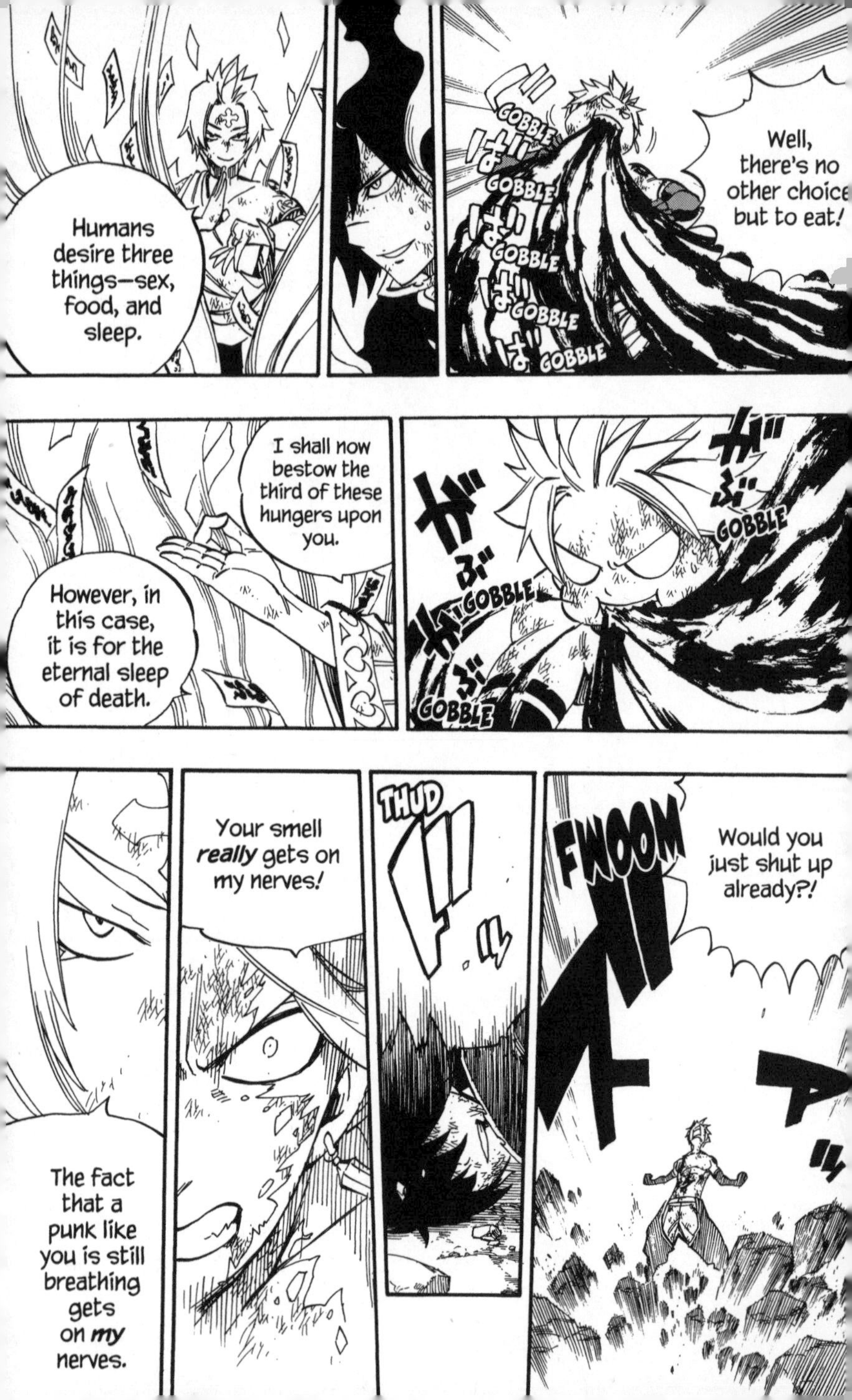
Well, there's no other choice but to eat!
GOBBLE
GOBBLE
GOBBLE
GOBBLE
GOBBLE
Humans desire three things—sex, food, and sleep.
GOBBLE
GOBBLE
GOBBLE
I shall now bestow the third of these hungers upon you.
However, in this case, it is for the eternal sleep of death.
Would you just shut up already?!
FWOOM
THUD
Your smell *really* gets on my nerves!
The fact that a punk like you is still breathing gets on *my* nerves.

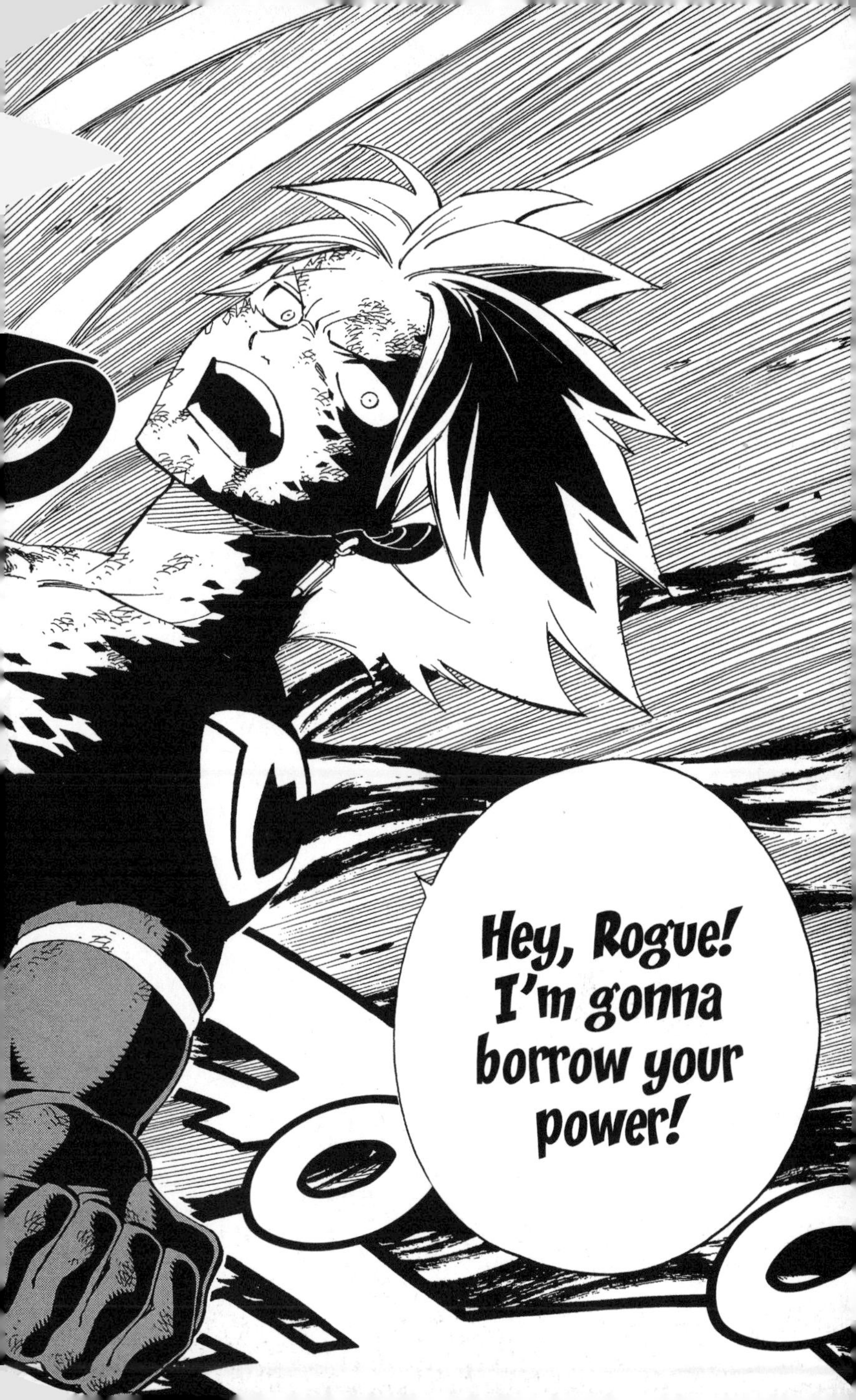
Hey, Rogue! I'm gonna borrow your power!

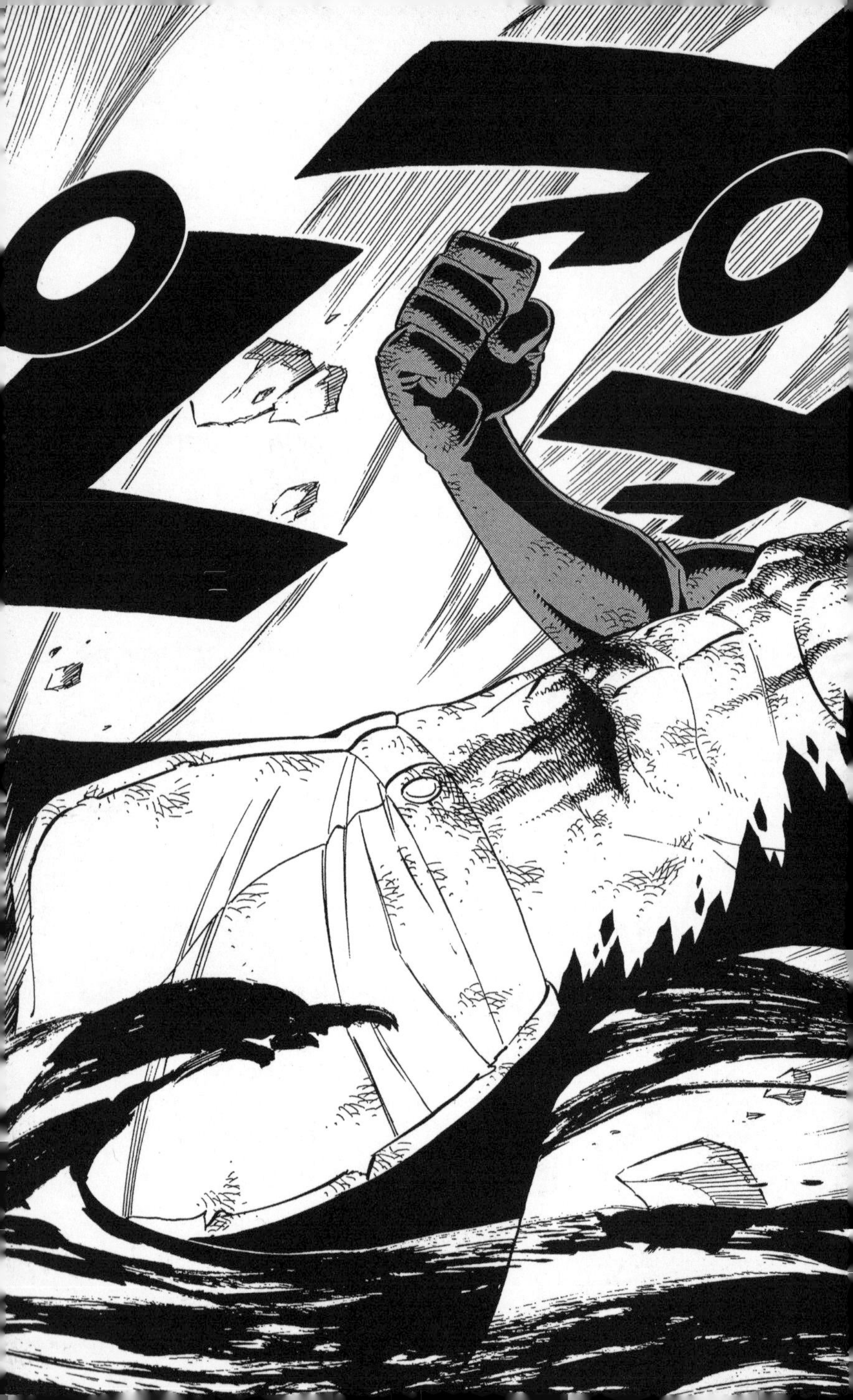

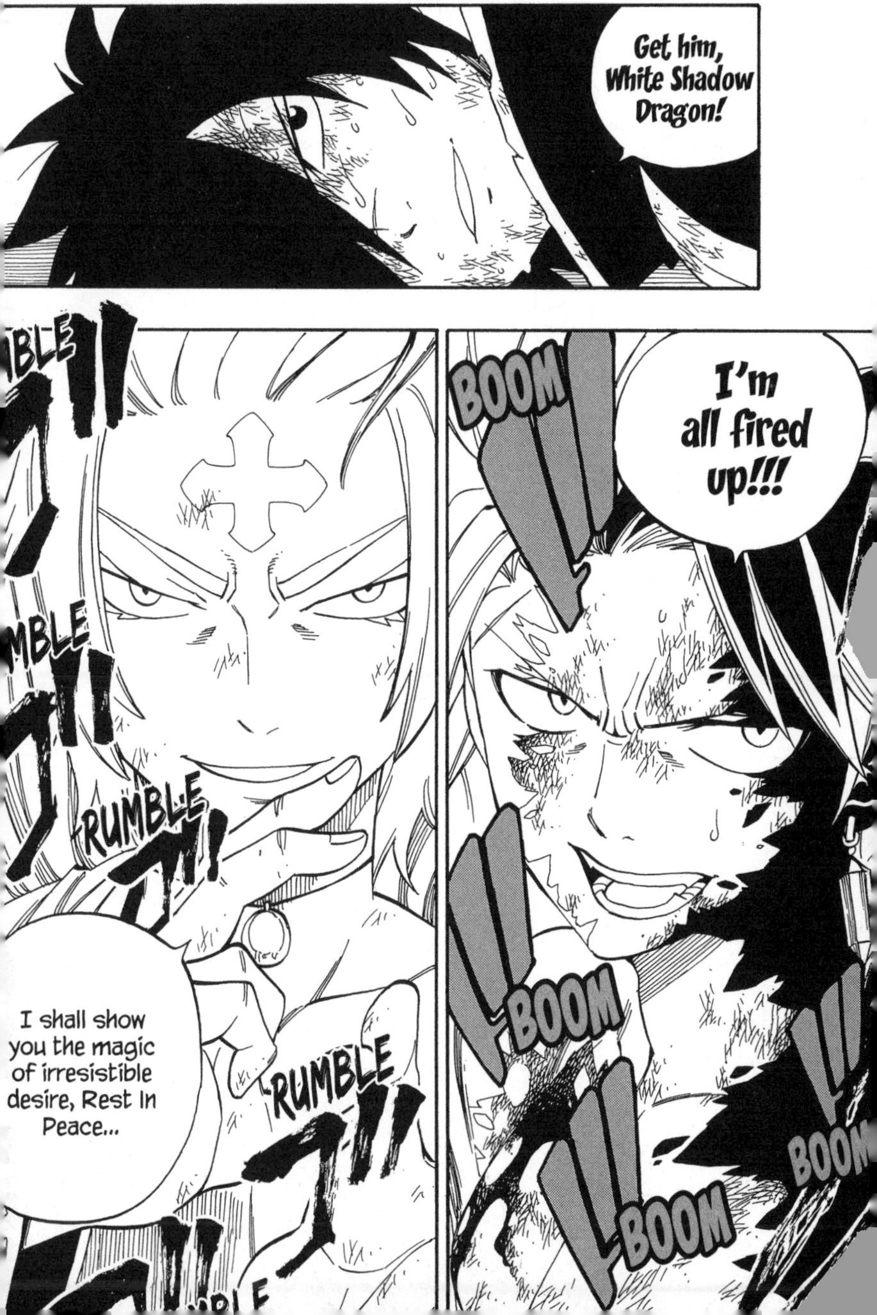
Get him, White Shadow Dragon!
BOOM
I'm all fired up!!!
BOOM
BOOM
BOOM
RUMBLE
I shall show you the magic of irresistible desire, Rest In Peace...
RUMBLE

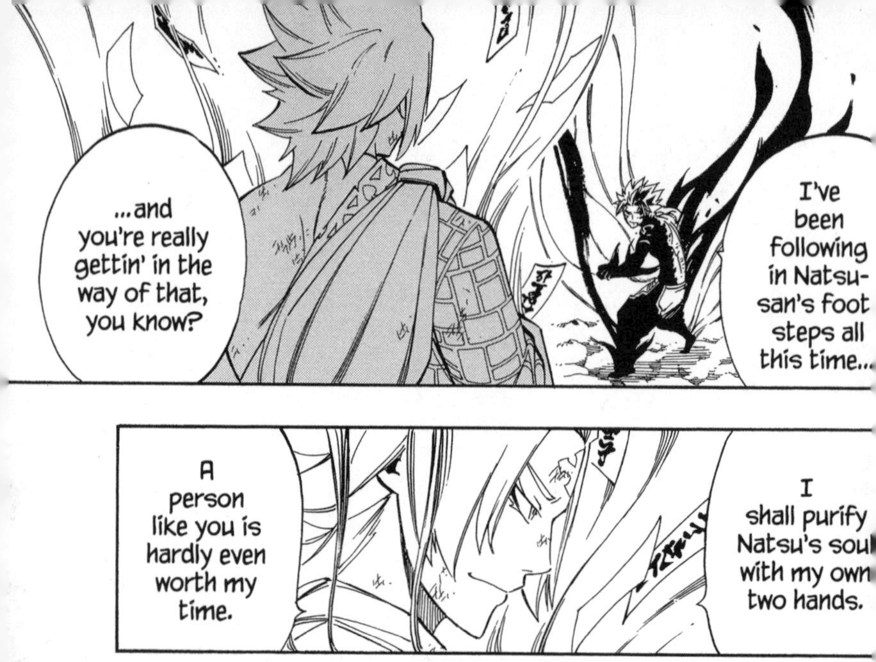
I've been following in Natsu-san's foot steps all this time...
...and you're really gettin' in the way of that, you know?
I shall purify Natsu's soul with my own two hands.
A person like you is hardly even worth my time.

Chapter 512: Sting, the White Shadow Dragon

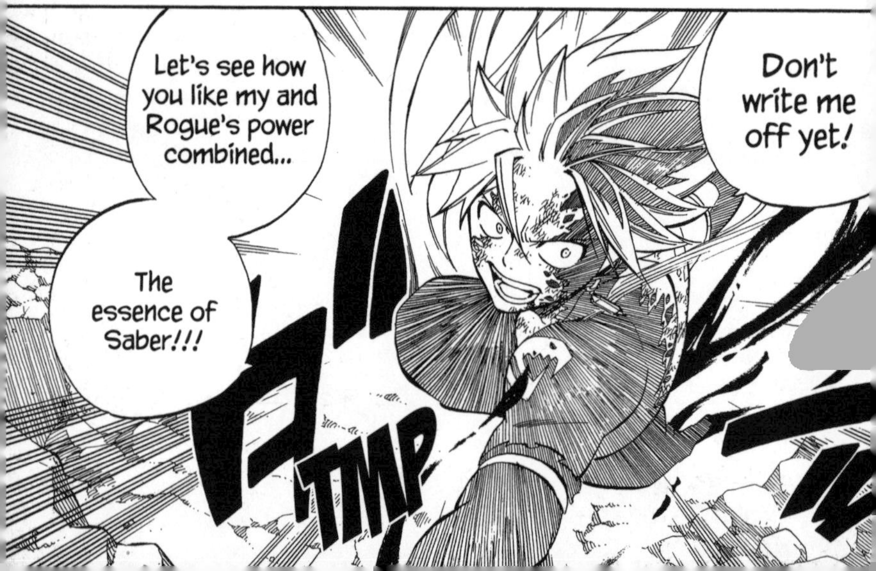
Don't write me off yet!
Let's see how you like my and Rogue's power combined...
The essence of Saber!!!
TMP

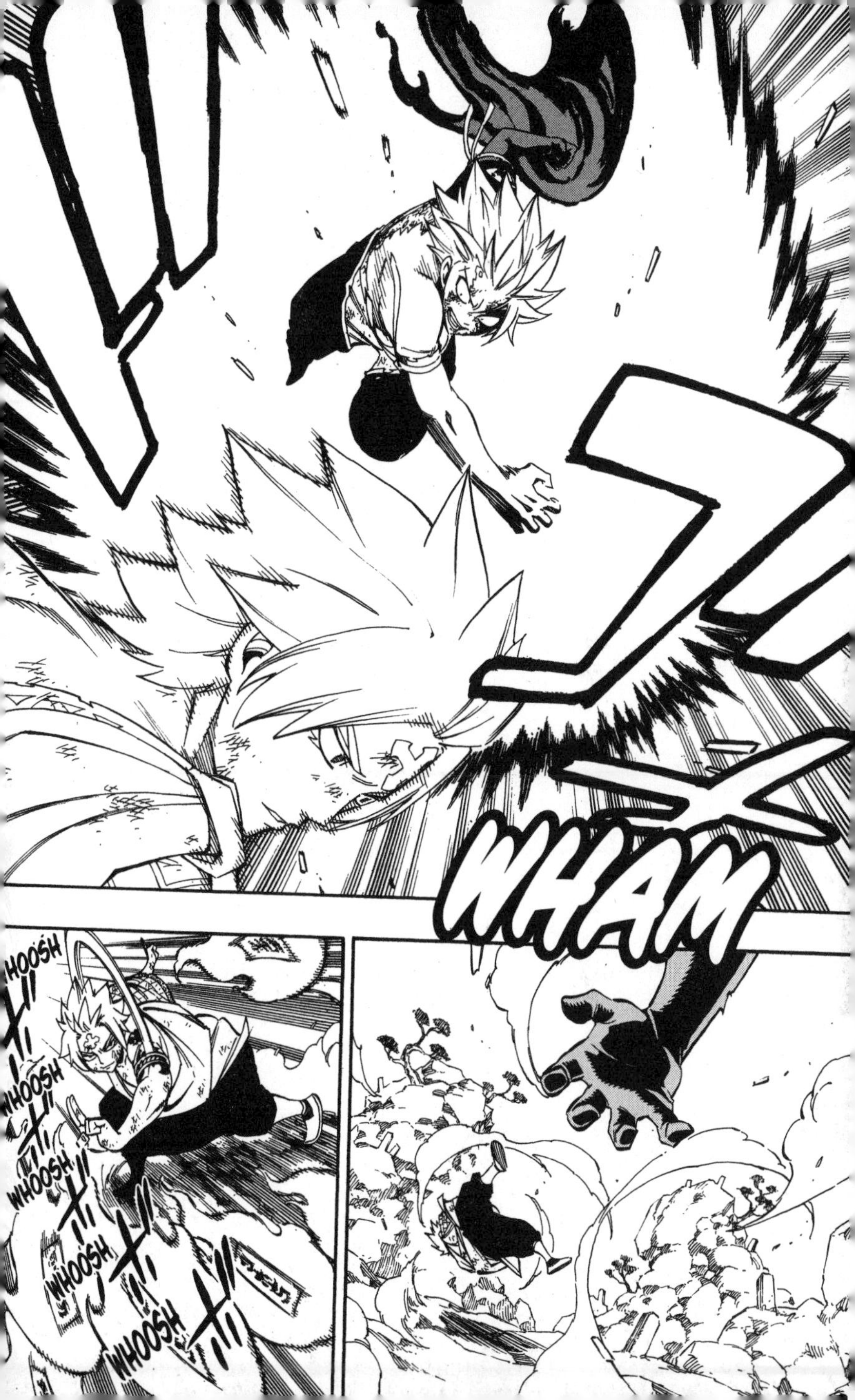
WHAM
WHOOSH
WHOOSH
WHOOSH
WHOOSH
WHOOSH
WHOOSH

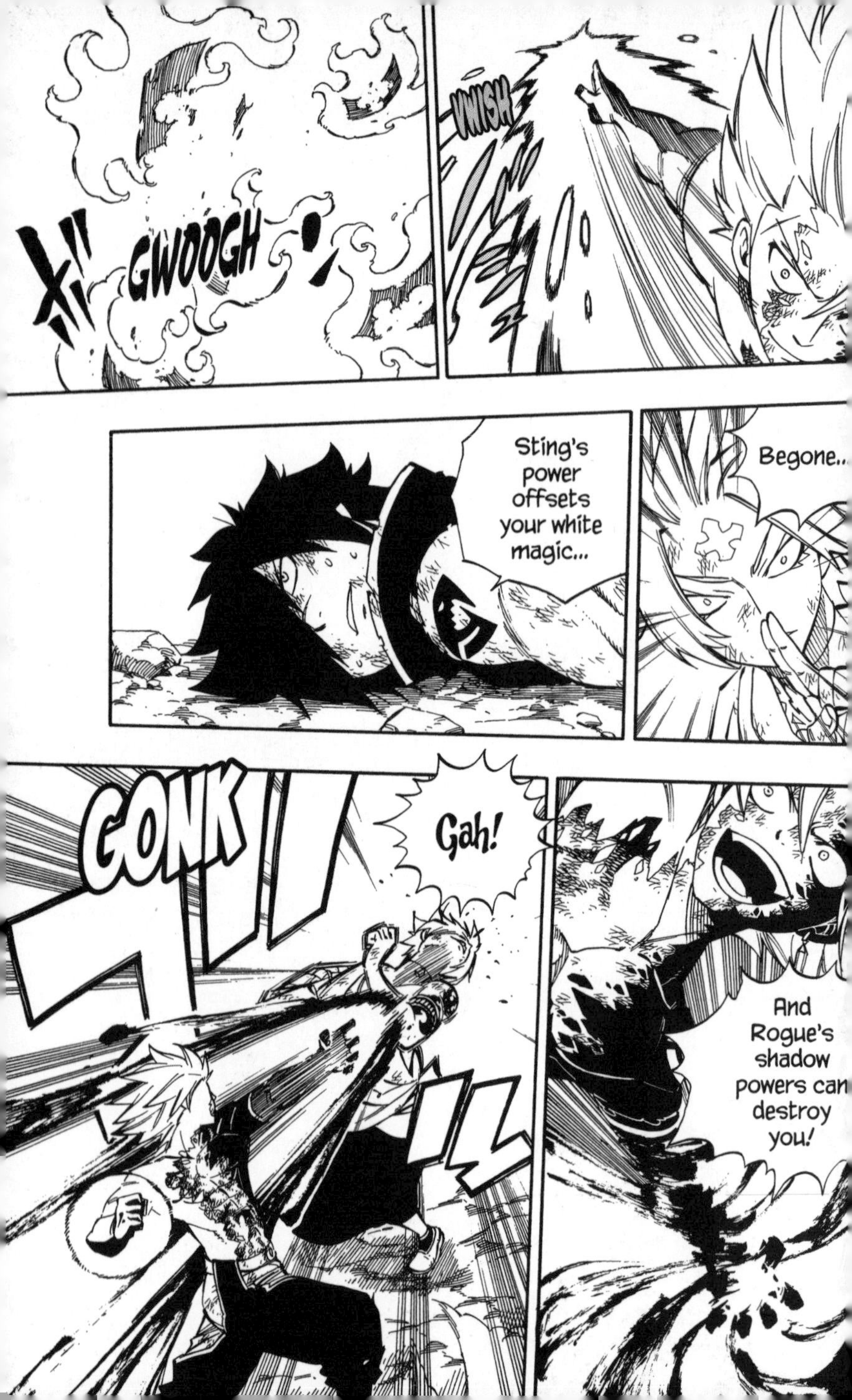
VWISH
GWOOGH
Begone...
Sting's power offsets your white magic...
And Rogue's shadow powers can destroy you!
GONK
Gah!

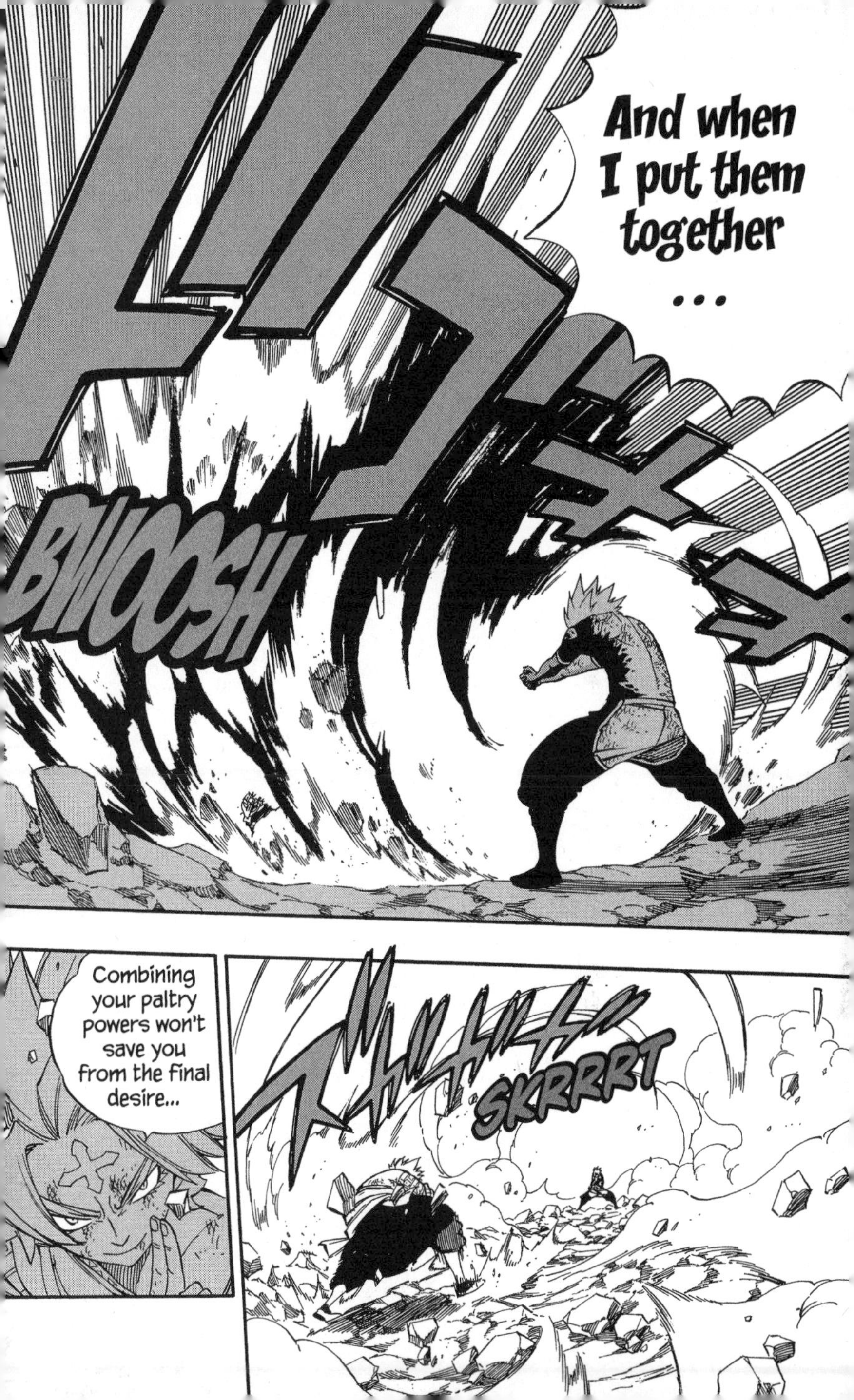
And when I put them together ...
BWOOSH
Combining your paltry powers won't save you from the final desire...
SKRRRT

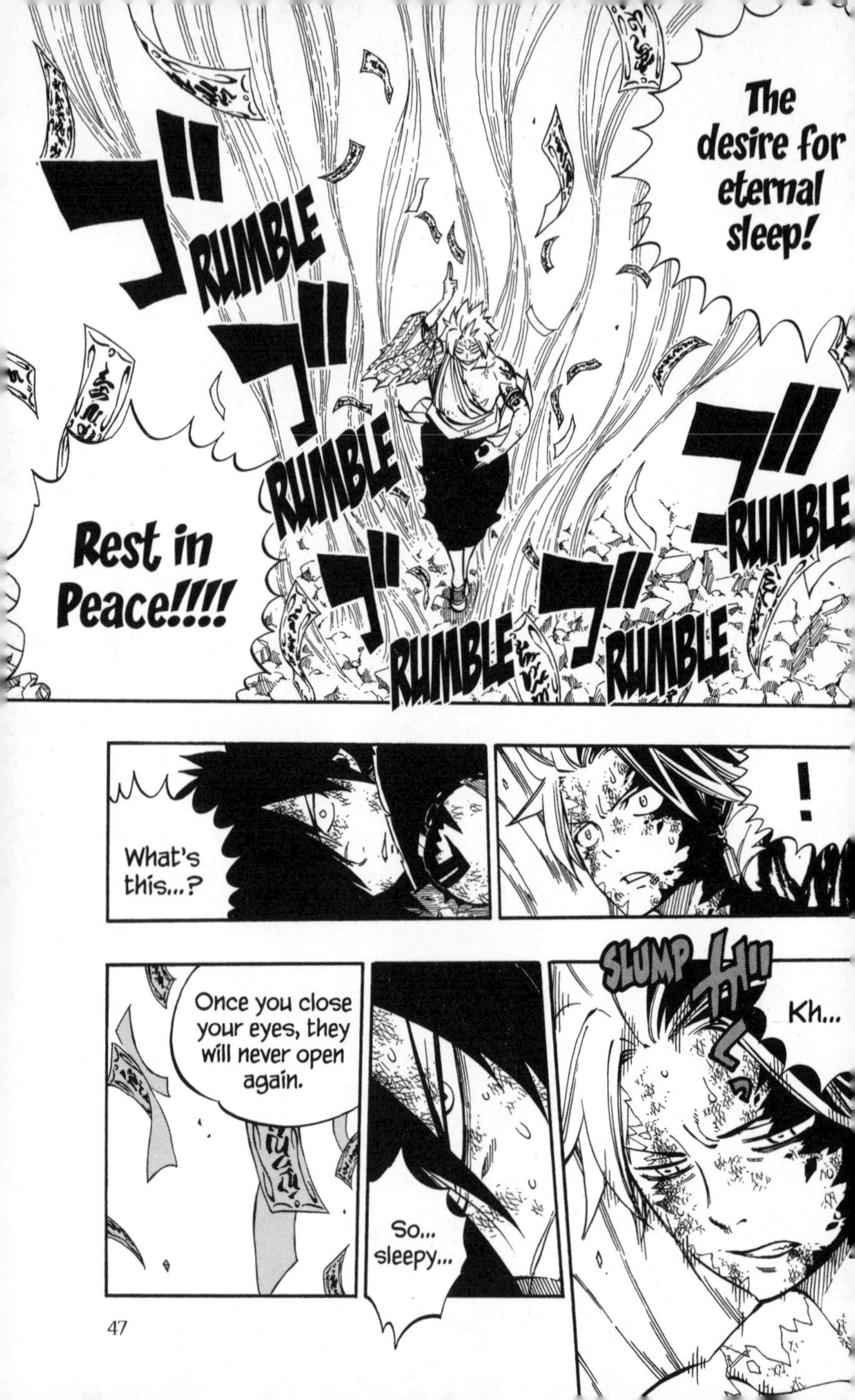
The desire for eternal sleep!
ゴ RUMBLE
ゴ RUMBLE
ゴ RUMBLE
ゴ RUMBLE
ゴ RUMBLE
Rest in Peace!!!!
!
What's this...?
SLUMP
Kh...
So... sleepy...
Once you close your eyes, they will never open again.

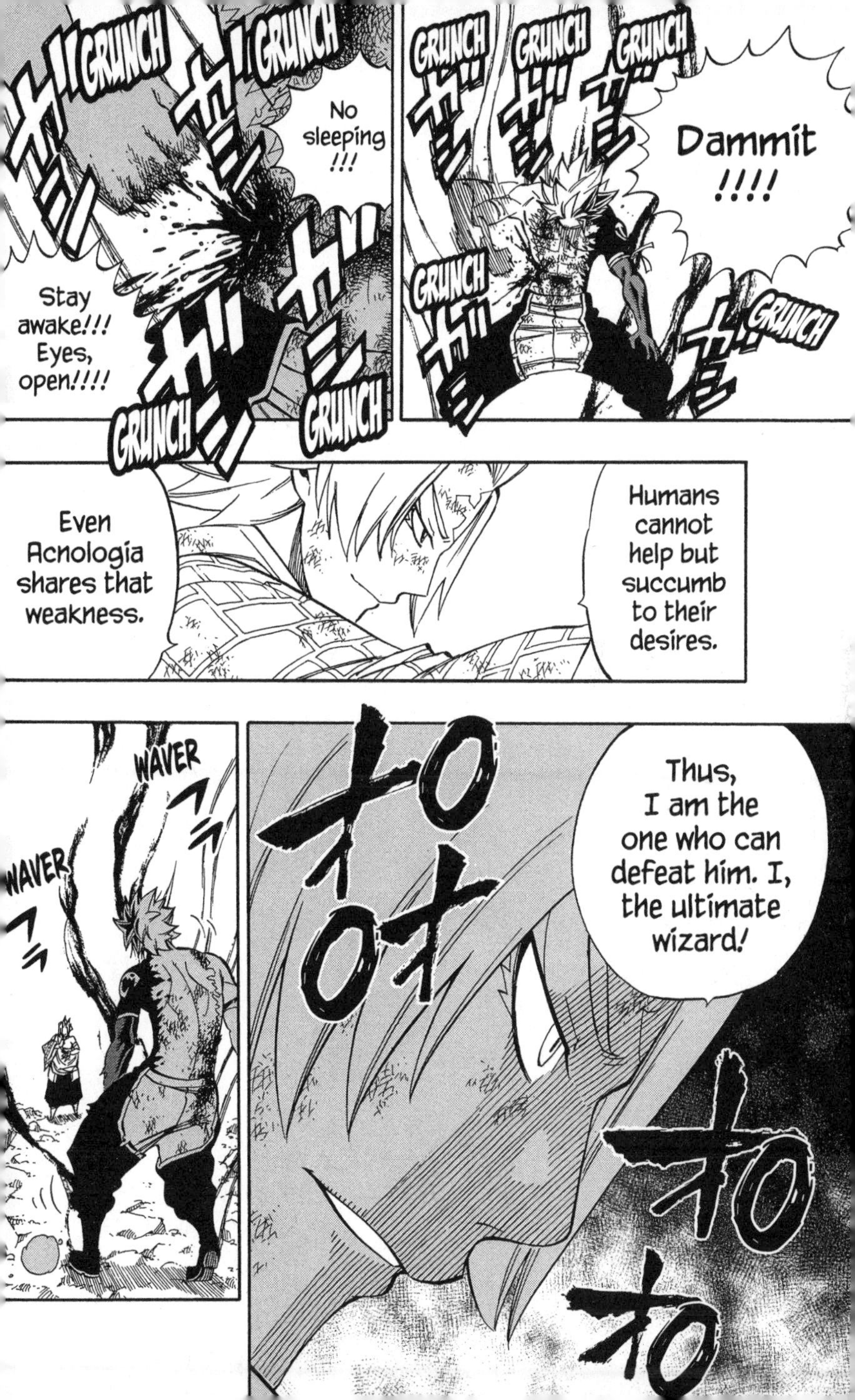
GRUNCH
GRUNCH
GRUNCH
Dammit!!!!
GRUNCH
GRUNCH
GRUNCH
GRUNCH
No sleeping!!!
Stay awake!!! Eyes, open!!!!
GRUNCH
GRUNCH
Humans cannot help but succumb to their desires.
Even Acnologia shares that weakness.
Thus, I am the one who can defeat him. I, the ultimate wizard!
WAVER
WAVER

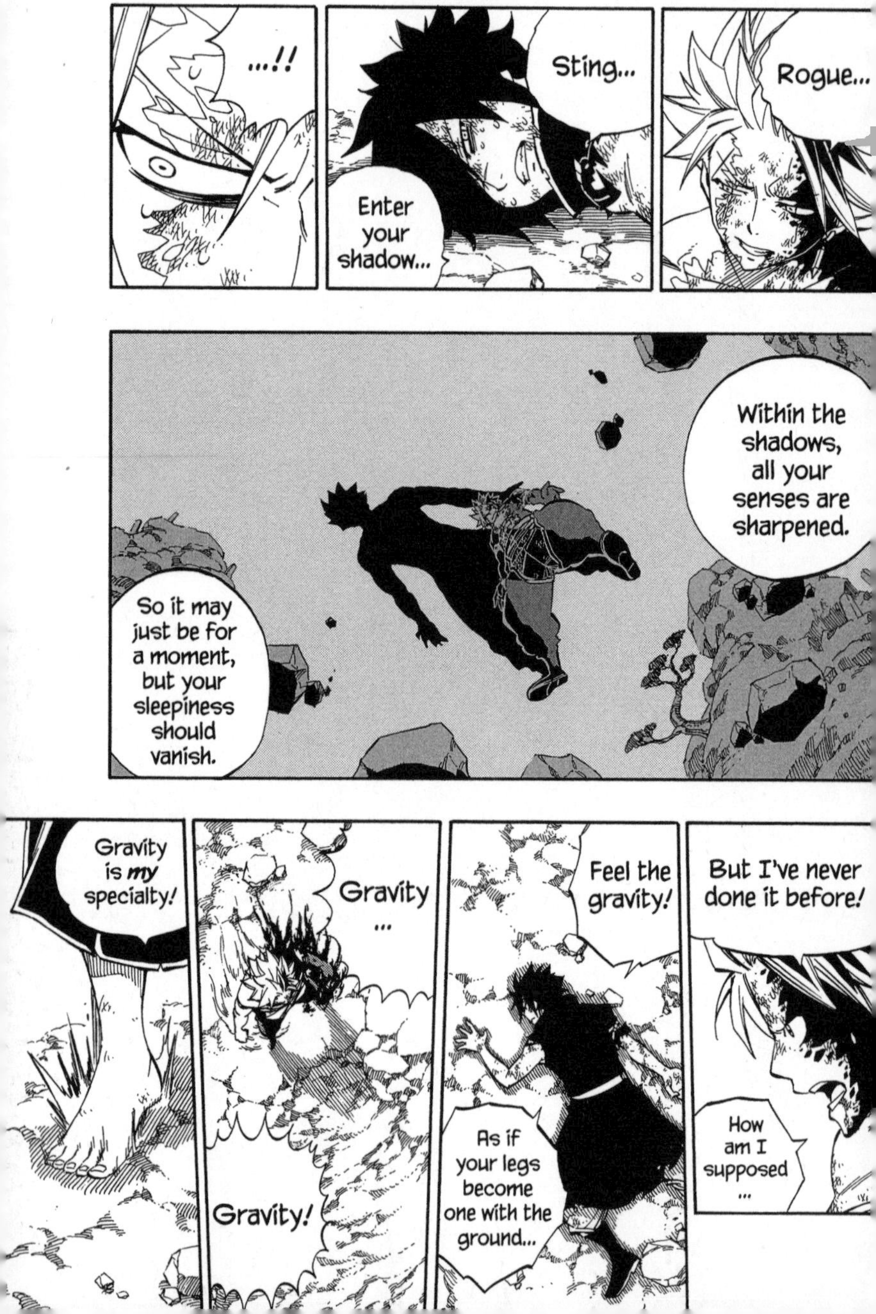
Rogue...
Sting...
Enter your shadow...
...!!
Within the shadows, all your senses are sharpened.
So it may just be for a moment, but your sleepiness should vanish.
But I've never done it before!
How am I supposed ...
Feel the gravity!
As if your legs become one with the ground...
Gravity ...
Gravity!
Gravity is *my* specialty!

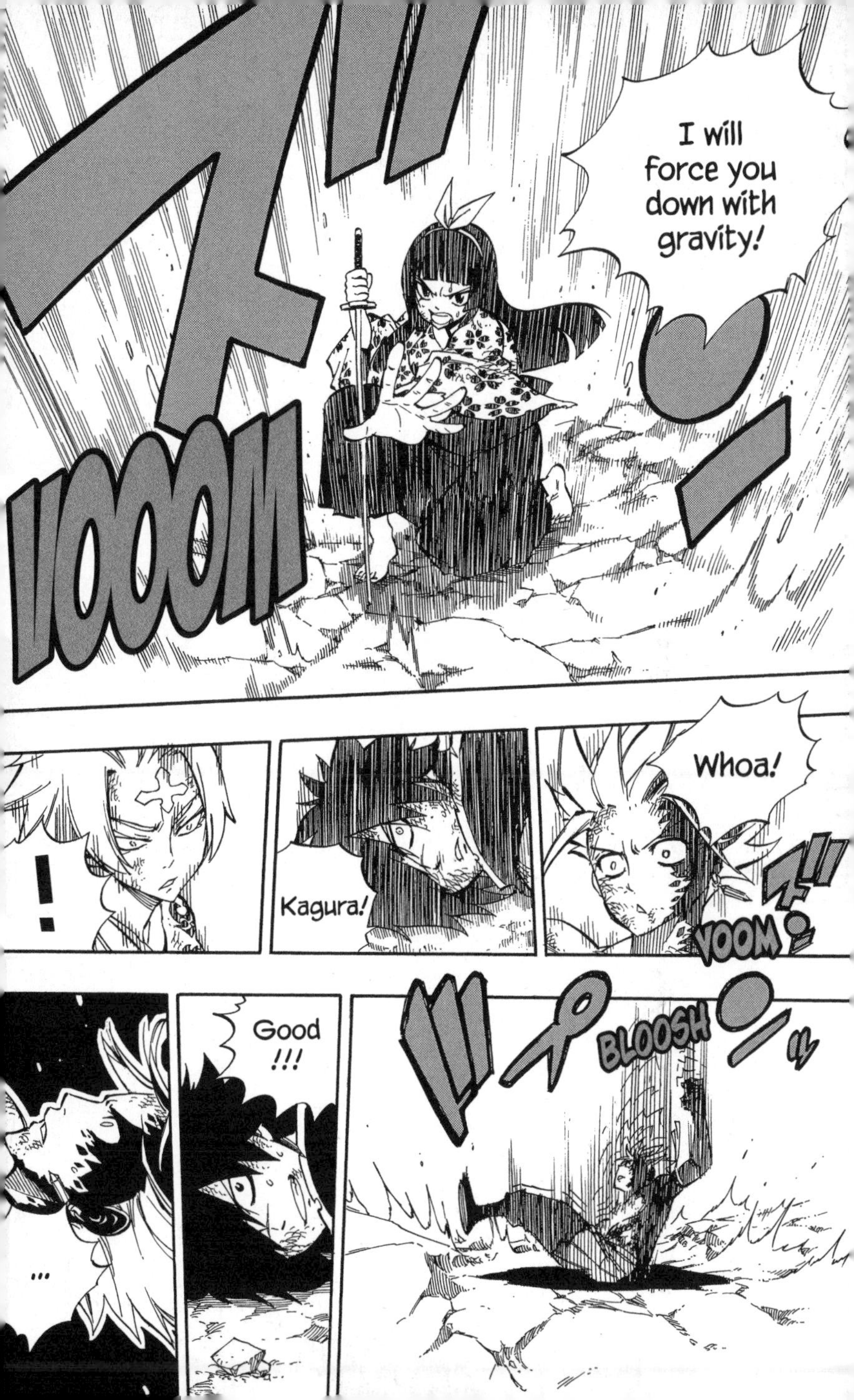
I will force you down with gravity!
VOOOM
Whoa!
VOOM
Kagura!
!
BLOOSH
Good !!!
...

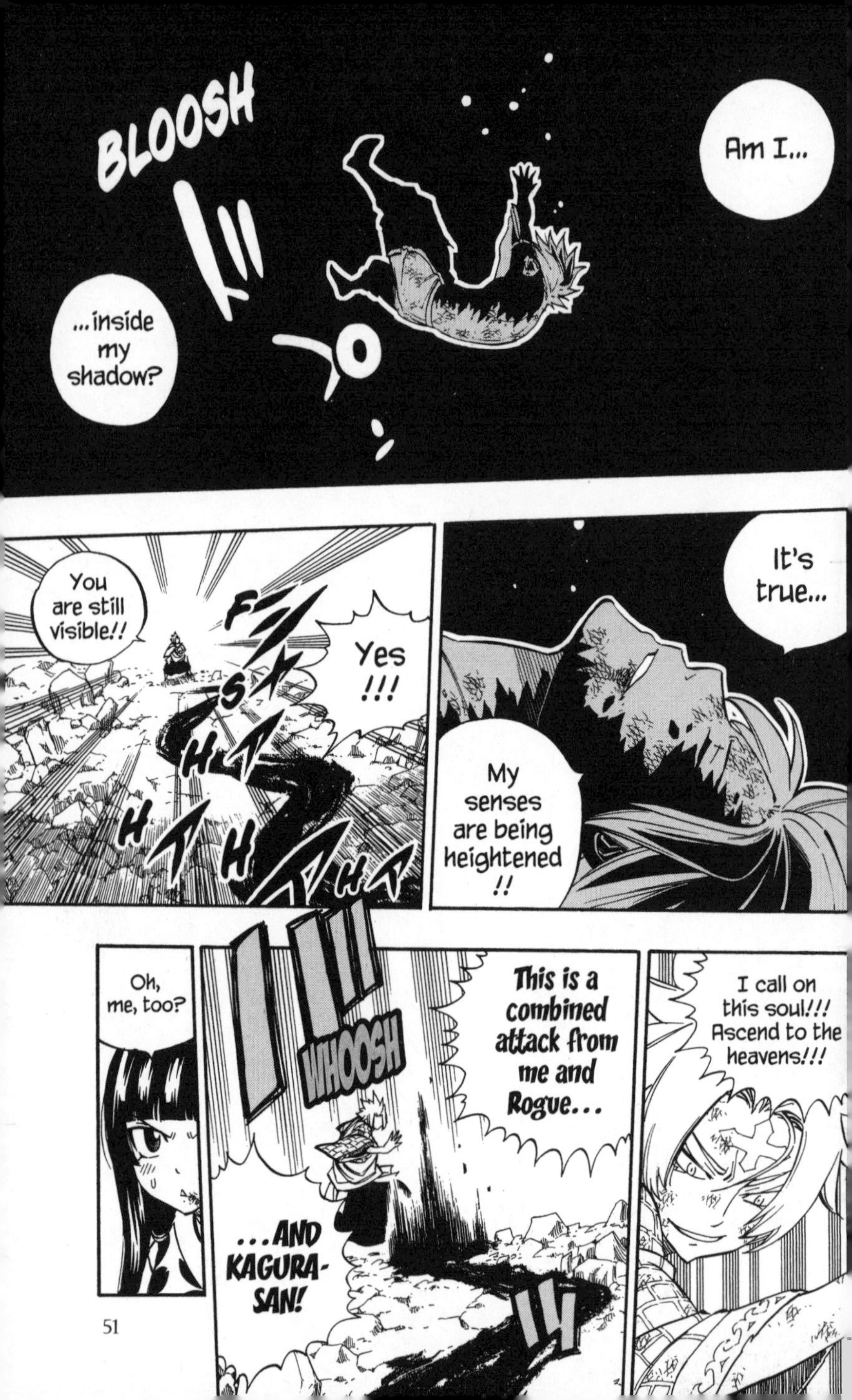
Am I...
BLOOSH
...inside my shadow?
It's true...
My senses are being heightened!!
Yes!!!
You are still visible!!
I call on this soul!!! Ascend to the heavens!!!
This is a combined attack from me and Rogue...
WHOOSH
...AND KAGURA-SAN!
Oh, me, too?

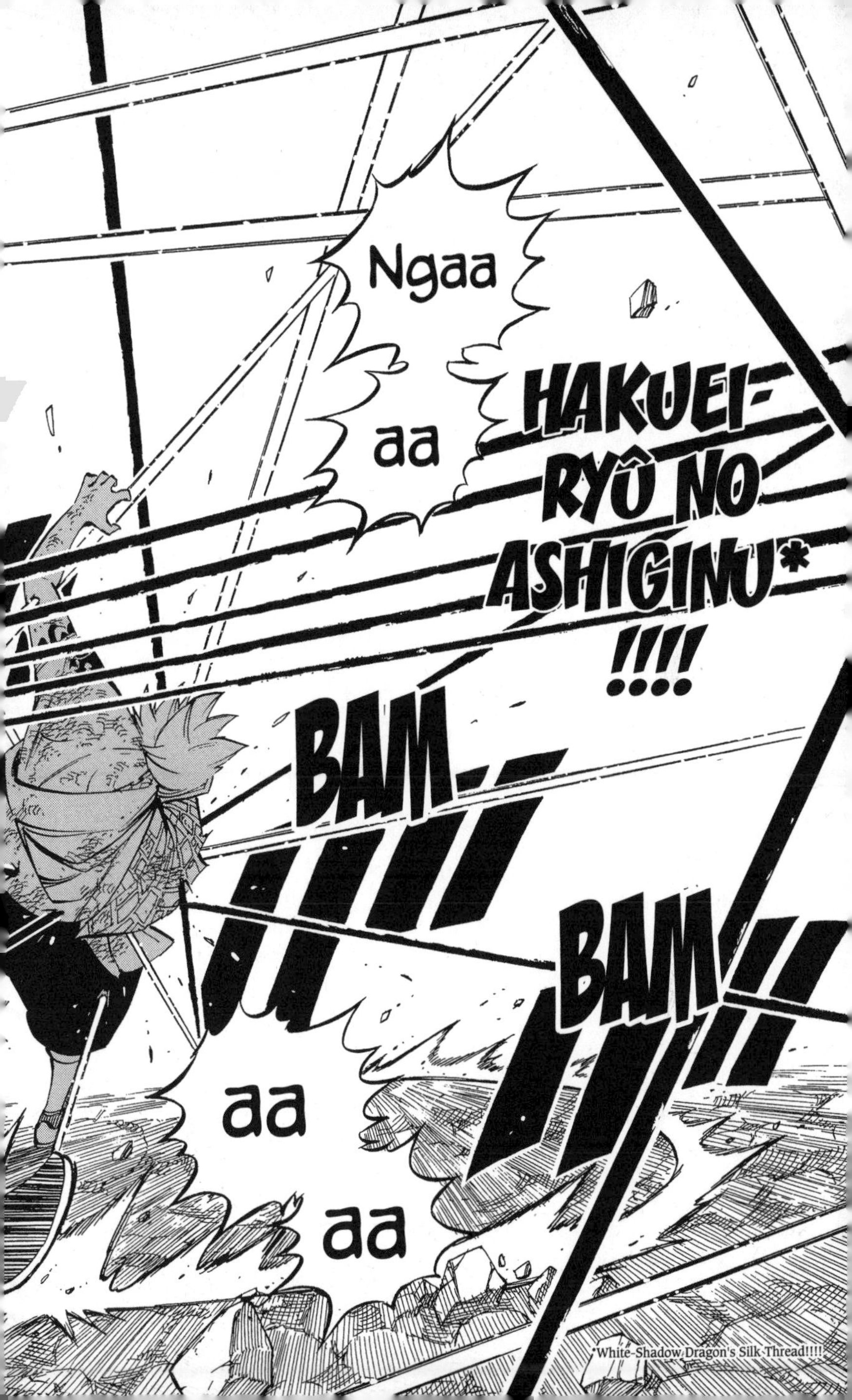
HAKUEI-RYÛ NO ASHIGINU* !!!!
Ngaa
aa
BAM
BAM
aa
aa
*White-Shadow Dragon's Silk Thread!!!!

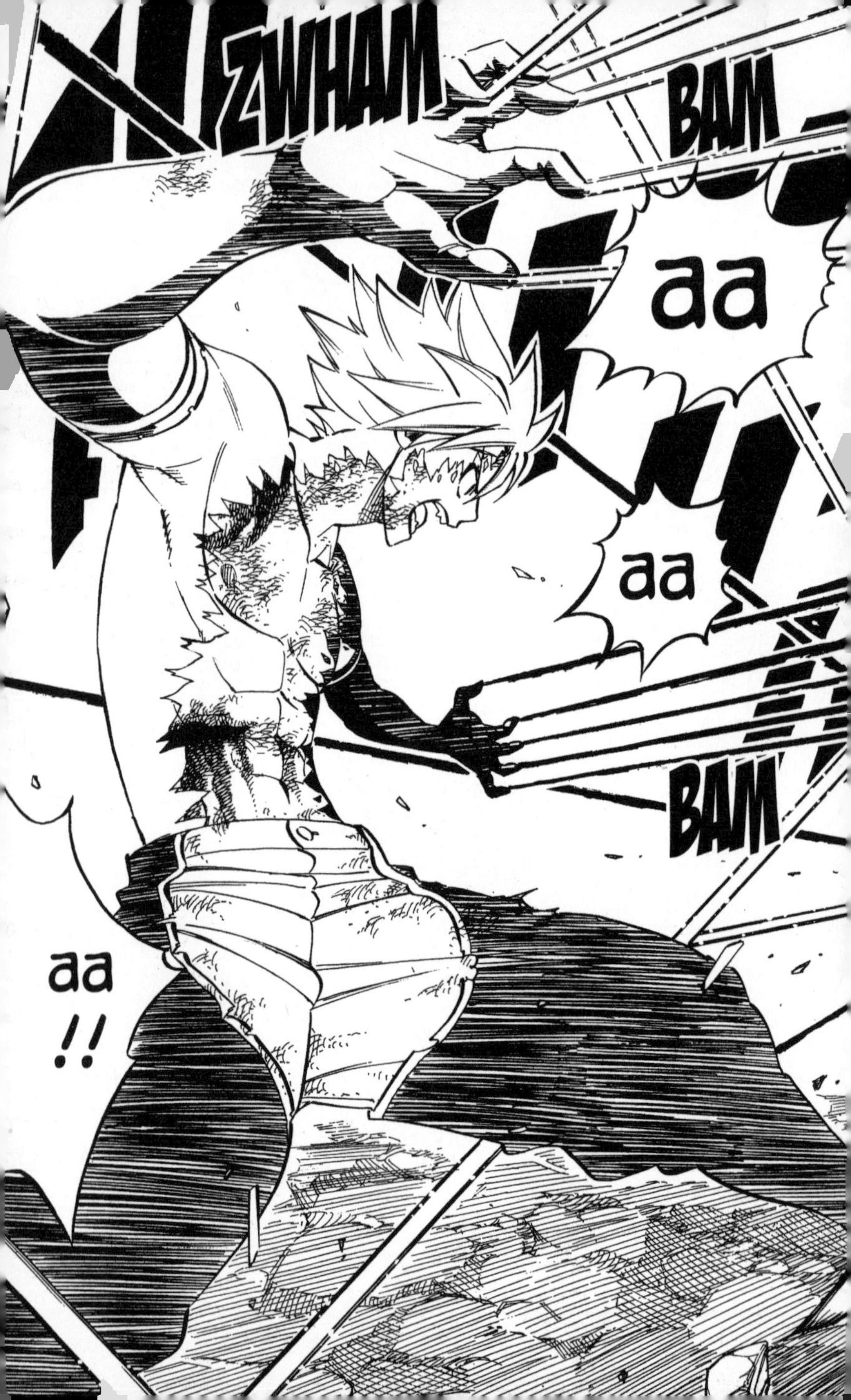
BAM
ZWHAM
aa
aa
BAM
aa
!!

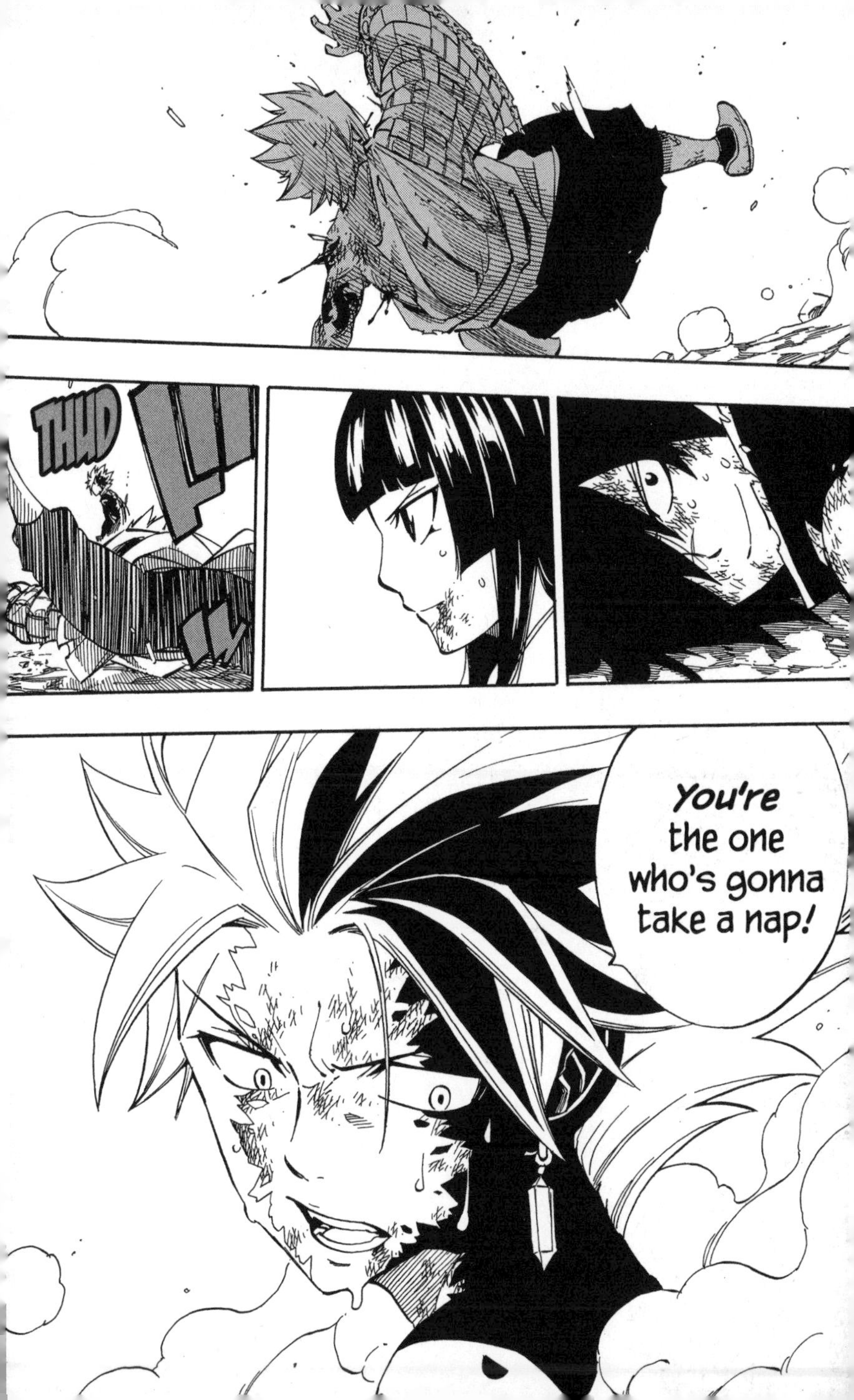
THUD
You're the one who's gonna take a nap!

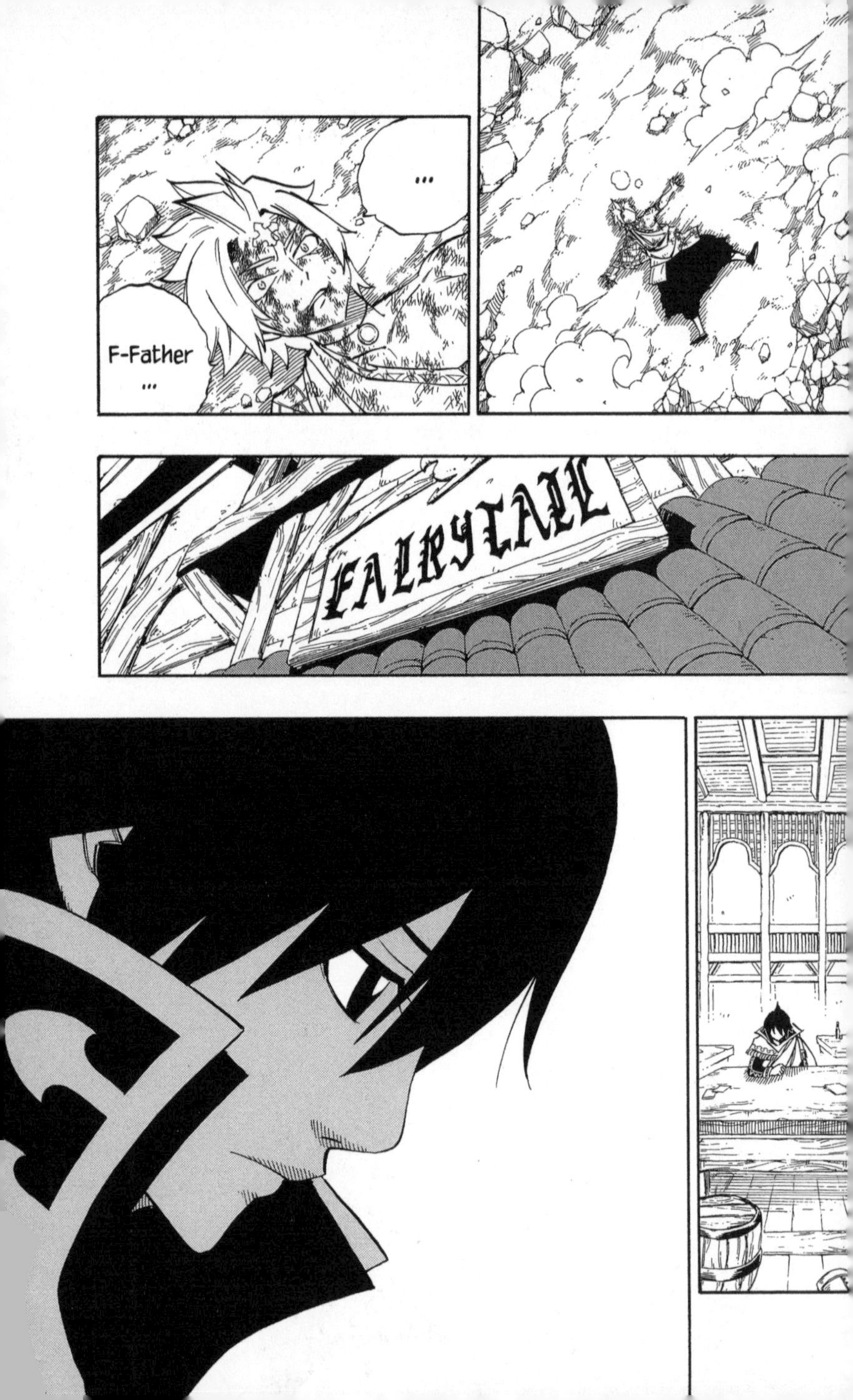
...
F-Father ...
FAIRYTAIL

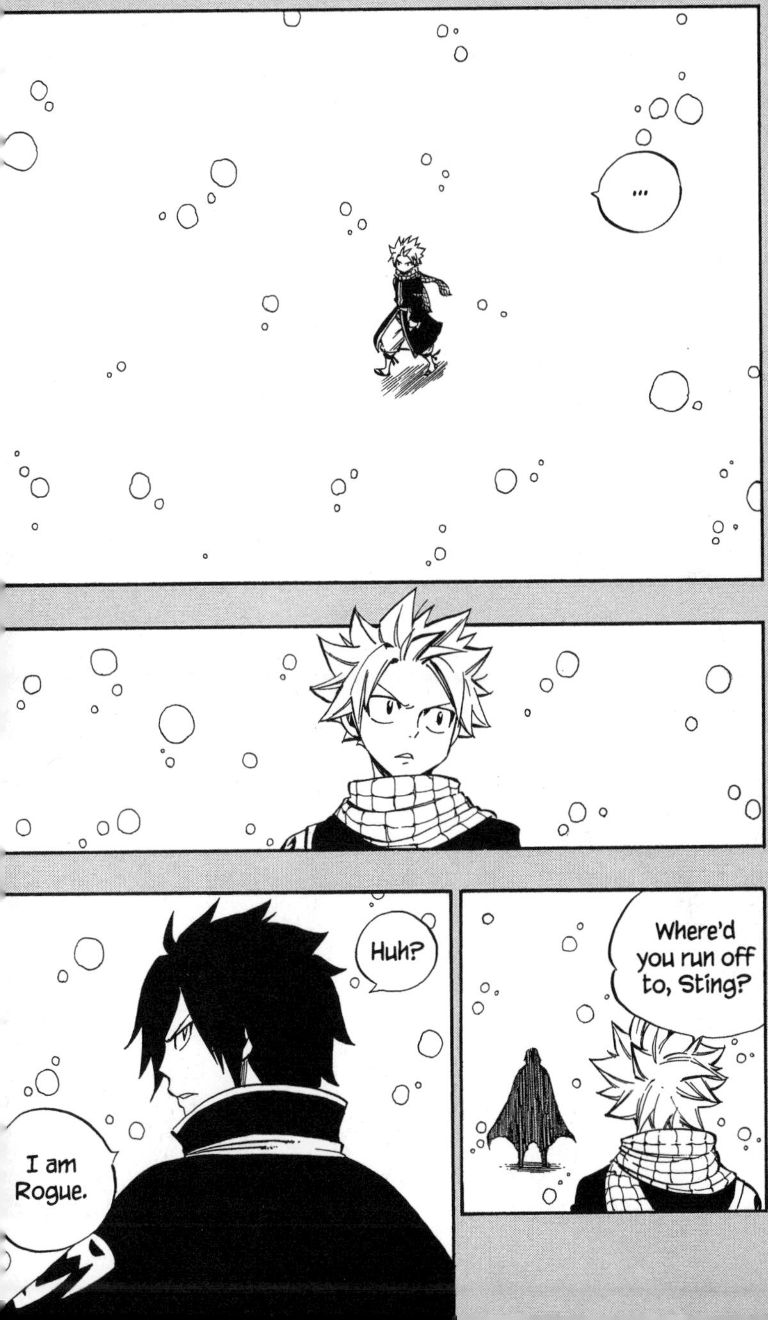
...
Where'd you run off to, Sting?
Huh?
I am Rogue.

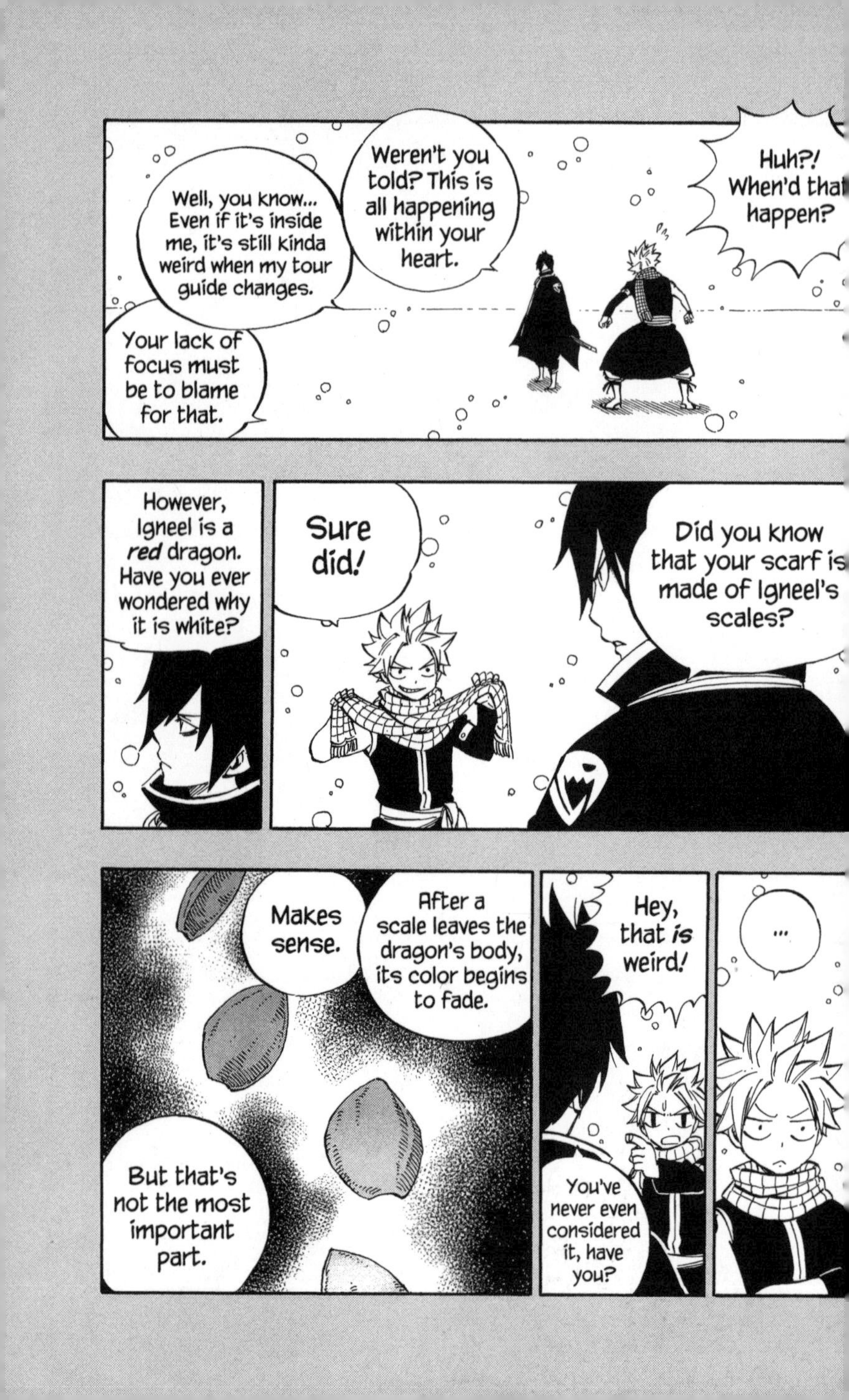

Huh?! When'd that happen?
Weren't you told? This is all happening within your heart.
Well, you know... Even if it's inside me, it's still kinda weird when my tour guide changes.
Your lack of focus must be to blame for that.
Did you know that your scarf is made of Igneel's scales?
Sure did!
However, Igneel is a *red* dragon. Have you ever wondered why it is white?
...
Hey, that *is* weird!
You've never even considered it, have you?
After a scale leaves the dragon's body, its color begins to fade.
Makes sense.
But that's not the most important part.

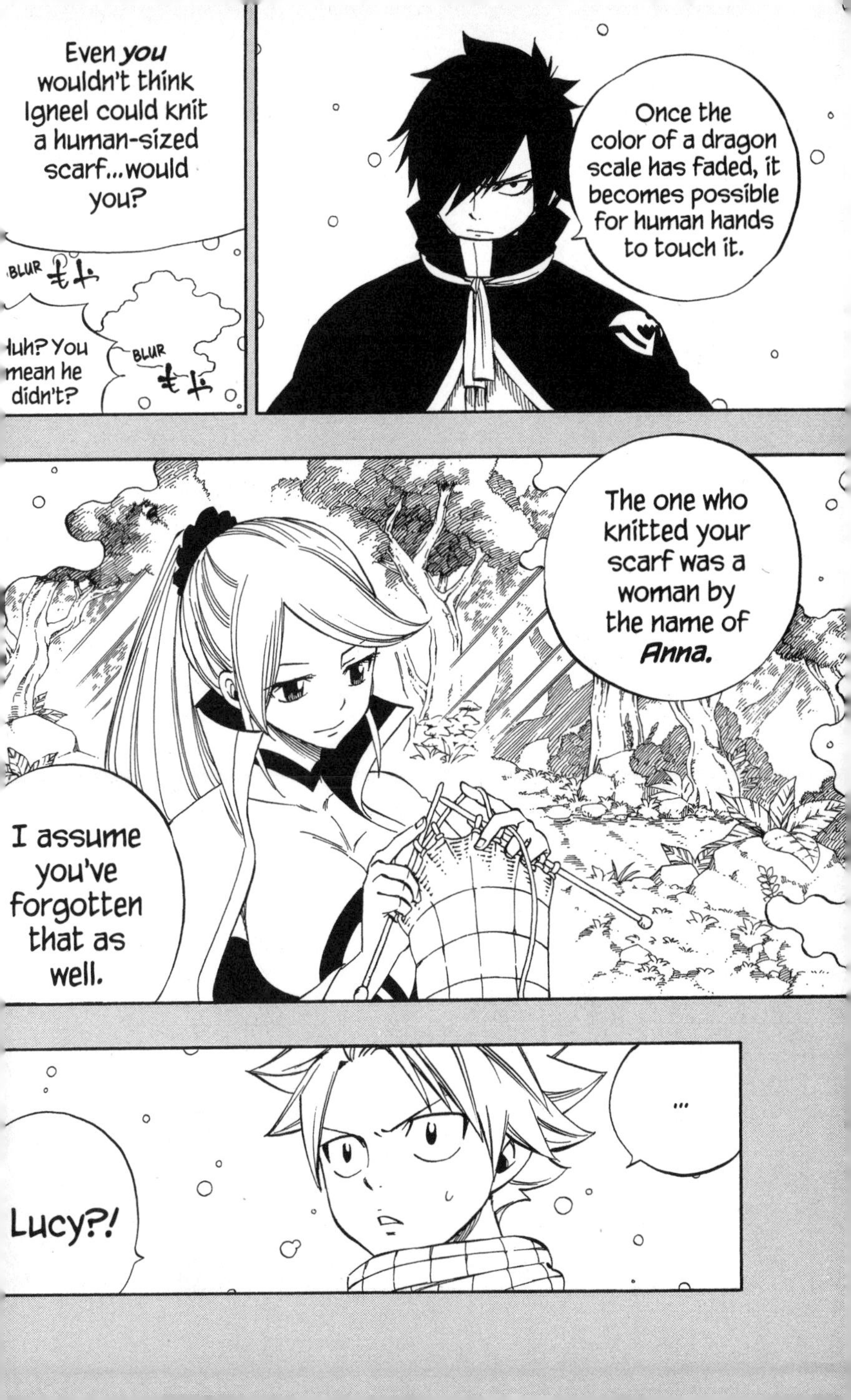
Once the color of a dragon scale has faded, it becomes possible for human hands to touch it.
Even *you* wouldn't think Igneel could knit a human-sized scarf...would you?
BLUR
Huh? You mean he didn't?
BLUR
The one who knitted your scarf was a woman by the name of *Anna.*
I assume you've forgotten that as well.
...
Lucy?!

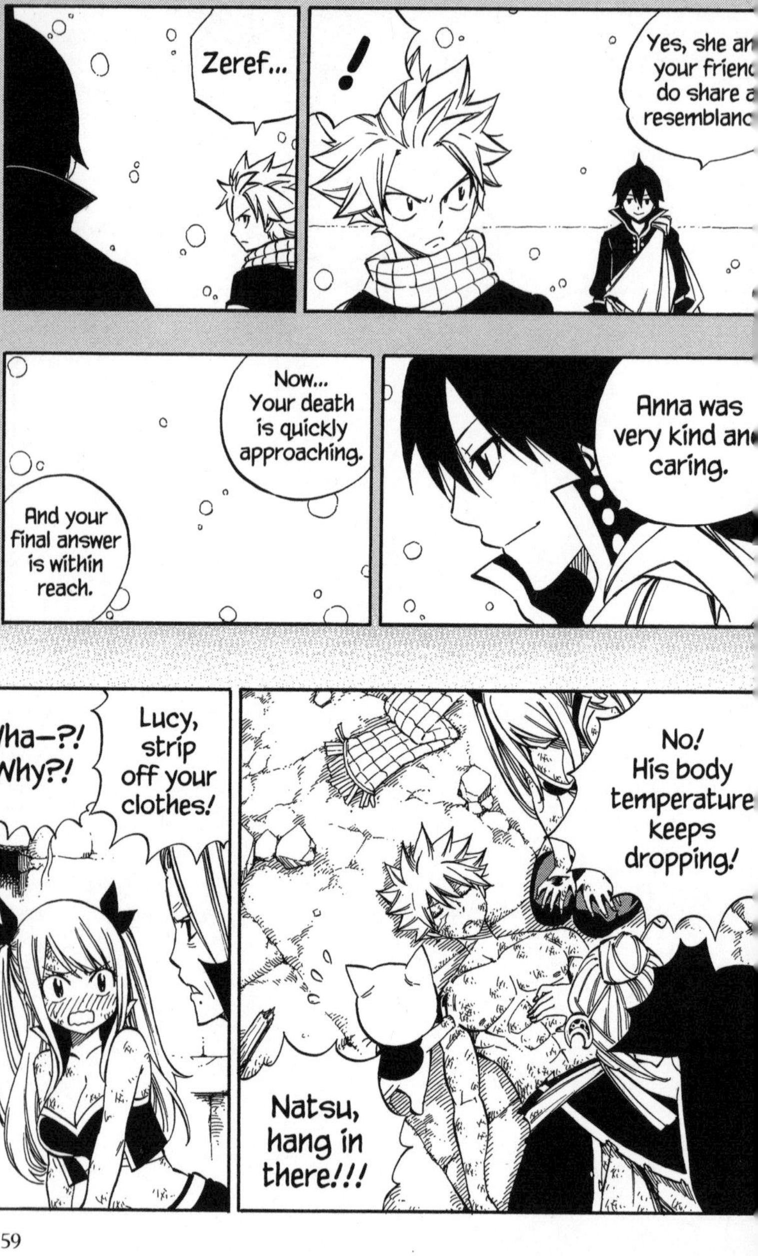

Yes, she ar your frien do share a resemblanc
!
Zeref...
Anna was very kind an caring.
Now... Your death is quickly approaching.
And your final answer is within reach.
No! His body temperature keeps dropping!
Natsu, hang in there!!!
Lucy, strip off your clothes!
Wha—?! Why?!

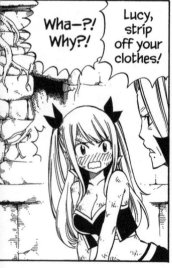

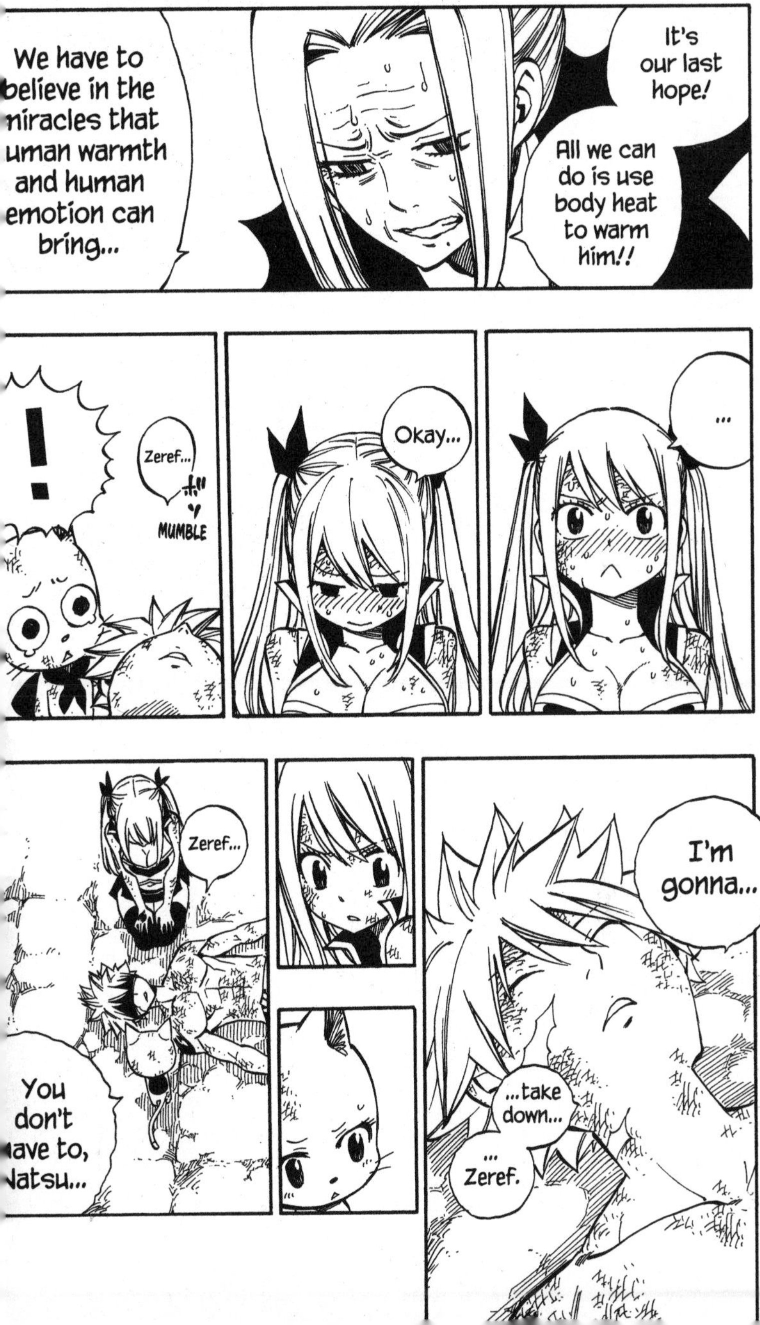
It's our last hope!
All we can do is use body heat to warm him!!
We have to believe in the niracles that uman warmth and human emotion can bring...
...
Okay...
!
Zeref...
MUMBLE
I'm gonna...
...take down...
... Zeref.
Zeref...
You don't ave to, Vatsu...

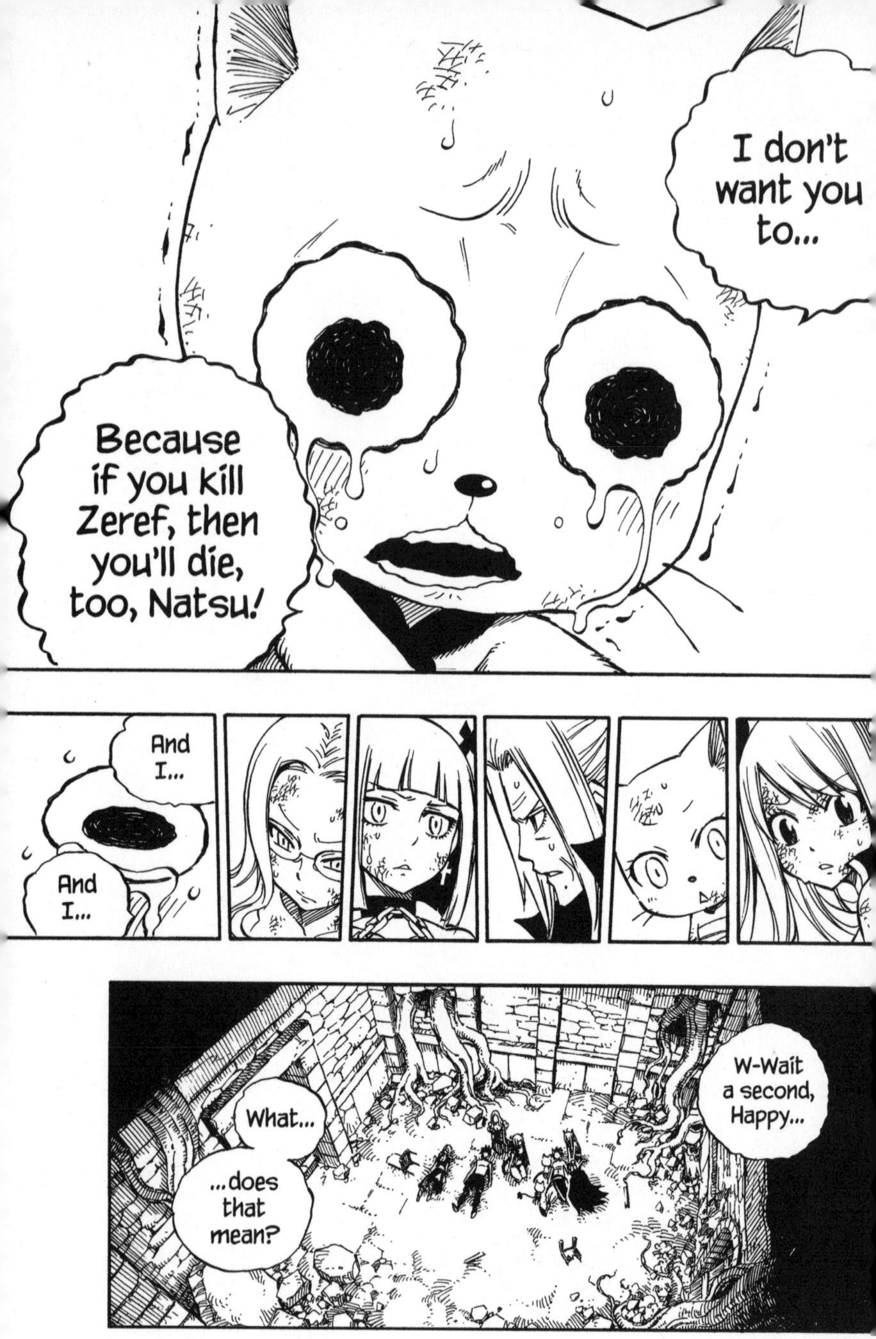
I don't want you to...
Because if you kill Zeref, then you'll die, too, Natsu!
And I...
And I...
W-Wait a second, Happy...
What...
...does that mean?

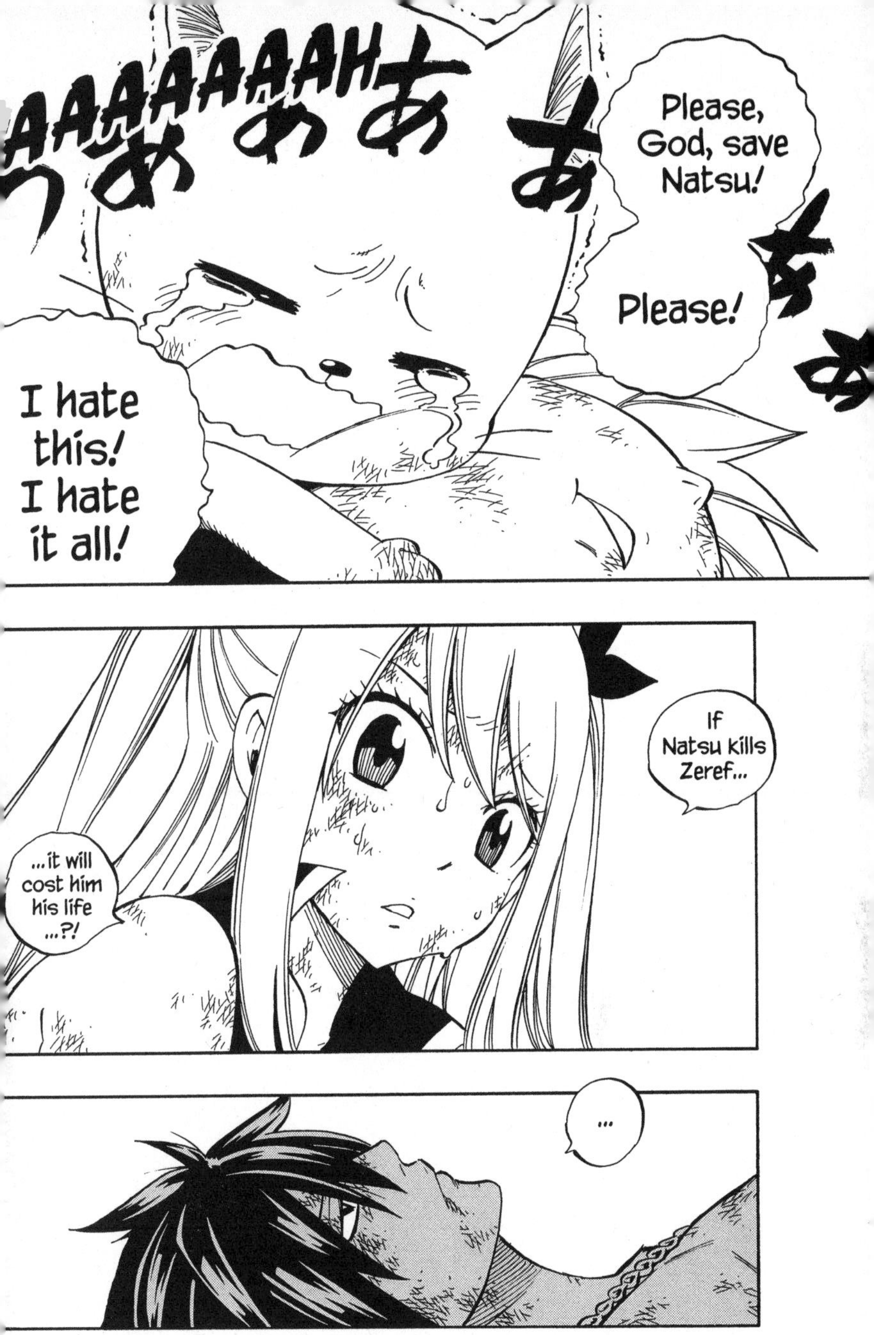
Please, God, save Natsu!
Please!
AAAAAAAH
I hate this! I hate it all!
If Natsu kills Zeref...
...it will cost him his life ...?!
...

FAIRY TAIL

フェアリーテイル

Chapter 513: Hanamaru

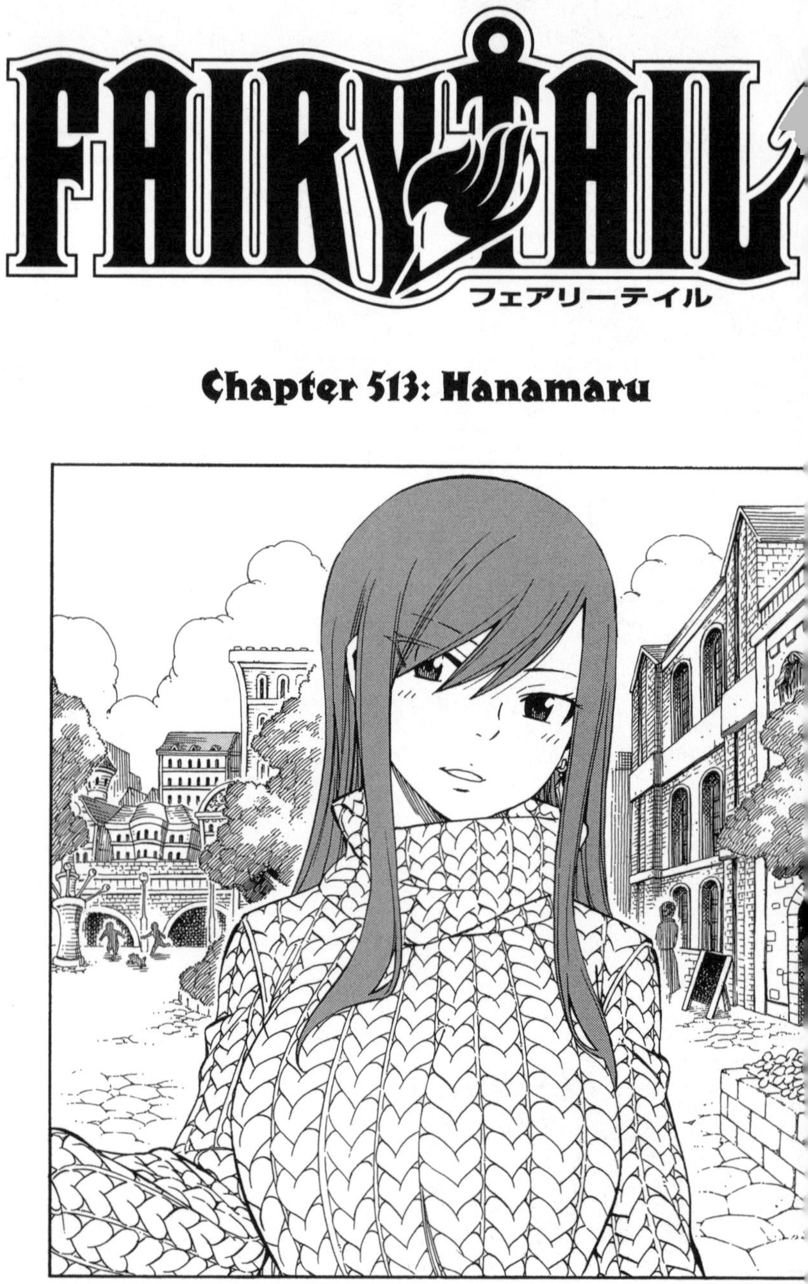

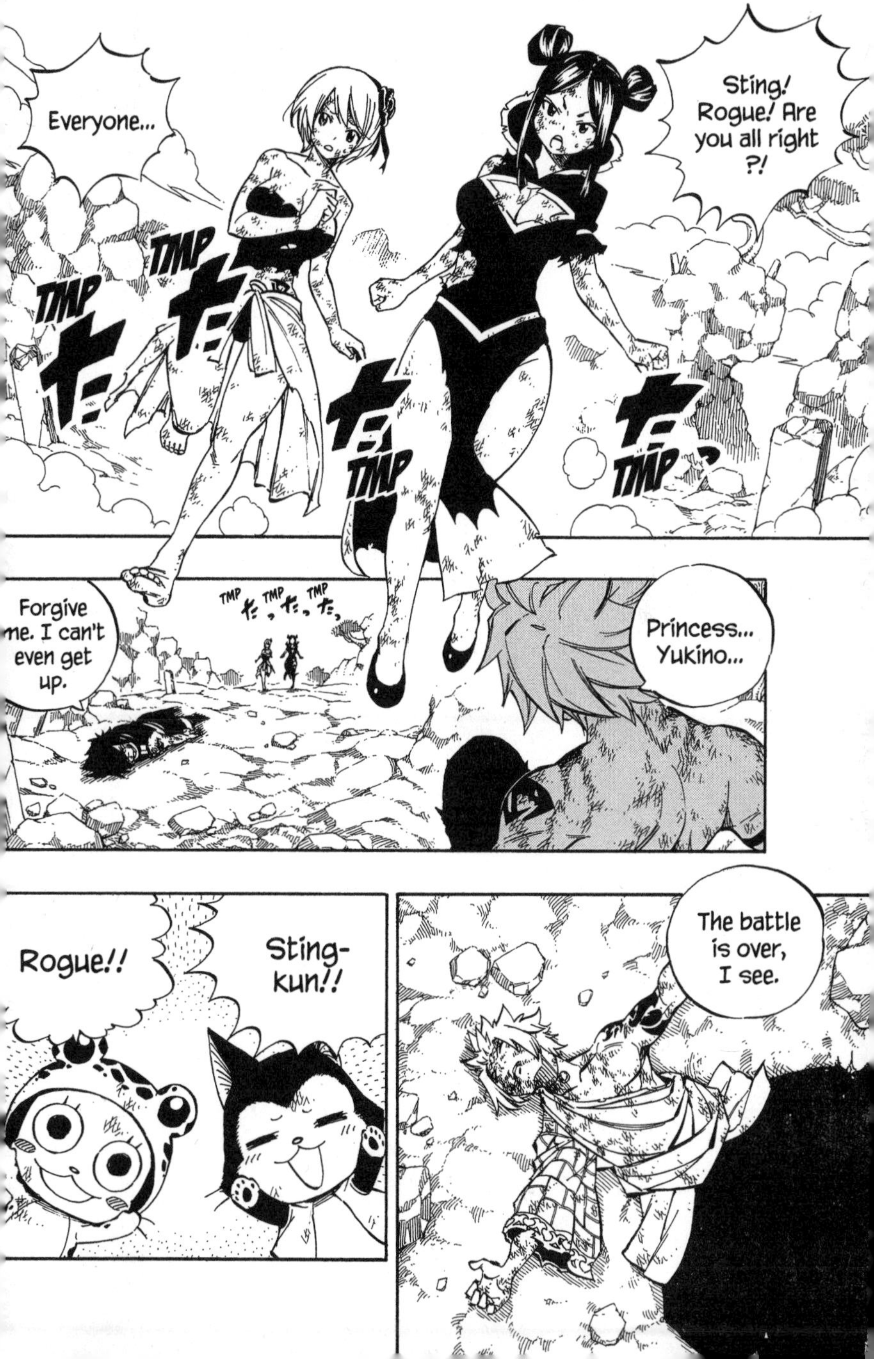
Sting! Rogue! Are you all right ?!
Everyone...
TMP
TMP
TMP
TMP
Princess... Yukino...
TMP TMP TMP
Forgive me. I can't even get up.
The battle is over, I see.
Sting-kun!!
Rogue!!

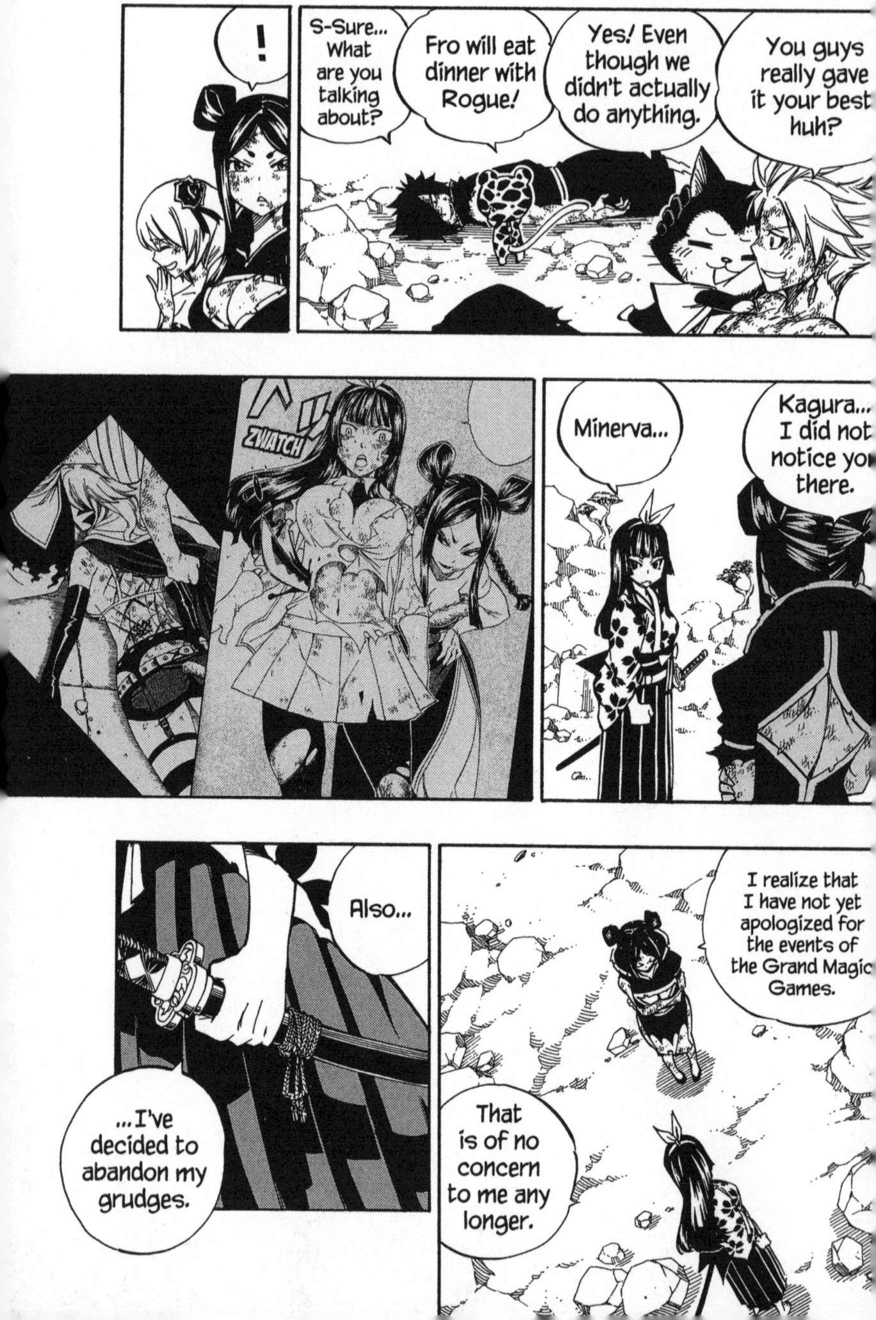
You guys really gave it your best huh?
Yes! Even though we didn't actually do anything.
Fro will eat dinner with Rogue!
S-Sure... What are you talking about?
!
Kagura... I did not notice yo there.
Minerva...
ZWATCH
I realize that I have not yet apologized for the events of the Grand Magic Games.
That is of no concern to me any longer.
Also...
...I've decided to abandon my grudges.

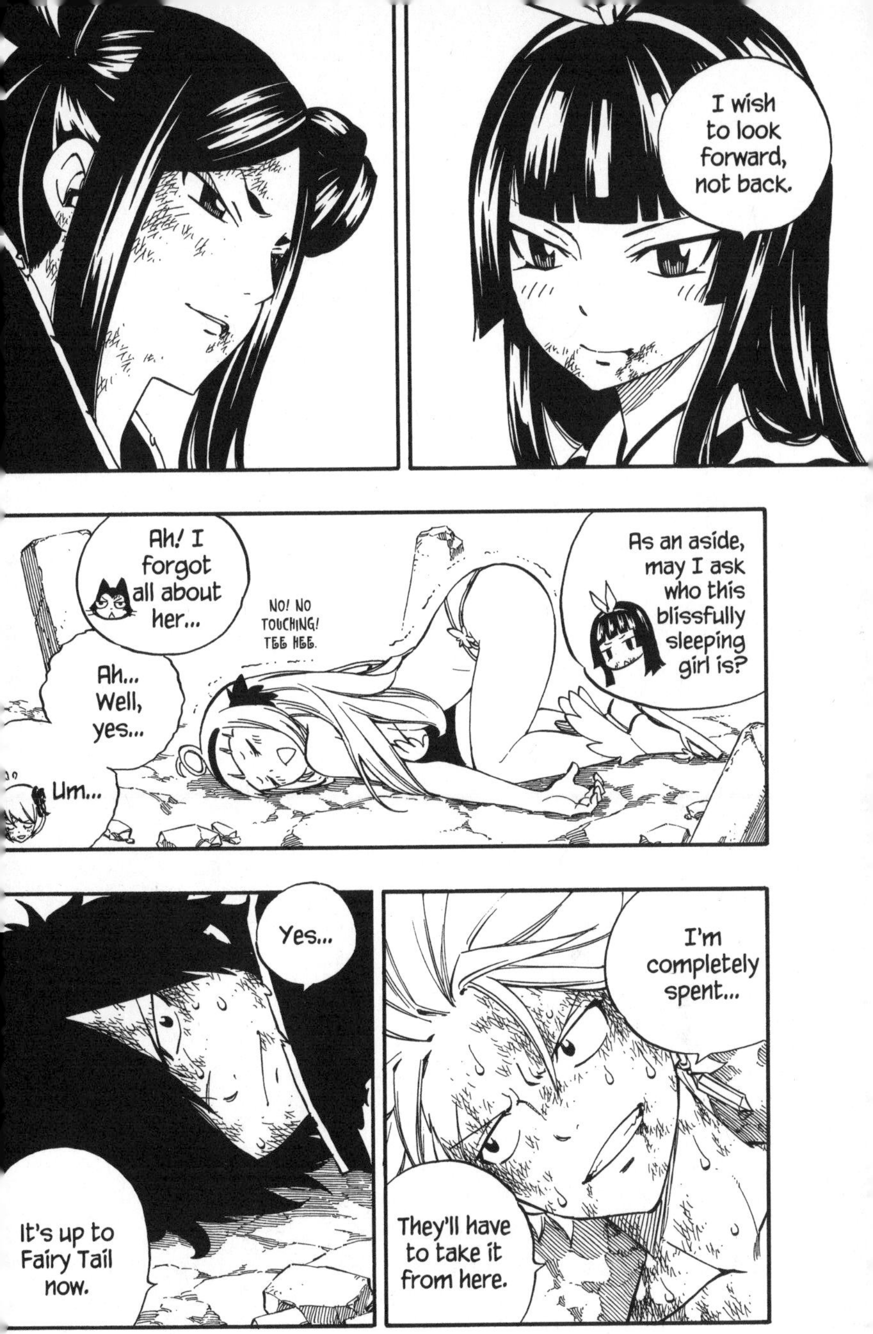
I wish to look forward, not back.
As an aside, may I ask who this blissfully sleeping girl is?
No! No touching! Tee hee.
Ah! I forgot all about her...
Ah... Well, yes...
Um...
I'm completely spent...
They'll have to take it from here.
Yes...
It's up to Fairy Tail now.

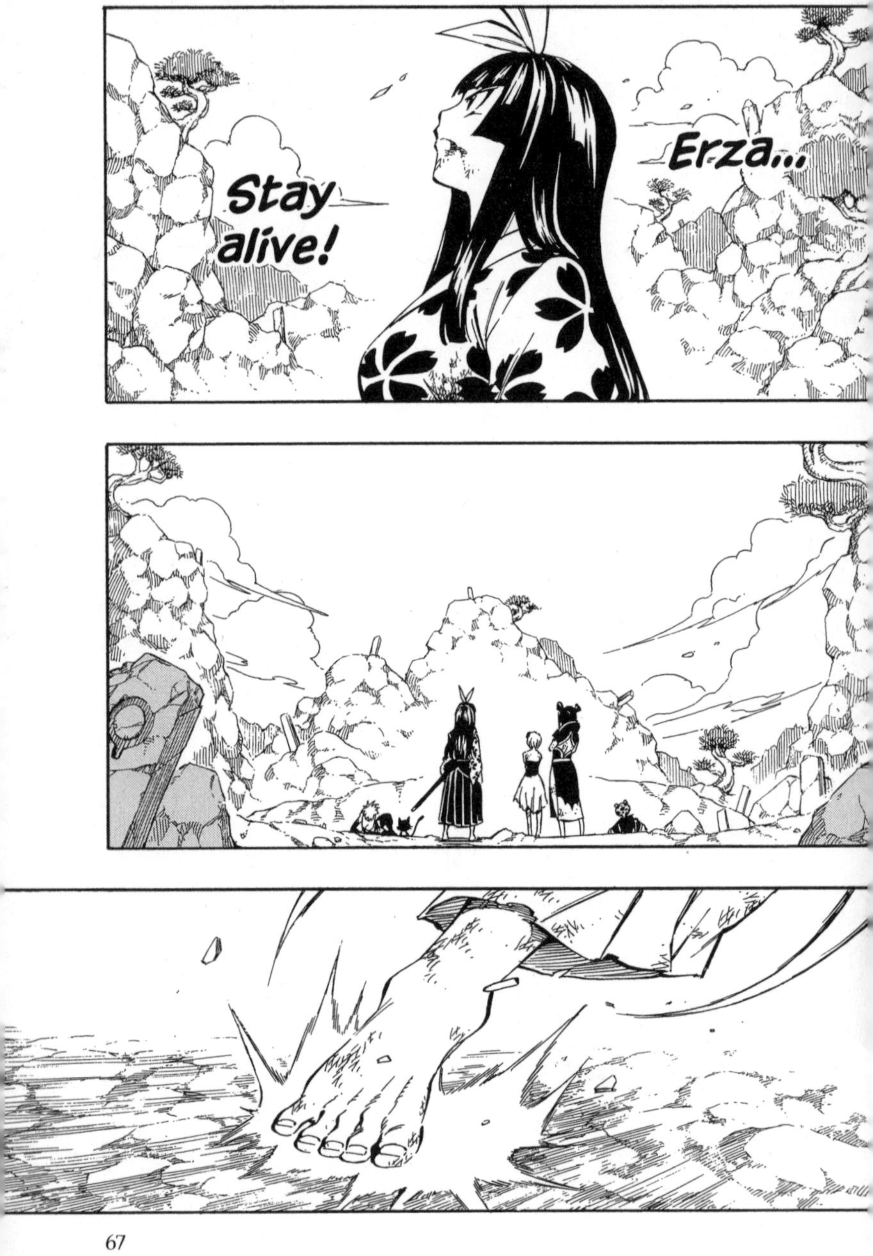
Erza...
Stay alive!

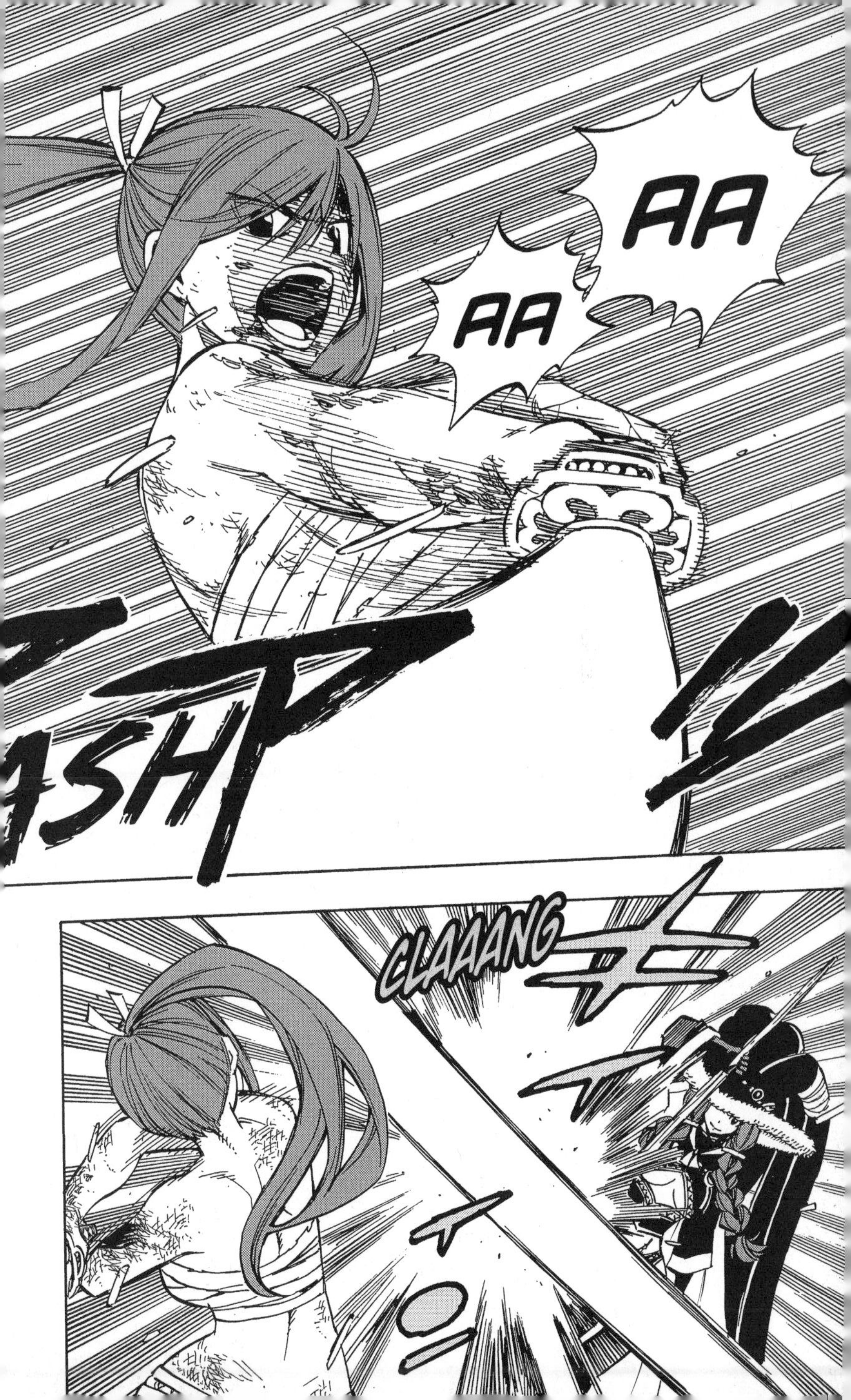
AA
AA
ASH
CLAAANG

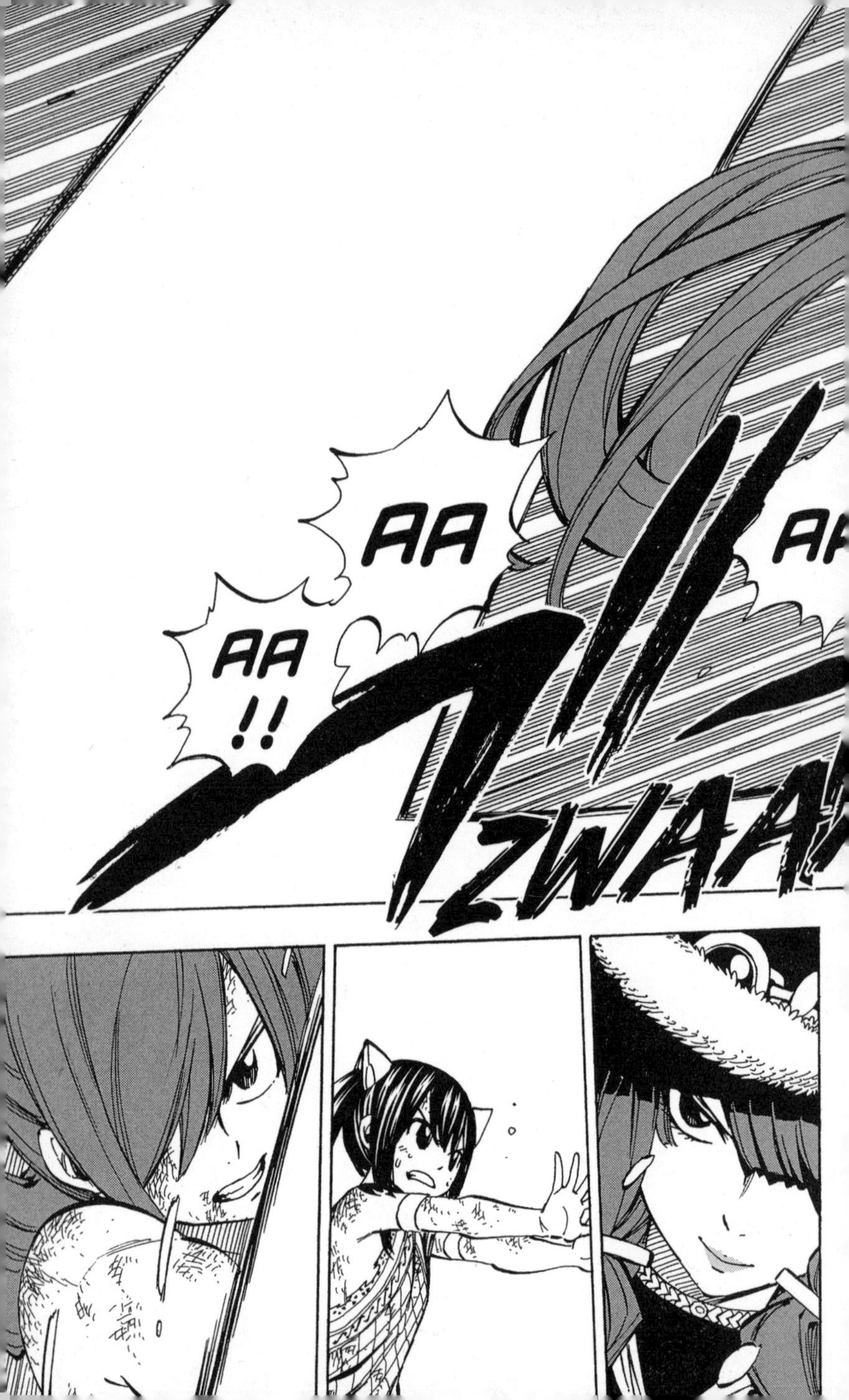
AA
AA!!
ZWAA

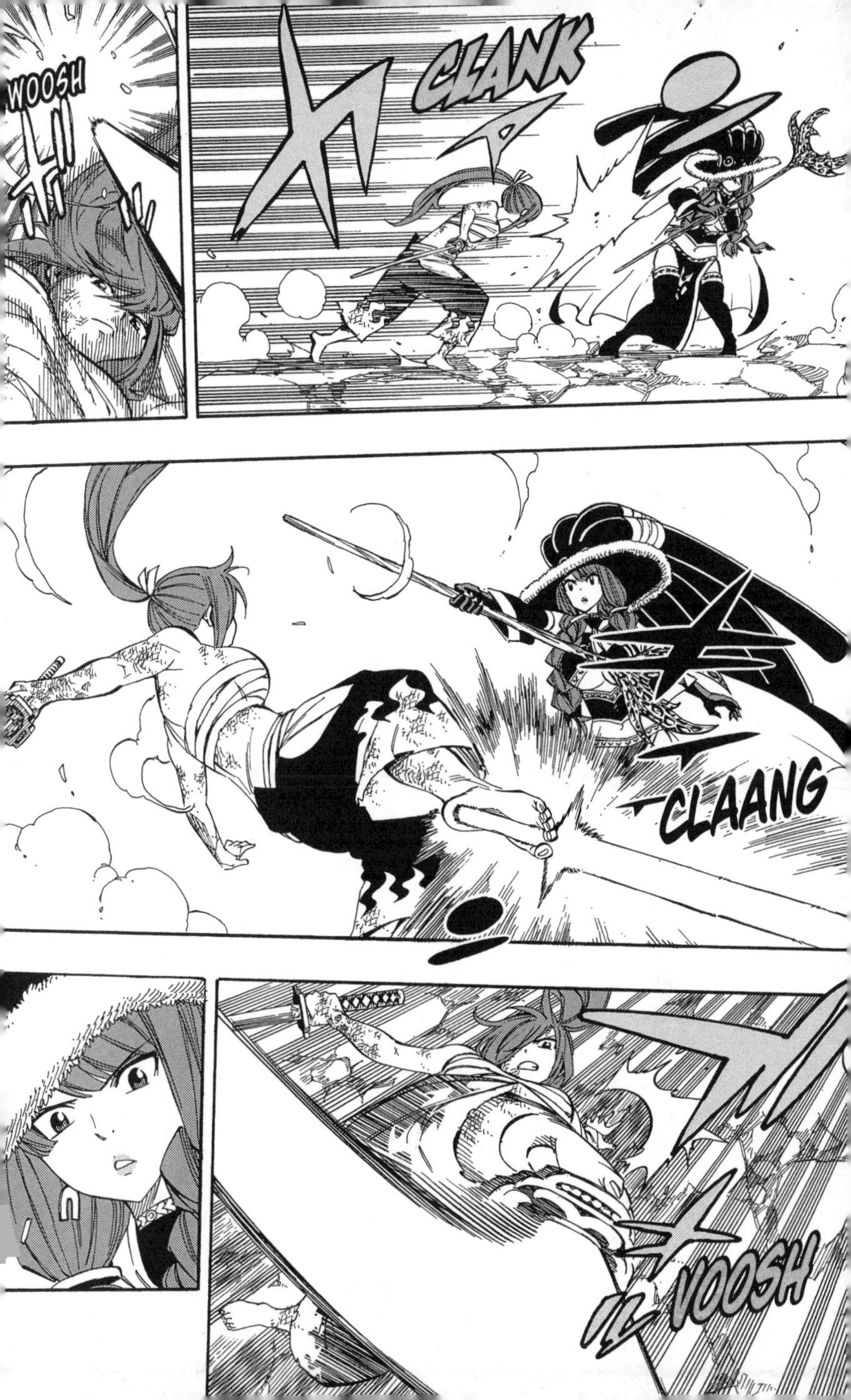
CLANK
WOOSH
CLAANG
VOOSH

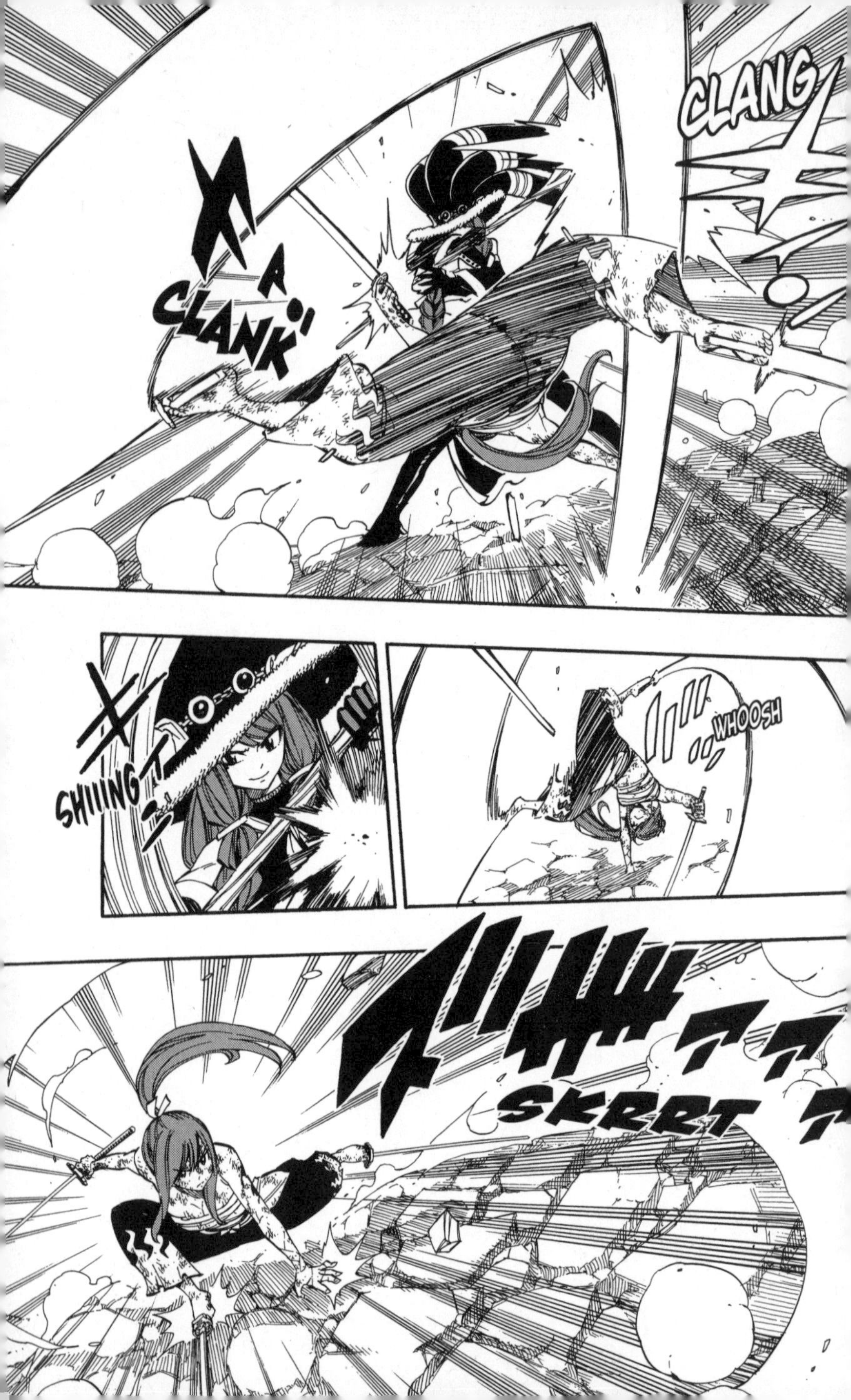
CLANG
CLANK
WHOOSH
SHIIING
SKRRT

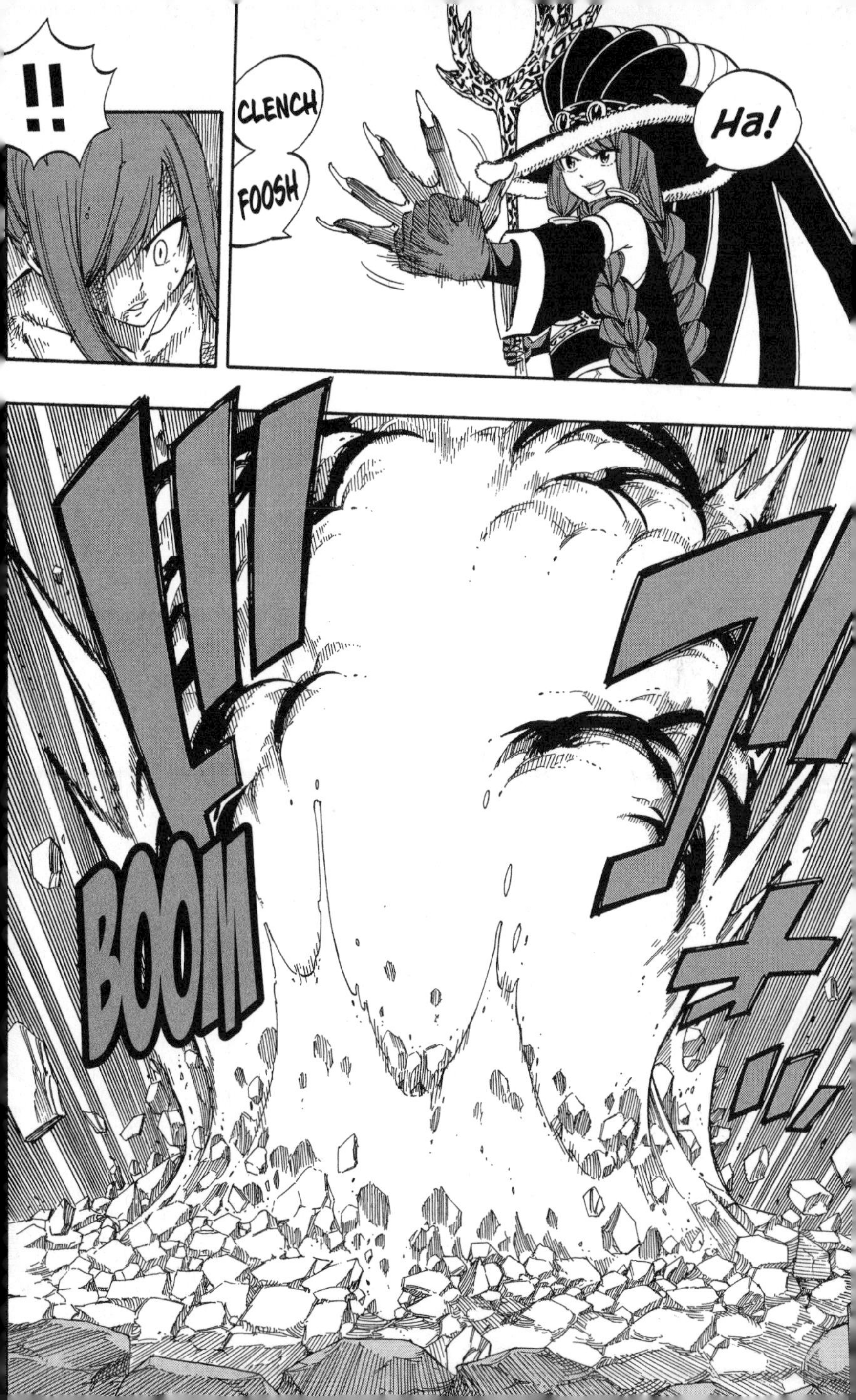
Ha!
CLENCH
FOOSH
!!
BOOM

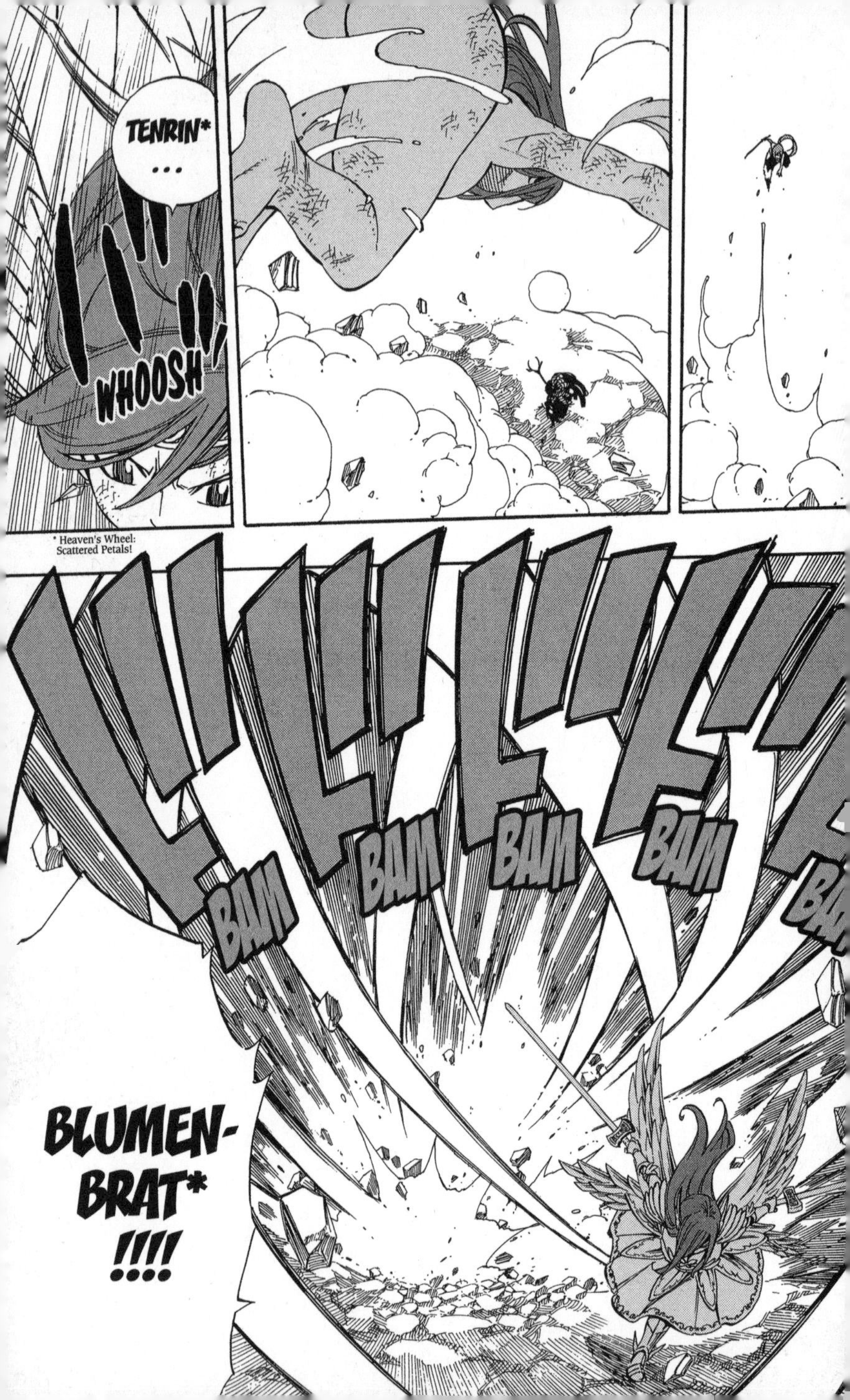
TENRIN* ...
WHOOSH
BAM
BAM
BAM
BAM
BLUMEN-BRAT* !!!!
* Heaven's Wheel: Scattered Petals!

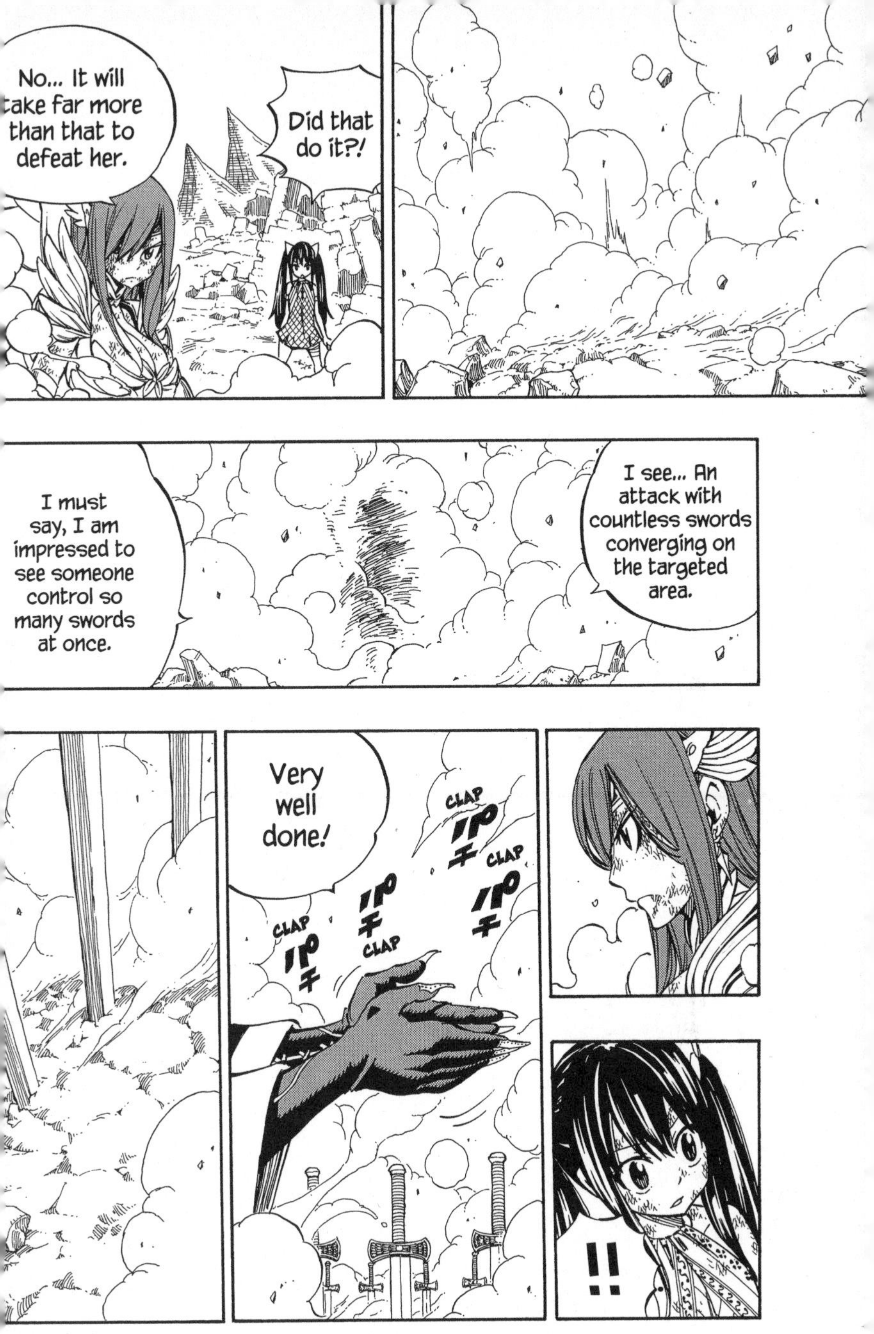
Did that do it?!
No... It will take far more than that to defeat her.
I see... An attack with countless swords converging on the targeted area.
I must say, I am impressed to see someone control so many swords at once.
!!
Very well done!
CLAP
CLAP
CLAP
CLAP

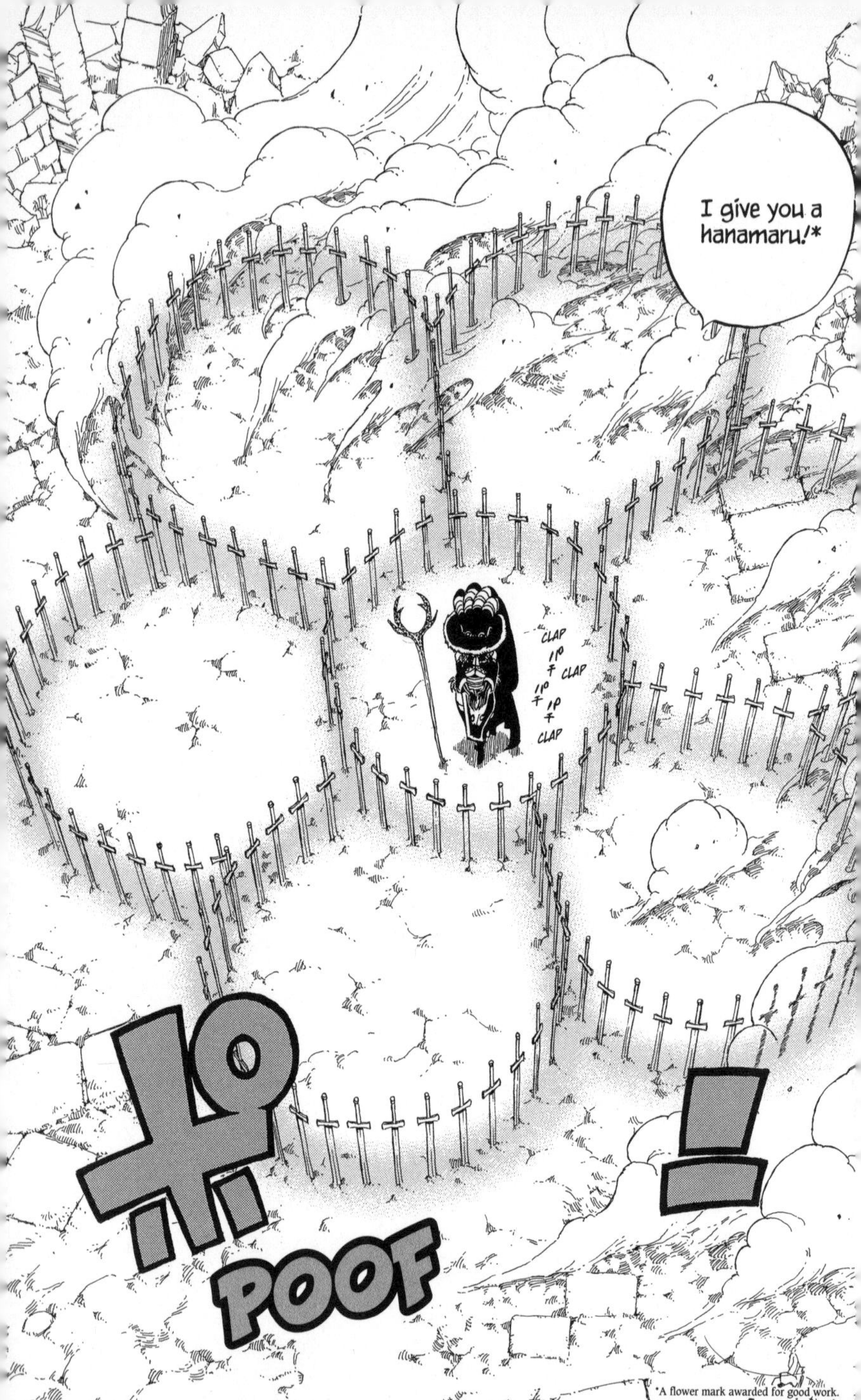
I give you a hanamaru!*
CLAP
CLAP
CLAP
POOF

*A flower mark awarded for good work.

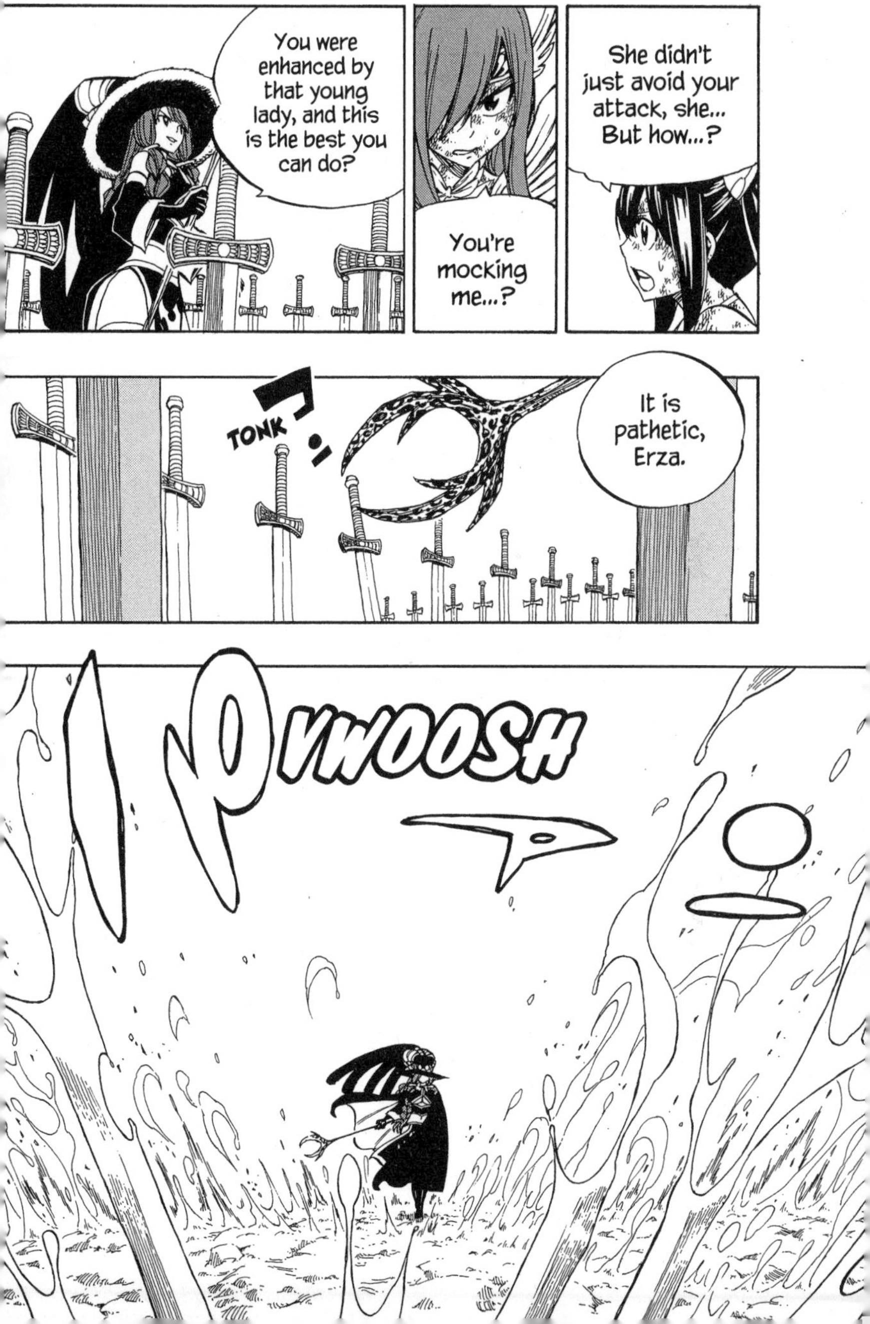
She didn't just avoid your attack, she... But how...?
You're mocking me...?
You were enhanced by that young lady, and this is the best you can do?
It is pathetic, Erza.
TONK
VWOOSH

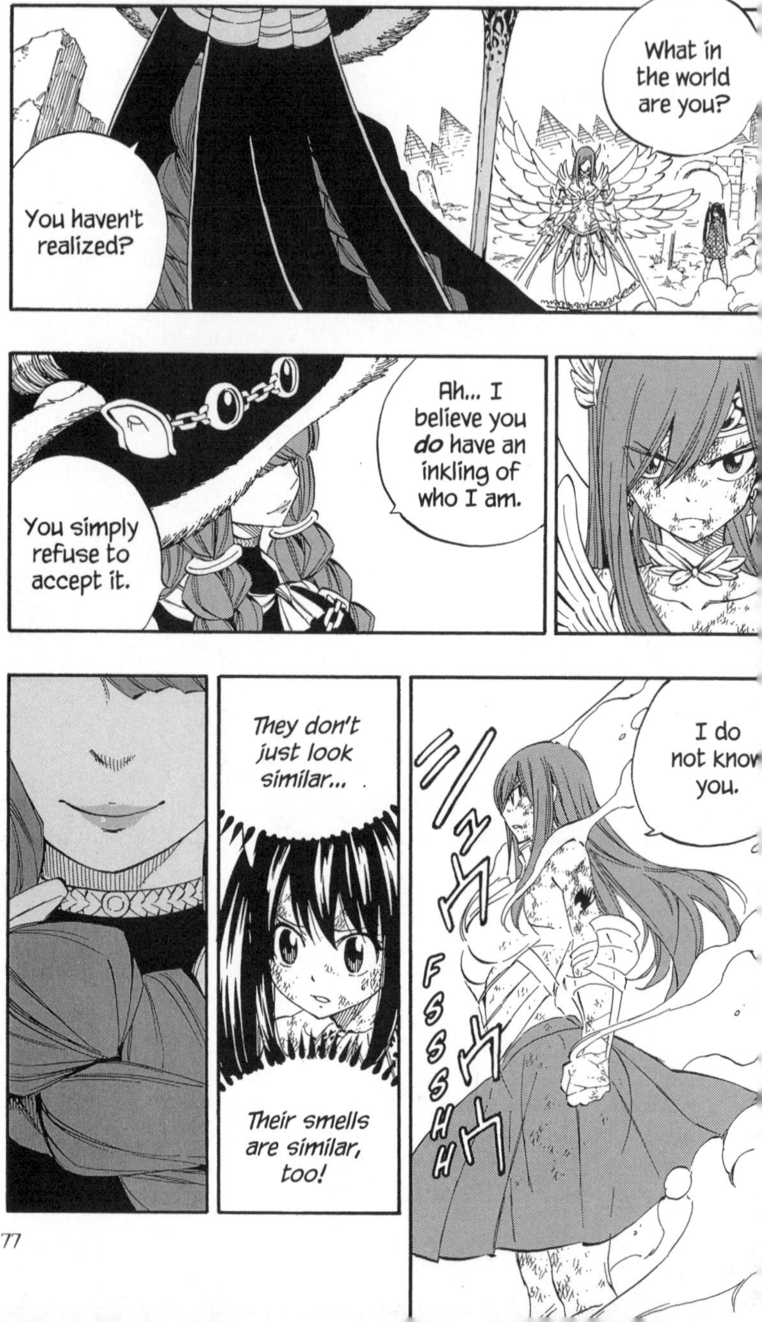
What in the world are you?
You haven't realized?
Ah... I believe you *do* have an inkling of who I am.
You simply refuse to accept it.
I do not know you.
FSSSHHH
They don't just look similar...
Their smells are similar, too!

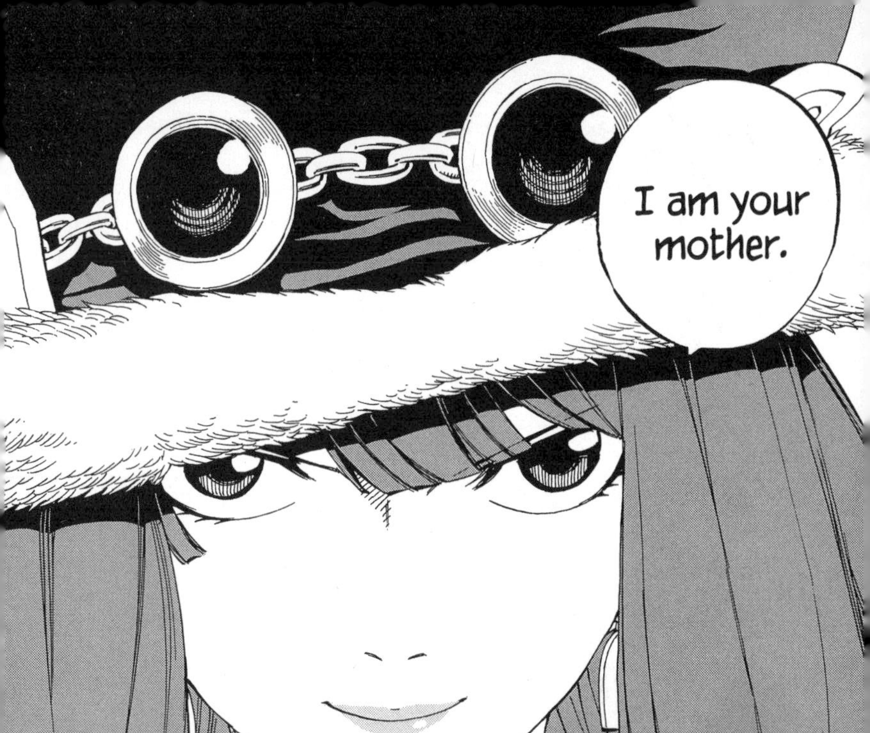
I am your mother.
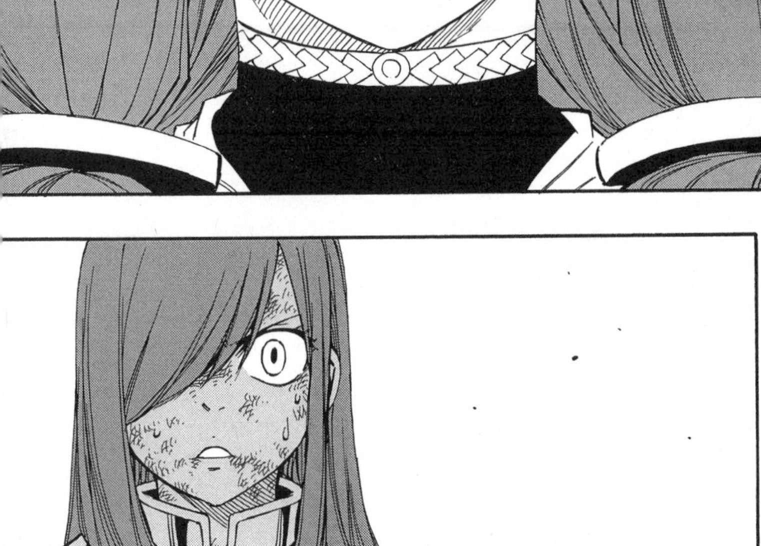

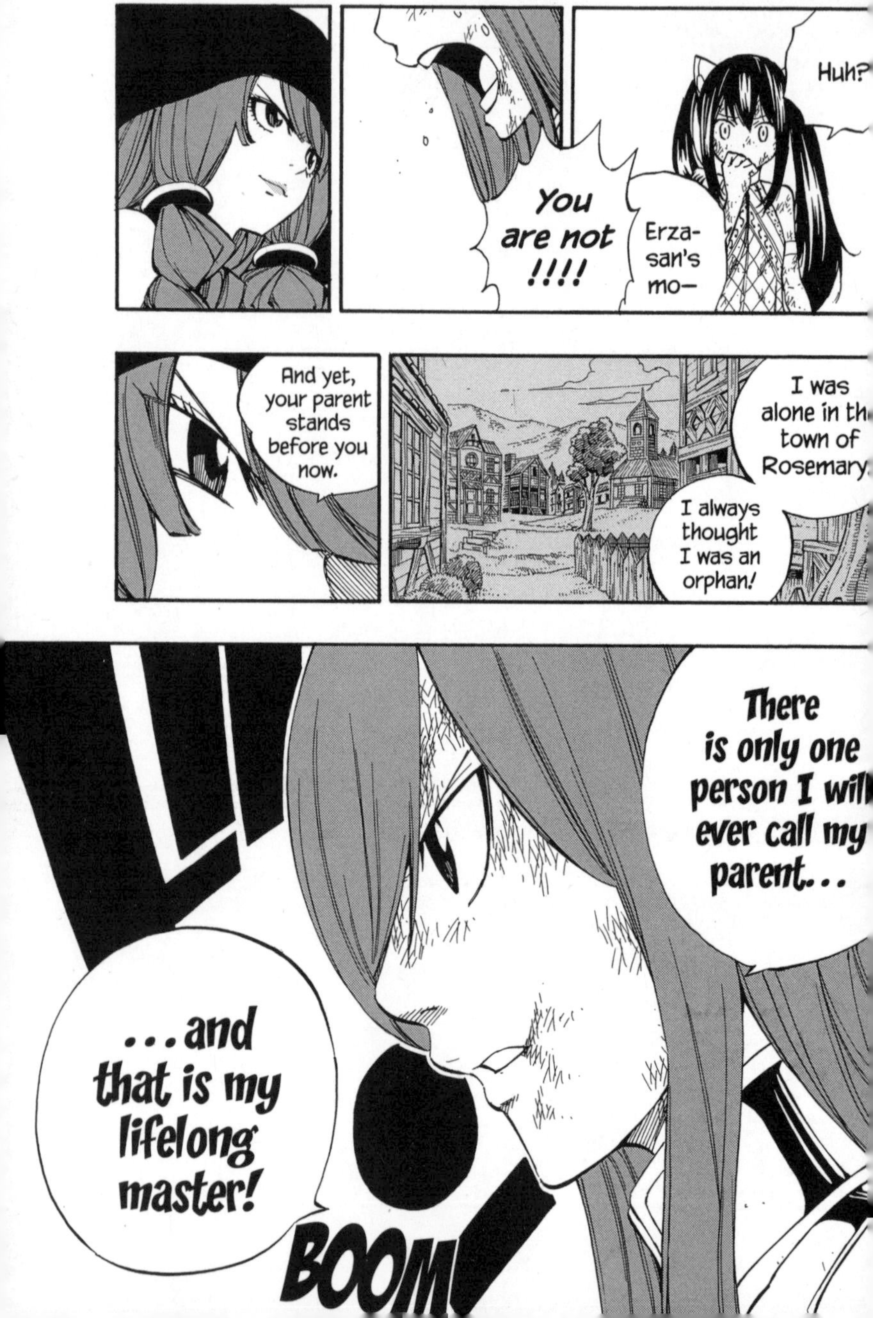
Huh?
Erza-san's mo—
You are not !!!!
I was alone in th town of Rosemary.
I always thought I was an orphan!
And yet, your parent stands before you now.
There is only one person I wil ever call my parent...
...and that is my lifelong master!
BOOM

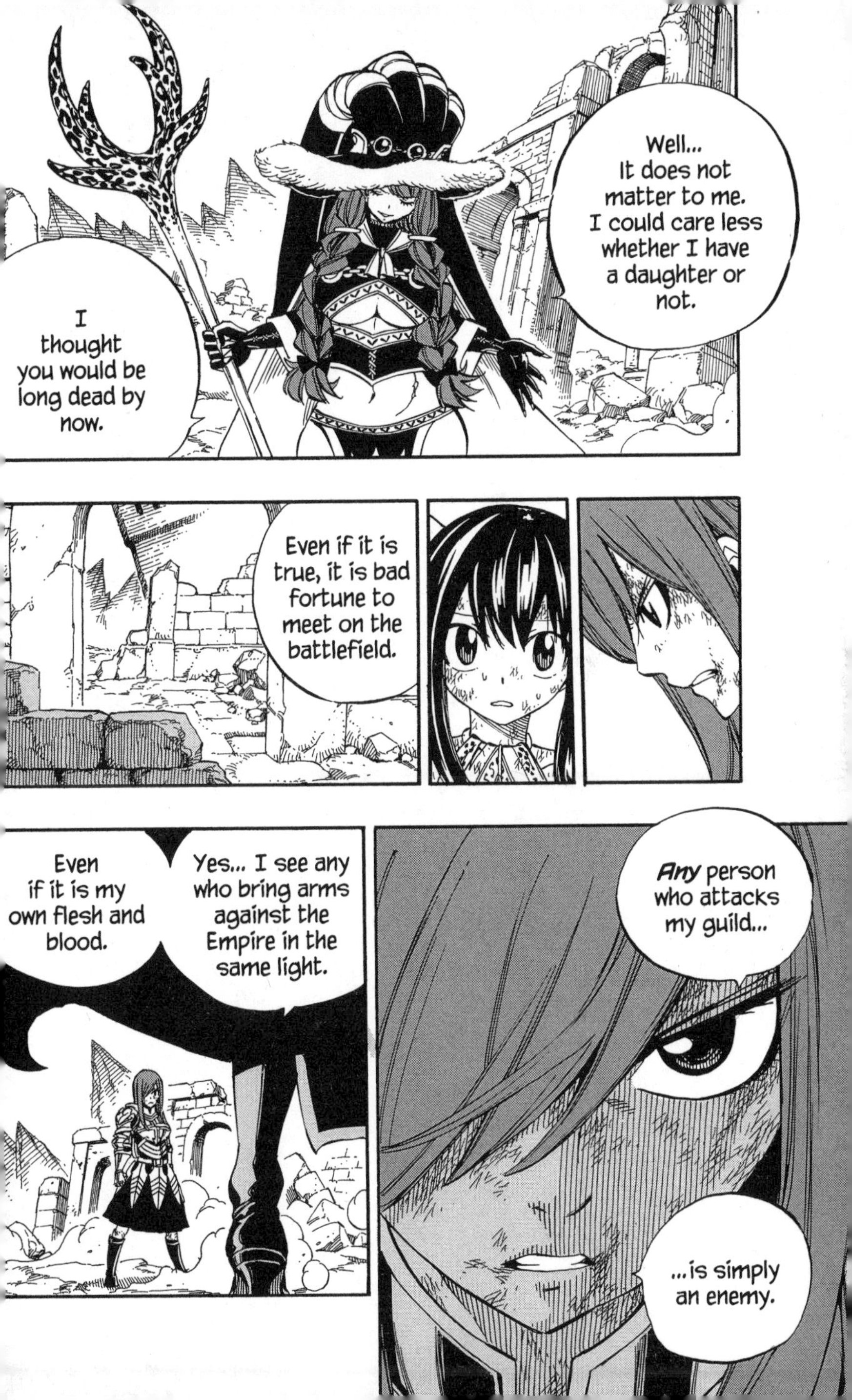
Well... It does not matter to me. I could care less whether I have a daughter or not.
I thought you would be long dead by now.
Even if it is true, it is bad fortune to meet on the battlefield.
Any person who attacks my guild...
...is simply an enemy.
Yes... I see any who bring arms against the Empire in the same light.
Even if it is my own flesh and blood.

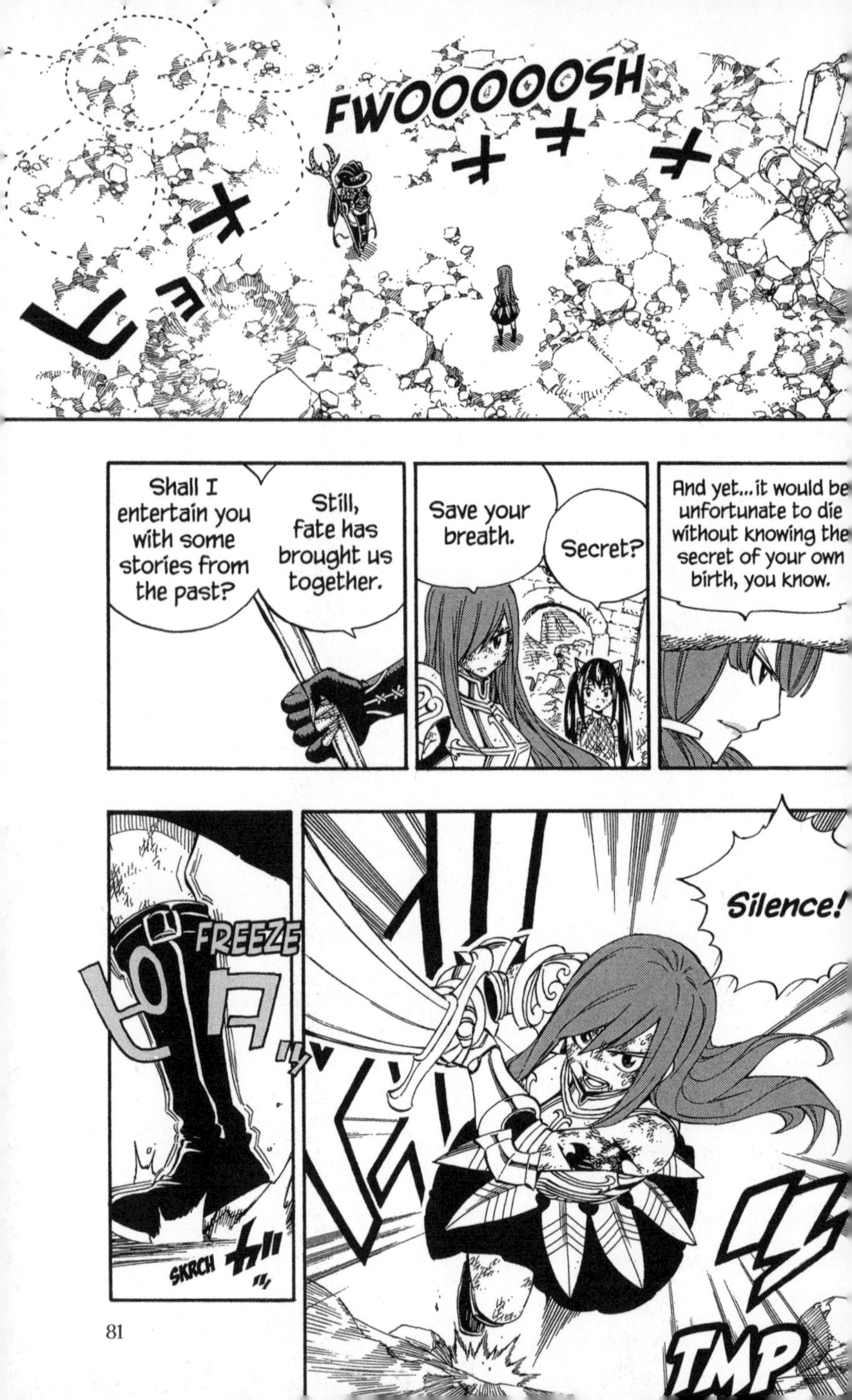

FWOOOOOSH
And yet...it would be unfortunate to die without knowing the secret of your own birth, you know.
Secret?
Save your breath.
Still, fate has brought us together.
Shall I entertain you with some stories from the past?
Silence!
TMP
FREEZE
SKRCH

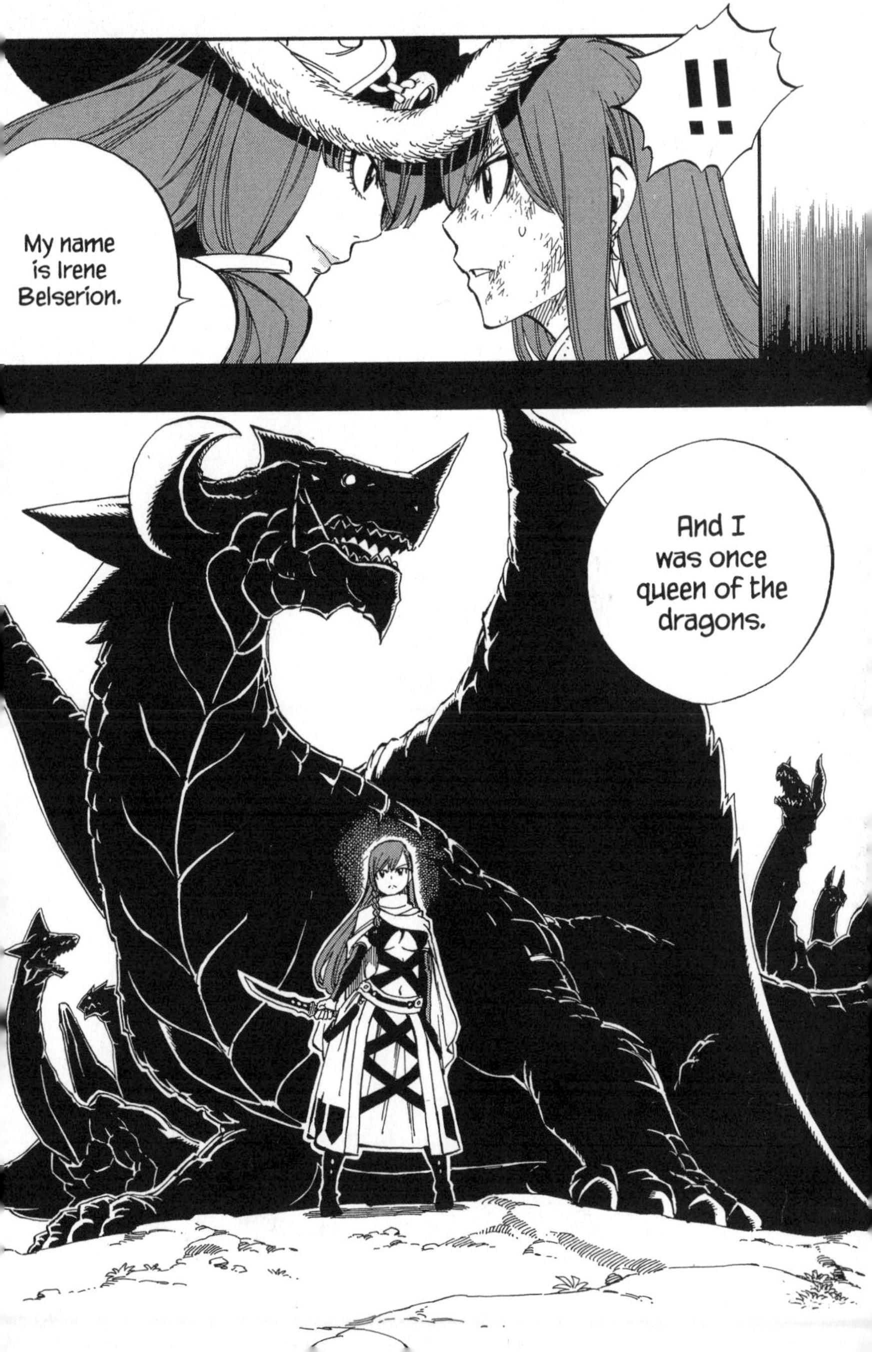
!!
My name is Irene Belserion.
And I was once queen of the dragons.

FAIRY TAIL

フェアリーテイル

Chapter 514: Dragon Seed

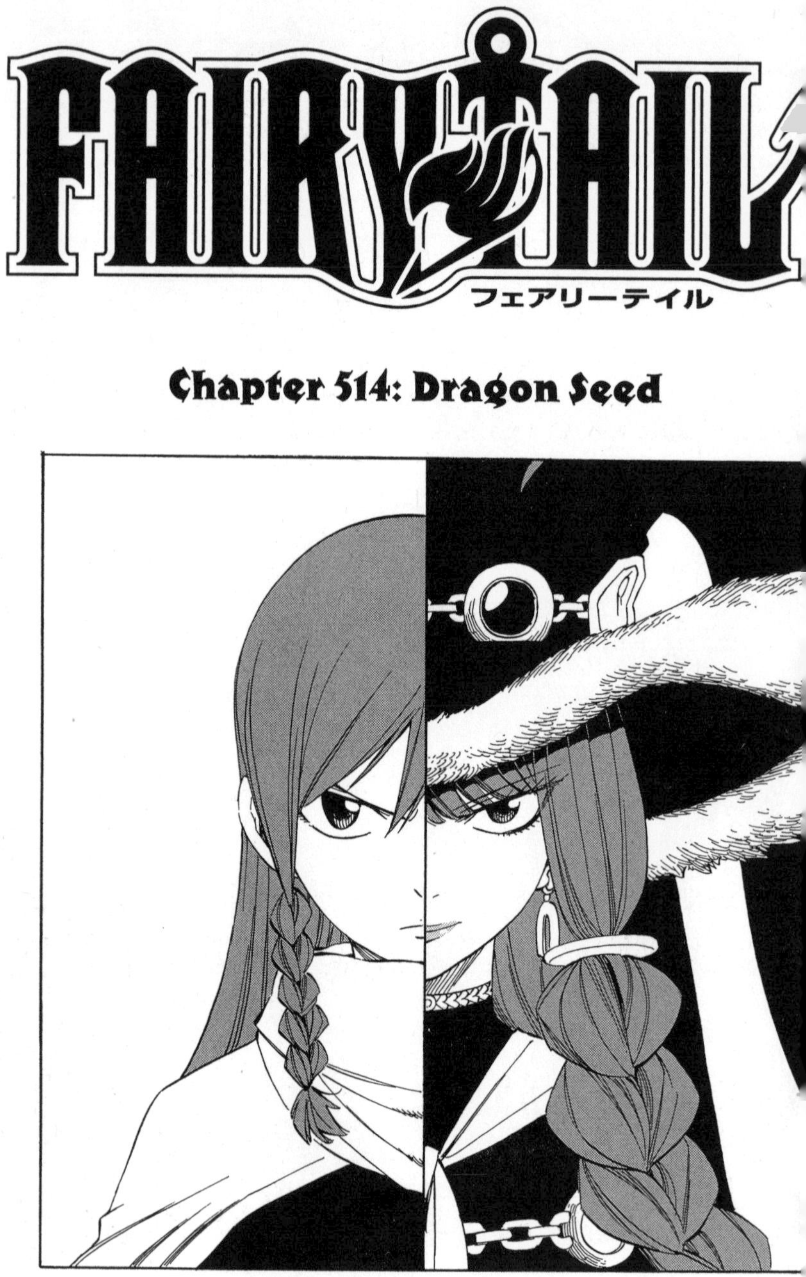

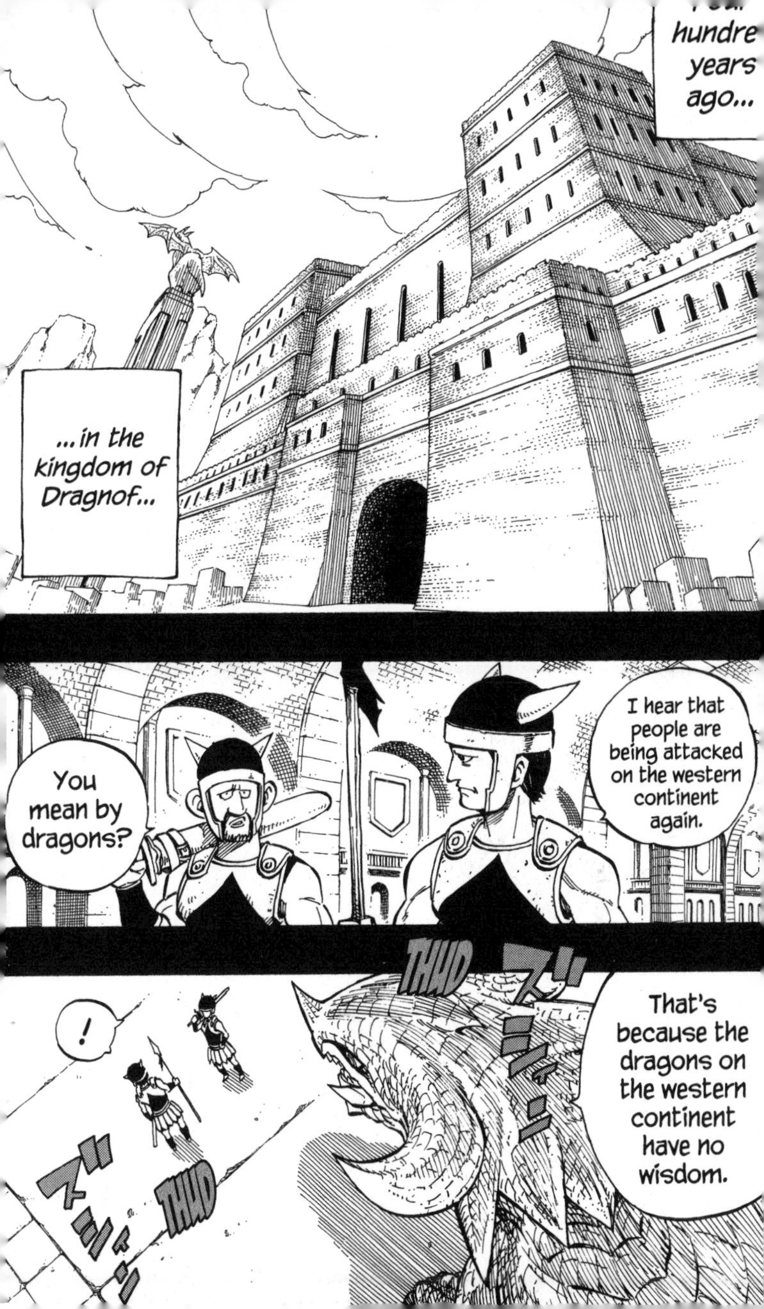

hundre years ago...
...in the kingdom of Dragnof...
I hear that people are being attacked on the western continent again.
You mean by dragons?
THUD
That's because the dragons on the western continent have no wisdom.
!
THUD

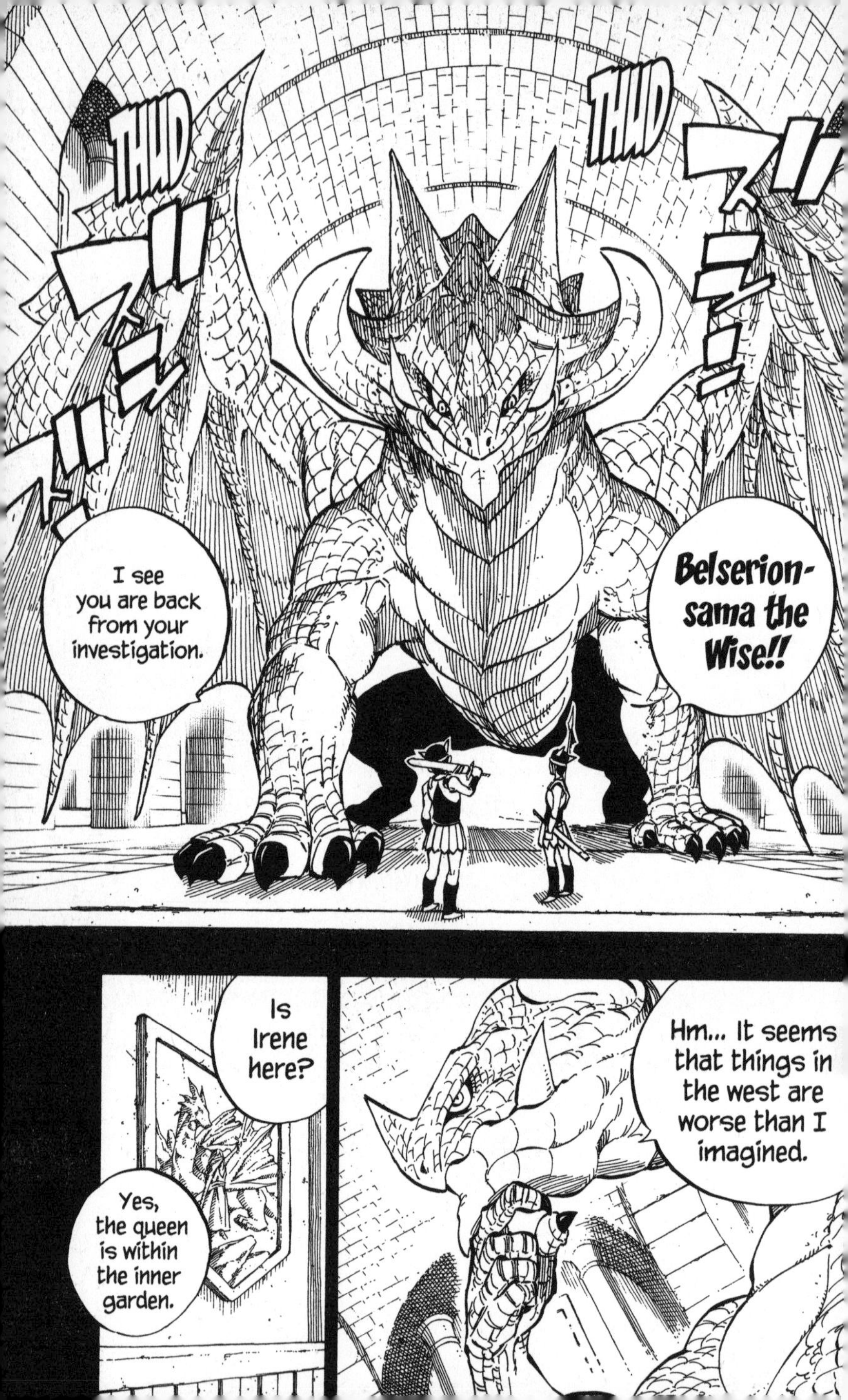
THUD
THUD
Belserion-sama the Wise!!
I see you are back from your investigation.
Hm... It seems that things in the west are worse than I imagined.
Is Irene here?
Yes, the queen is within the inner garden.

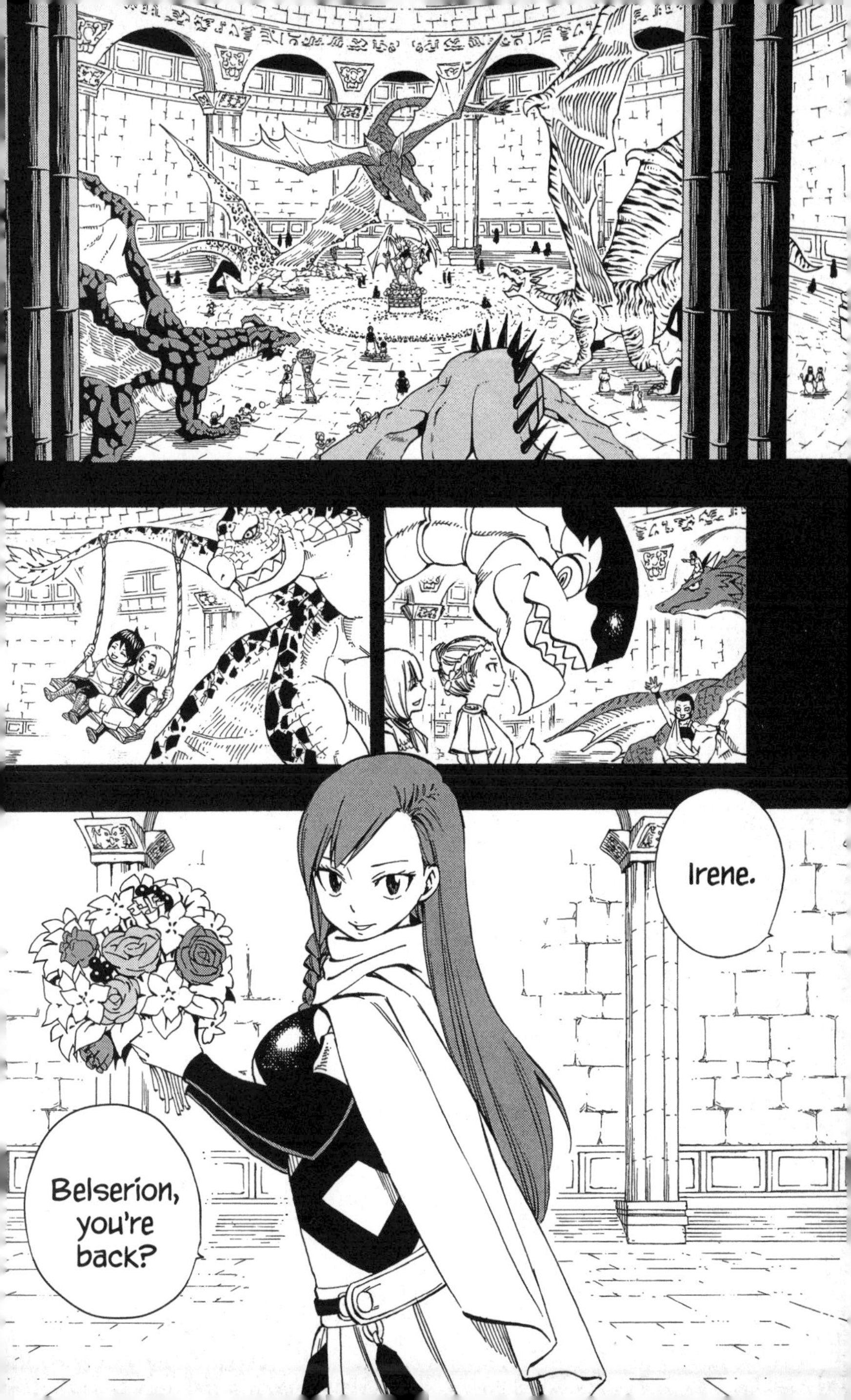
Irene.
Belserion, you're back?

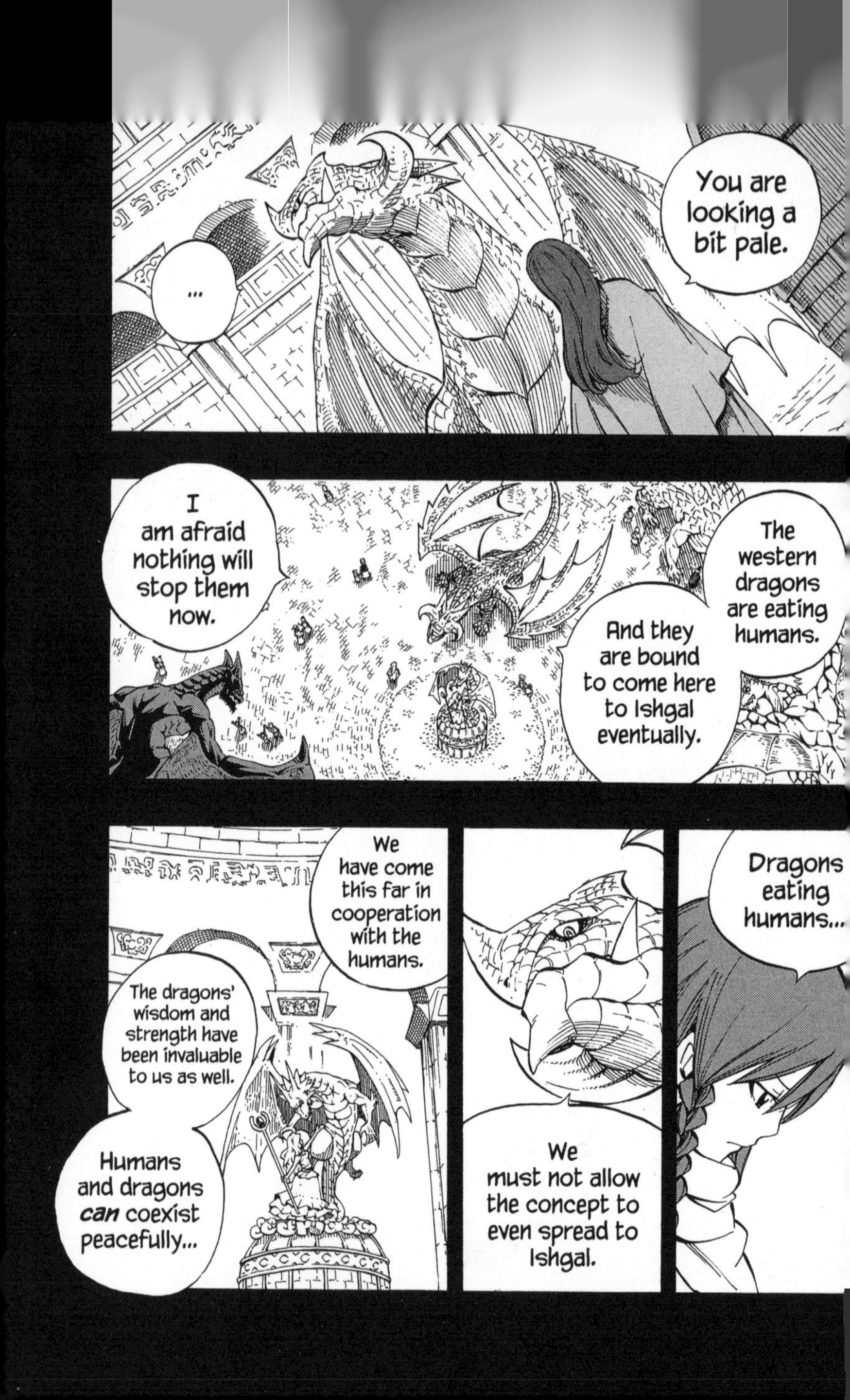
You are looking a bit pale.
...
The western dragons are eating humans.
And they are bound to come here to Ishgal eventually.
I am afraid nothing will stop them now.
Dragons eating humans...
We must not allow the concept to even spread to Ishgal.
We have come this far in cooperation with the humans.
The dragons' wisdom and strength have been invaluable to us as well.
Humans and dragons *can* coexist peacefully...

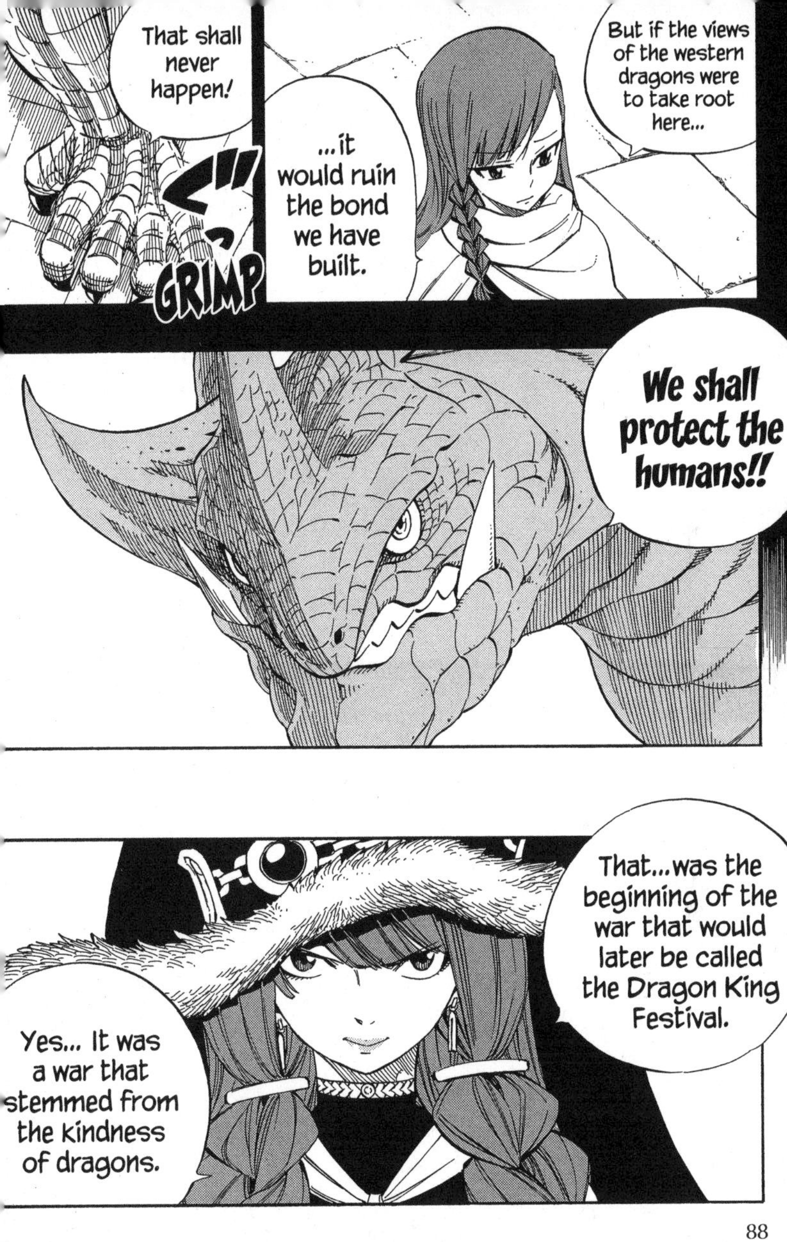

But if the views of the western dragons were to take root here...
...it would ruin the bond we have built.
That shall never happen!
ぐっ
GRIMP
We shall protect the humans!!
That...was the beginning of the war that would later be called the Dragon King Festival.
Yes... It was a war that stemmed from the kindness of dragons.

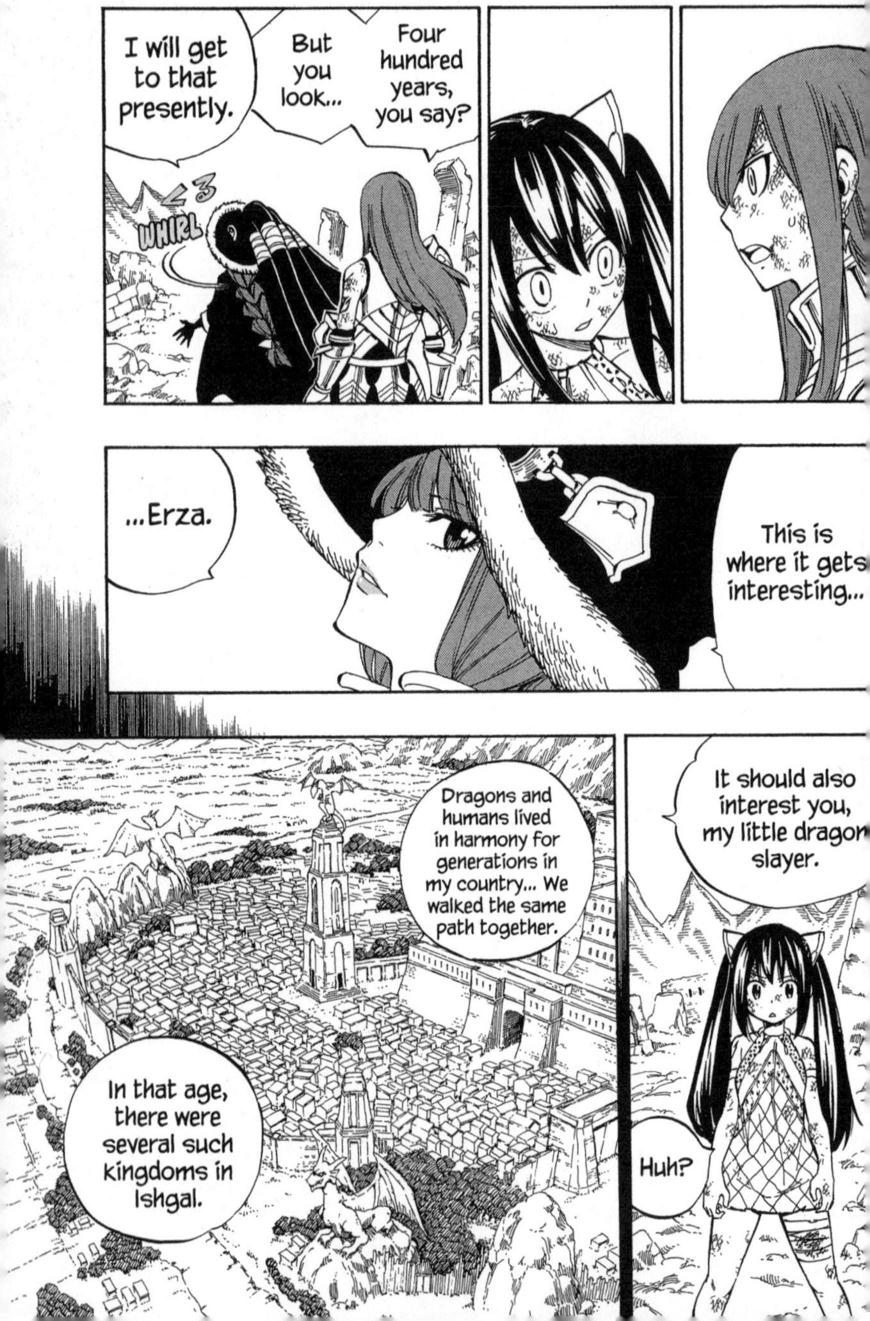
Four hundred years, you say?
But you look...
I will get to that presently.
WHIRL
This is where it gets interesting...
...Erza.
It should also interest you, my little dragon slayer.
Huh?
Dragons and humans lived in harmony for generations in my country... We walked the same path together.
In that age, there were several such kingdoms in Ishgal.

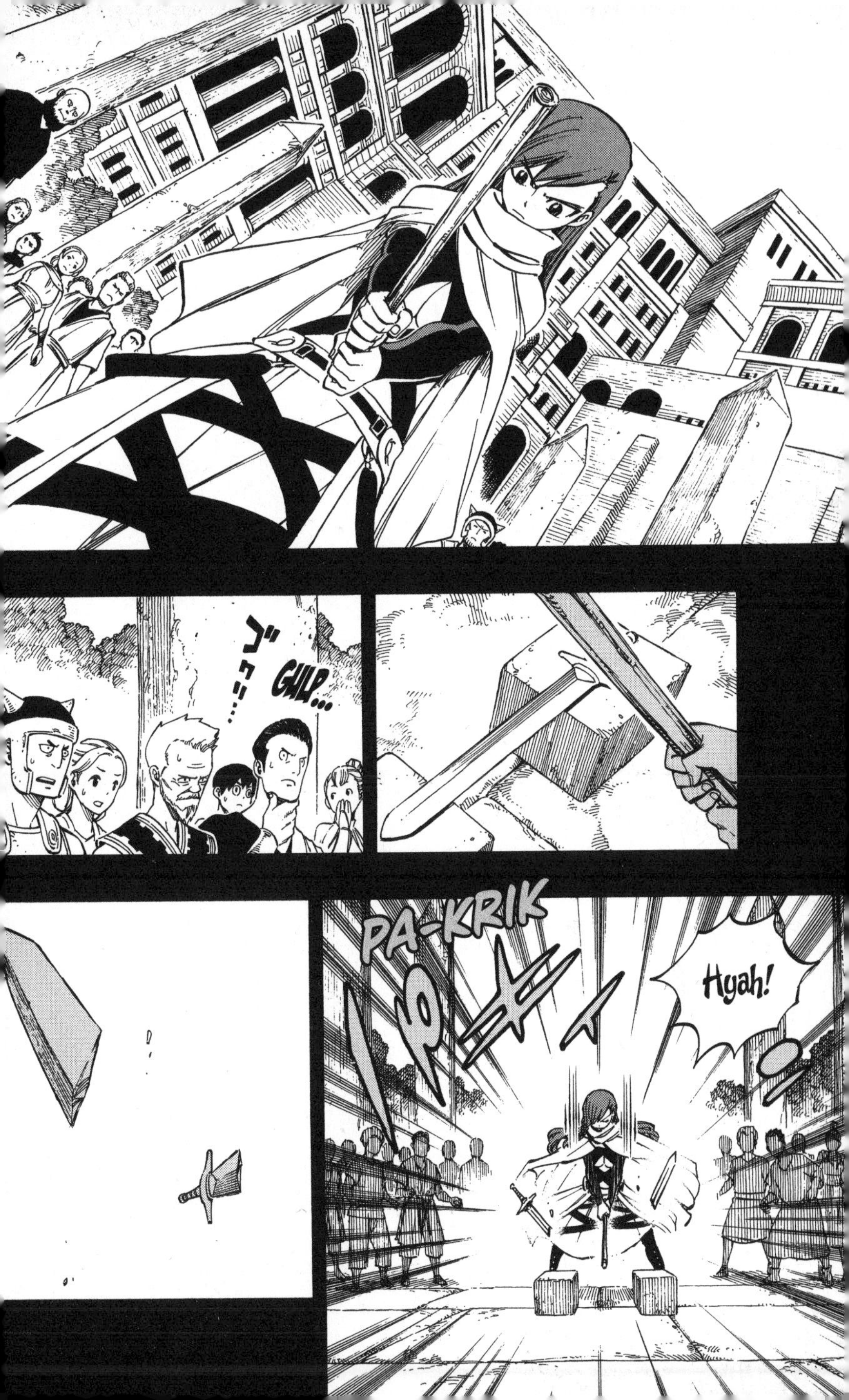
ゴクッ…
GULP...
PA-KRIK
Hyah!

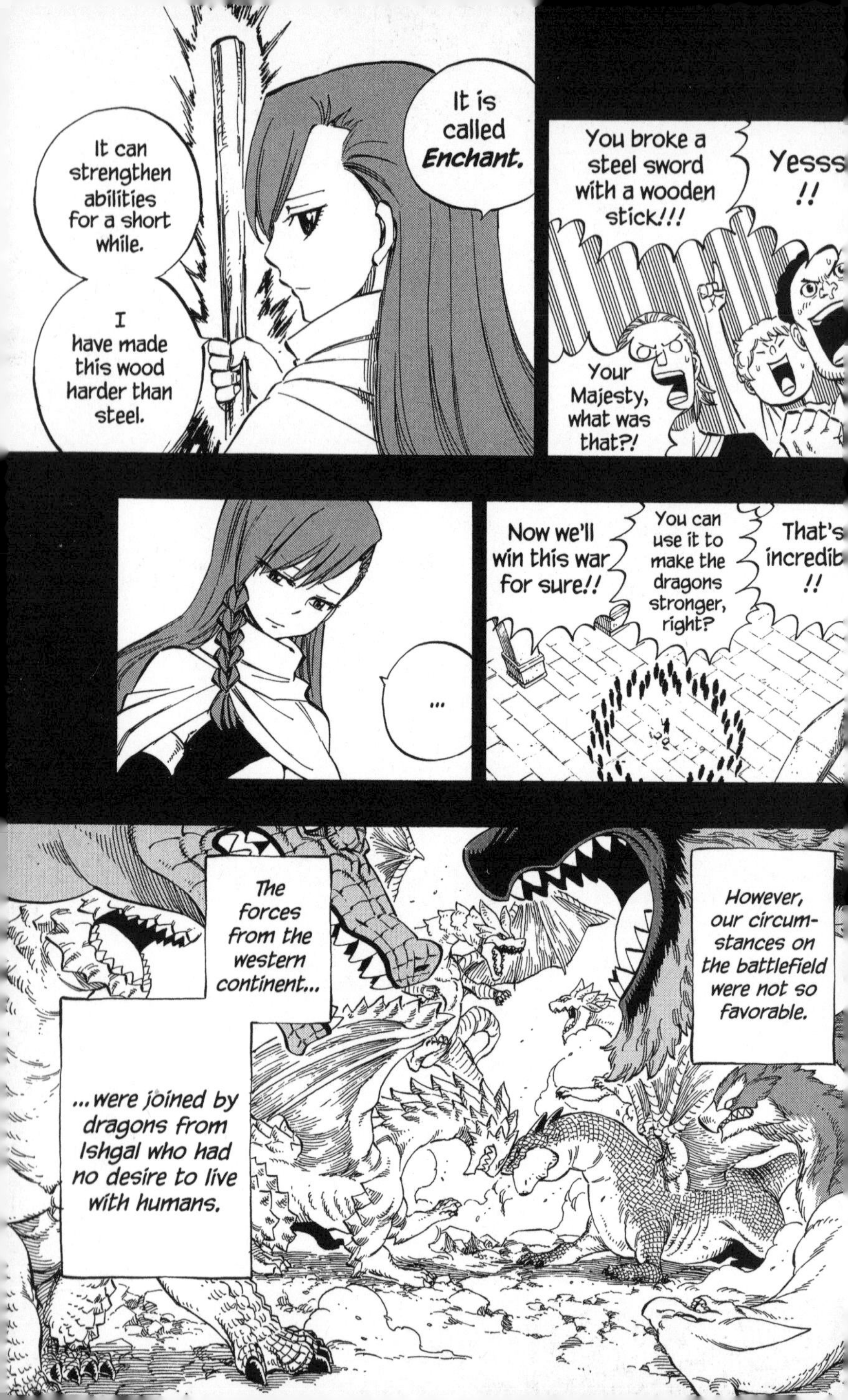

Yesss !!
You broke a steel sword with a wooden stick!!!
Your Majesty, what was that?!
It is called *Enchant.*
It can strengthen abilities for a short while.
I have made this wood harder than steel.
That's incredib !!
You can use it to make the dragons stronger, right?
Now we'll win this war for sure!!
...
However, our circum-stances on the battlefield were not so favorable.
The forces from the western continent...
...were joined by dragons from Ishgal who had no desire to live with humans.

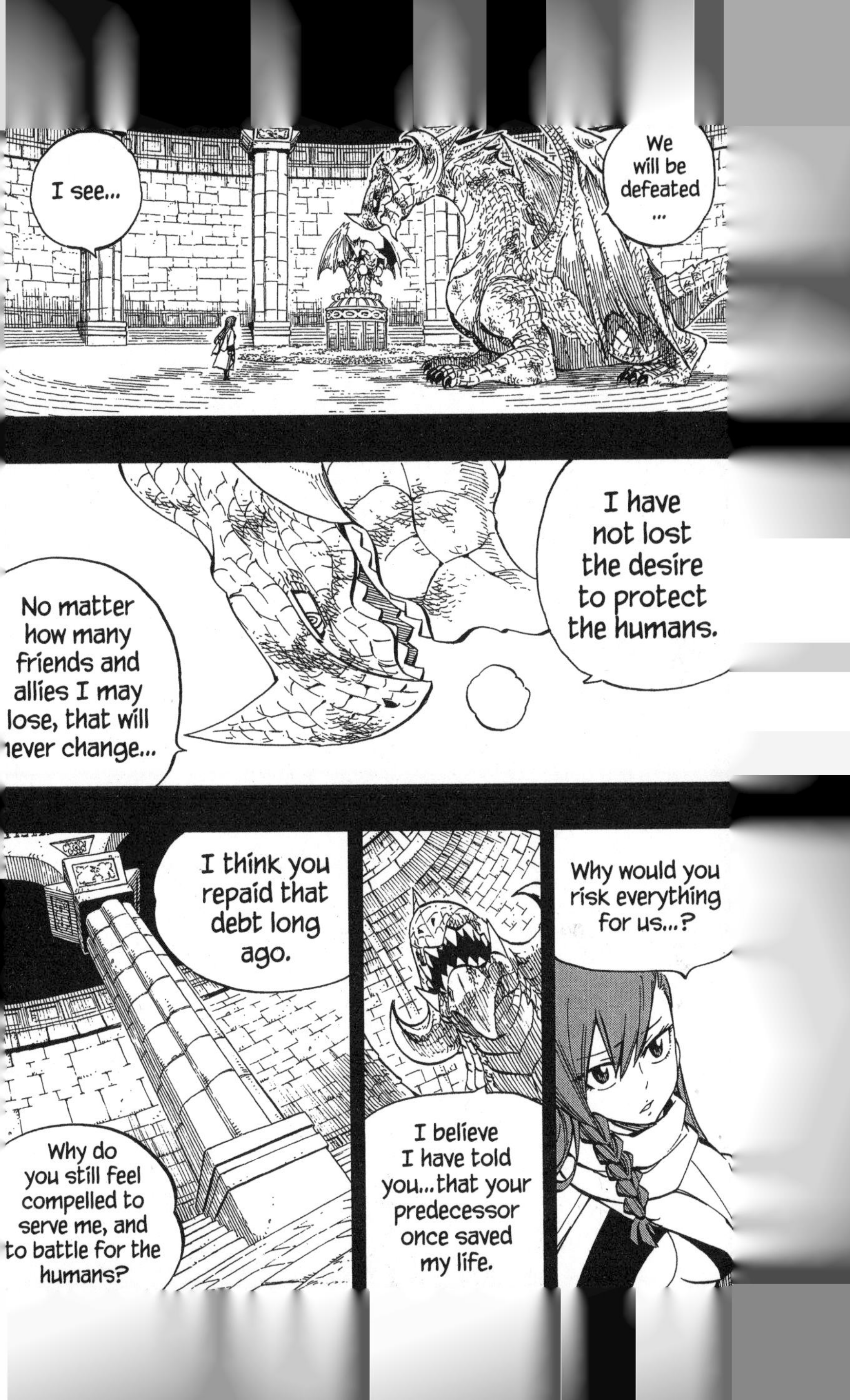
We will be defeated ...
I see...
I have not lost the desire to protect the humans.
No matter how many friends and allies I may lose, that will never change...
Why would you risk everything for us...?
I believe I have told you...that your predecessor once saved my life.
I think you repaid that debt long ago.
Why do you still feel compelled to serve me, and to battle for the humans?

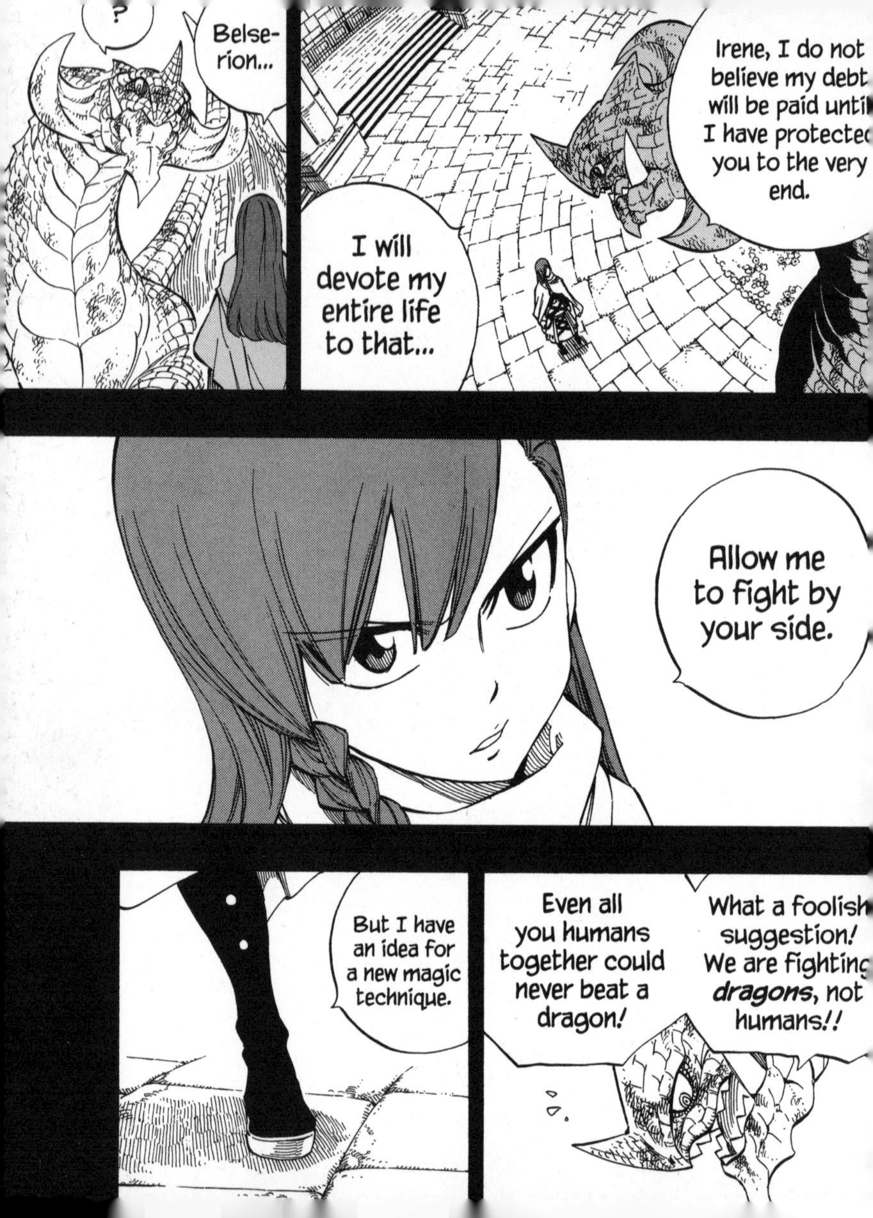
Irene, I do not believe my debt will be paid unti I have protecte you to the very end.
I will devote my entire life to that...
Belse-rion...
?
Allow me to fight by your side.
What a foolis suggestion! We are fightin *dragons*, not humans!!
Even all you humans together could never beat a dragon!
But I have an idea for a new magic technique.

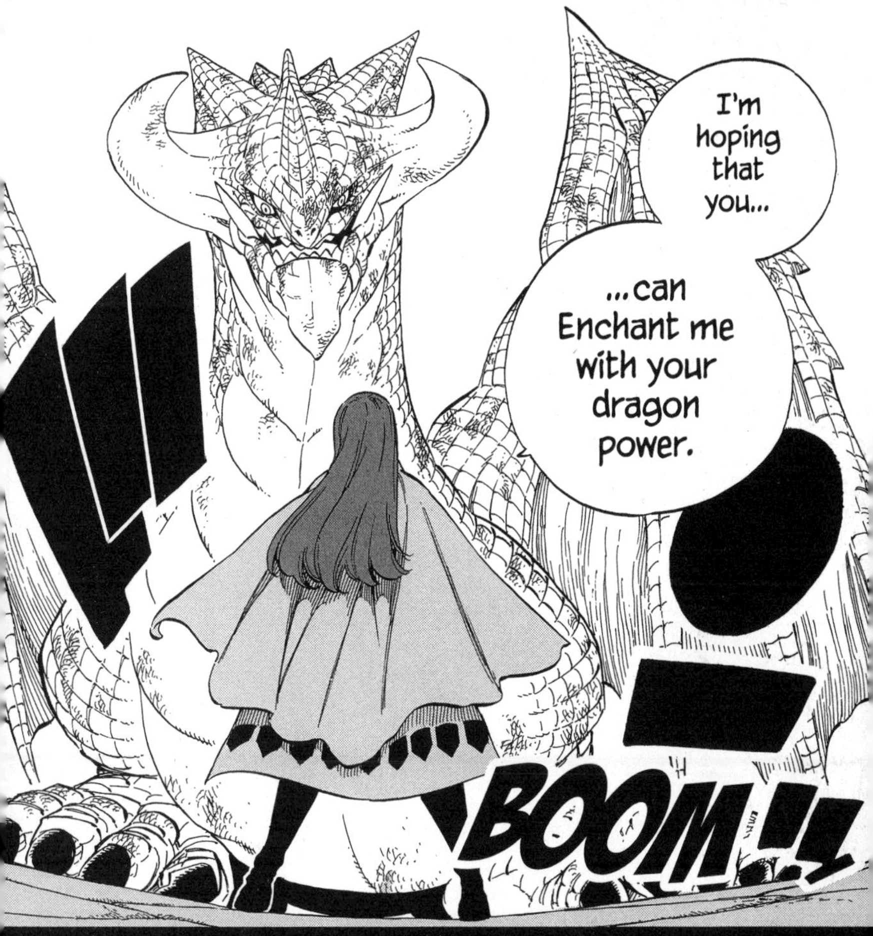
I'm hoping that you...
...can Enchant me with your dragon power.
BOOM!!
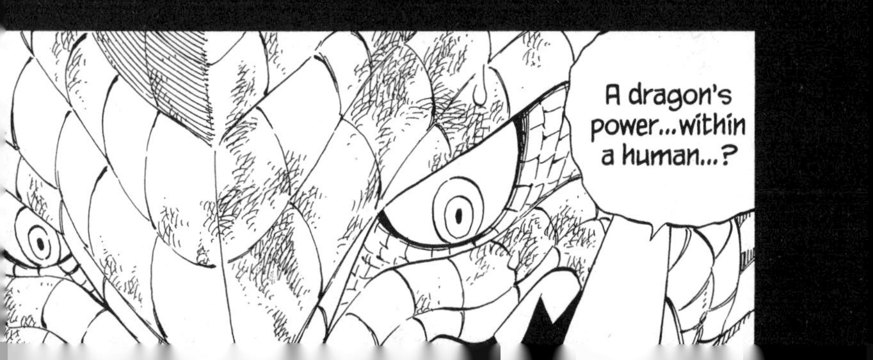
A dragon's power...within a human...?

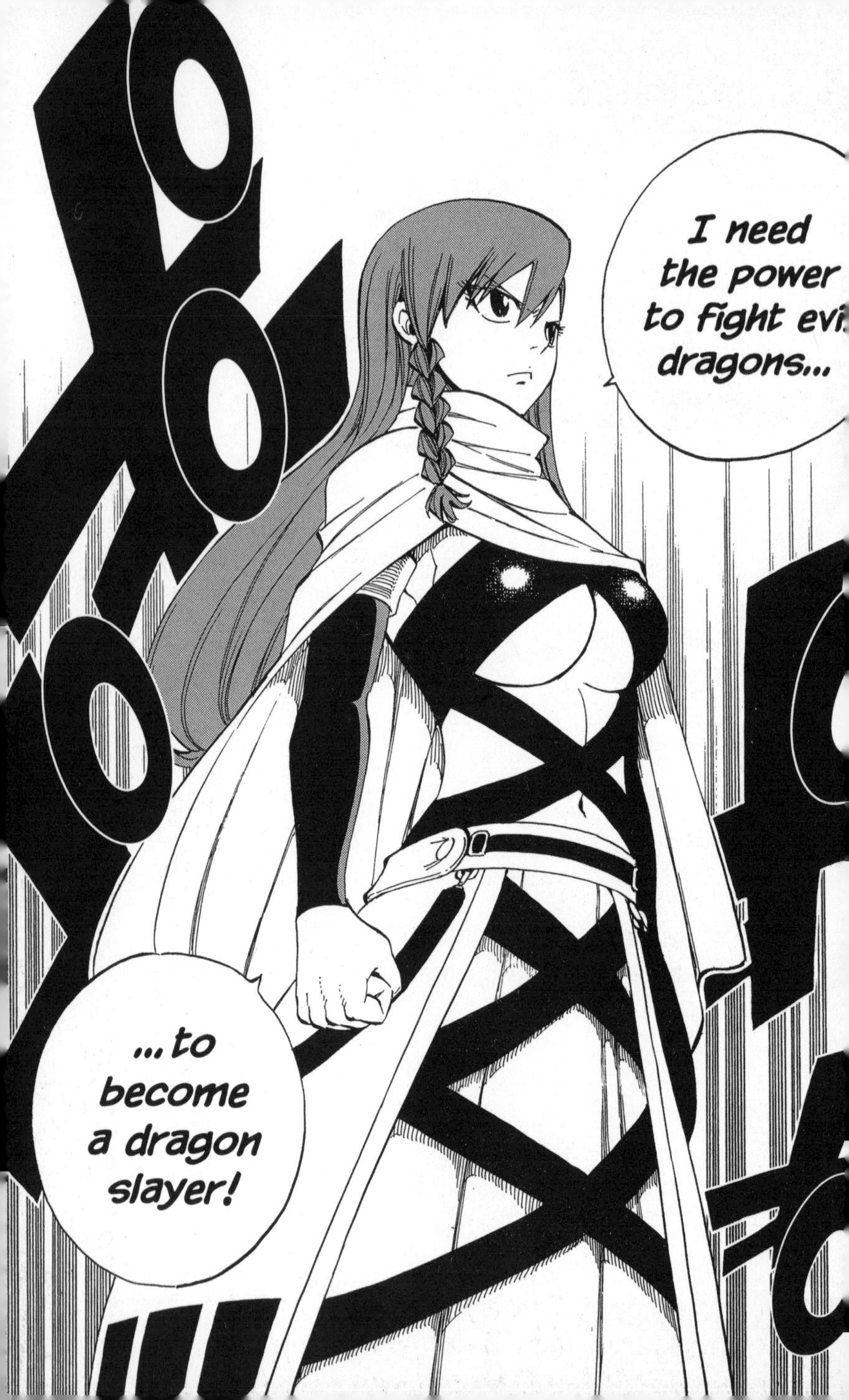
I need the power to fight evi dragons...
...to become a dragon slayer!

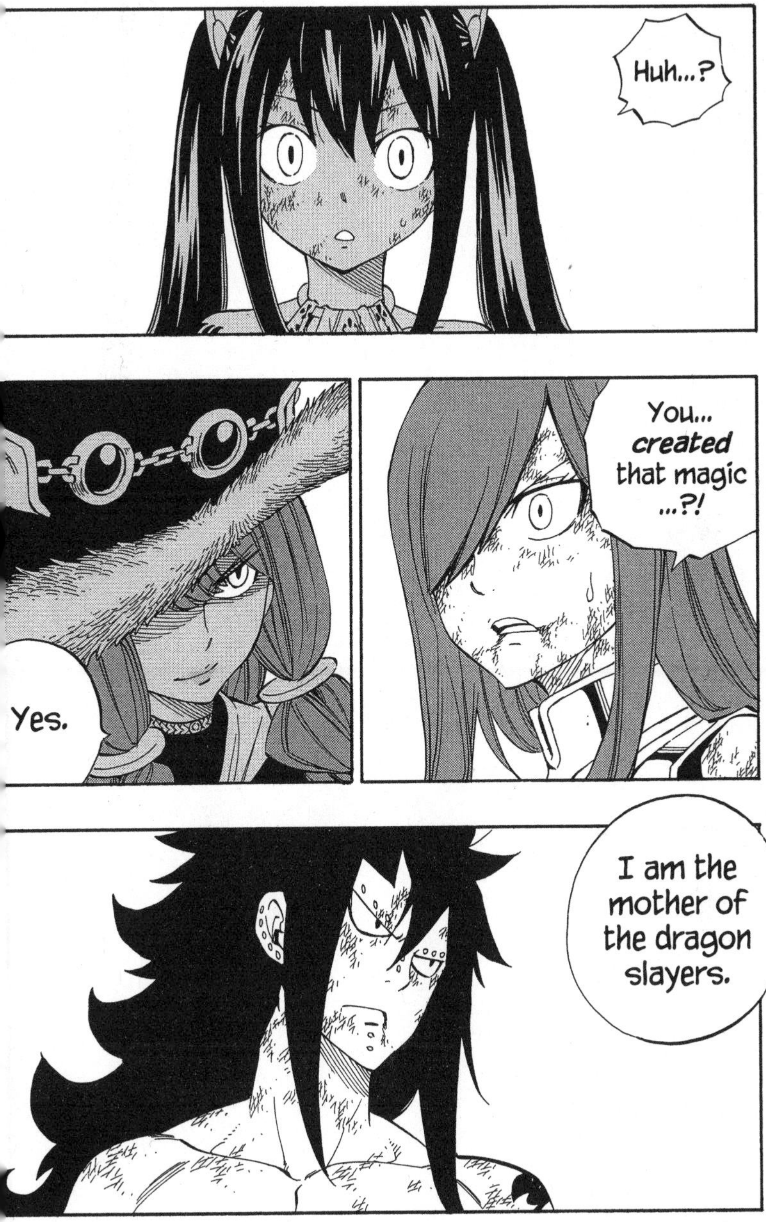
Huh...?
You... *created* that magic ...?!
Yes.
I am the mother of the dragon slayers.

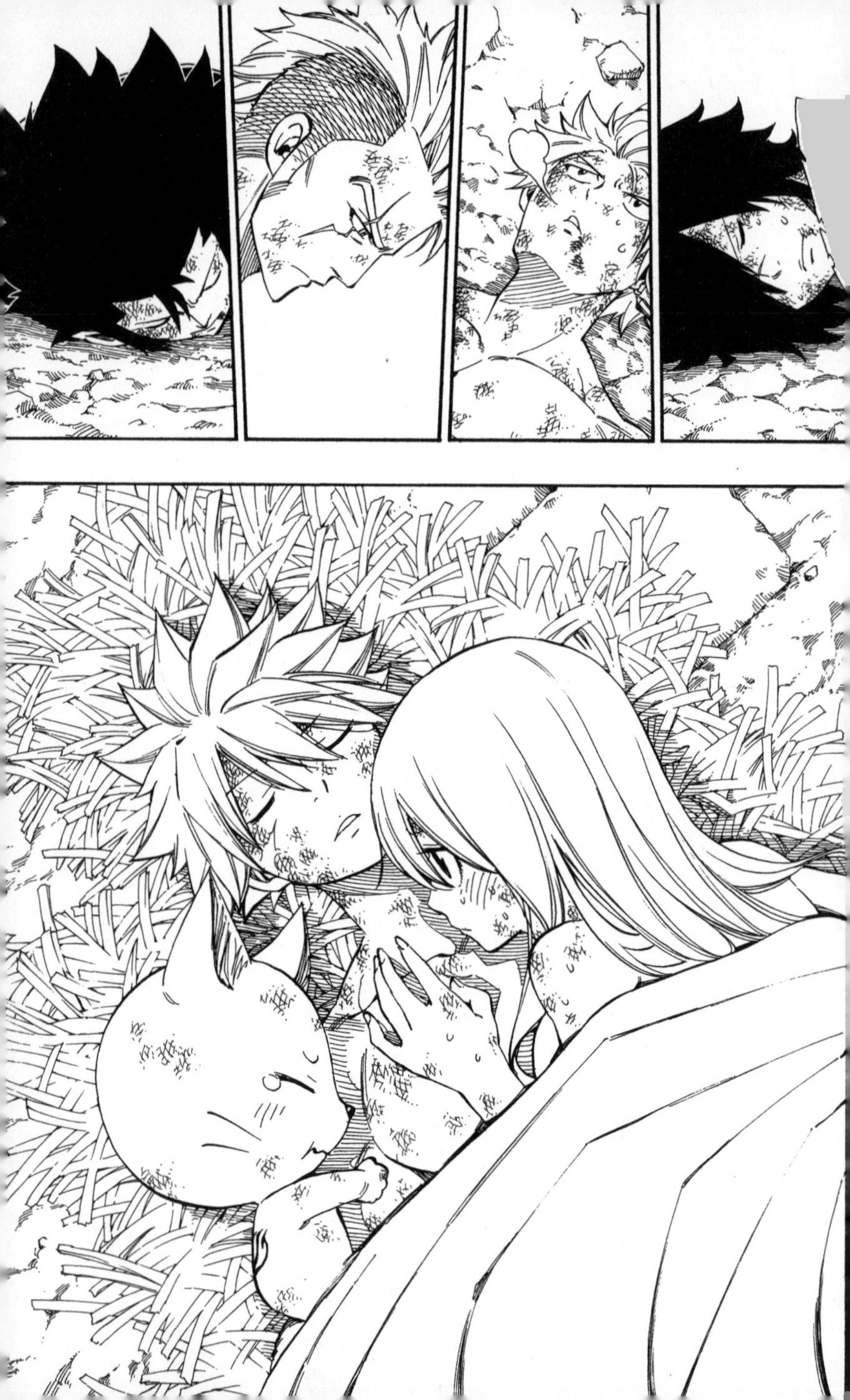

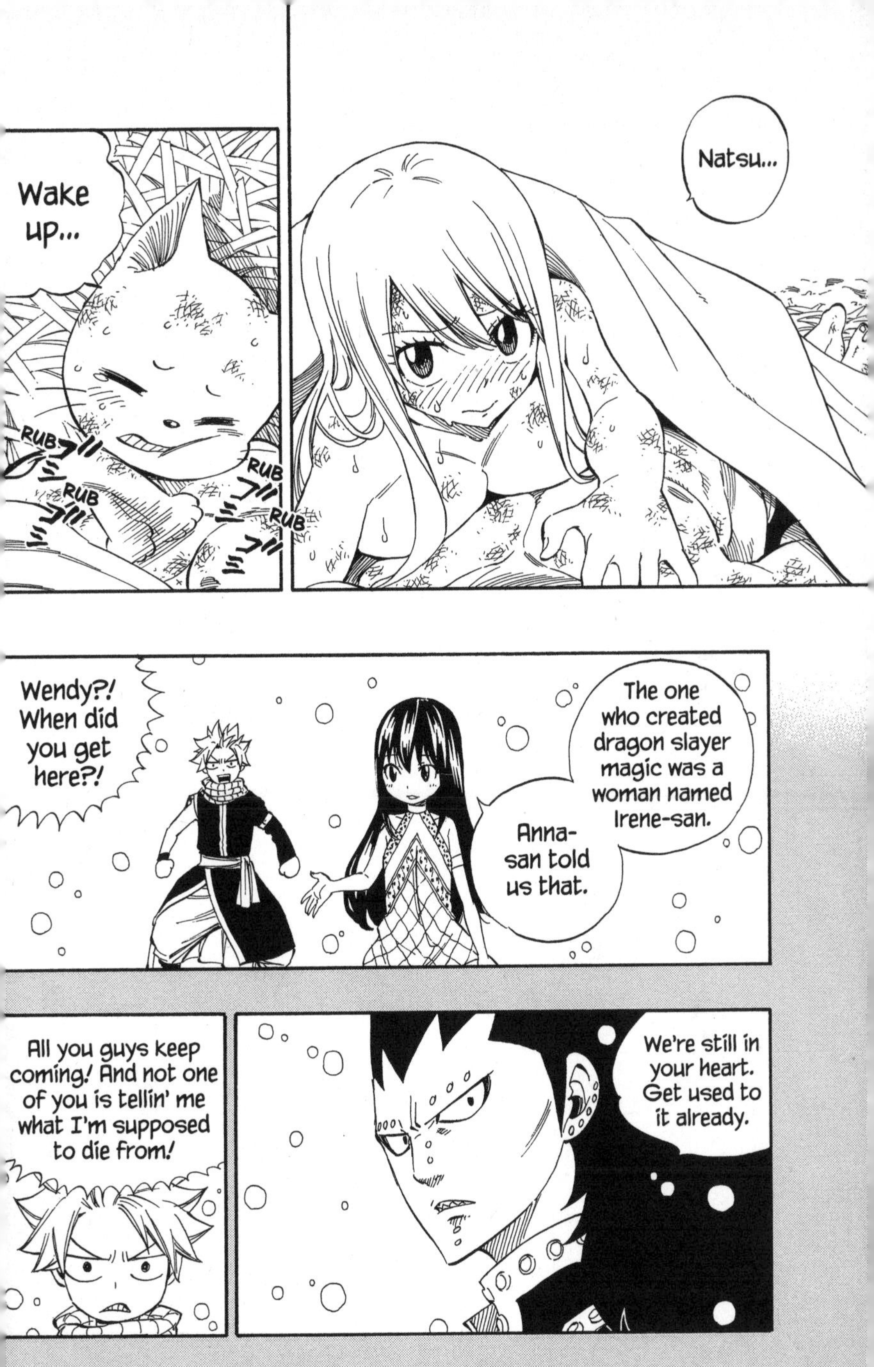
Natsu...
Wake up...
RUB
RUB
RUB
RUB
The one who created dragon slayer magic was a woman named Irene-san.
Anna-san told us that.
Wendy?! When did you get here?!
We're still in your heart. Get used to it already.
All you guys keep coming! And not one of you is tellin' me what I'm supposed to die from!

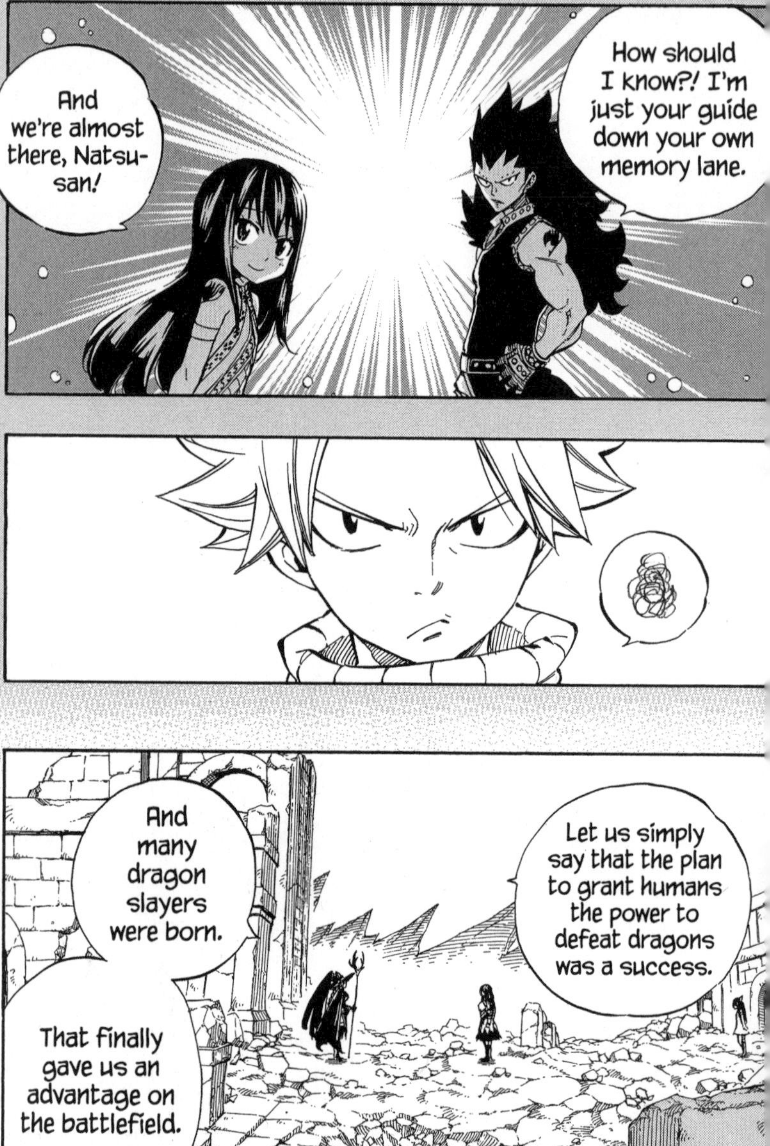
How should I know?! I'm just your guide down your own memory lane.
And we're almost there, Natsu-san!
Let us simply say that the plan to grant humans the power to defeat dragons was a success.
And many dragon slayers were born.
That finally gave us an advantage on the battlefield.

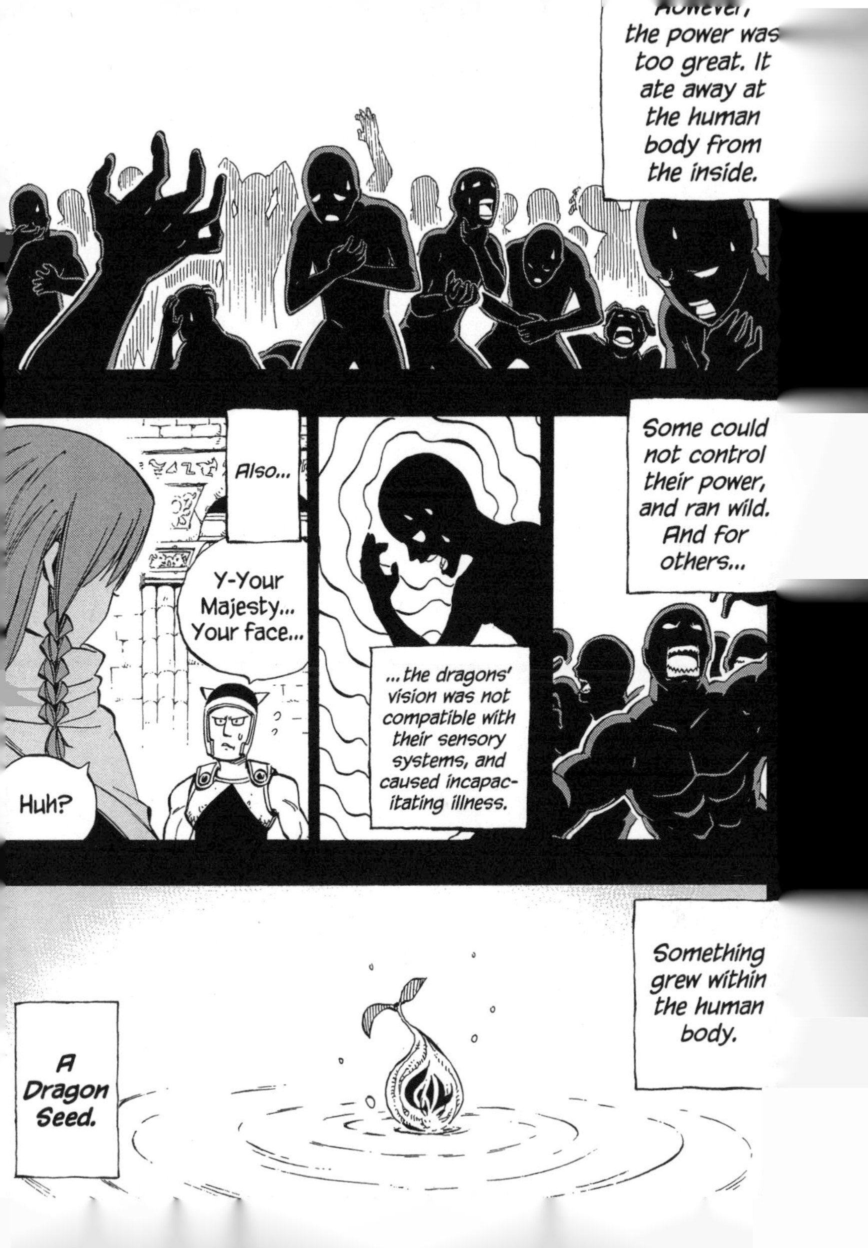
the power was too great. It ate away at the human body from the inside.
Some could not control their power, and ran wild. And for others...
...the dragons' vision was not compatible with their sensory systems, and caused incapacitating illness.
Also...
Y-Your Majesty... Your face...
Huh?
Something grew within the human body.
A Dragon Seed.

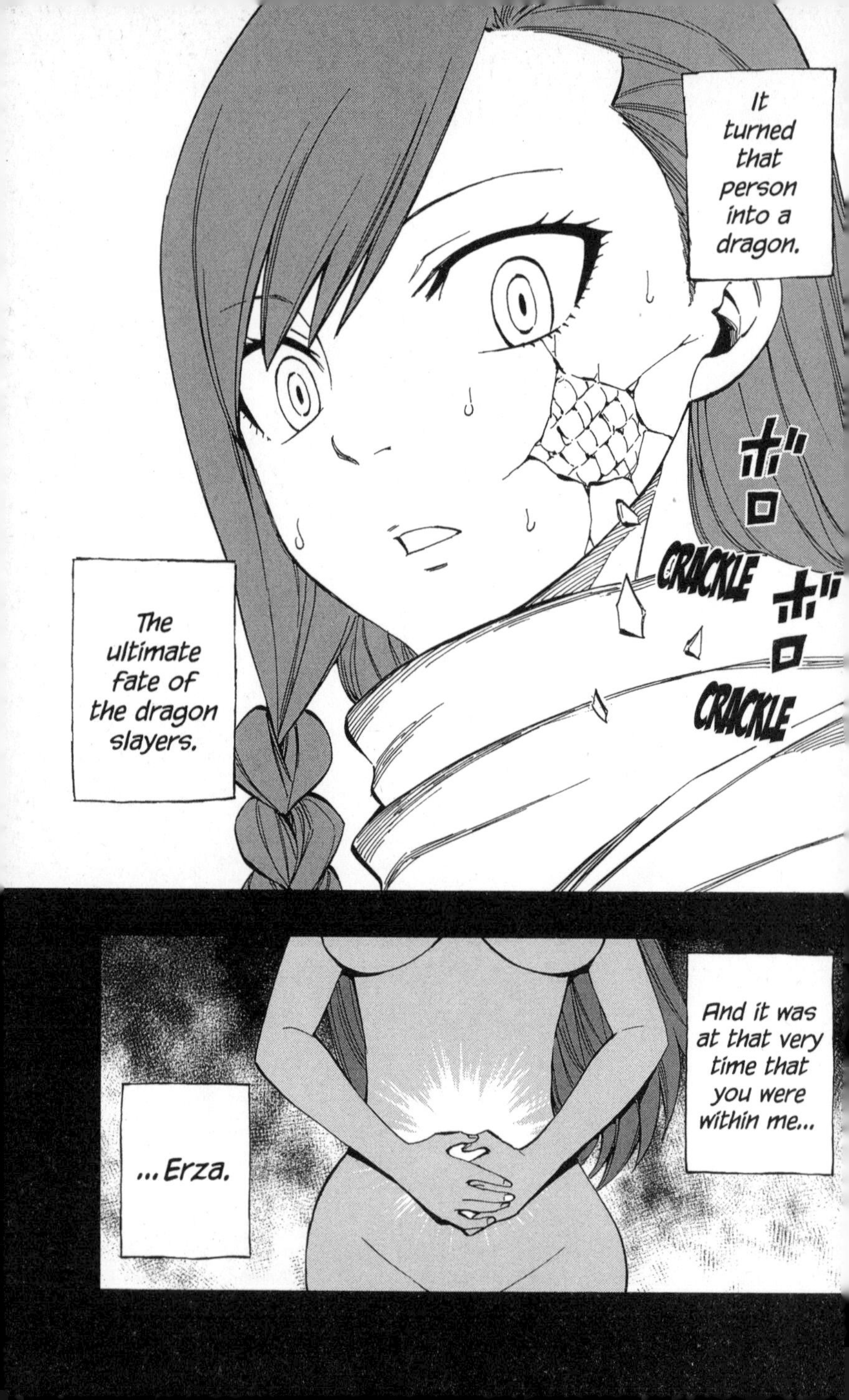
It turned that person into a dragon.
ボロ
CRACKLE
ボロ
CRACKLE
The ultimate fate of the dragon slayers.
And it was at that very time that you were within me...
...Erza.

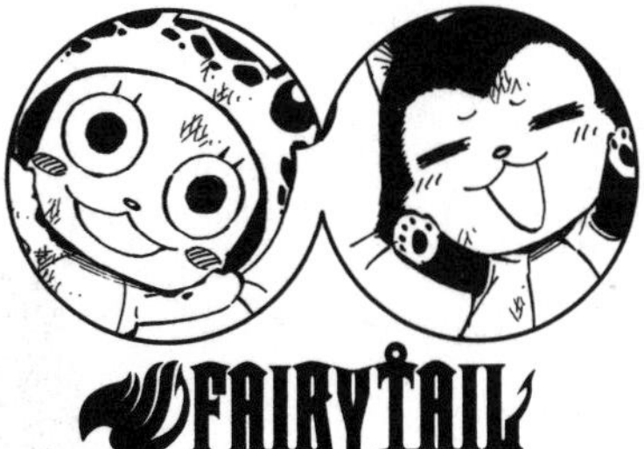

FAIRY TAIL

Chapter 515: I Am You...You Are Me

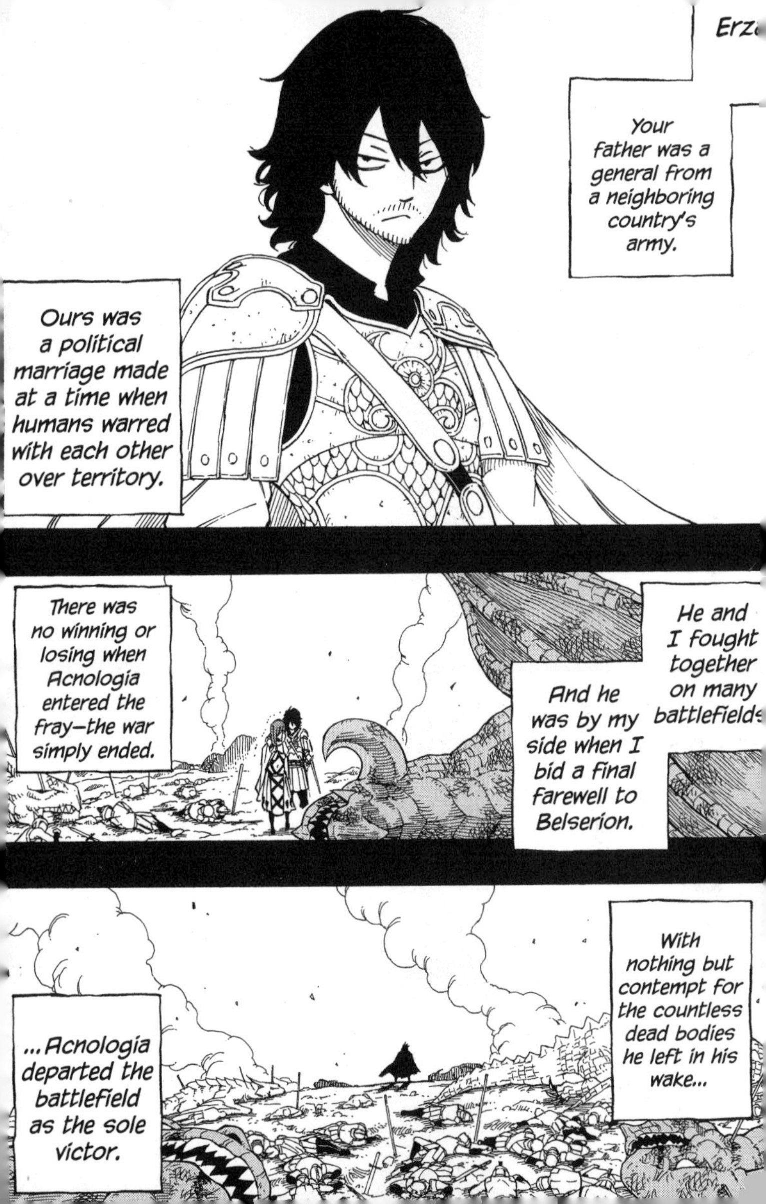
Erz
Your father was a general from a neighboring country's army.
Ours was a political marriage made at a time when humans warred with each other over territory.
He and I fought together on many battlefield
And he was by my side when I bid a final farewell to Belserion.
There was no winning or losing when Acnologia entered the fray—the war simply ended.
With nothing but contempt for the countless dead bodies he left in his wake...
...Acnologia departed the battlefield as the sole victor.

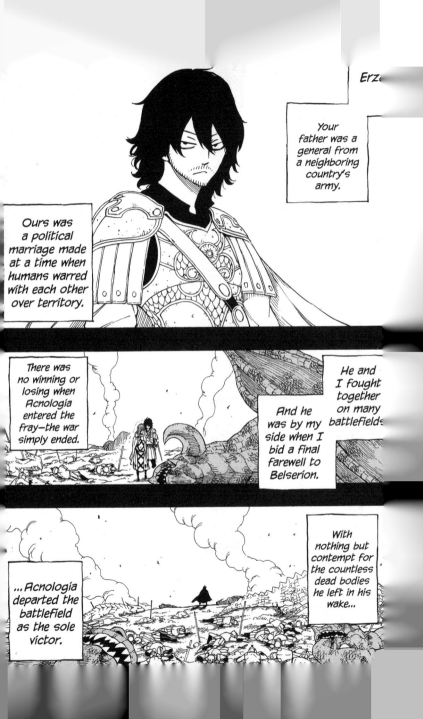

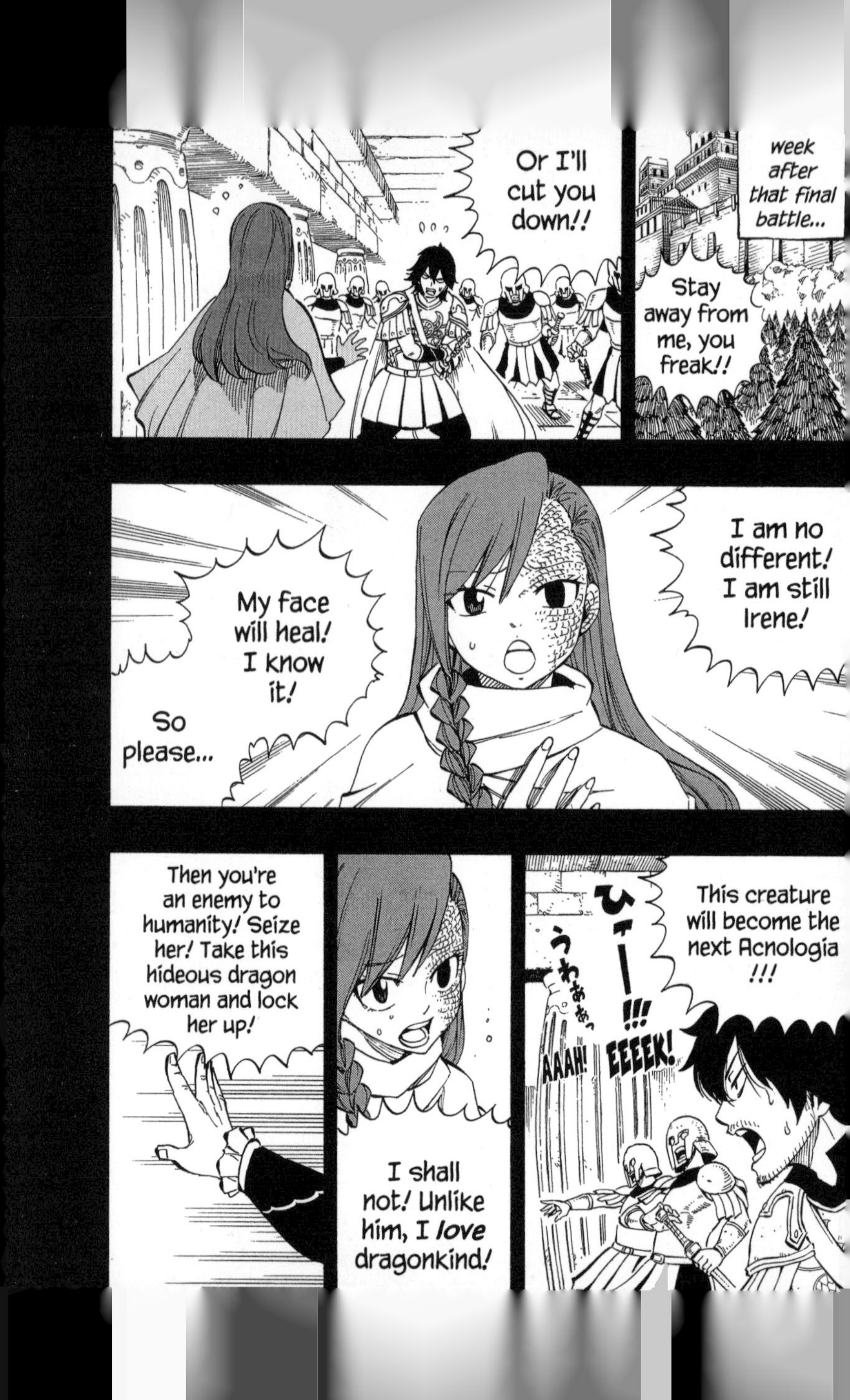
week after that final battle...
Stay away from me, you freak!!
Or I'll cut you down!!
I am no different! I am still Irene!
My face will heal! I know it!
So please...
This creature will become the next Acnologia!!!
ひー!!!
EEEEK!
うわあぁっ
AAAH!
I shall not! Unlike him, I love dragonkind!
Then you're an enemy to humanity! Seize her! Take this hideous dragon woman and lock her up!

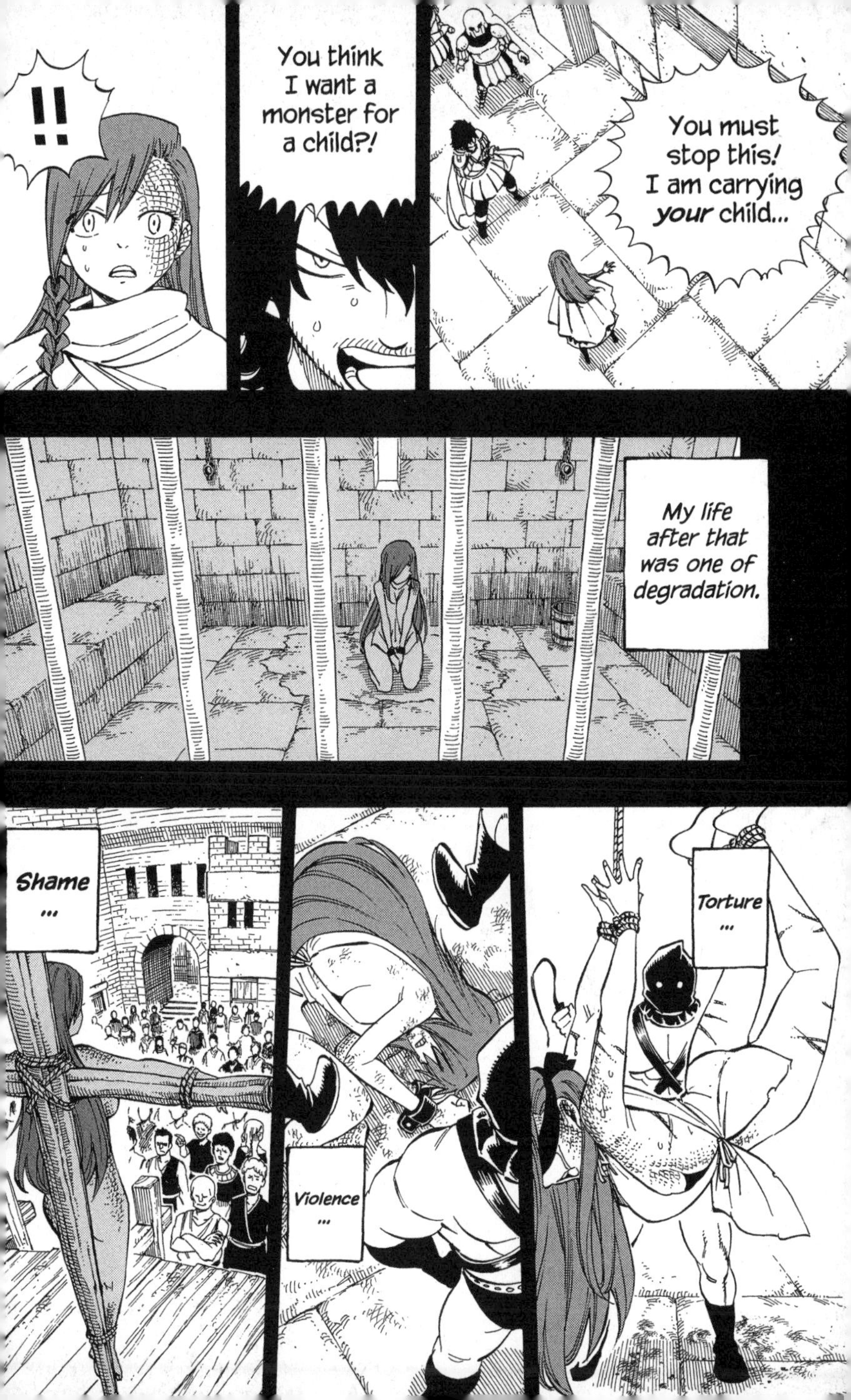
You must stop this! I am carrying *your* child...
You think I want a monster for a child?!
!!
My life after that was one of degradation.
Torture ...
Violence ...
Shame ...

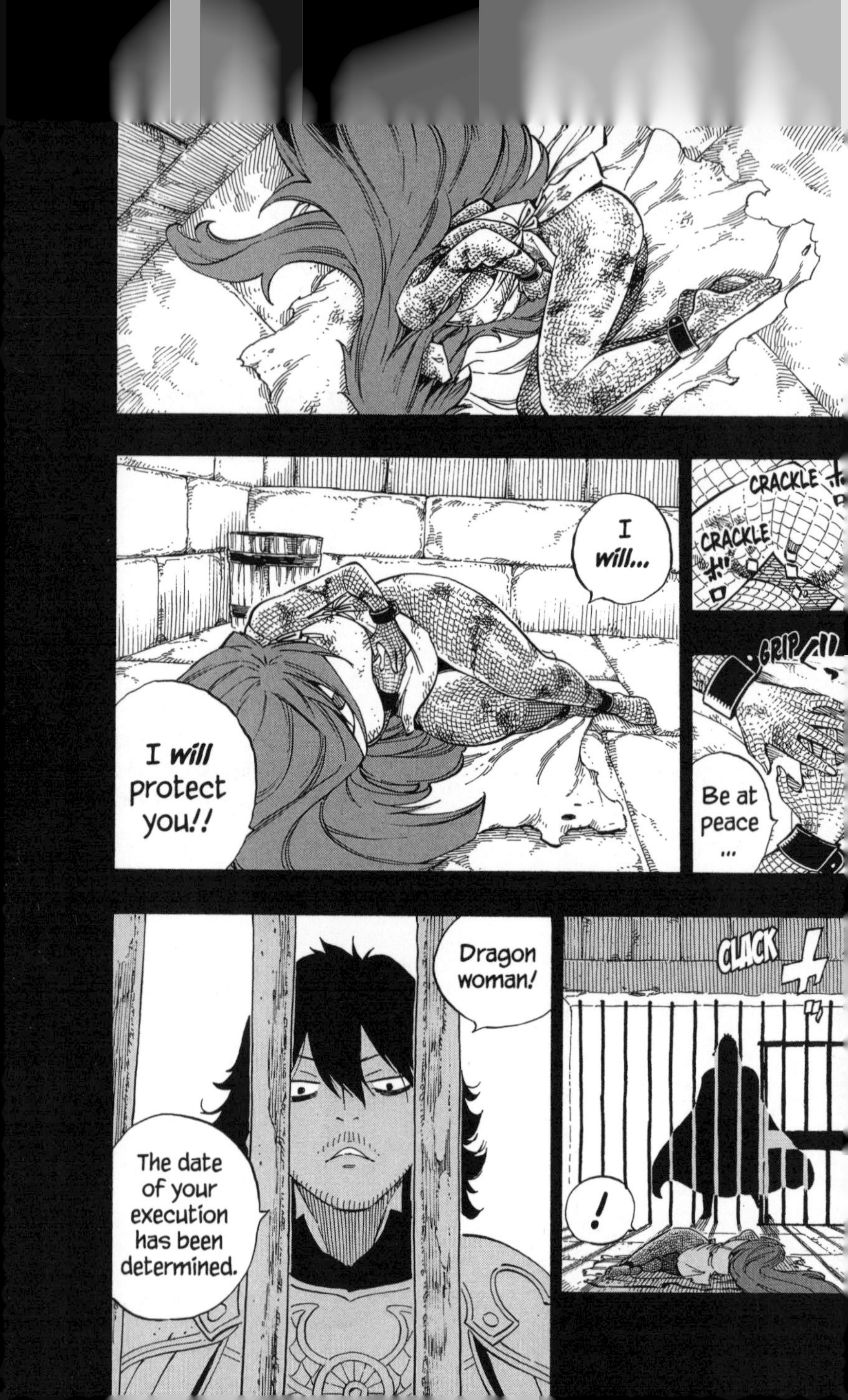
CRACKLE
CRACKLE
GRIP
Be at peace ...
I will...
I will protect you!!
CLACK
!
Dragon woman!
The date of your execution has been determined.

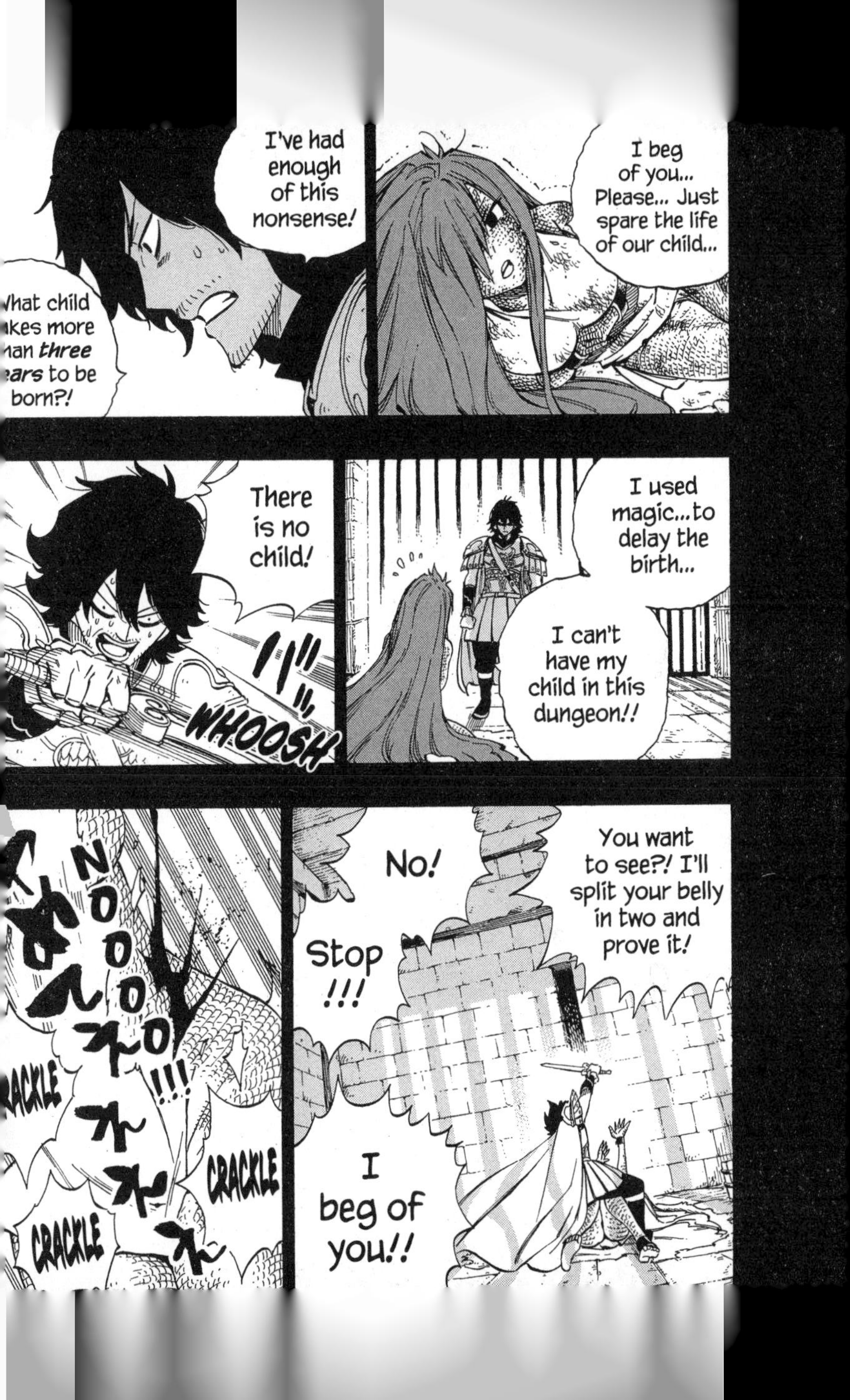
I beg of you... Please... Just spare the life of our child...
I've had enough of this nonsense!
hat child kes more han three ears to be born?!
I used magic...to delay the birth...
I can't have my child in this dungeon!!
There is no child!
WHOOSH
You want to see?! I'll split your belly in two and prove it!
No!
Stop!!!
I beg of you!!
NOOOOO!!!
CRACKLE
CRACKLE
CRACKLE

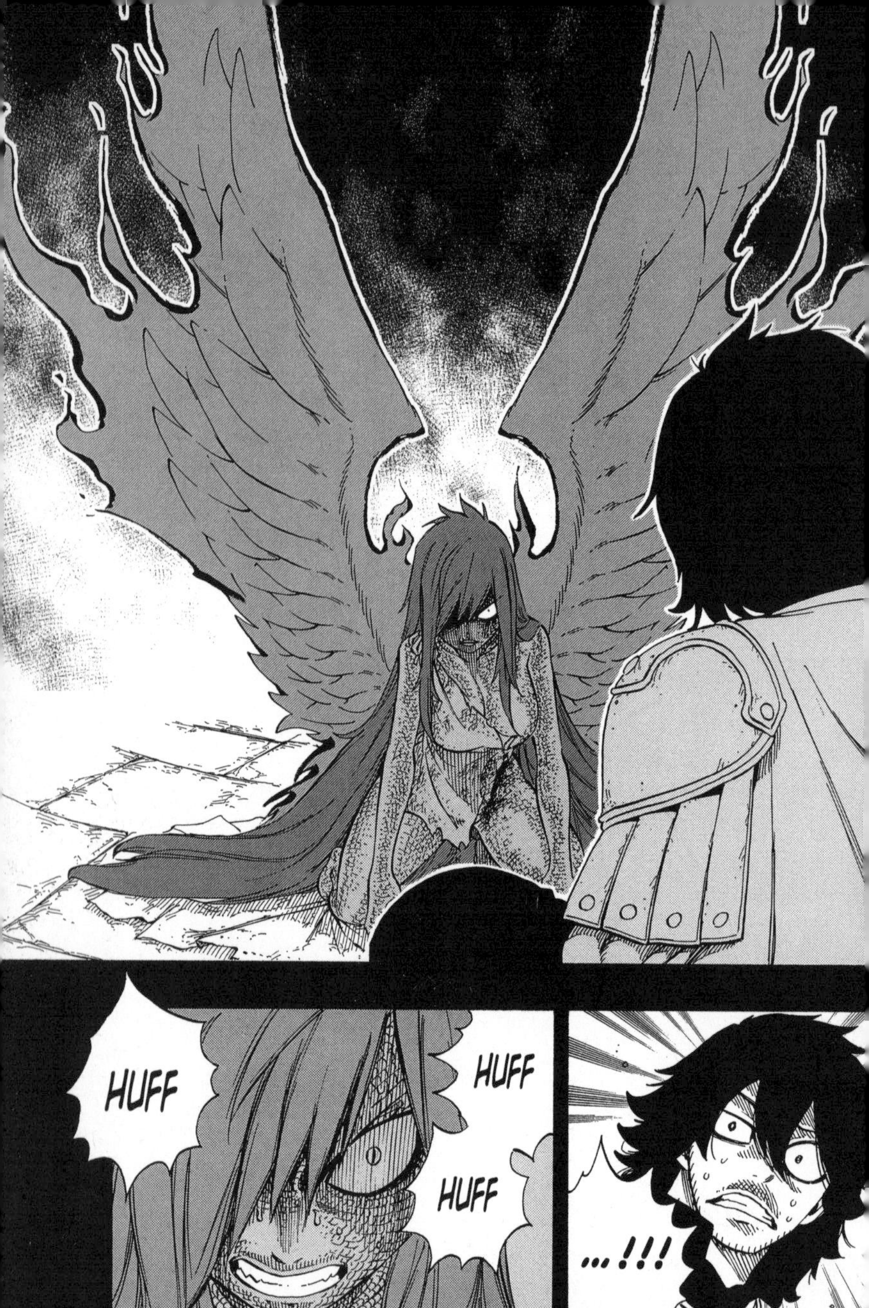
...!!!
HUFF
HUFF
HUFF

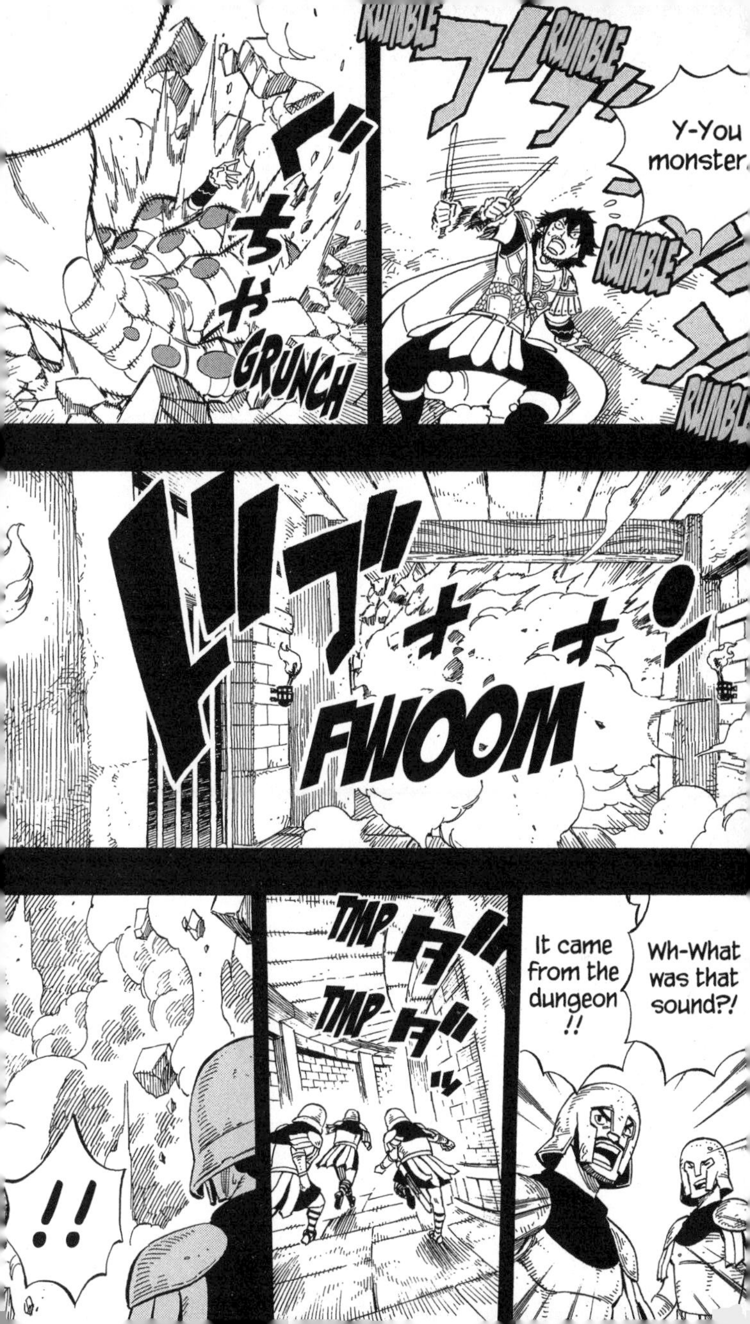

RUMBLE
RUMBLE
Y-You monster
RUMBLE
RUMBL
RUMBLE
GRUNCH
FWOOM
Wh-What was that sound?!
It came from the dungeon!!
TMP
TMP
!!

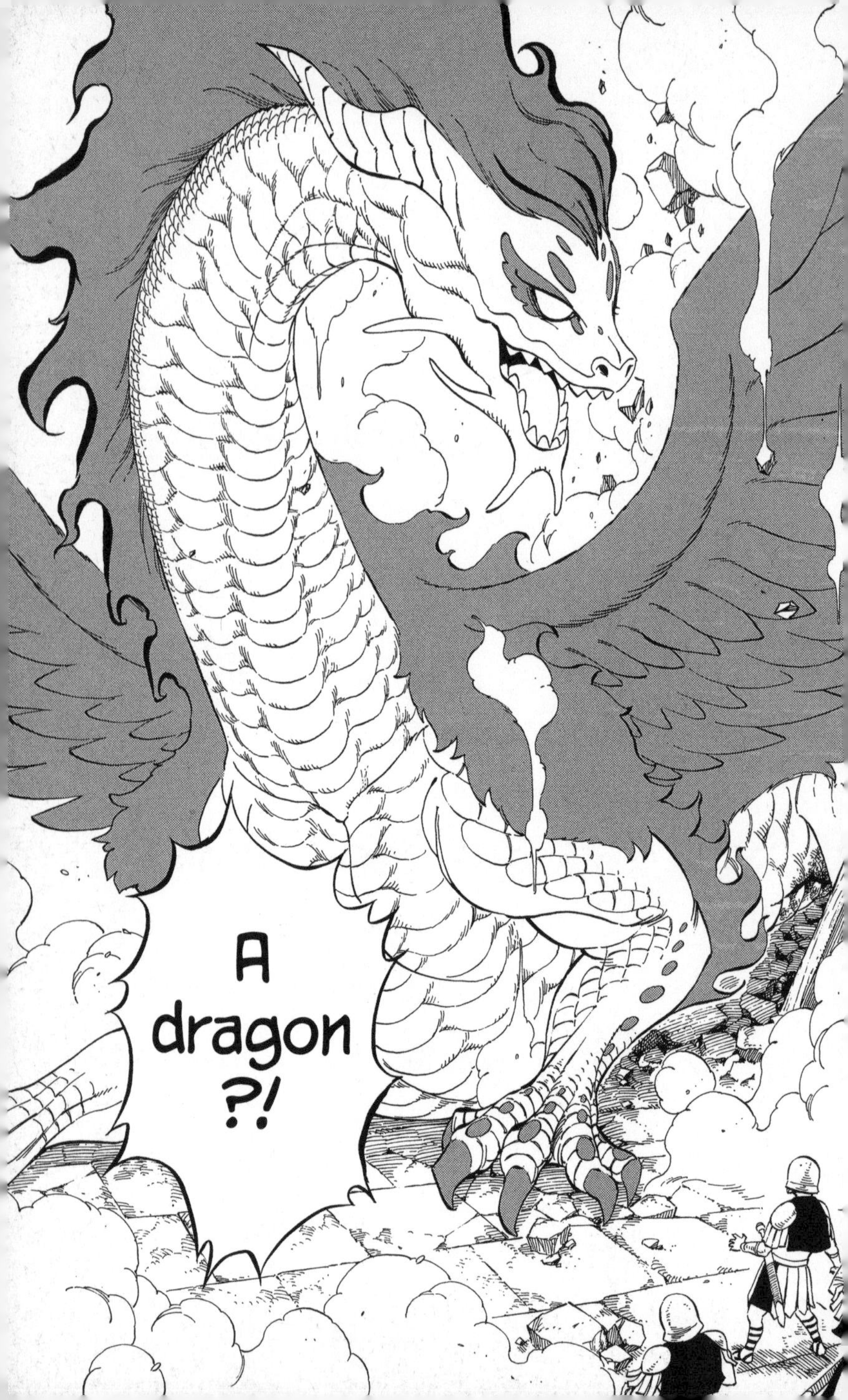
A dragon ?!

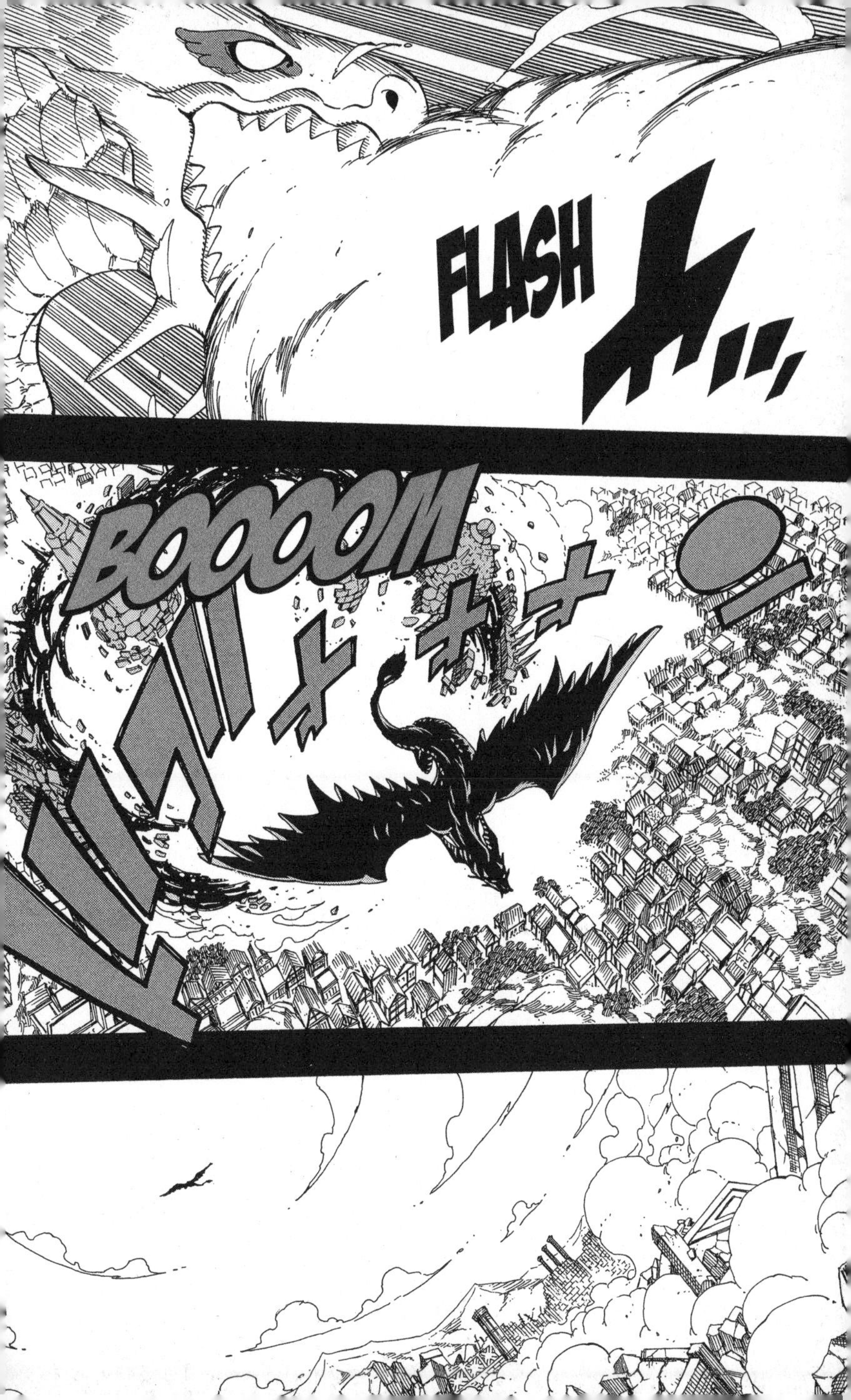
FLASH
BOOOOM

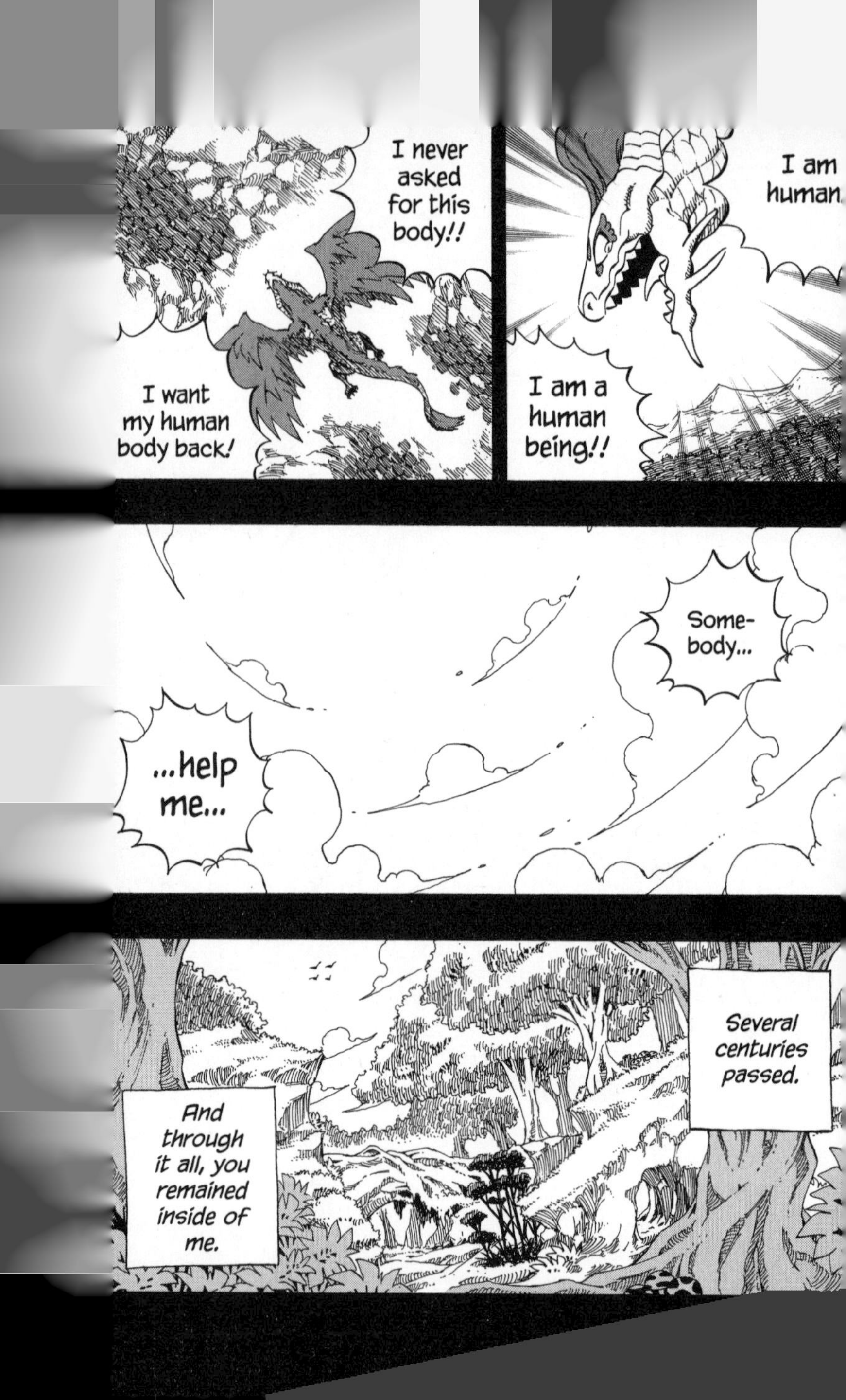
I am human.
I am a human being!!
I never asked for this body!!
I want my human body back!
Some-body...
...help me...
Several centuries passed.
And through it all, you remained inside of me.

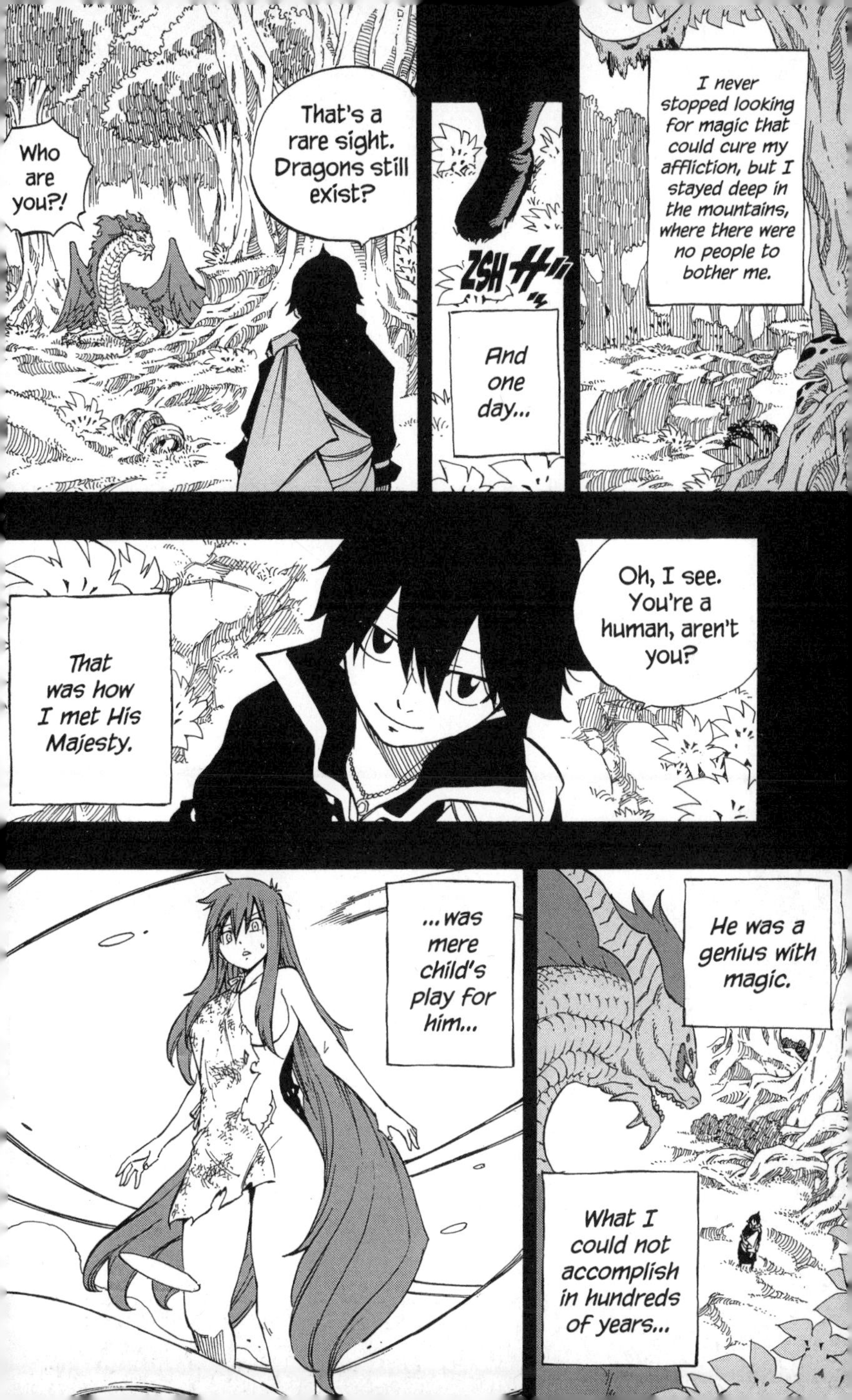
I never stopped looking for magic that could cure my affliction, but I stayed deep in the mountains, where there were no people to bother me.
ZSH
And one day...
That's a rare sight. Dragons still exist?
Who are you?!
Oh, I see. You're a human, aren't you?
That was how I met His Majesty.
He was a genius with magic.
What I could not accomplish in hundreds of years...
...was mere child's play for him...

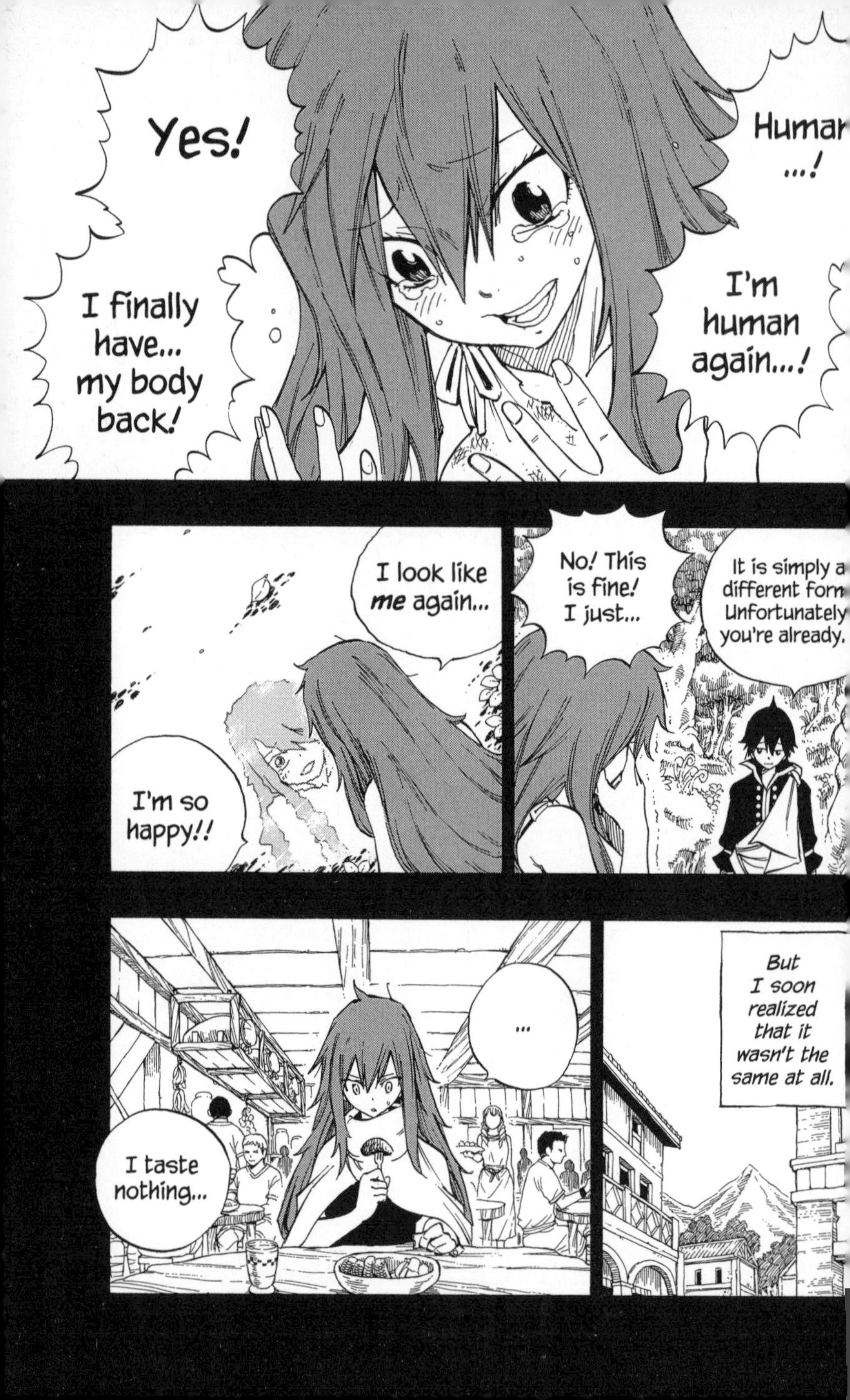
Human ...!
I'm human again...!
Yes!
I finally have... my body back!
It is simply a different form Unfortunately you're already.
No! This is fine! I just...
I look like *me* again...
I'm so happy!!
But I soon realized that it wasn't the same at all.
...
I taste nothing...

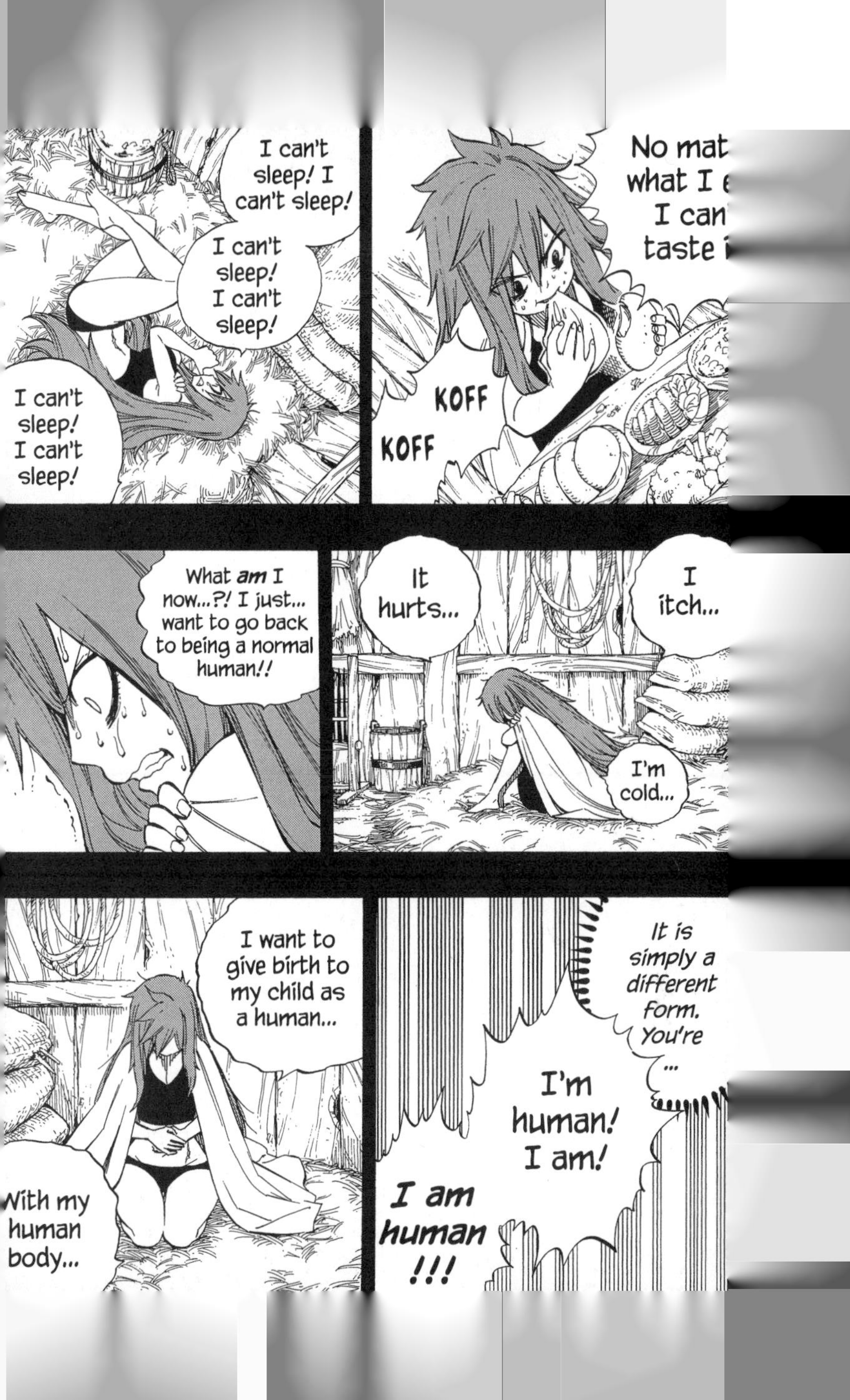
No mat
what I e
I can
taste i
KOFF
KOFF
I can't sleep! I can't sleep!
I can't sleep! I can't sleep!
I can't sleep! I can't sleep!
I itch...
It hurts...
I'm cold...
What *am* I now...?! I just... want to go back to being a normal human!!
It is simply a different form. You're ...
I'm human! I am!
I am human !!!
I want to give birth to my child as a human...
With my human body...

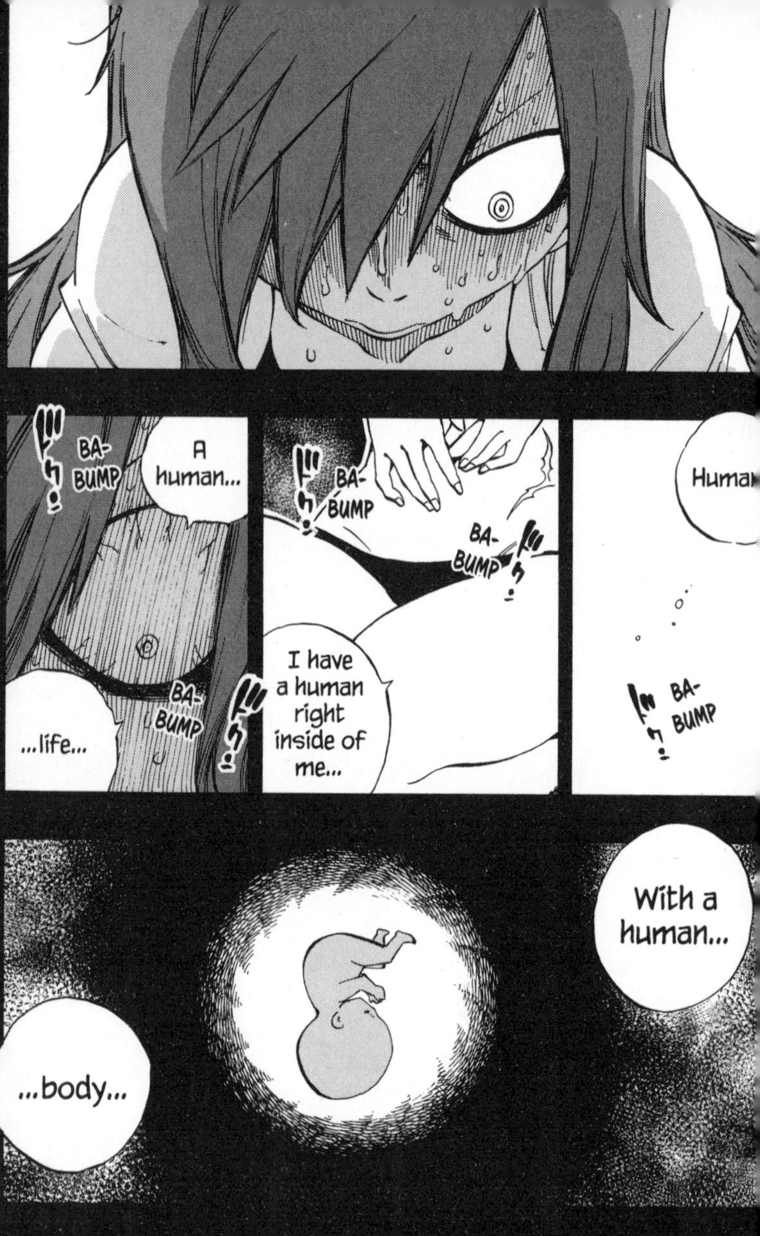
Huma
BA-BUMP
BA-BUMP
BA-BUMP
I have a human right inside of me...
A human...
BA-BUMP
BA-BUMP
...life...
With a human...
...body...

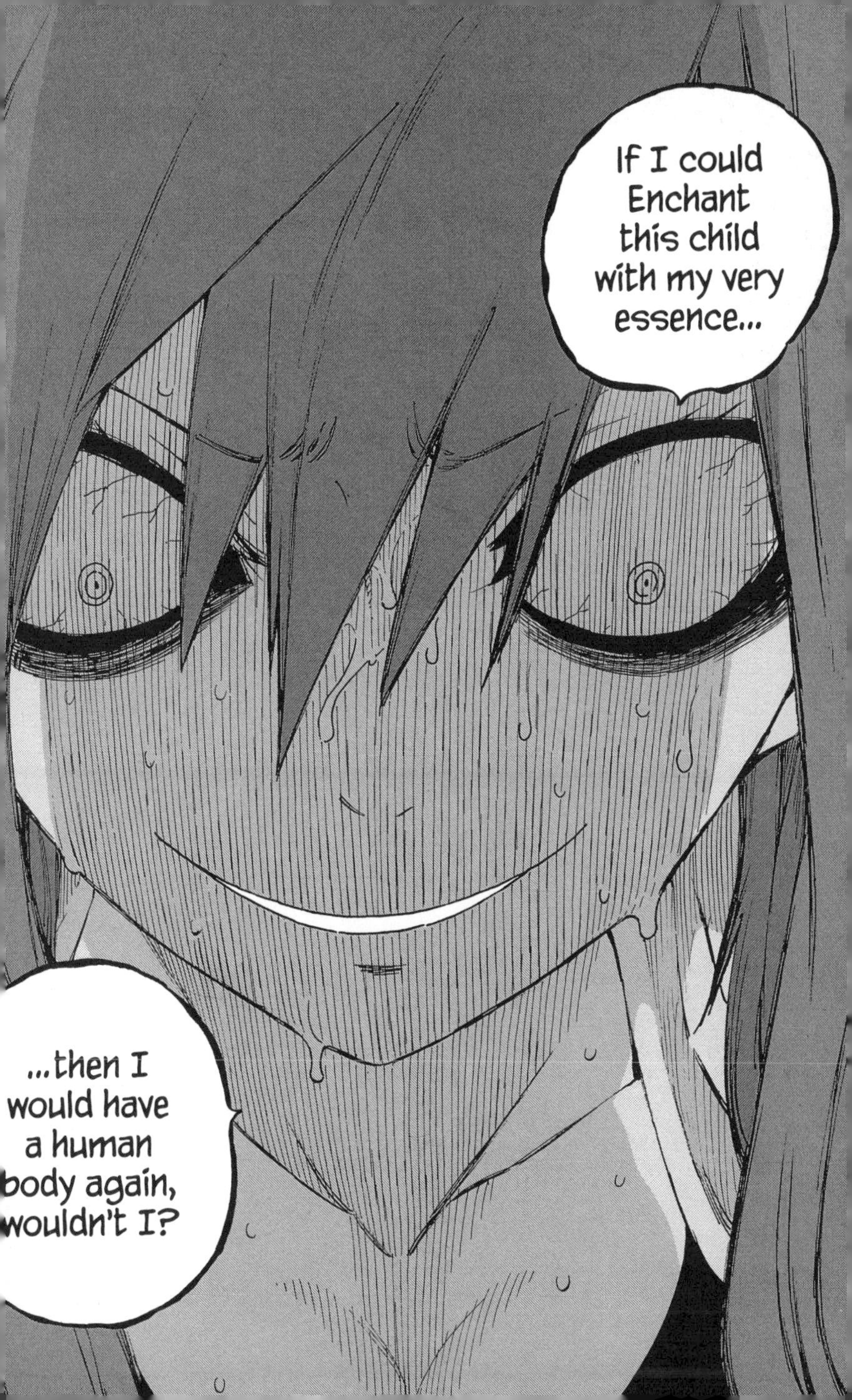
If I could Enchant this child with my very essence...
...then I would have a human body again, wouldn't I?

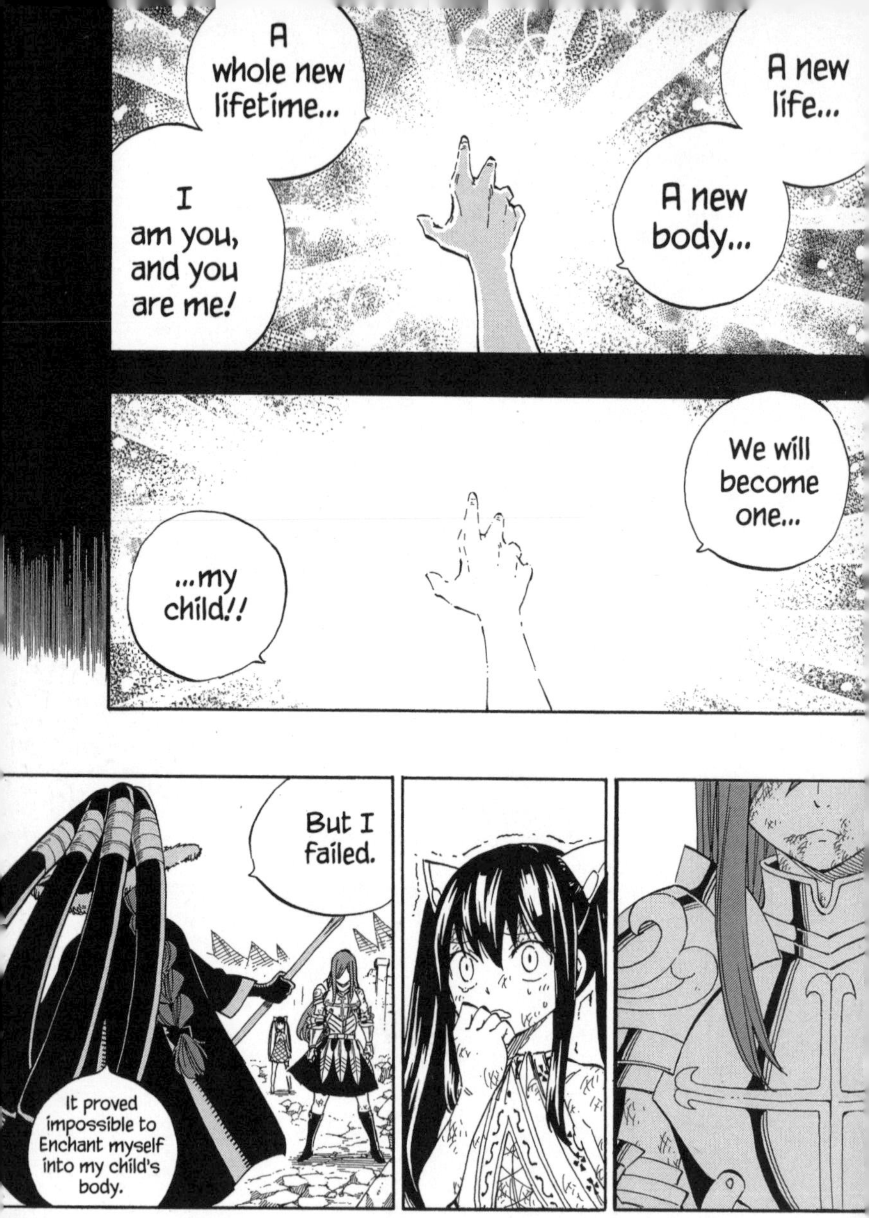
A new life...
A whole new lifetime...
A new body...
I am you, and you are me!
We will become one...
...my child!!
But I failed.
It proved impossible to Enchant myself into my child's body.

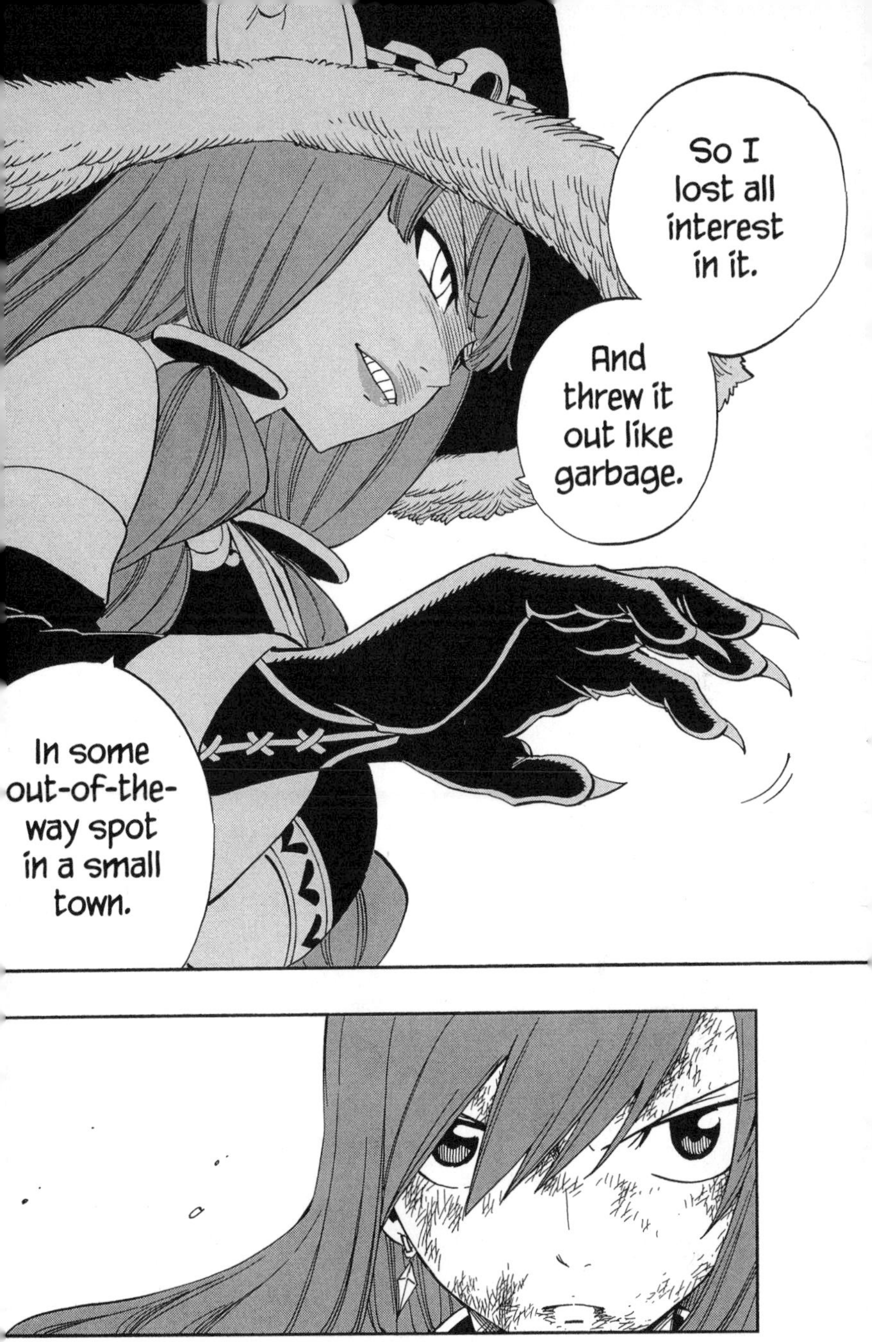
So I lost all interest in it.
And threw it out like garbage.
In some out-of-the-way spot in a small town.

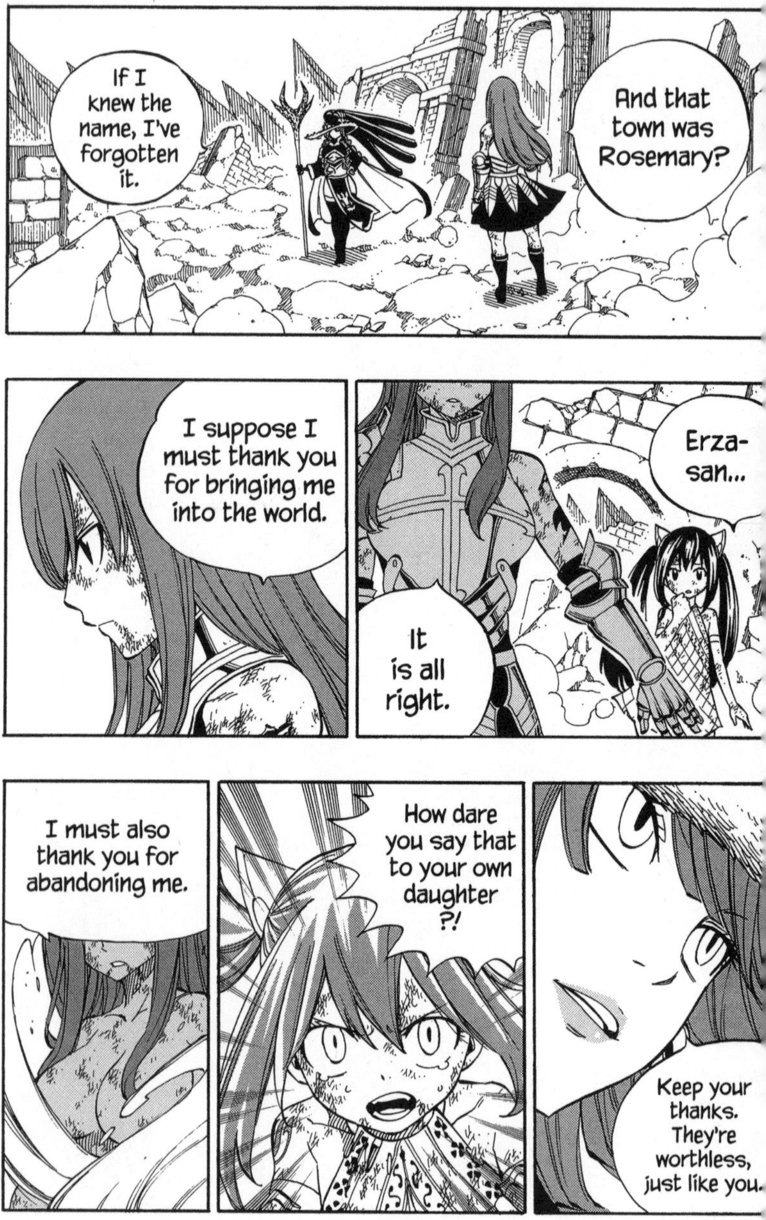
And that town was Rosemary?
If I knew the name, I've forgotten it.
Erza-san...
It is all right.
I suppose I must thank you for bringing me into the world.
Keep your thanks. They're worthless, just like you.
How dare you say that to your own daughter?!
I must also thank you for abandoning me.

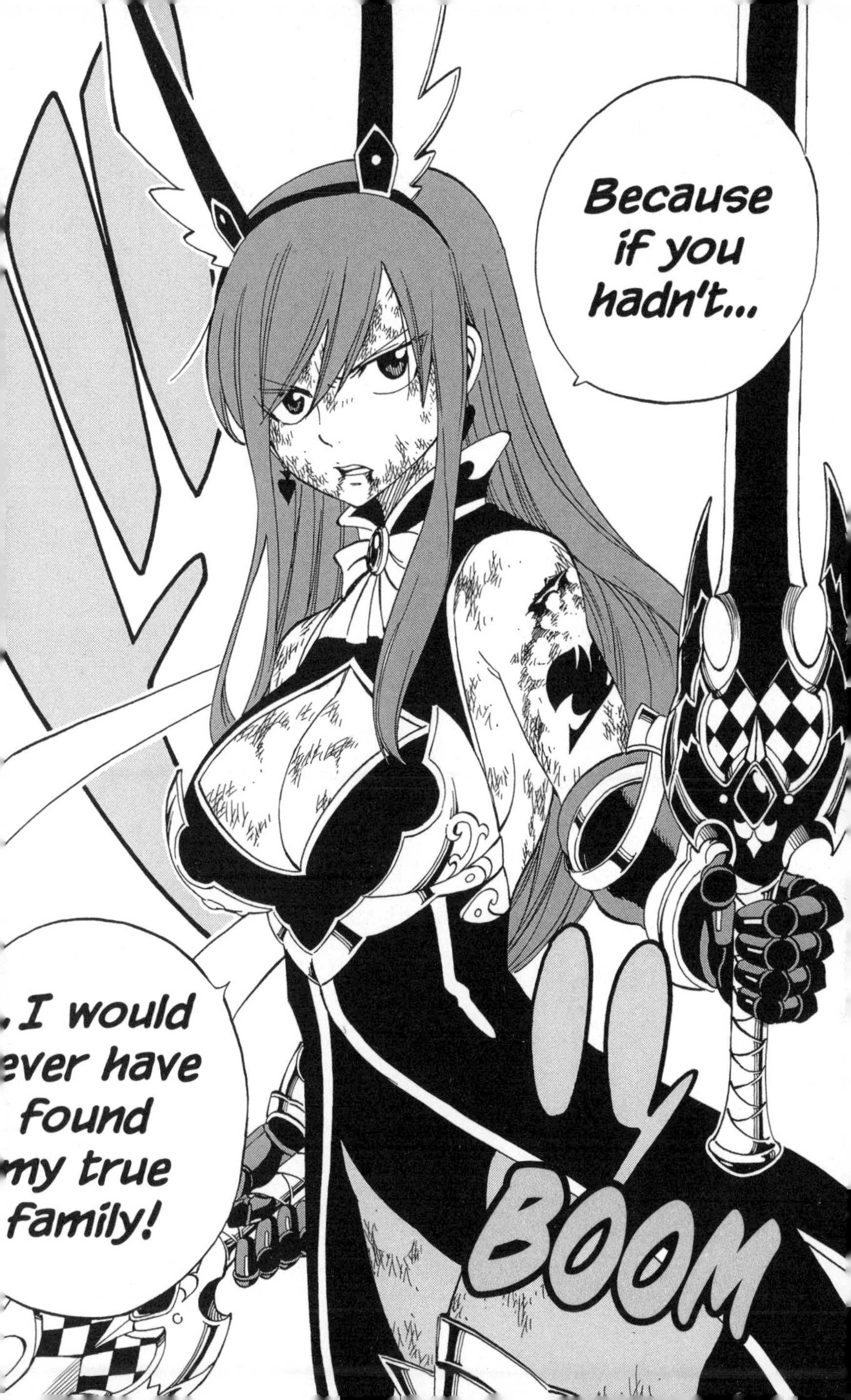
Because if you hadn't...
...I would never have found my true family!
BOOM

FAIRY TAIL

フェアリーテイル

Chapter 516: The Essence of Enchant

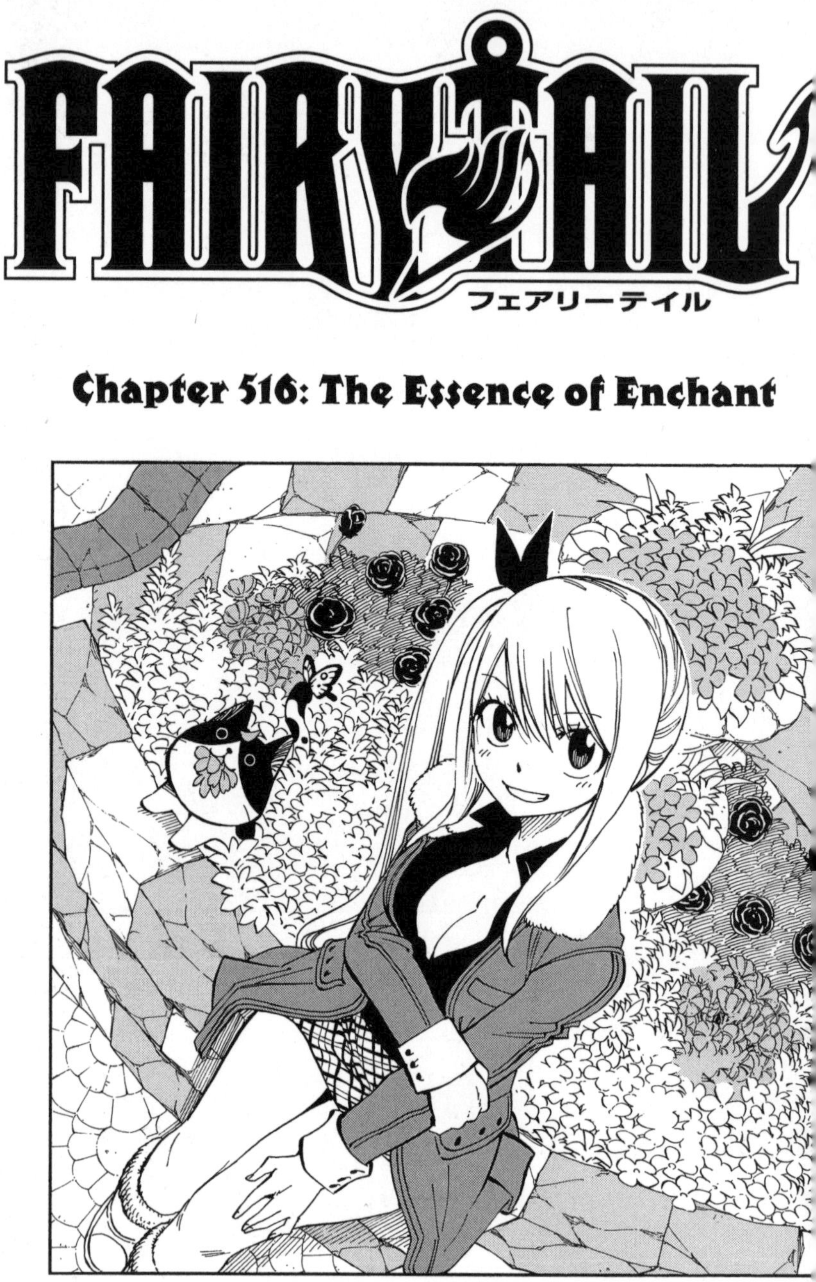

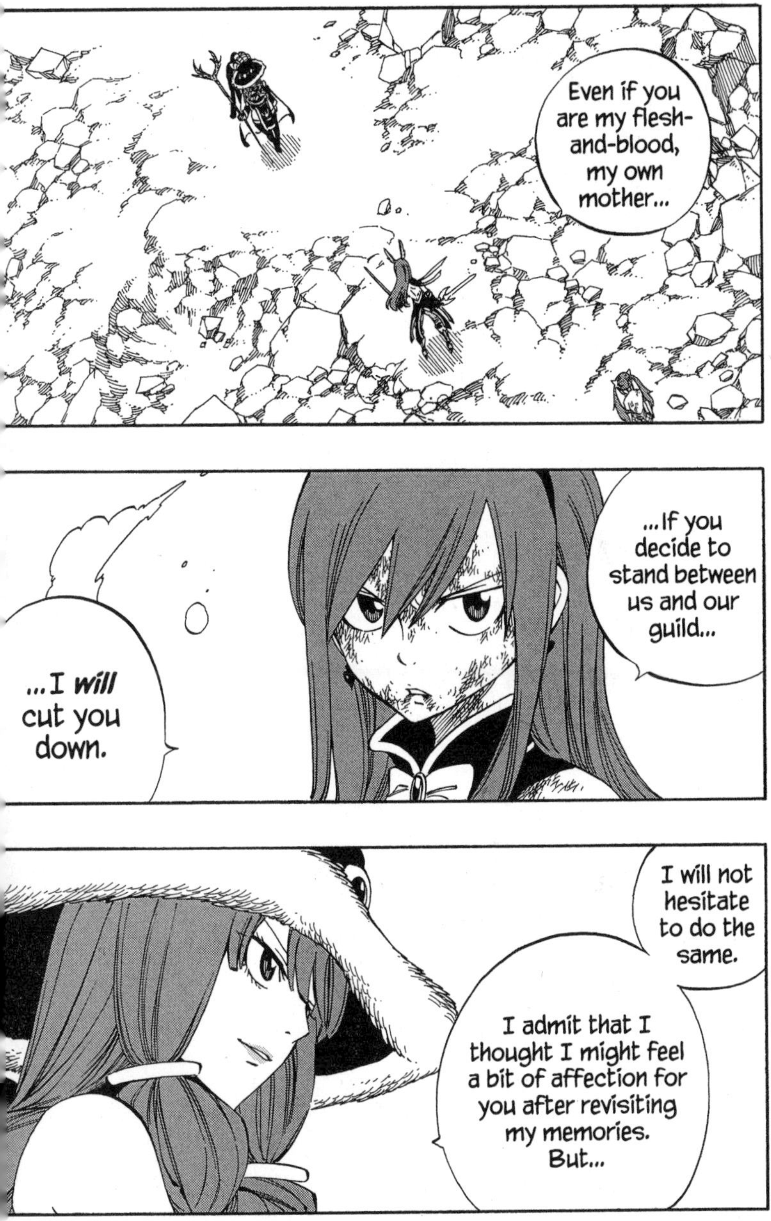
Even if you are my flesh-and-blood, my own mother...
...If you decide to stand between us and our guild...
...I *will* cut you down.
I will not hesitate to do the same.
I admit that I thought I might feel a bit of affection for you after revisiting my memories. But...

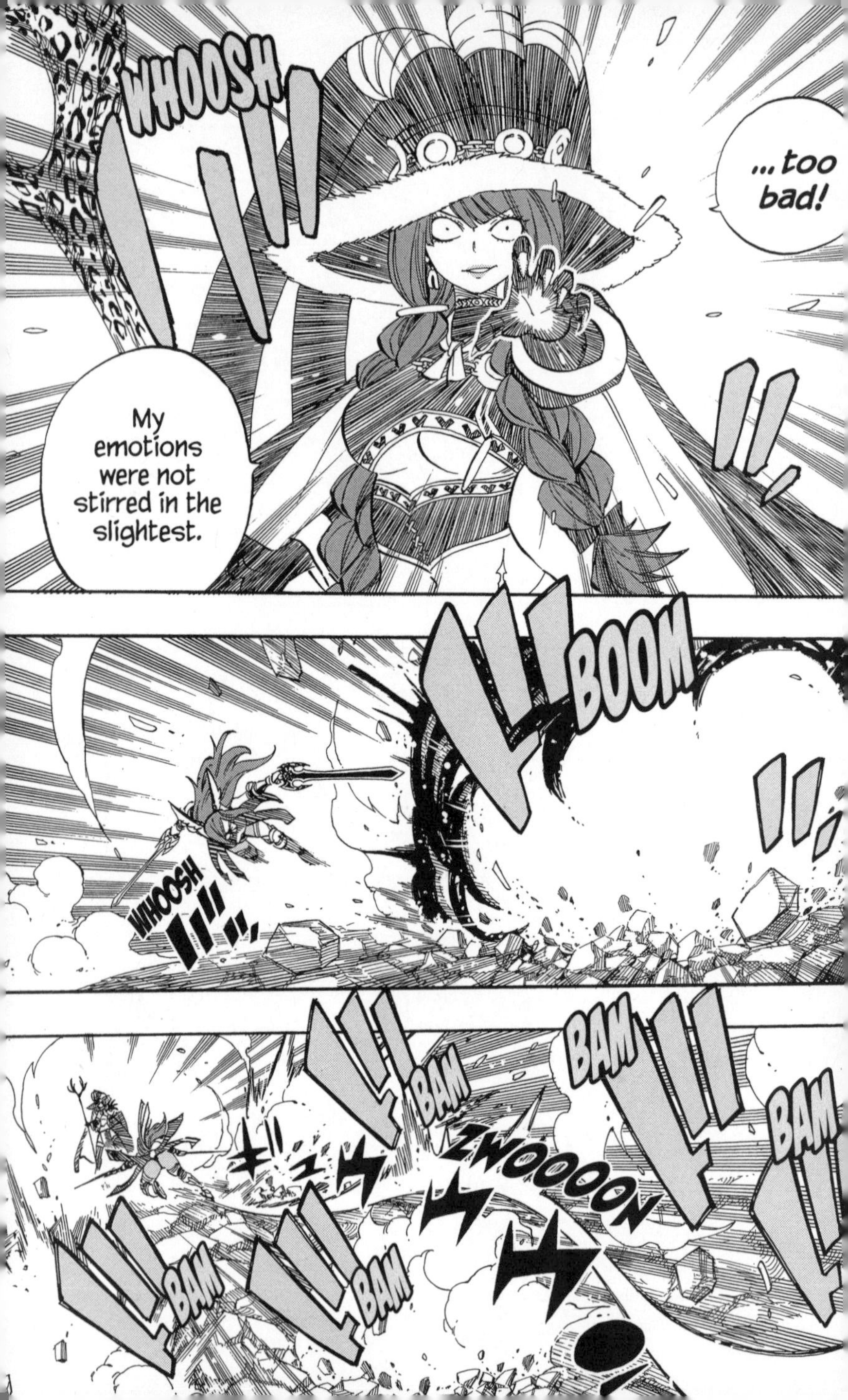
...too bad!
WHOOSH
My emotions were not stirred in the slightest.
BOOM
WHOOSH
BAM
BAM
BAM
ZWOOOON
BAM
BAM

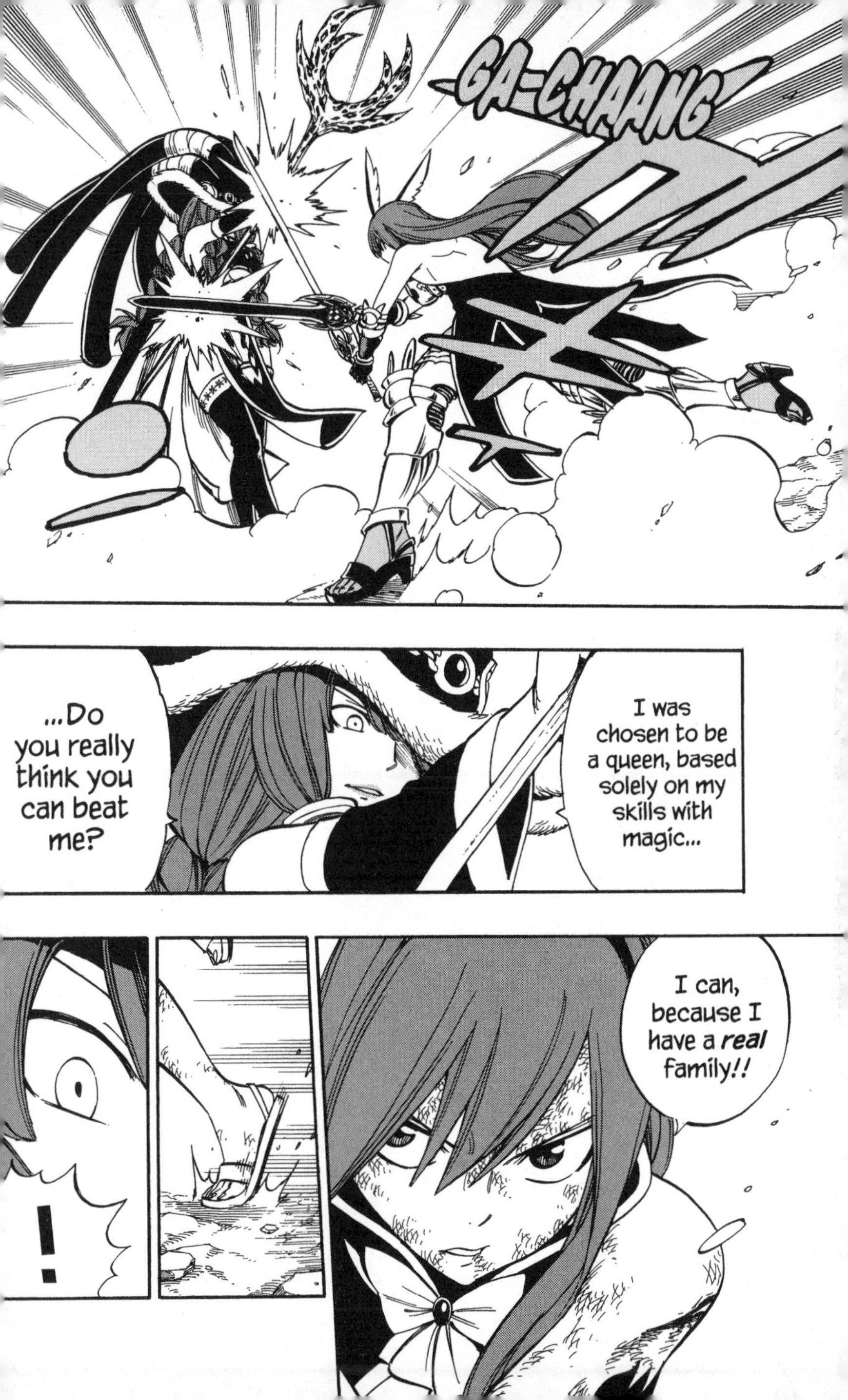
GA-CHAANG
I was chosen to be a queen, based solely on my skills with magic...
...Do you really think you can beat me?
I can, because I have a *real* family!!
!!

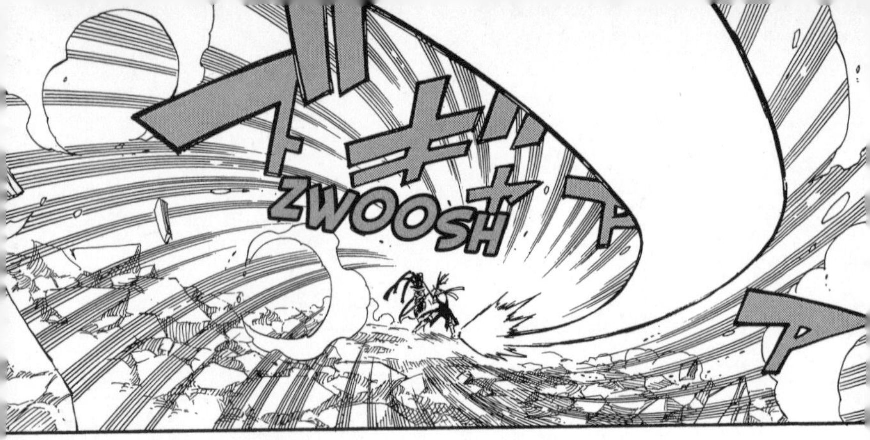
ZWOOSH

*Sky Dragon's Wing Attac

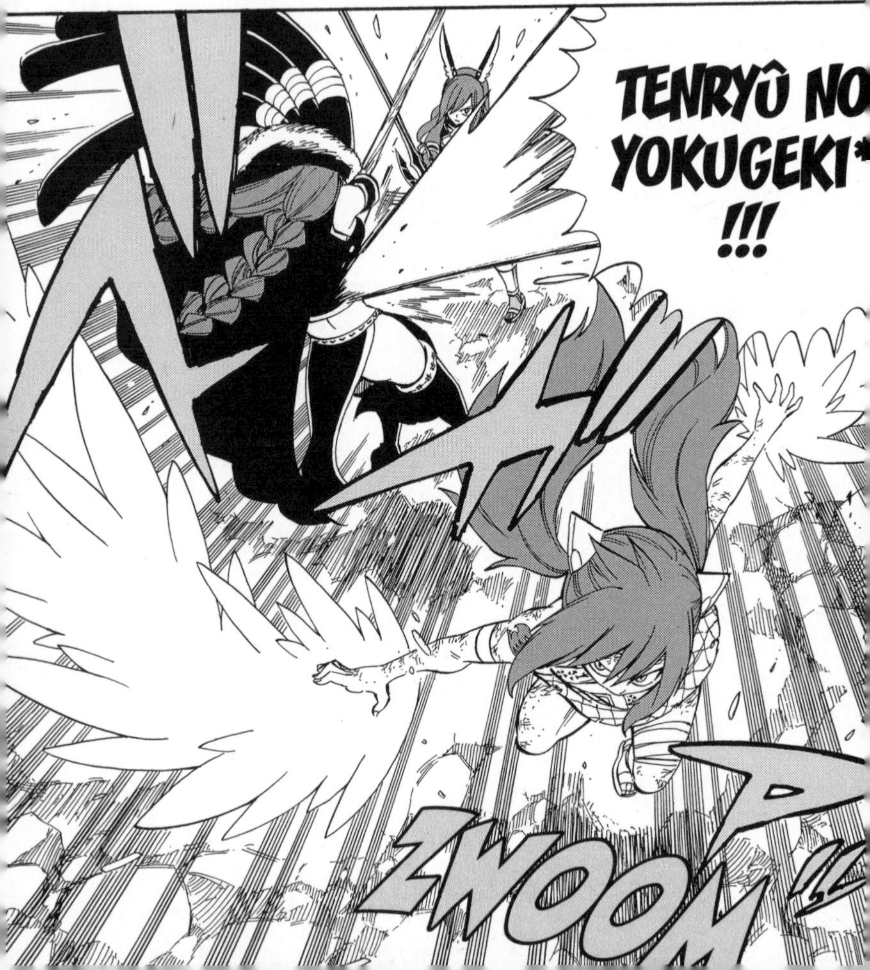
TENRYÛ NO YOKUGEKI* !!!
ZWOOM

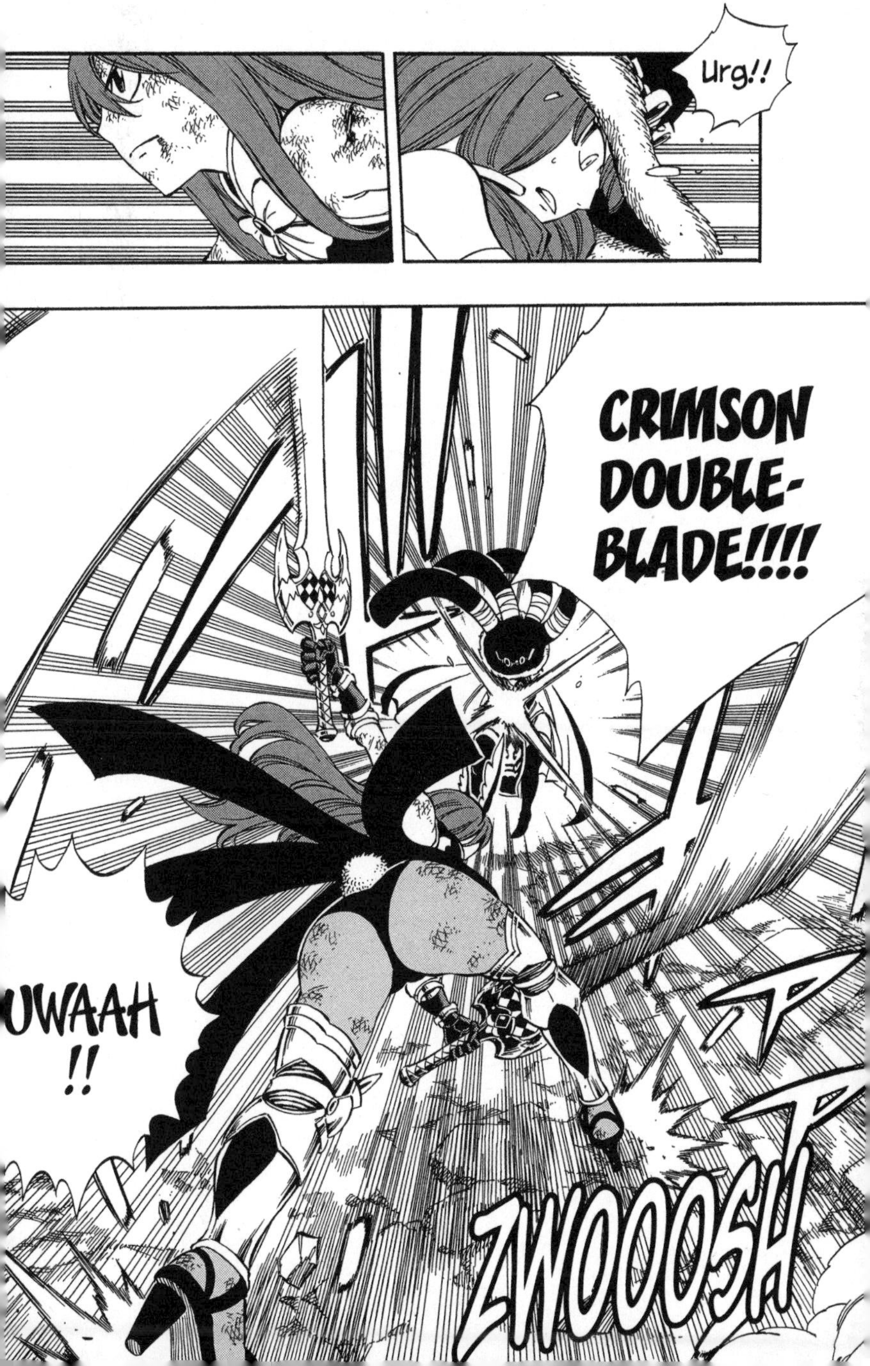
Urg!!
CRIMSON DOUBLE-BLADE!!!!
UWAAH!!
ZWOOOSH

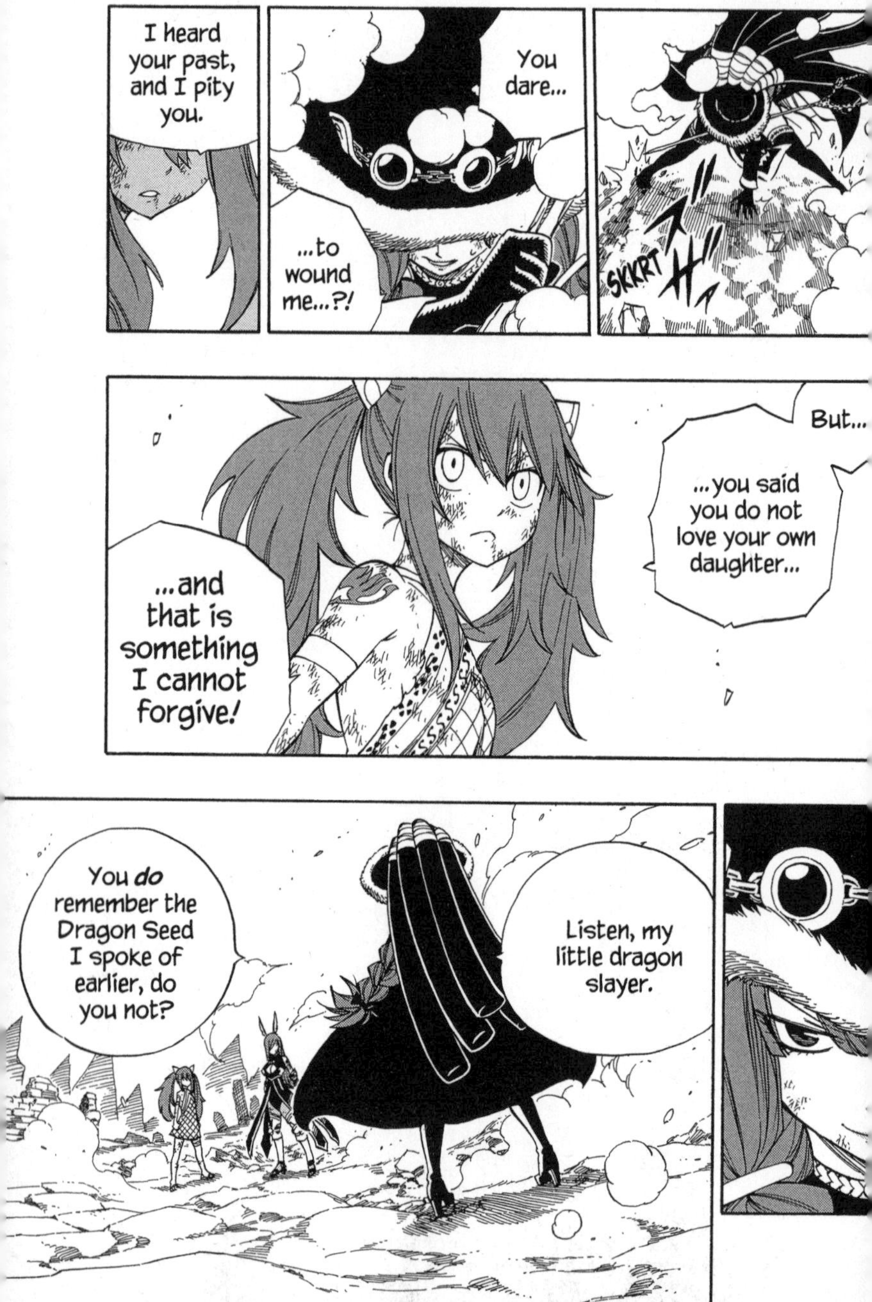
SKKRT
You dare...
...to wound me...?!
I heard your past, and I pity you.
But...
...you said you do not love your own daughter...
...and that is something I cannot forgive!
Listen, my little dragon slayer.
You *do* remember the Dragon Seed I spoke of earlier, do you not?

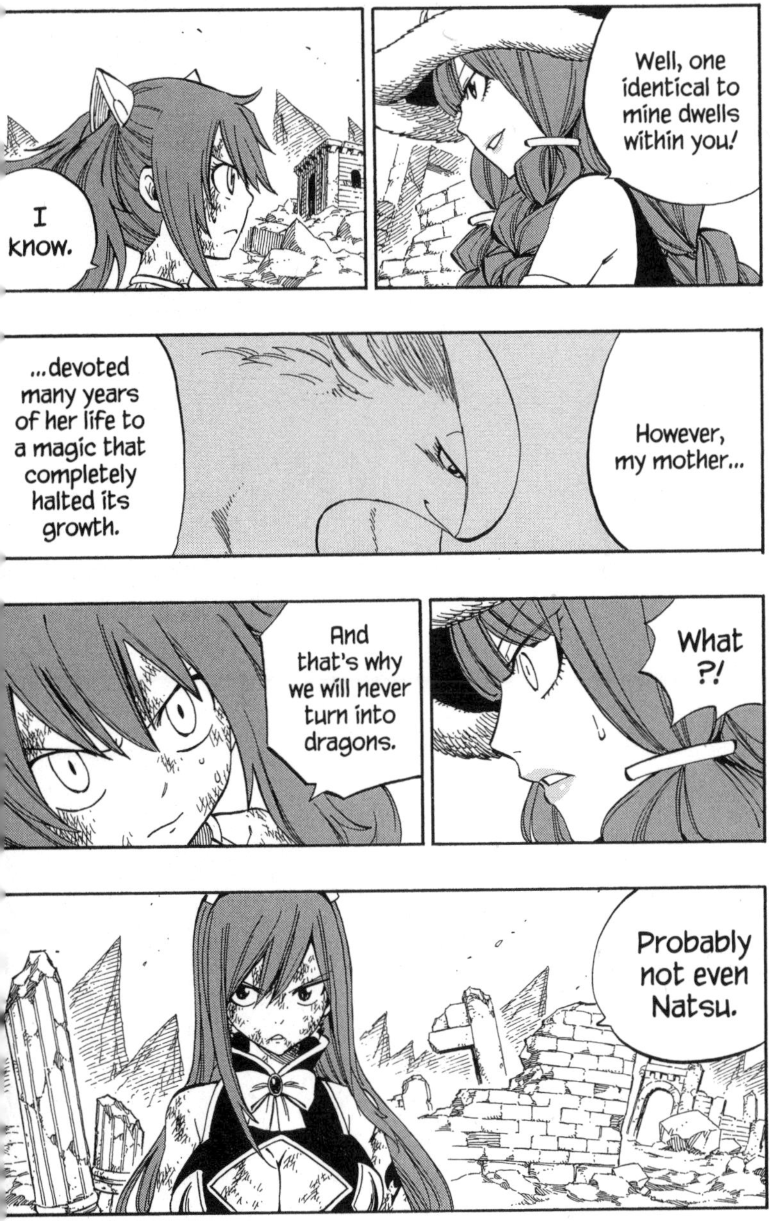

Well, one identical to mine dwells within you!
I know.
However, my mother...
...devoted many years of her life to a magic that completely halted its growth.
What?!
And that's why we will never turn into dragons.
Probably not even Natsu.

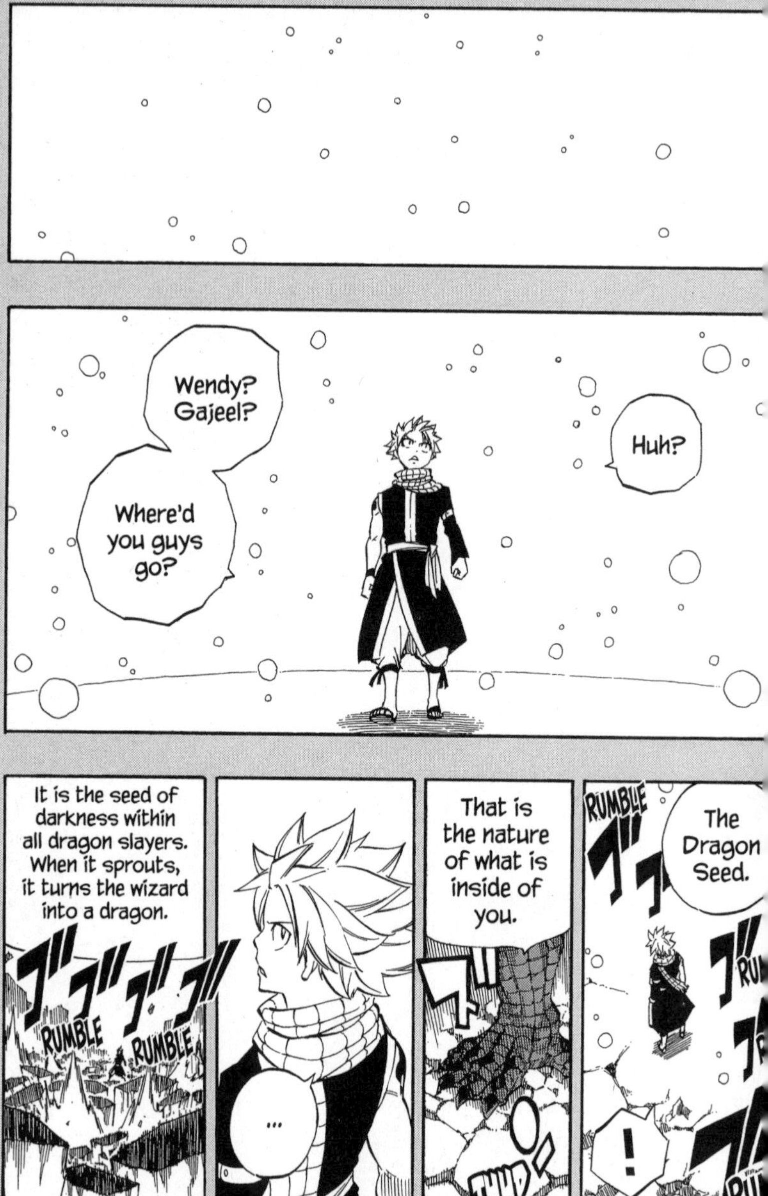
Huh?
Wendy? Gajeel?
Where'd you guys go?
RUMBLE
The Dragon Seed.
!
RUMBLE
That is the nature of what is inside of you.
THUD
...
It is the seed of darkness within all dragon slayers. When it sprouts, it turns the wizard into a dragon.
RUMBLE
RUMBLE

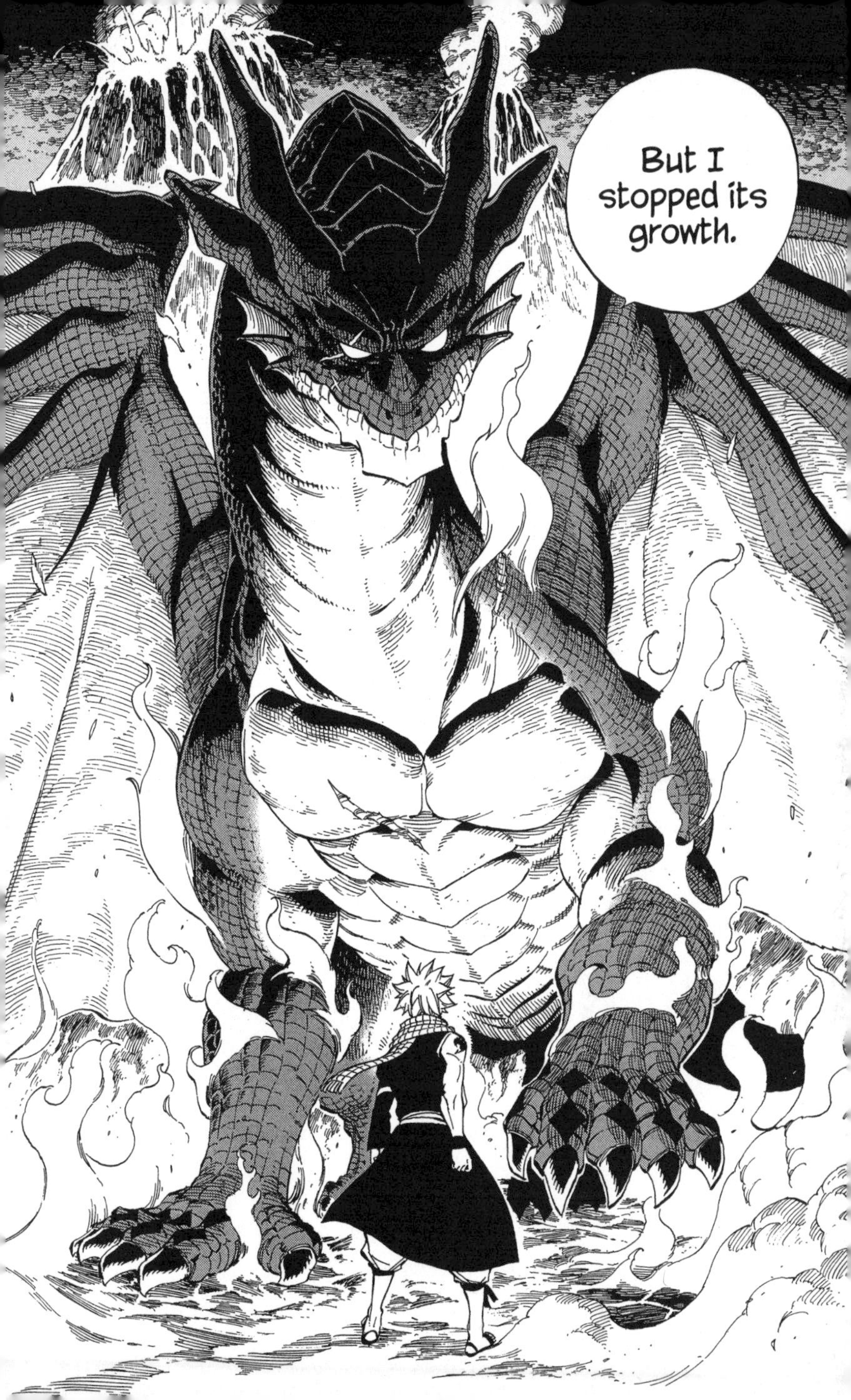
But I stopped its growth.

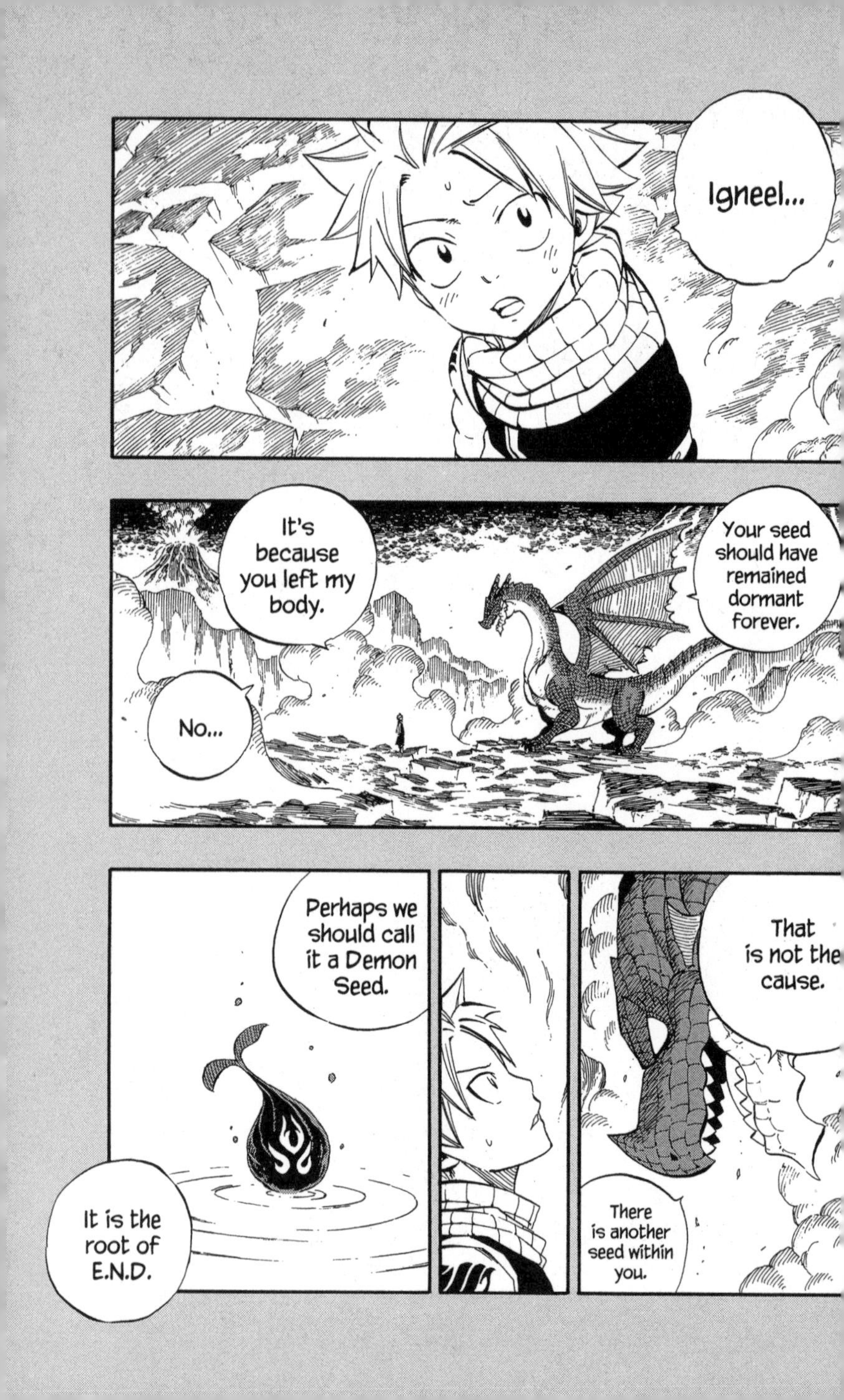
Igneel...
Your seed should have remained dormant forever.
It's because you left my body.
No...
That is not the cause.
There is another seed within you.
Perhaps we should call it a Demon Seed.
It is the root of E.N.D.

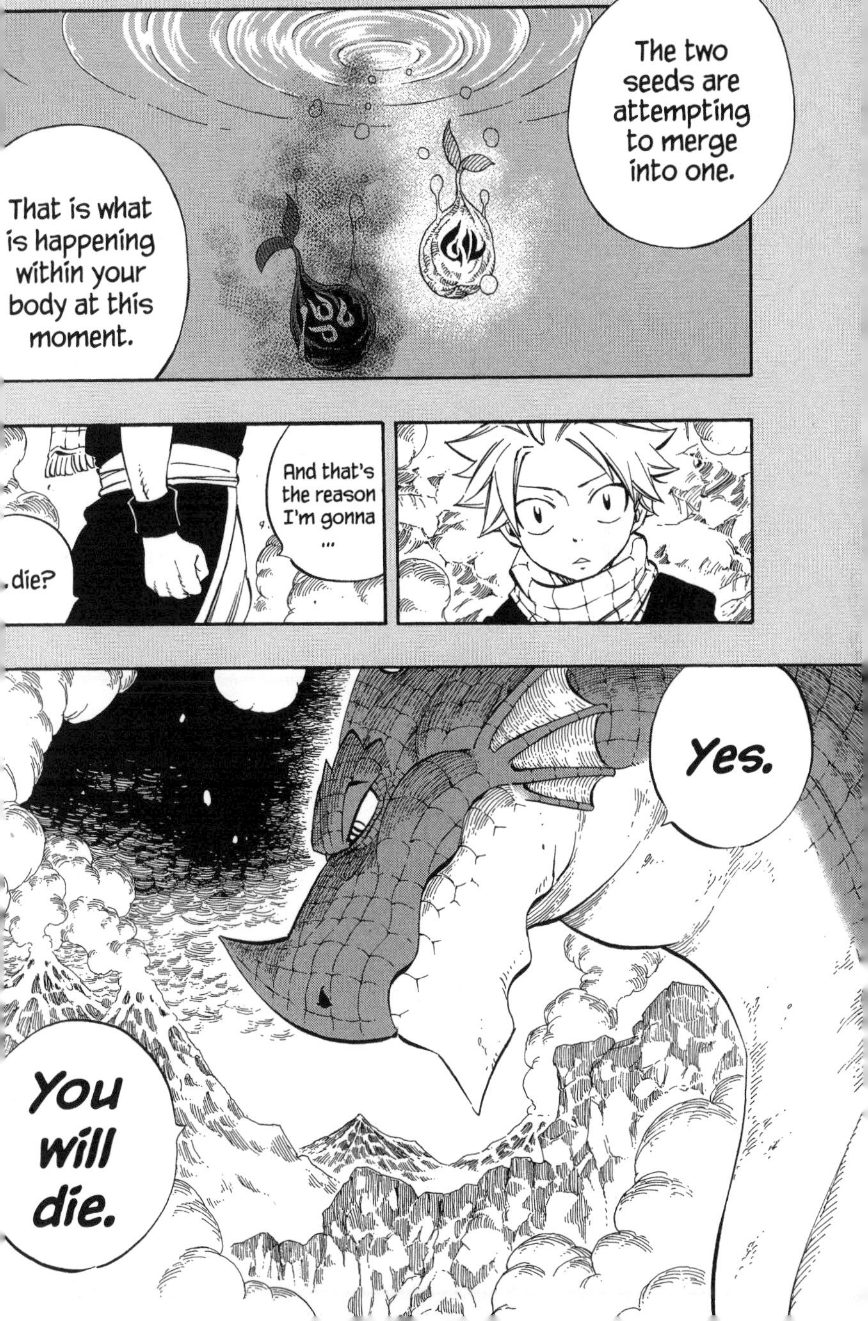

The two seeds are attempting to merge into one.
That is what is happening within your body at this moment.
And that's the reason I'm gonna ...
.die?
Yes.
You will die.

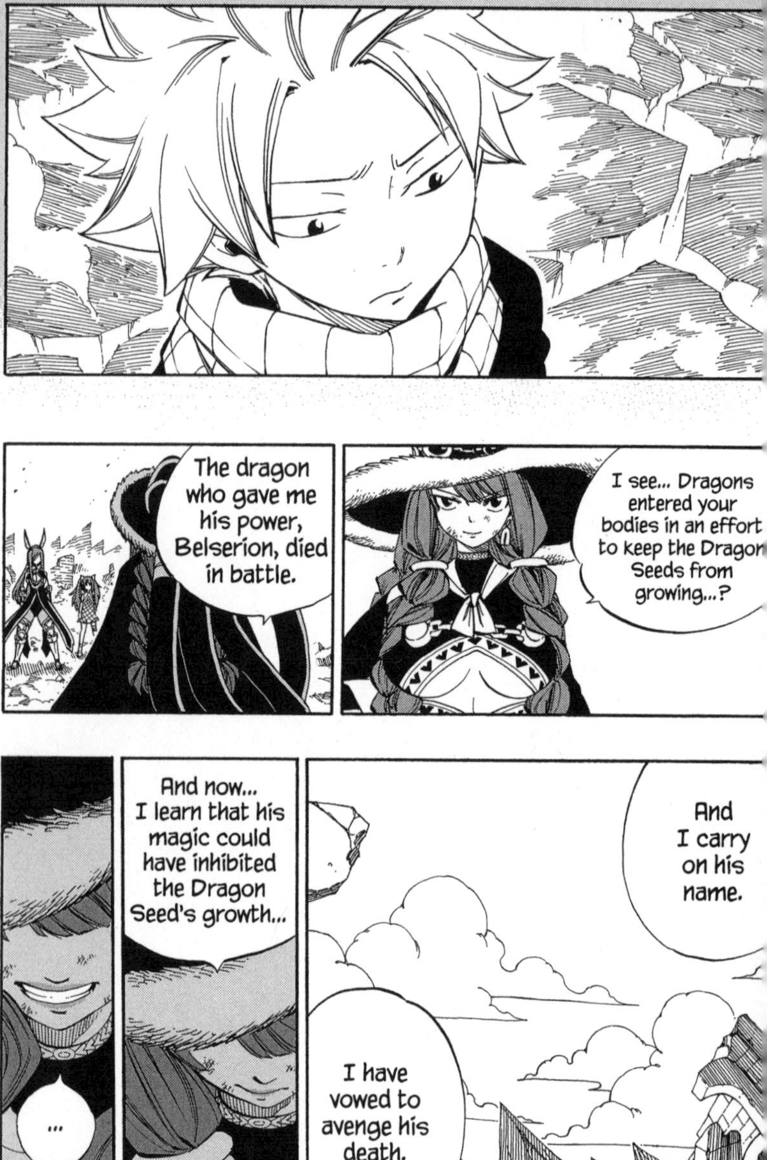
I see... Dragons entered your bodies in an effort to keep the Dragon Seeds from growing...?
The dragon who gave me his power, Belserion, died in battle.
And I carry on his name.
I have vowed to avenge his death.
And now... I learn that his magic could have inhibited the Dragon Seed's growth...
...

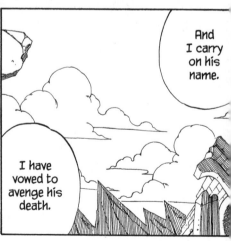

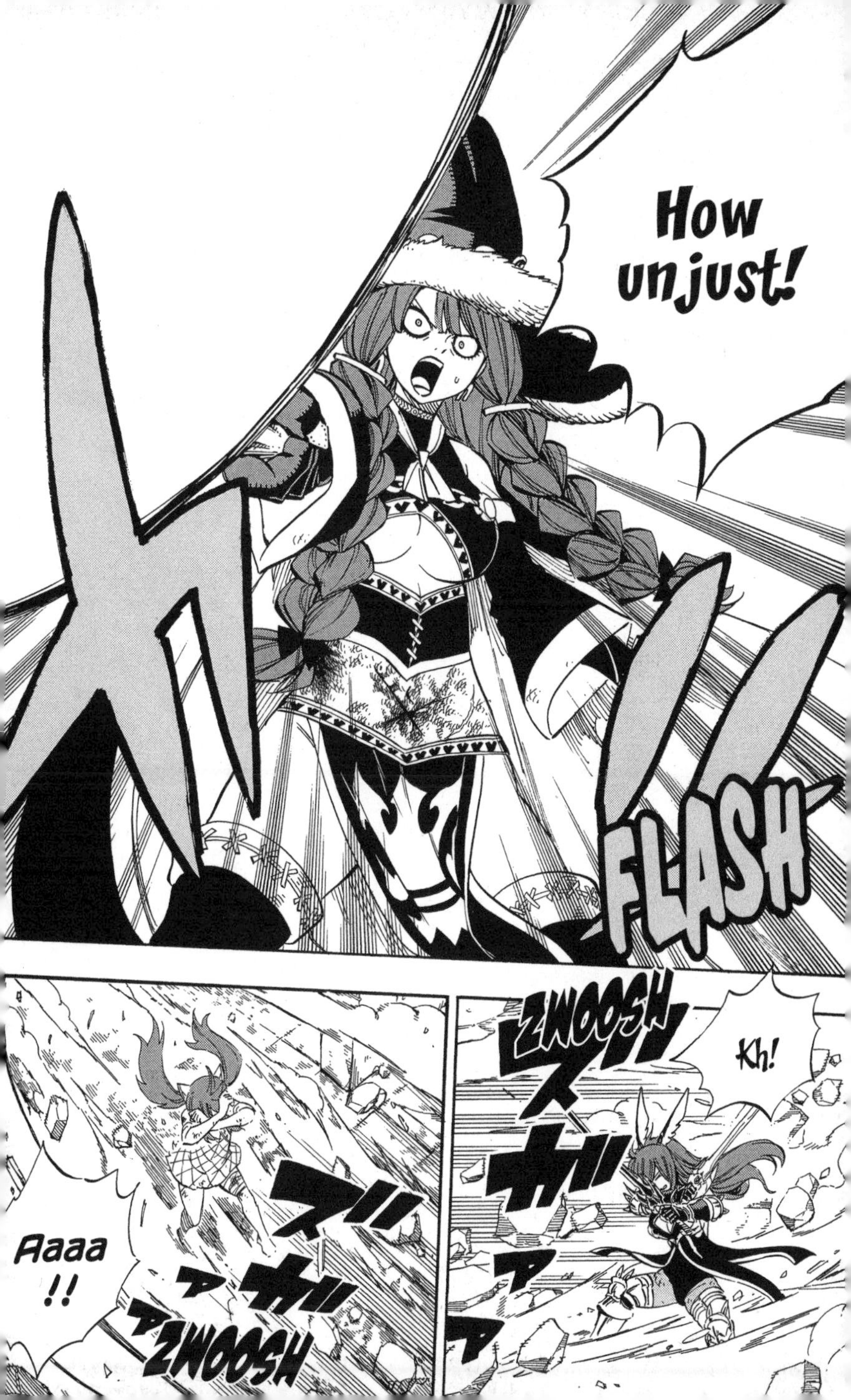
How unjust!
FLASH
ZWOOSH
Kh!
Aaaa !!
ZWOOSH

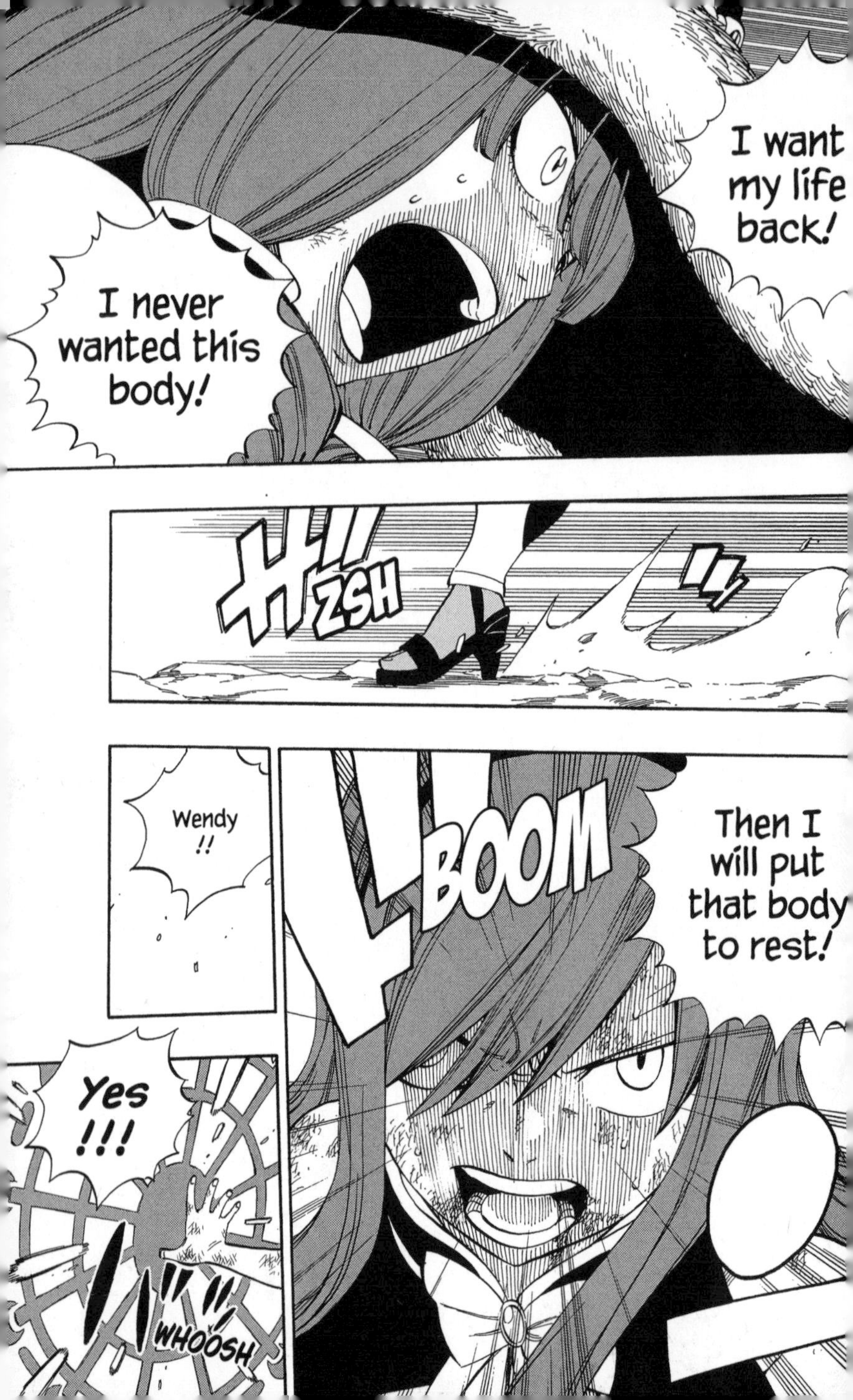
I want my life back!
I never wanted this body!
ZSH
Then I will put that body to rest!
BOOM
Wendy !!
Yes !!!
WHOOSH

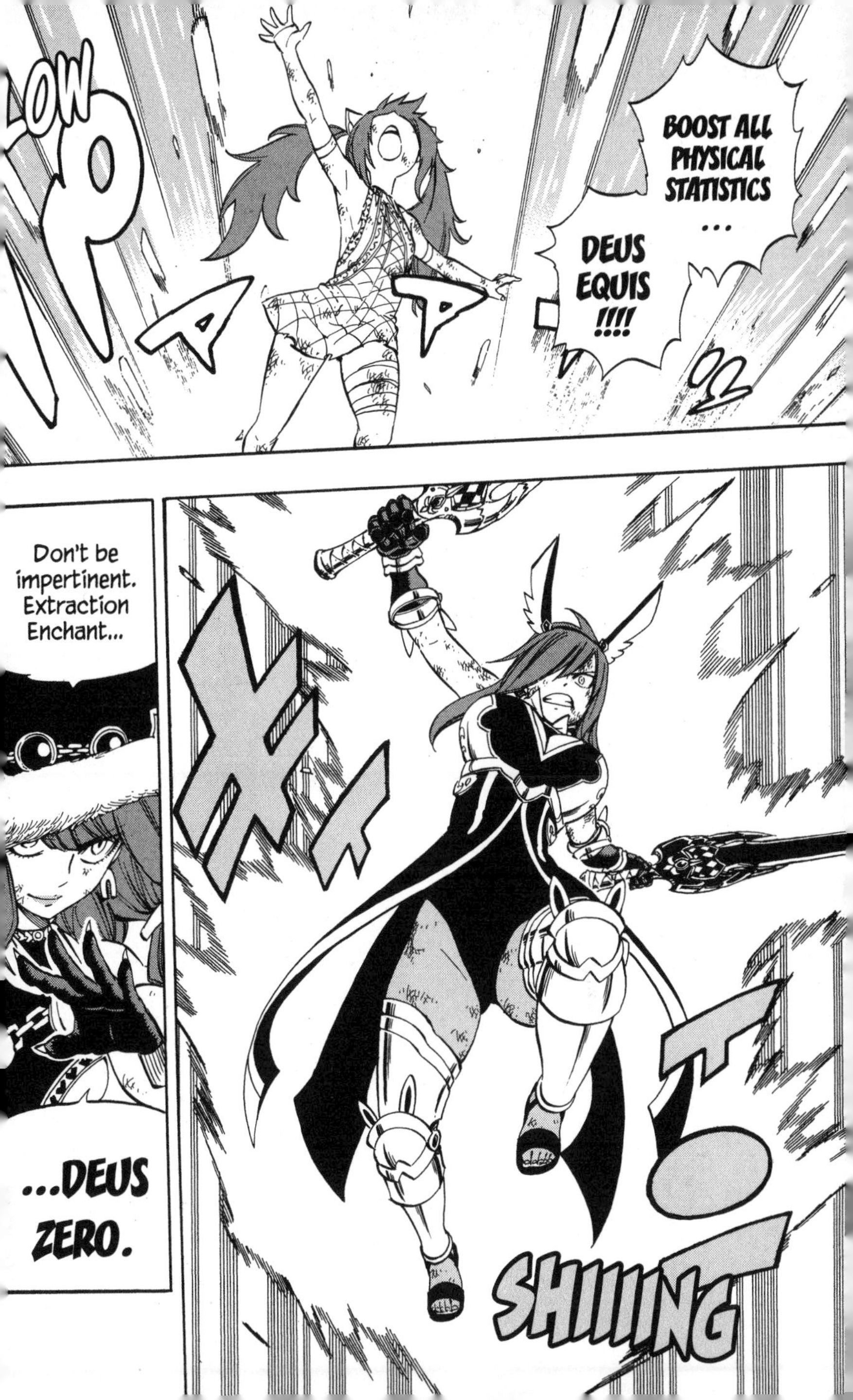
BOOST ALL PHYSICAL STATISTICS ...
DEUS EQUIS !!!!
SHIIING
Don't be impertinent. Extraction Enchant...
...DEUS ZERO.

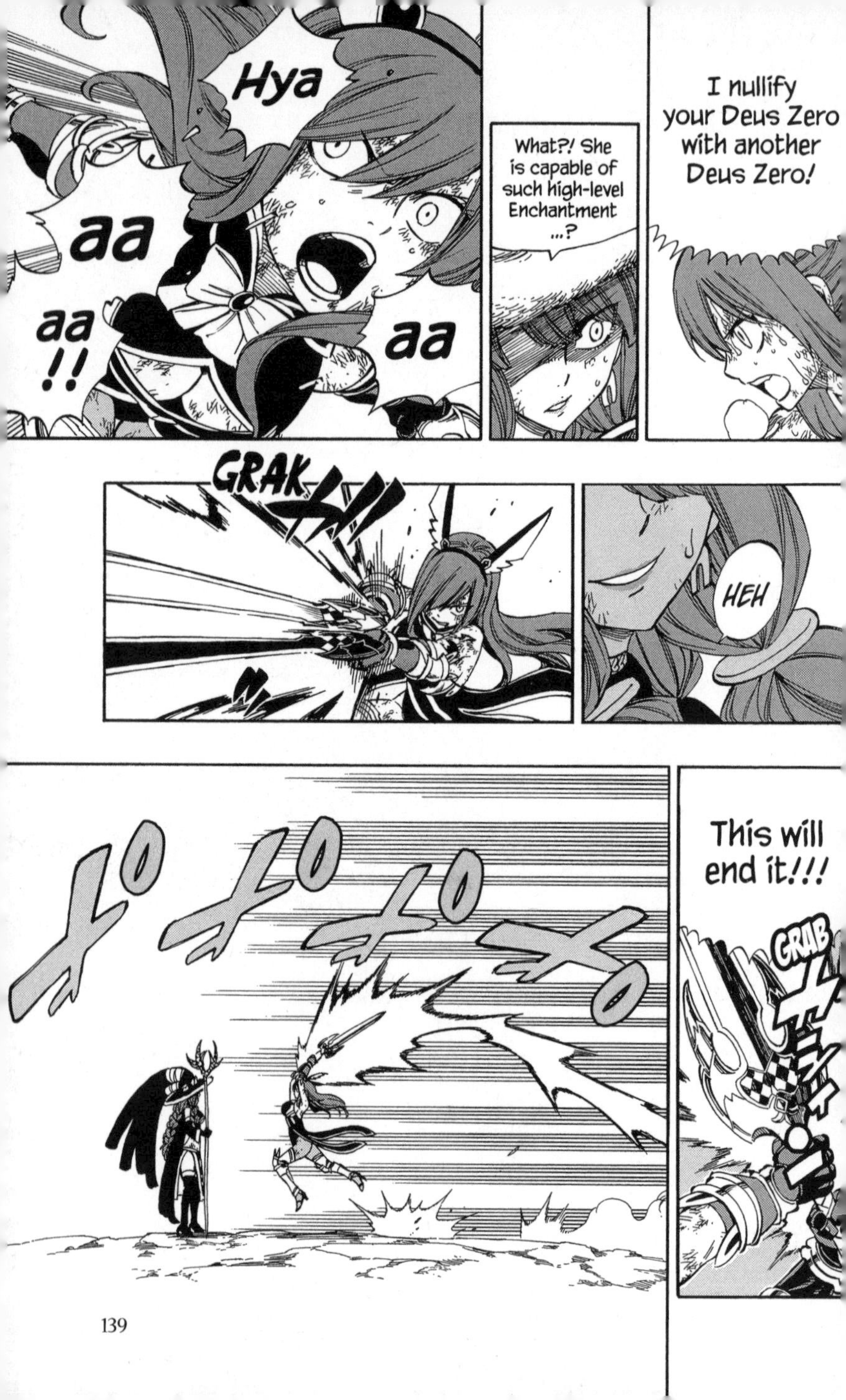
I nullify your Deus Zero with another Deus Zero!
What?! She is capable of such high-level Enchantment ...?
Hya
aa
aa
aa
!!
HEH
GRAK
This will end it!!!
GRAB

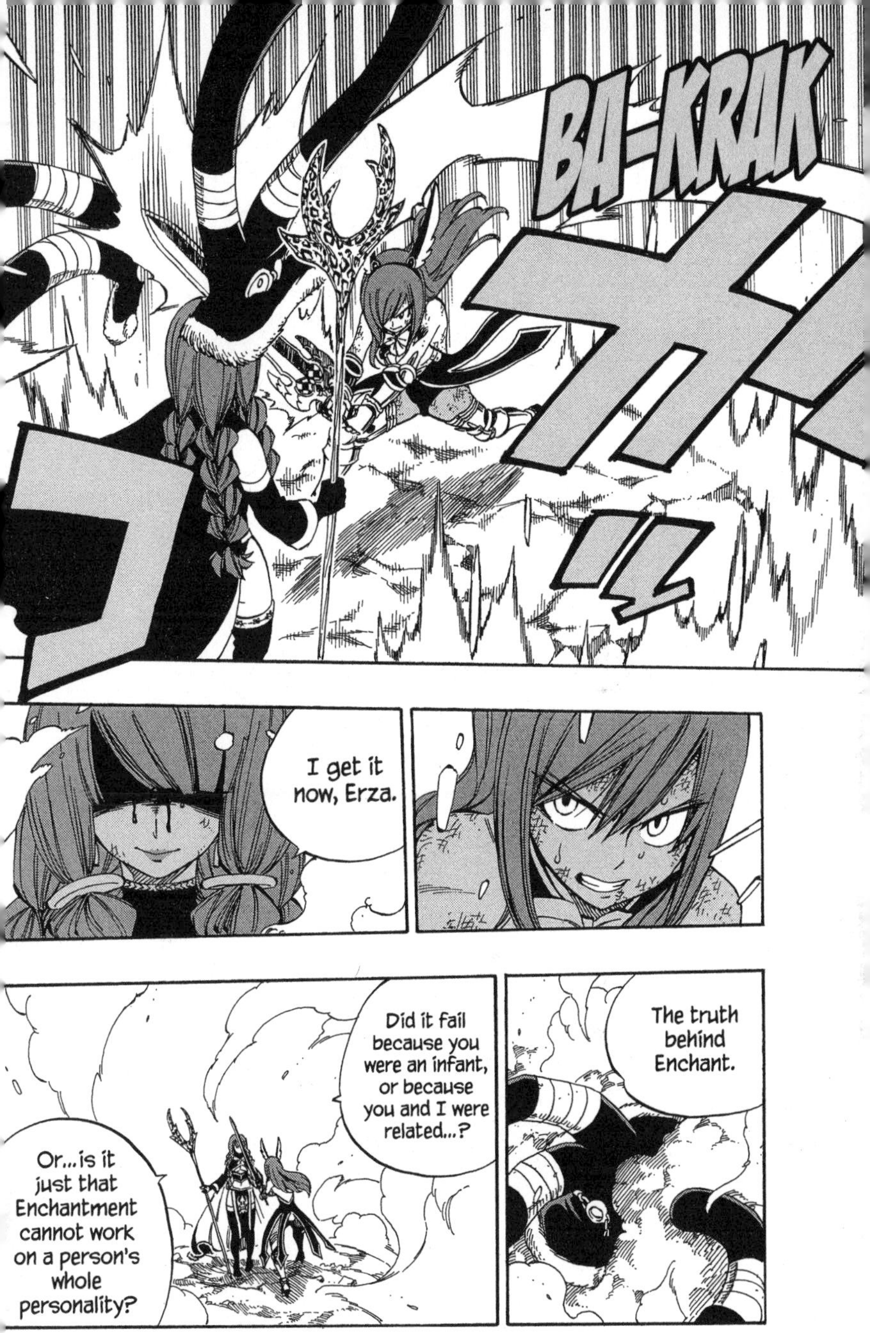
BA-KRAK
I get it now, Erza.
The truth behind Enchant.
Did it fail because you were an infant, or because you and I were related...?
Or...is it just that Enchantment cannot work on a person's whole personality?

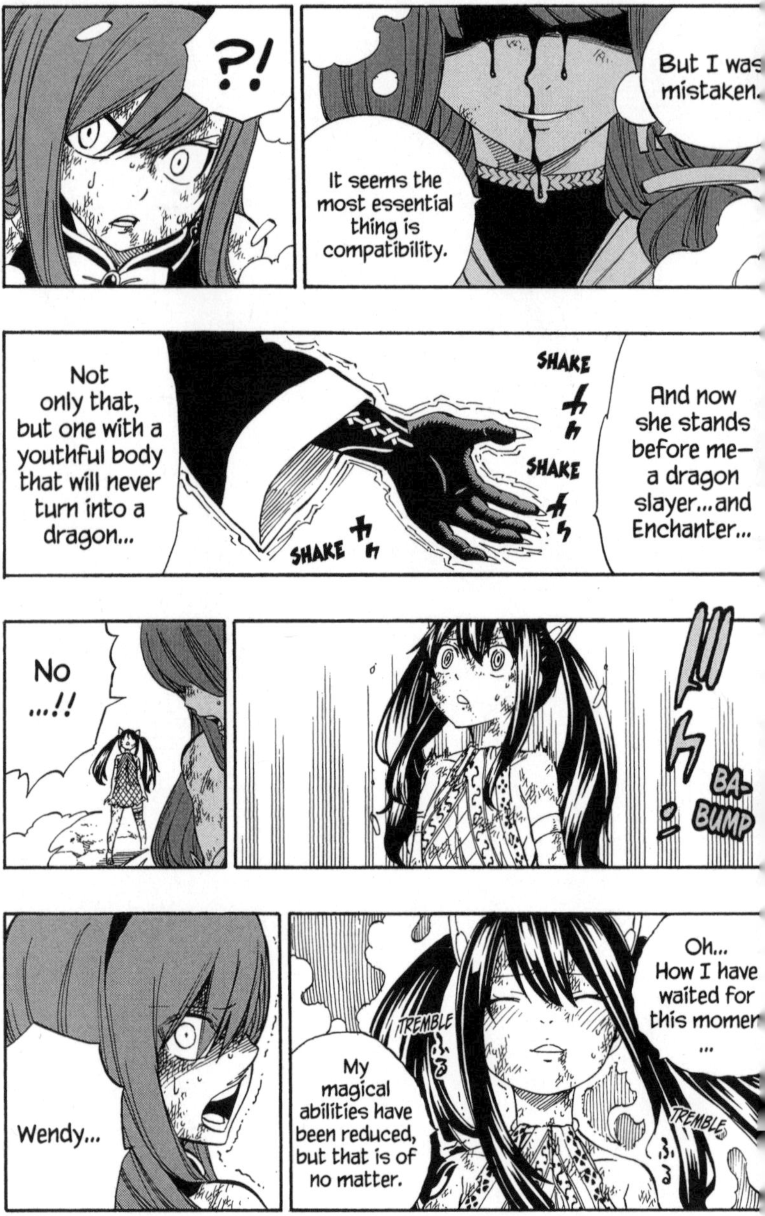
But I was mistaken.
It seems the most essential thing is compatibility.
?!
And now she stands before me—a dragon slayer...and Enchanter...
SHAKE
SHAKE
SHAKE
Not only that, but one with a youthful body that will never turn into a dragon...
BA-BUMP
No ...!!
Oh... How I have waited for this momen ...
TREMBLE
TREMBLE
My magical abilities have been reduced, but that is of no matter.
Wendy...

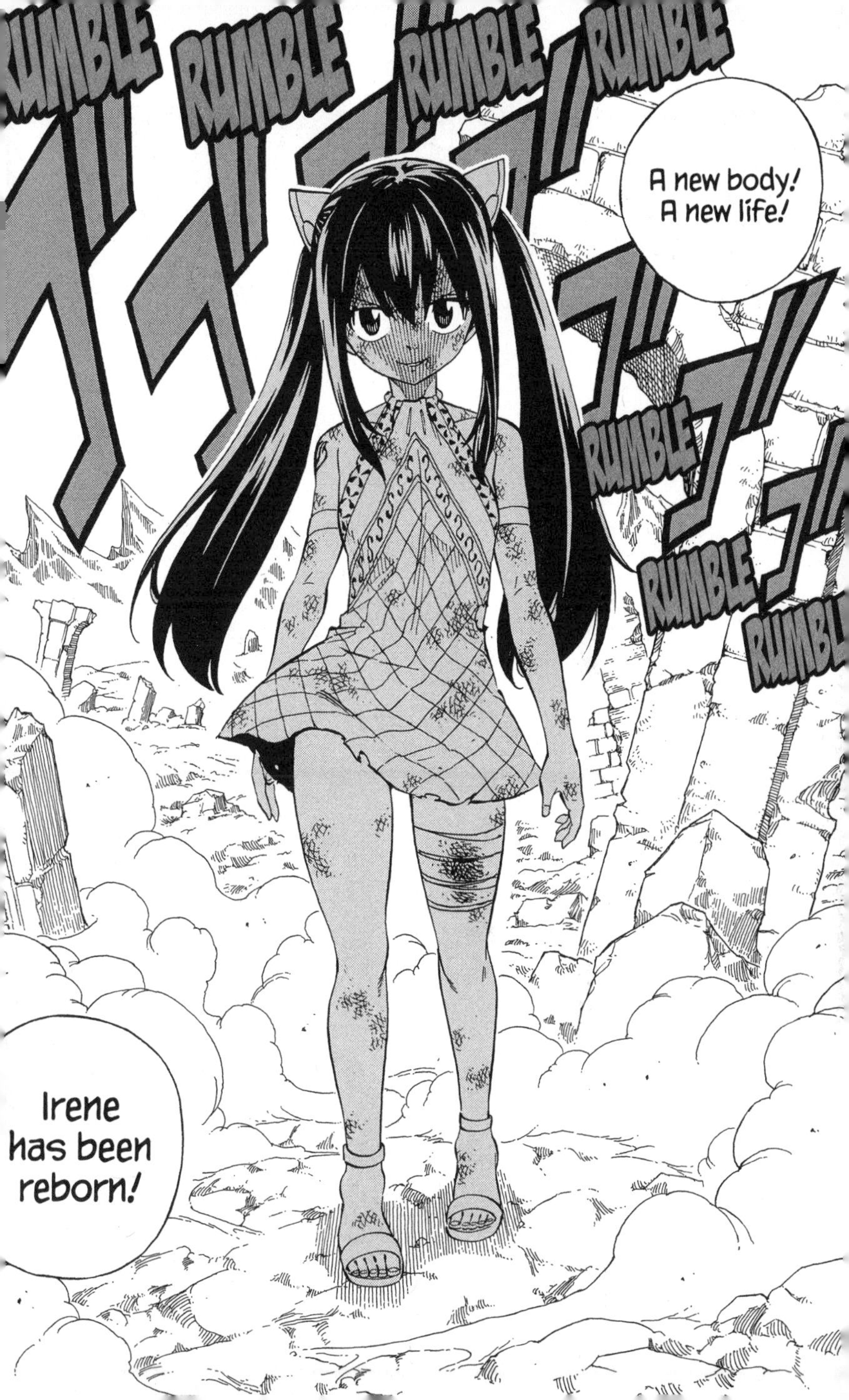
RUMBLE RUMBLE RUMBLE RUMBLE
A new body! A new life!
RUMBLE RUMBLE RUMBL
Irene has been reborn!

FAIRY TAIL

Chapter 517: Wendy Belserion

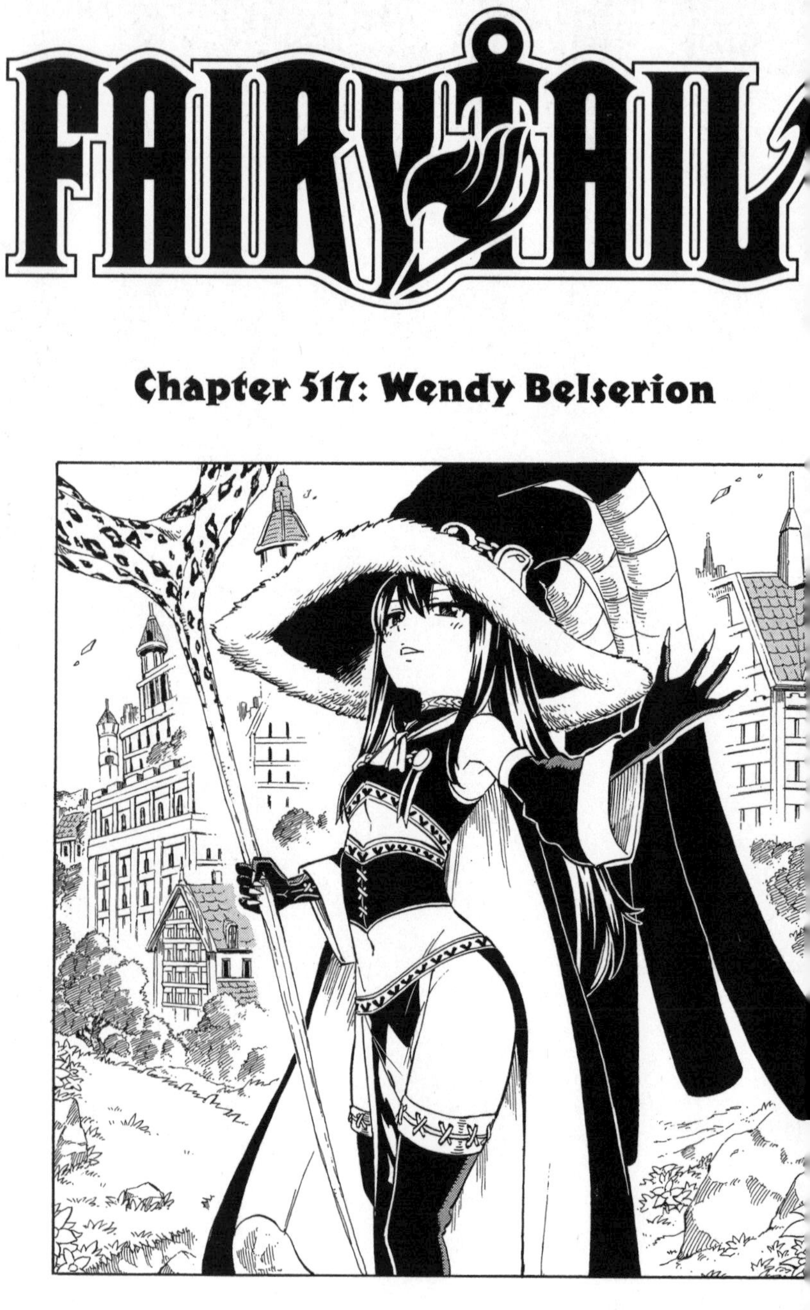

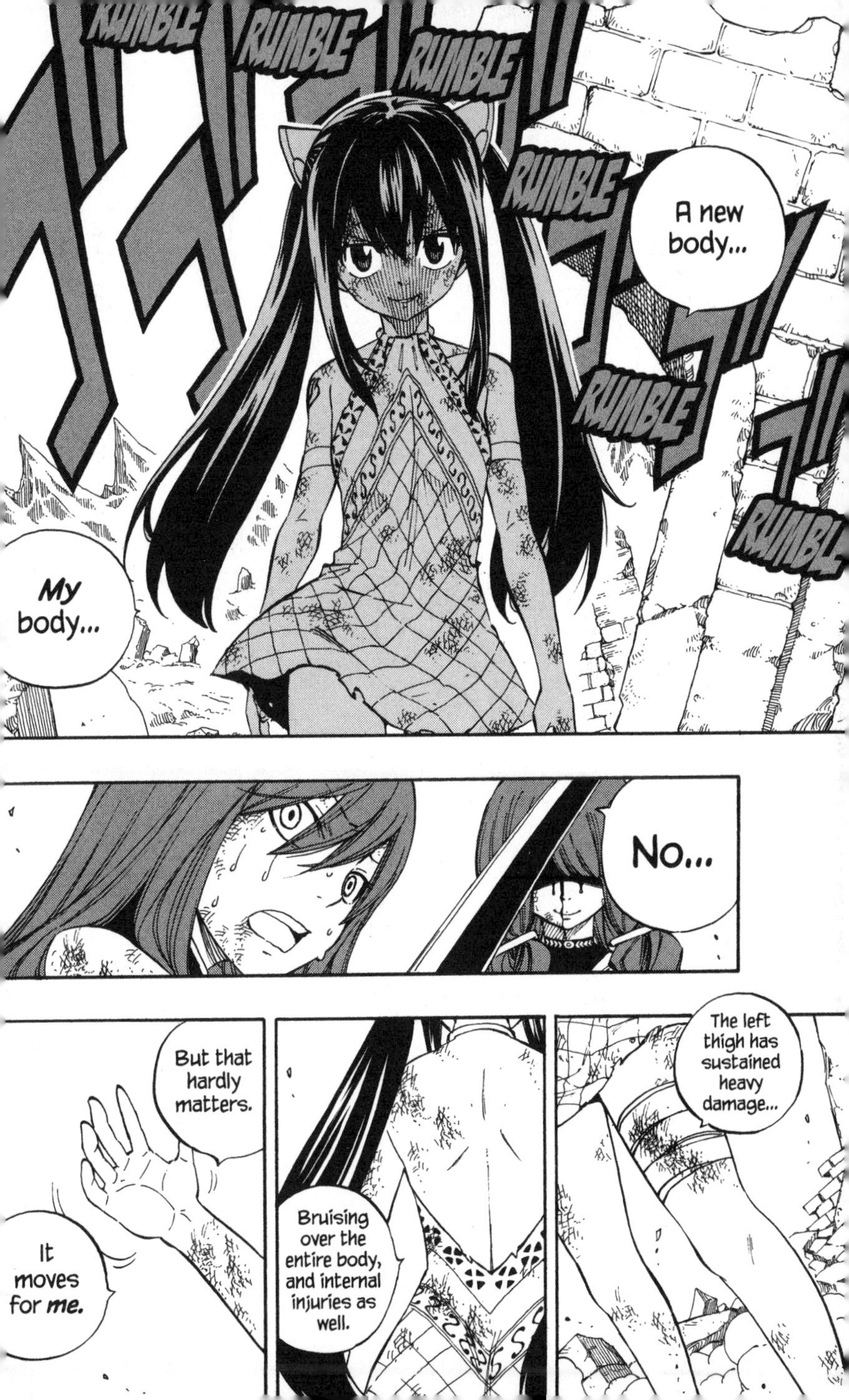
RUMBLE
RUMBLE
RUMBLE
RUMBLE
RUMBLE
RUMBLE
A new body...
My body...
No...
The left thigh has sustained heavy damage...
Bruising over the entire body, and internal injuries as well.
But that hardly matters.
It moves for me.

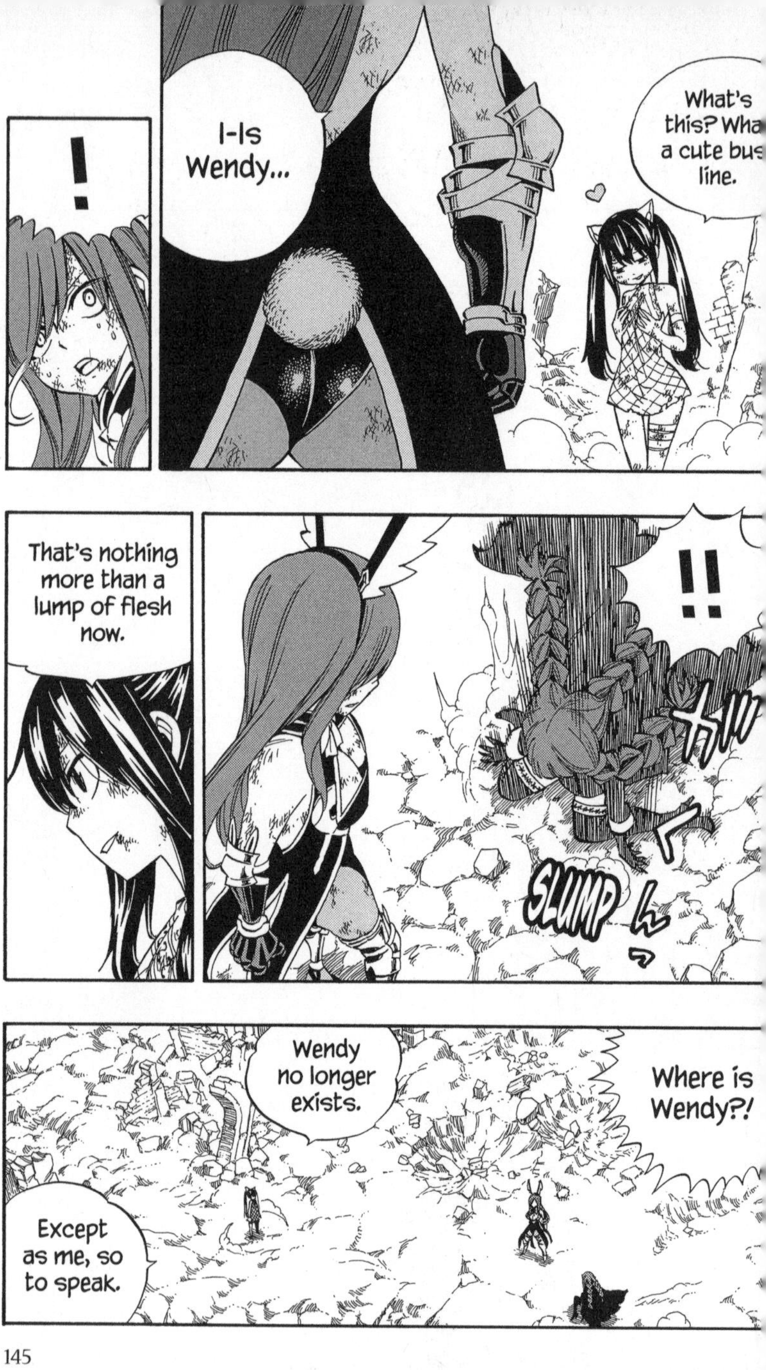
What's this? Wha
a cute bus
line.
I-Is Wendy...
!
!!
SLUMP
That's nothing more than a lump of flesh now.
Where is Wendy?!
Wendy no longer exists.
Except as me, so to speak.

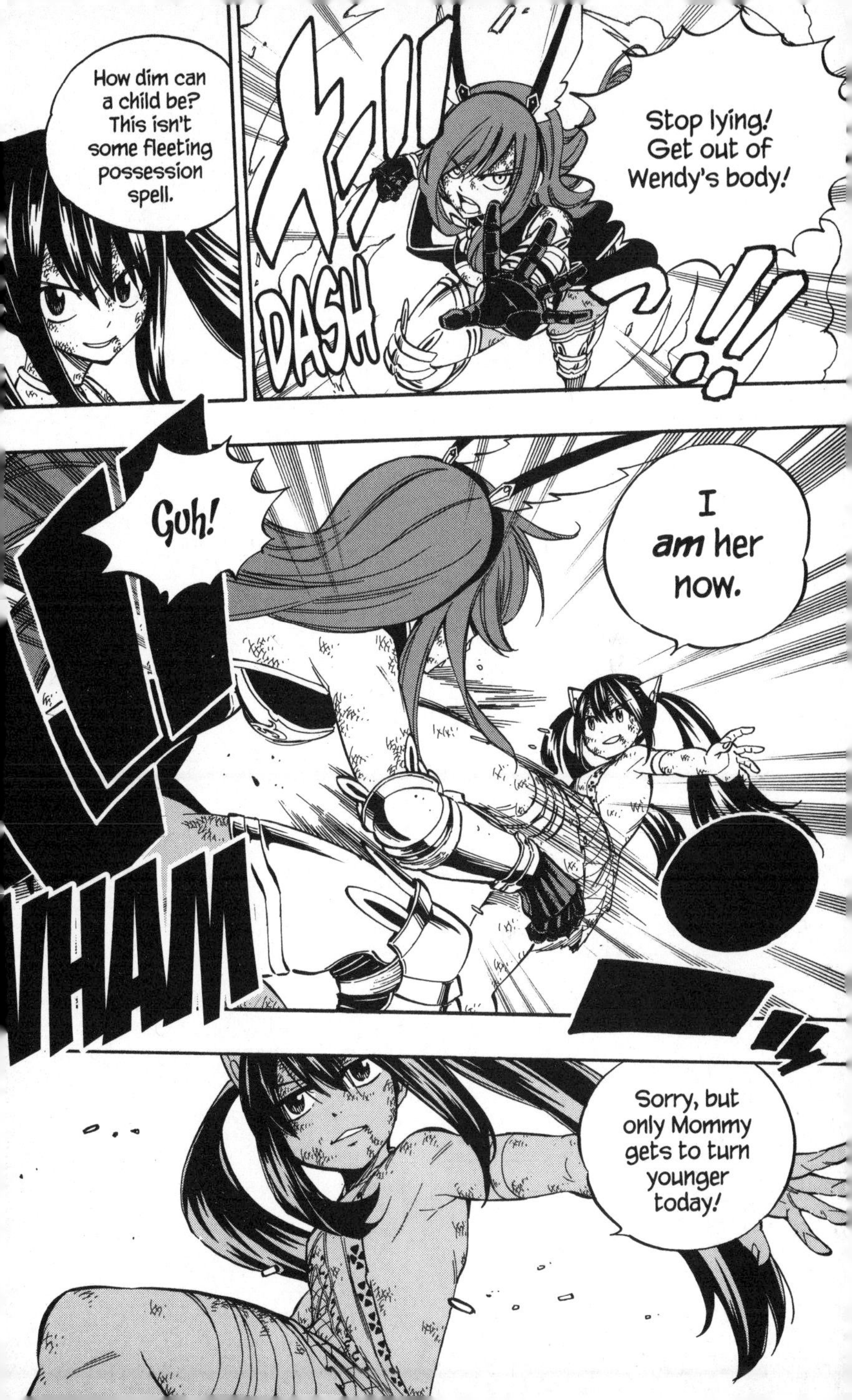
Stop lying! Get out of Wendy's body!
DASH
!!
How dim can a child be? This isn't some fleeting possession spell.
I am her now.
Guh!
WHAM
Sorry, but only Mommy gets to turn younger today!

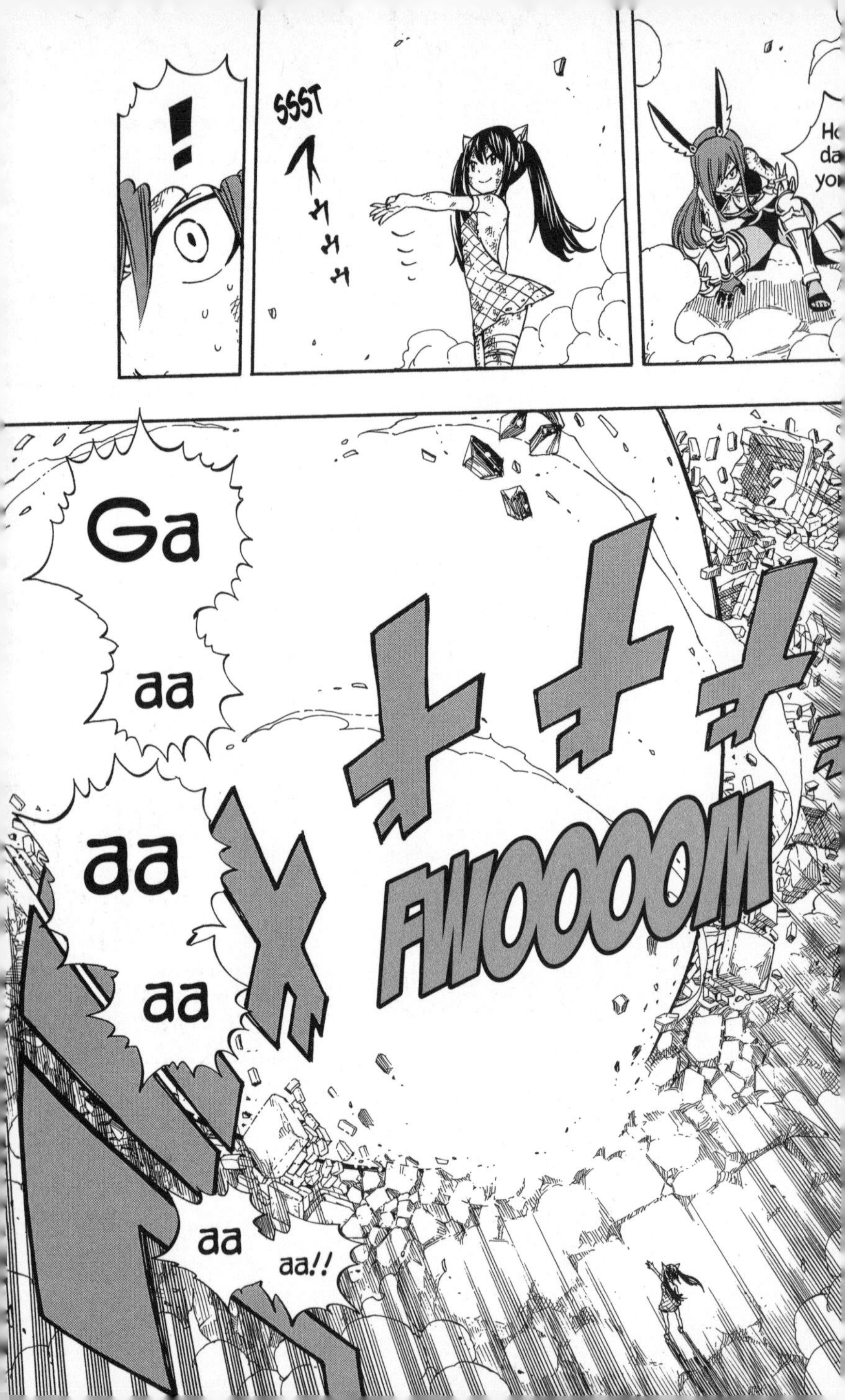
SSST
!
Ga aa aa aa aa aa!!
FWOOOOM

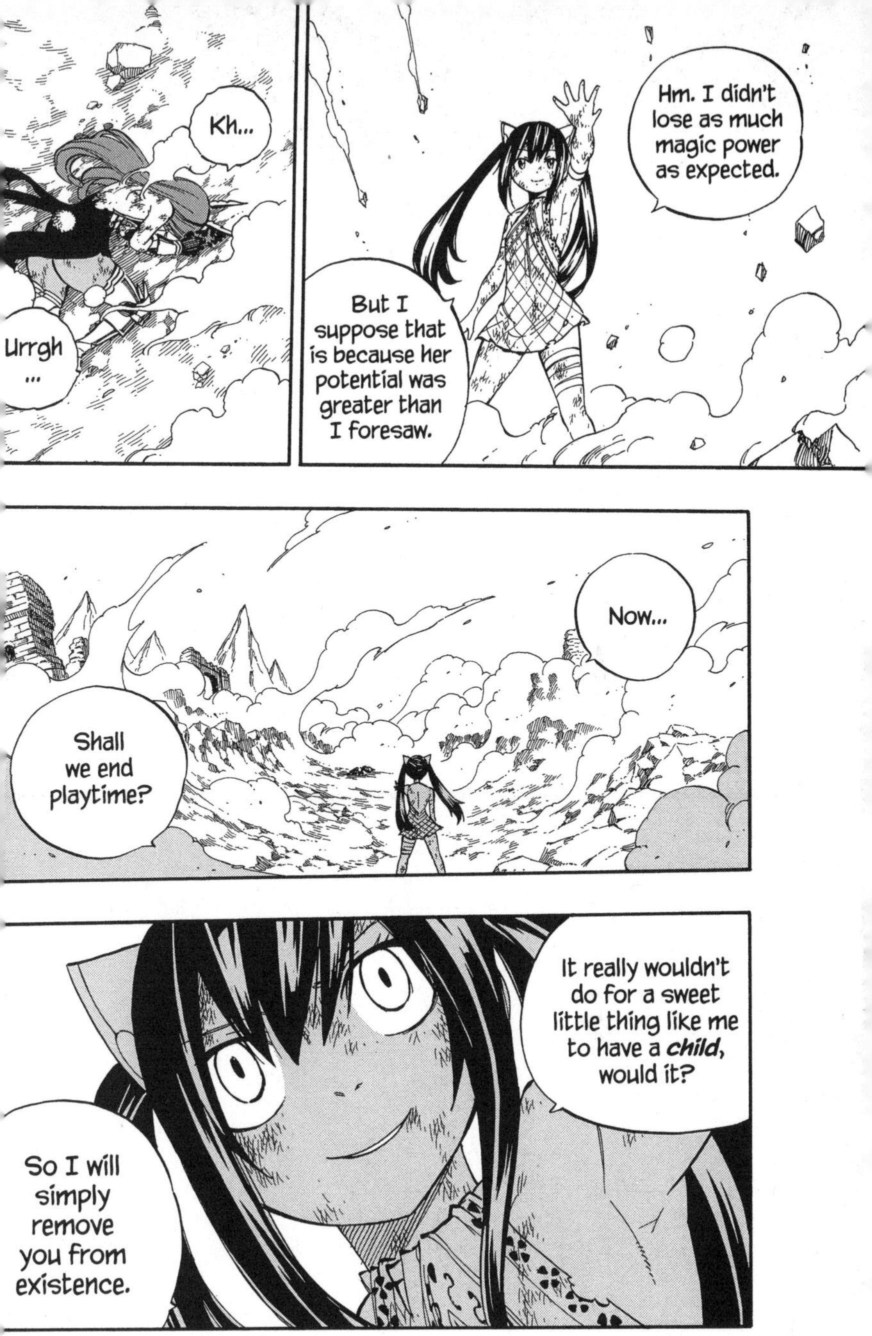
Hm. I didn't lose as much magic power as expected.
But I suppose that is because her potential was greater than I foresaw.
Kh...
Urrgh ...
Now...
Shall we end playtime?
It really wouldn't do for a sweet little thing like me to have a *child*, would it?
So I will simply remove you from existence.

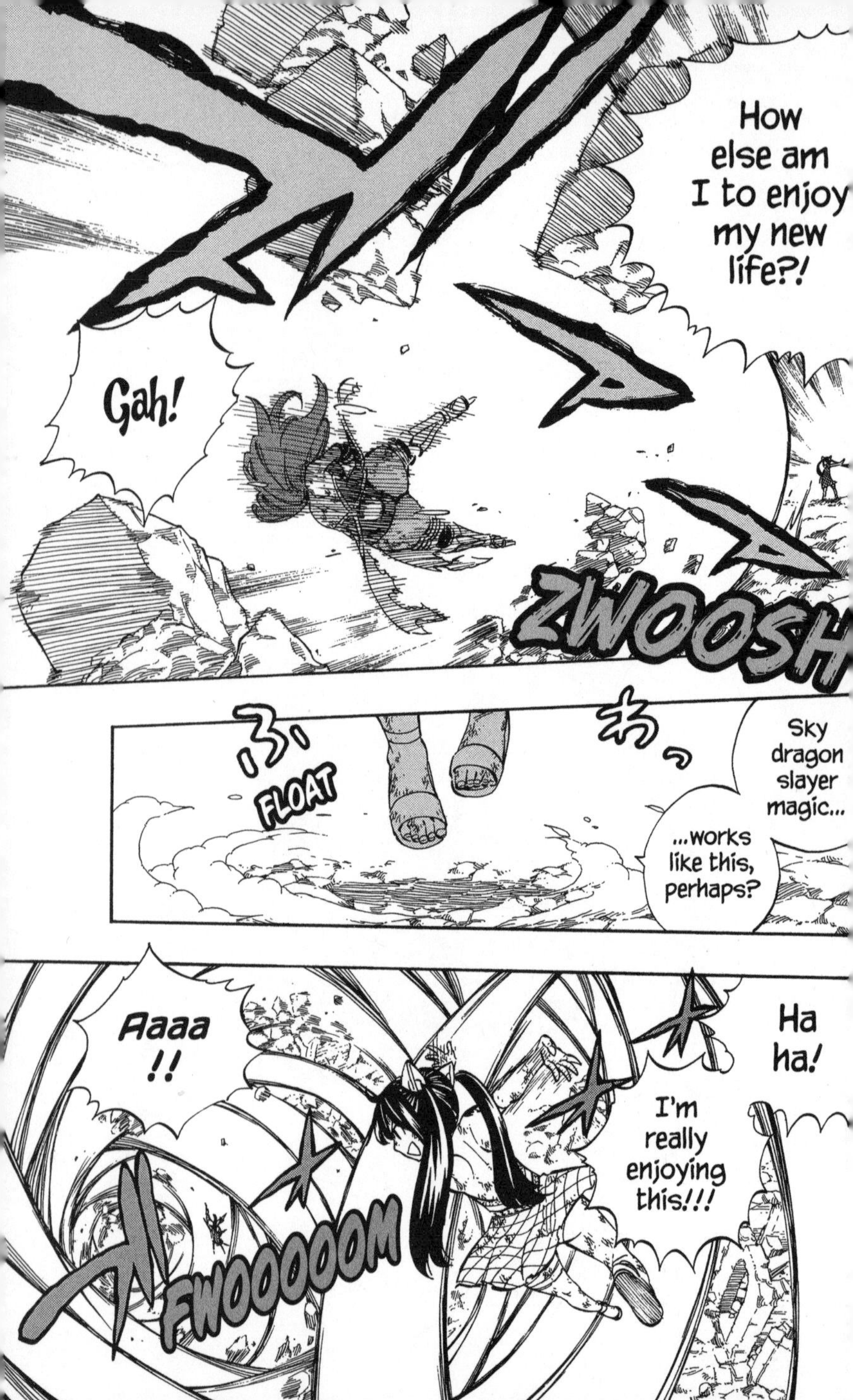
How else am I to enjoy my new life?!
Gah!
ZWOOSH
Sky dragon slayer magic...
...works like this, perhaps?
わっ
ふ
FLOAT
Ha ha!
I'm really enjoying this!!!
Aaaa !!
FWOOOOOM

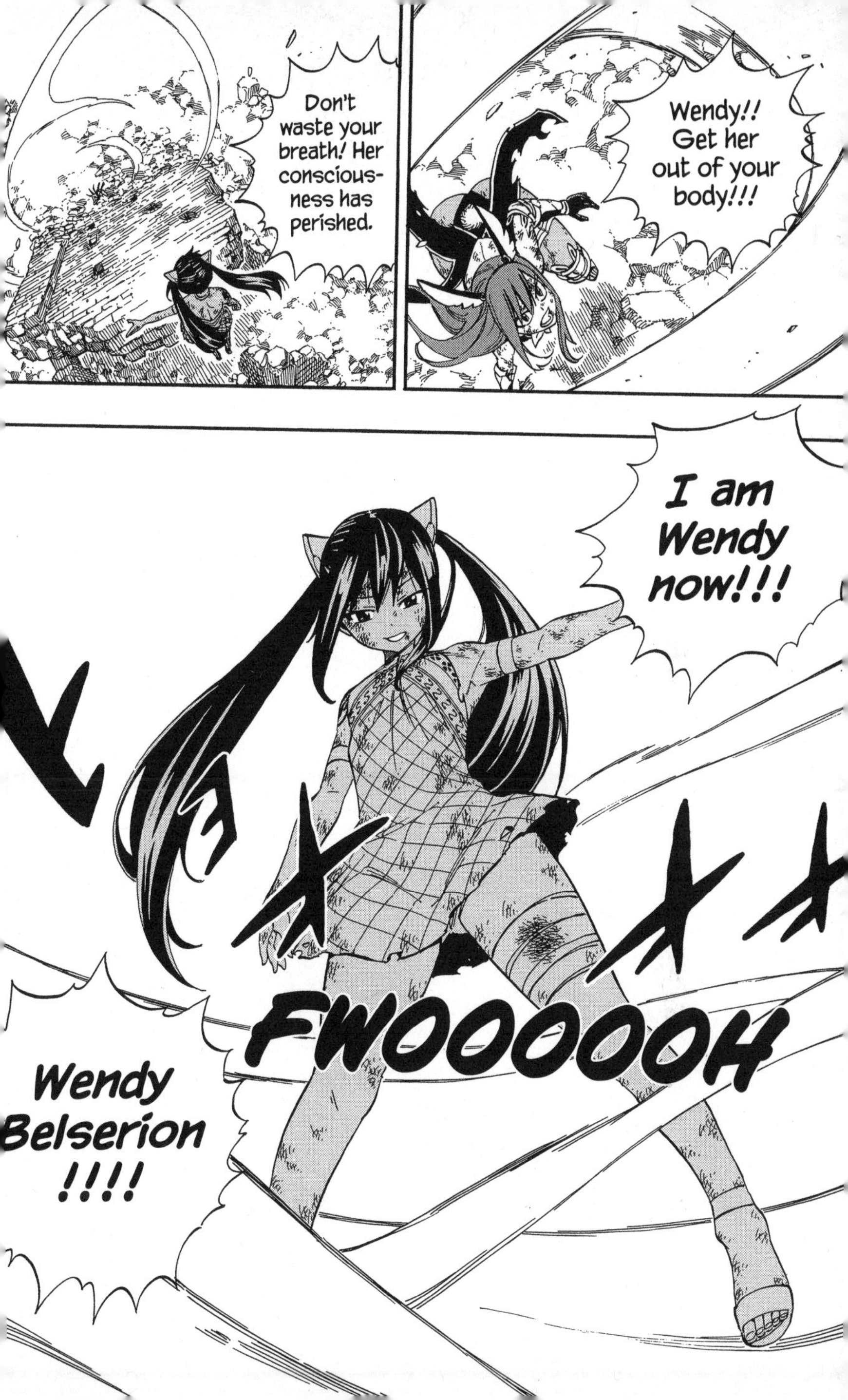
Wendy!! Get her out of your body!!!
Don't waste your breath! Her conscious-ness has perished.
I am Wendy now!!!
FWOOOOOH
Wendy Belserion !!!!

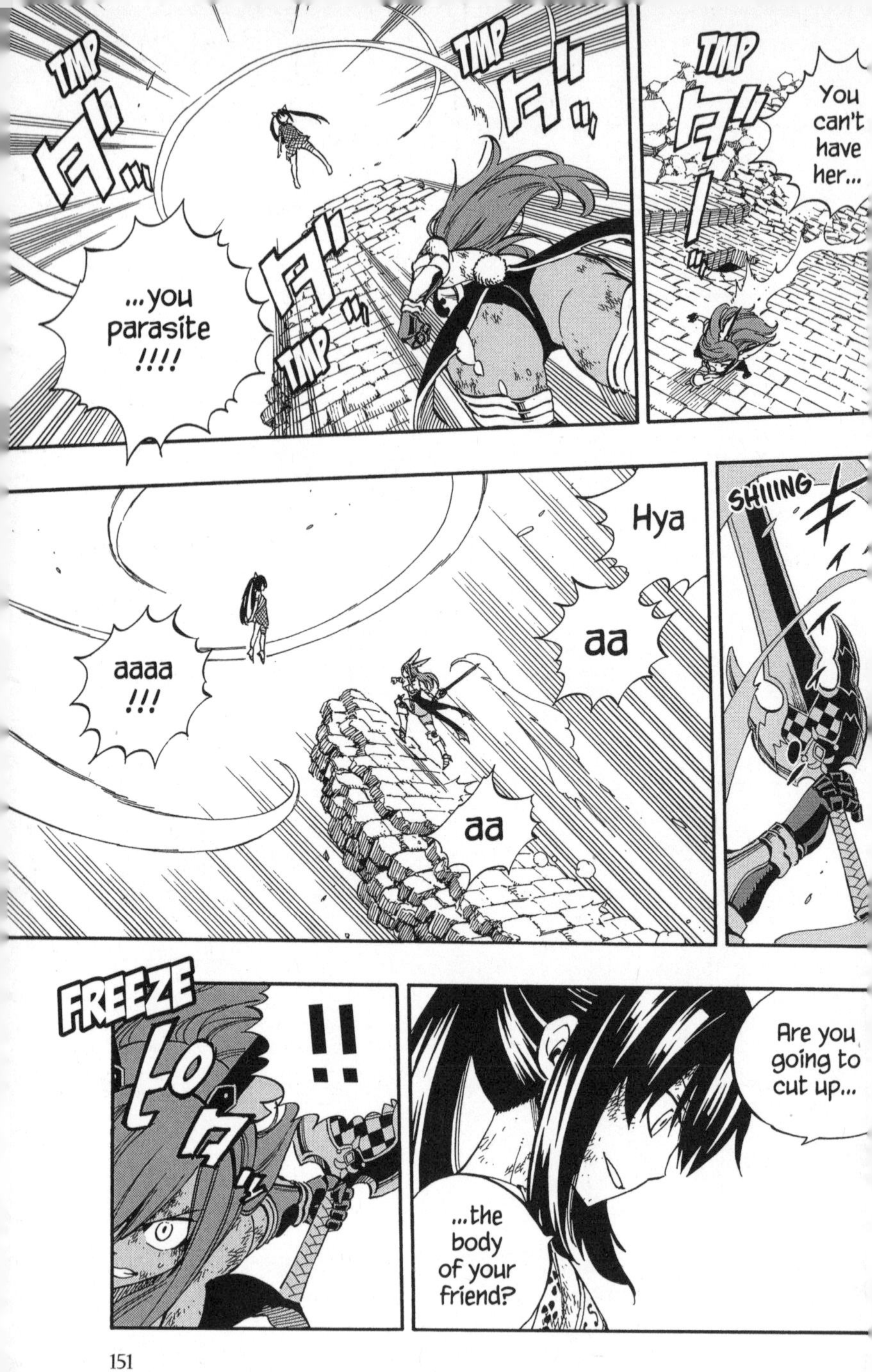
TMP
You can't have her...
TMP
TMP
TMP
...you parasite!!!!
SHIIING
Hya
aa
aa
aaaa!!!
Are you going to cut up...
...the body of your friend?
FREEZE
!!

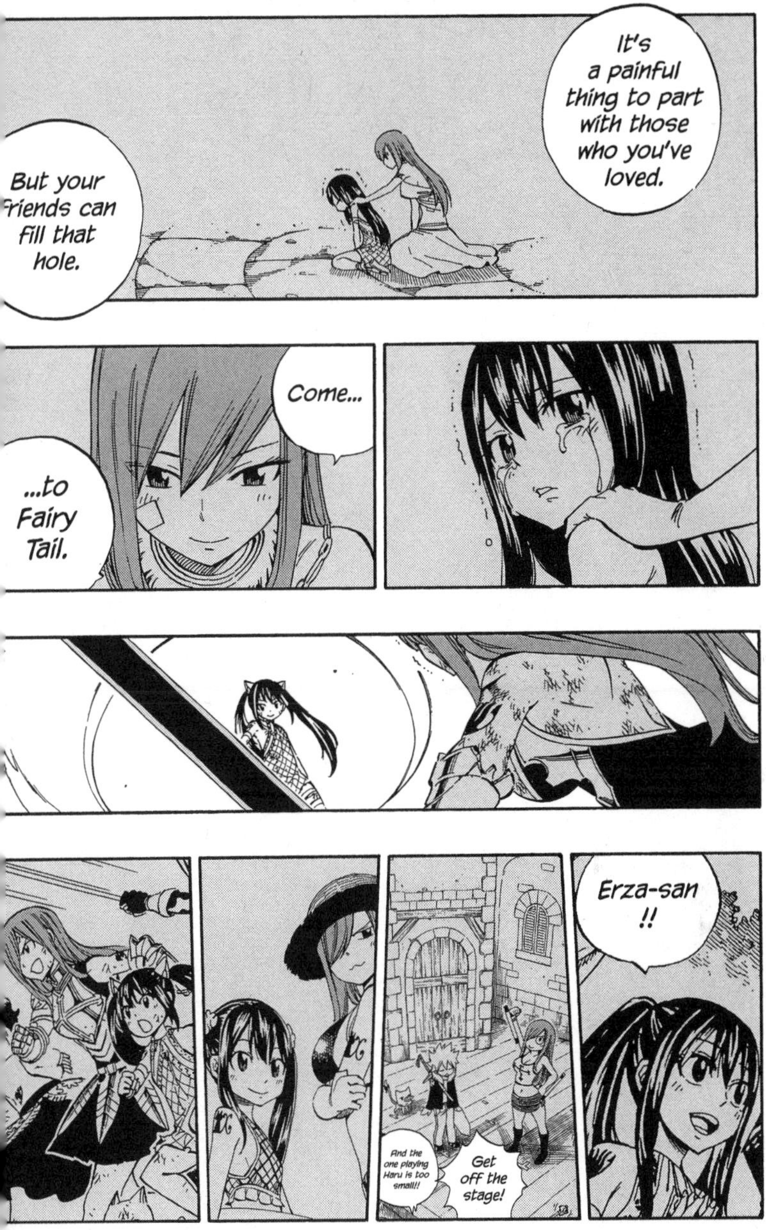
It's a painful thing to part with those who you've loved.
But your friends can fill that hole.
Come...
...to Fairy Tail.
Erza-san !!
Get off the stage!
And the one playing Haru is too small!!

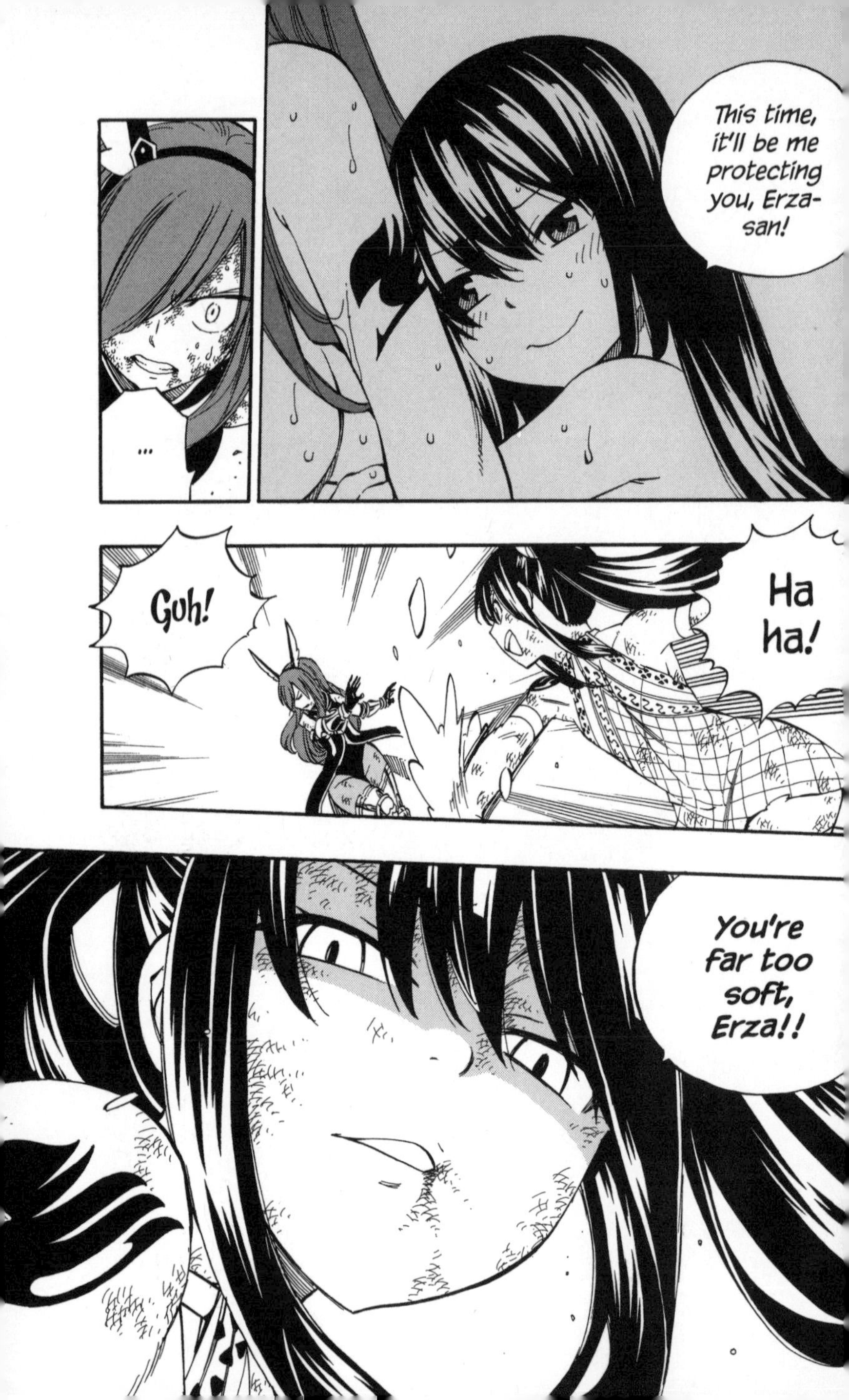
This time, it'll be me protecting you, Erza-san!
...
Ha ha!
Guh!
You're far too soft, Erza!!

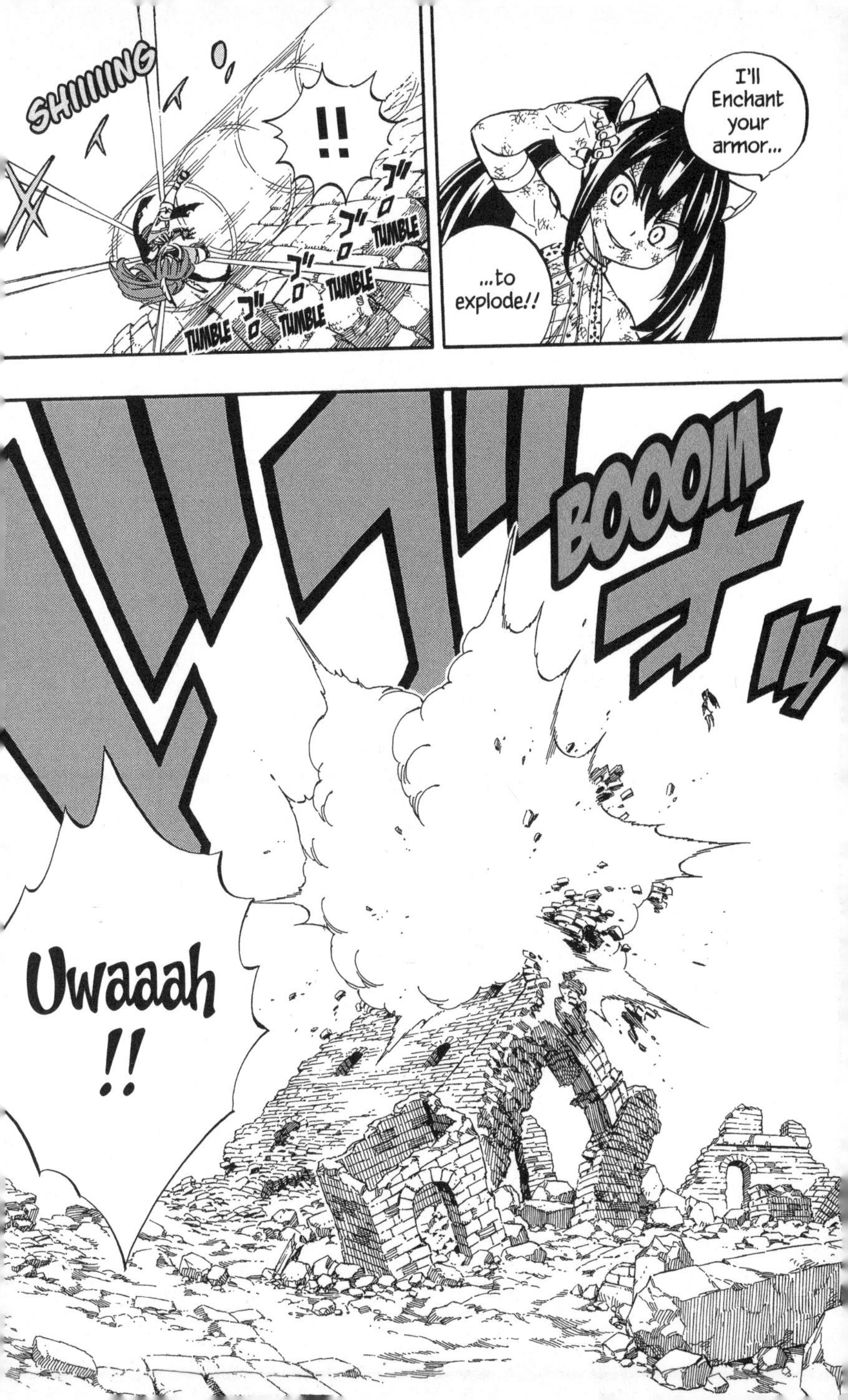
I'll Enchant your armor...
...to explode!!
SHIIIIING
!!
ゴロ
TUMBLE
ゴロ
TUMBLE
ゴロ
TUMBLE
ゴロ
TUMBLE
BOOOM
Uwaaah !!

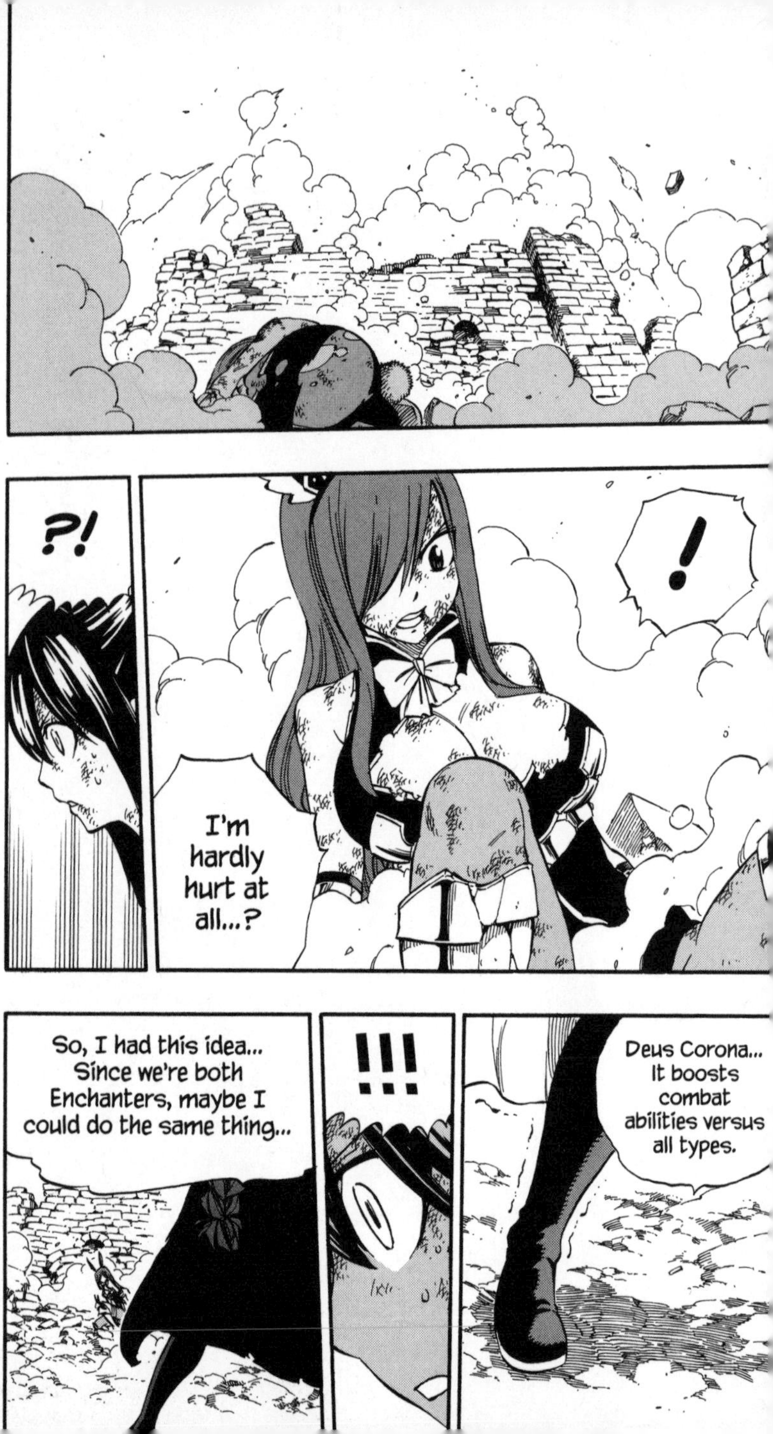
!
I'm hardly hurt at all...?
?!
Deus Corona... It boosts combat abilities versus all types.
!!!
So, I had this idea... Since we're both Enchanters, maybe I could do the same thing...

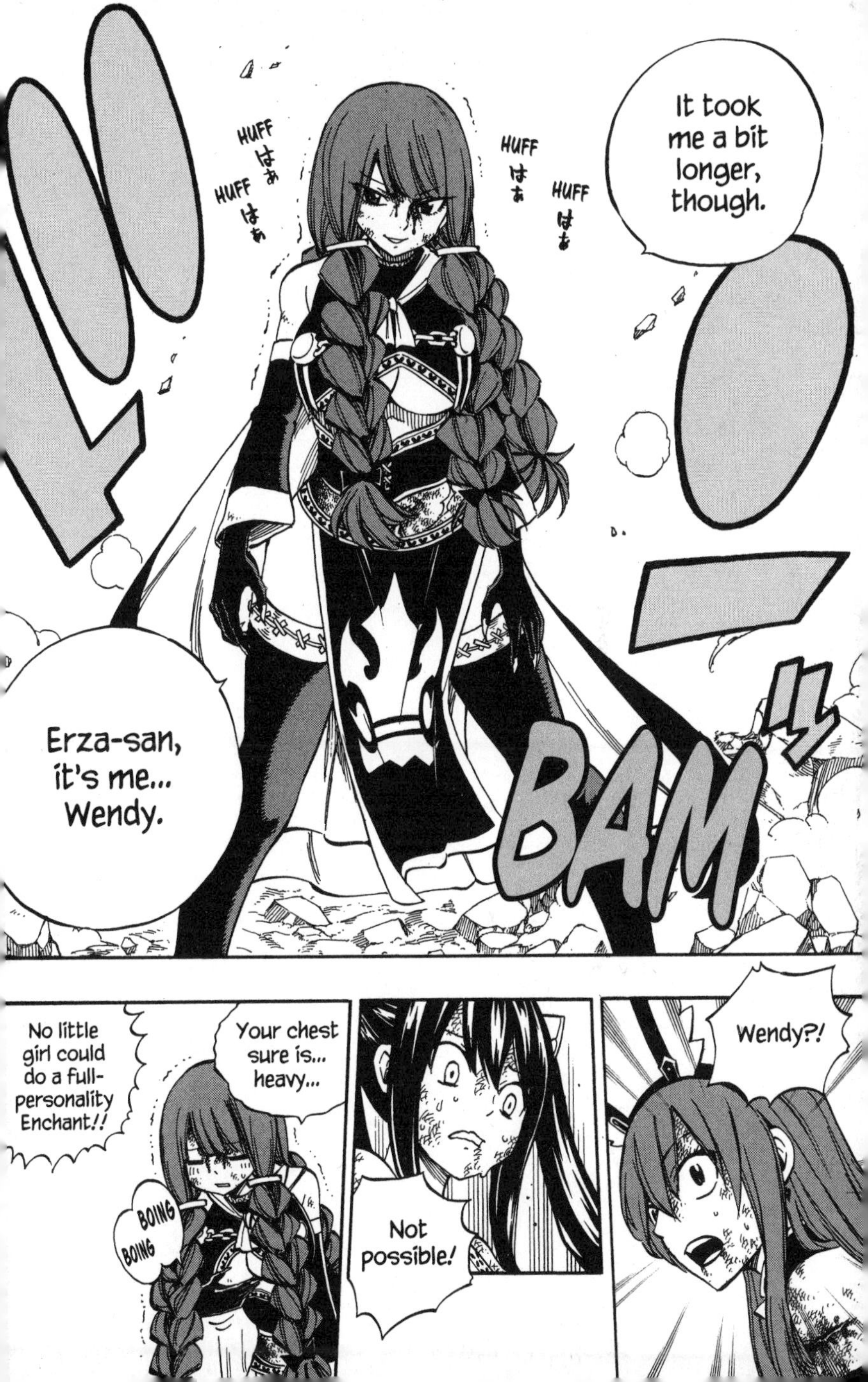
It took me a bit longer, though.
HUFF はぁ
HUFF はぁ
HUFF はぁ
HUFF はぁ
BAM
Erza-san, it's me... Wendy.
Wendy?!
Not possible!
Your chest sure is... heavy...
No little girl could do a full-personality Enchant!!
BOING BOING

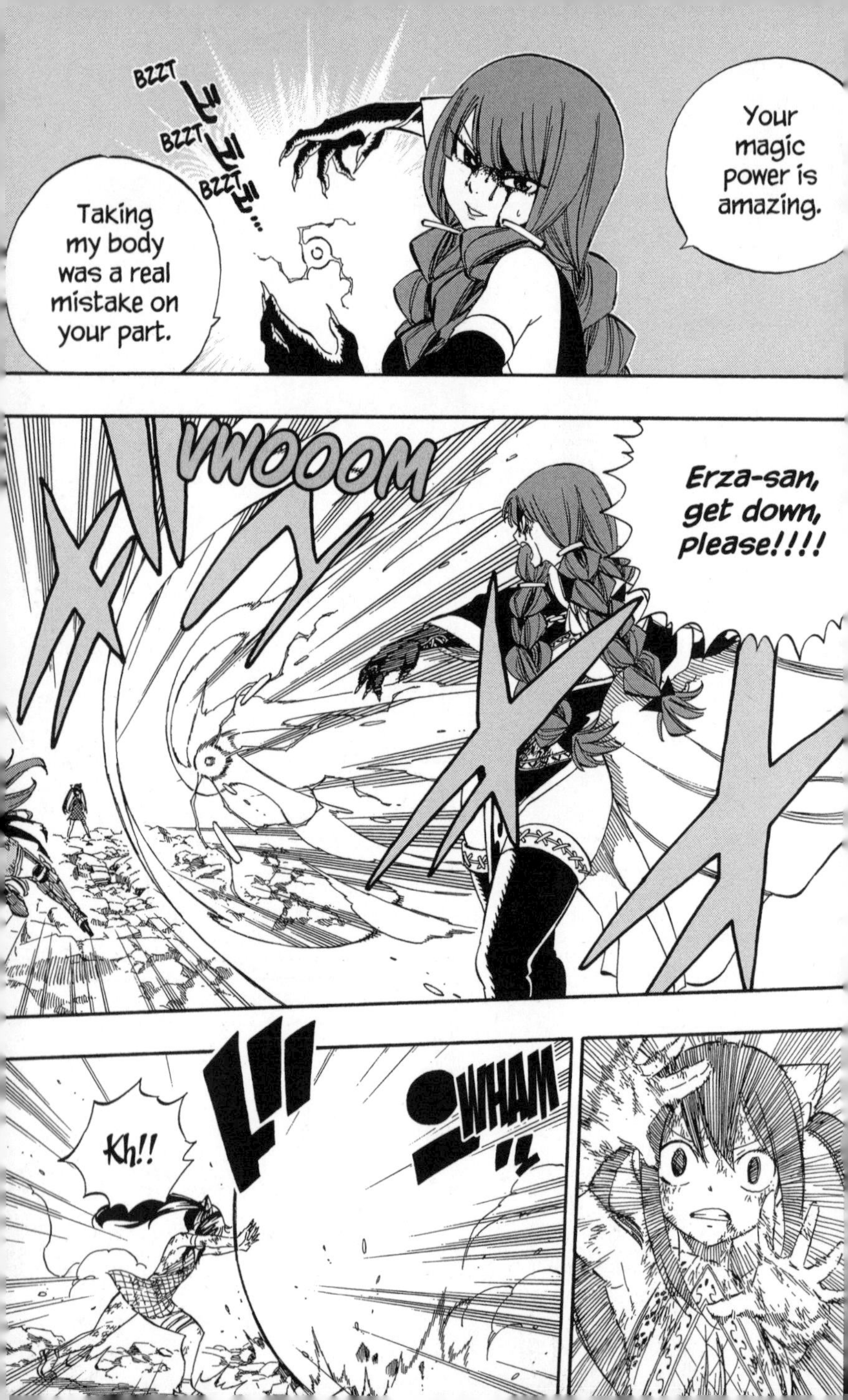
Your magic power is amazing.
BZZT
BZZT
BZZT
Taking my body was a real mistake on your part.
Erza-san, get down, please!!!!
VWOOOM
WHAM
Kh!!

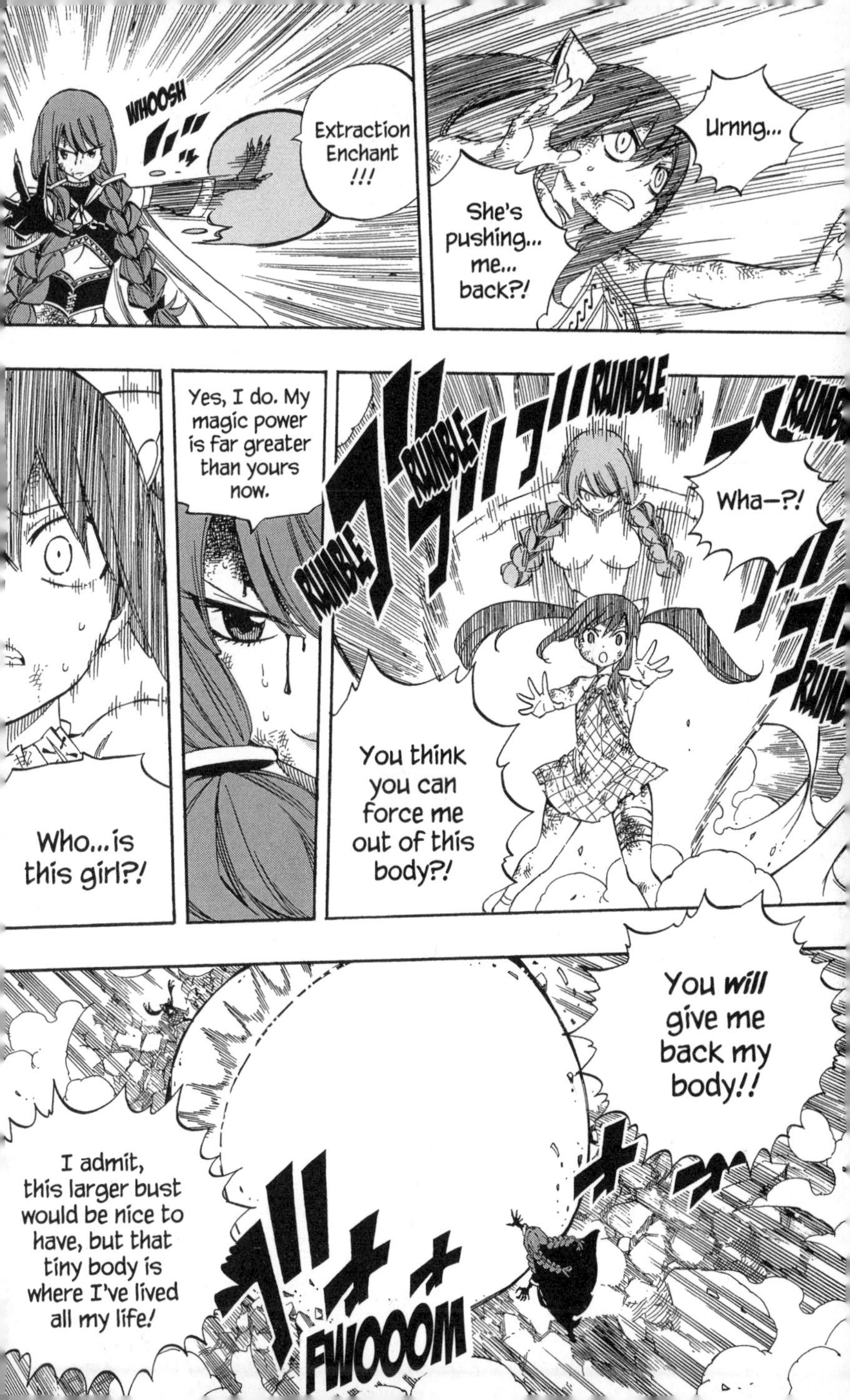
Urnng...
She's pushing... me... back?!
WHOOSH
Extraction Enchant !!!
RUMBLE
RUMBLE
RUMBLE
Wha—?!
You think you can force me out of this body?!
Yes, I do. My magic power is far greater than yours now.
Who...is this girl?!
You will give me back my body!!
I admit, this larger bust would be nice to have, but that tiny body is where I've lived all my life!
FWOOOM

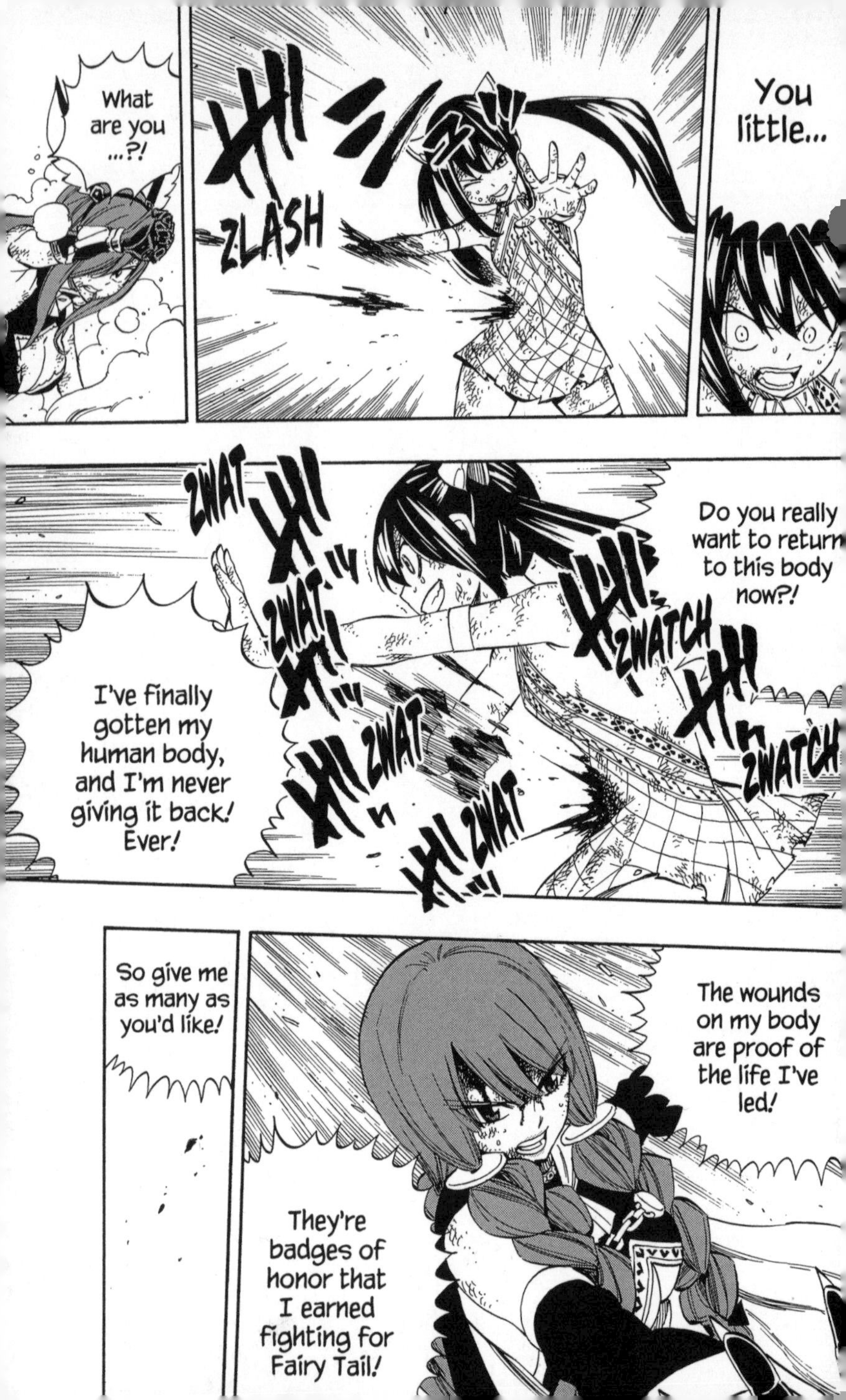
You little...
ZLASH
What are you ...?!
Do you really want to return to this body now?!
ZWATCH
ZWATCH
ZWAT
ZWAT
ZWAT
ZWAT
I've finally gotten my human body, and I'm never giving it back! Ever!
The wounds on my body are proof of the life I've led!
They're badges of honor that I earned fighting for Fairy Tail!
So give me as many as you'd like!

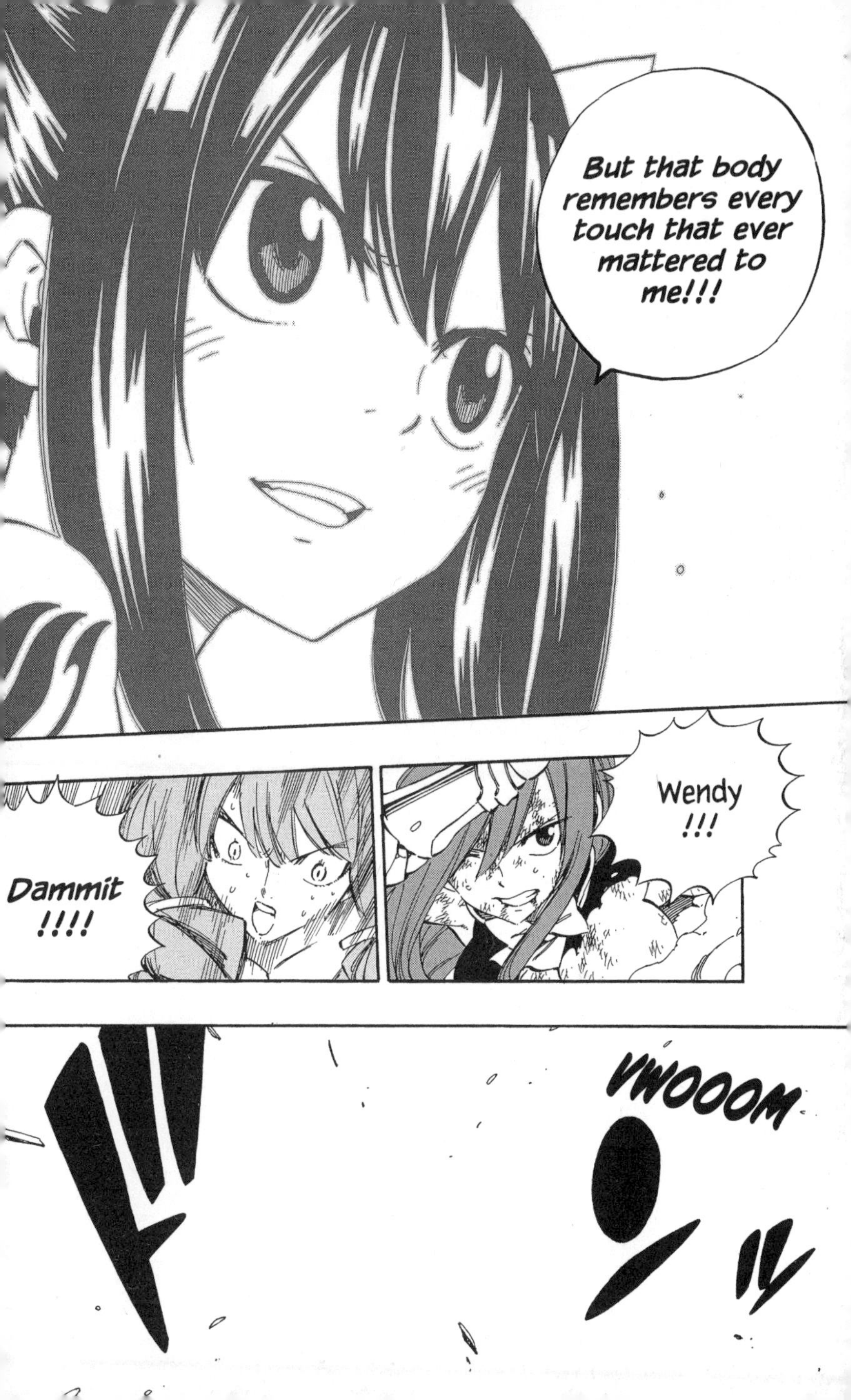
But that body remembers every touch that ever mattered to me!!!
Wendy !!!
Dammit !!!!
VWOOOM

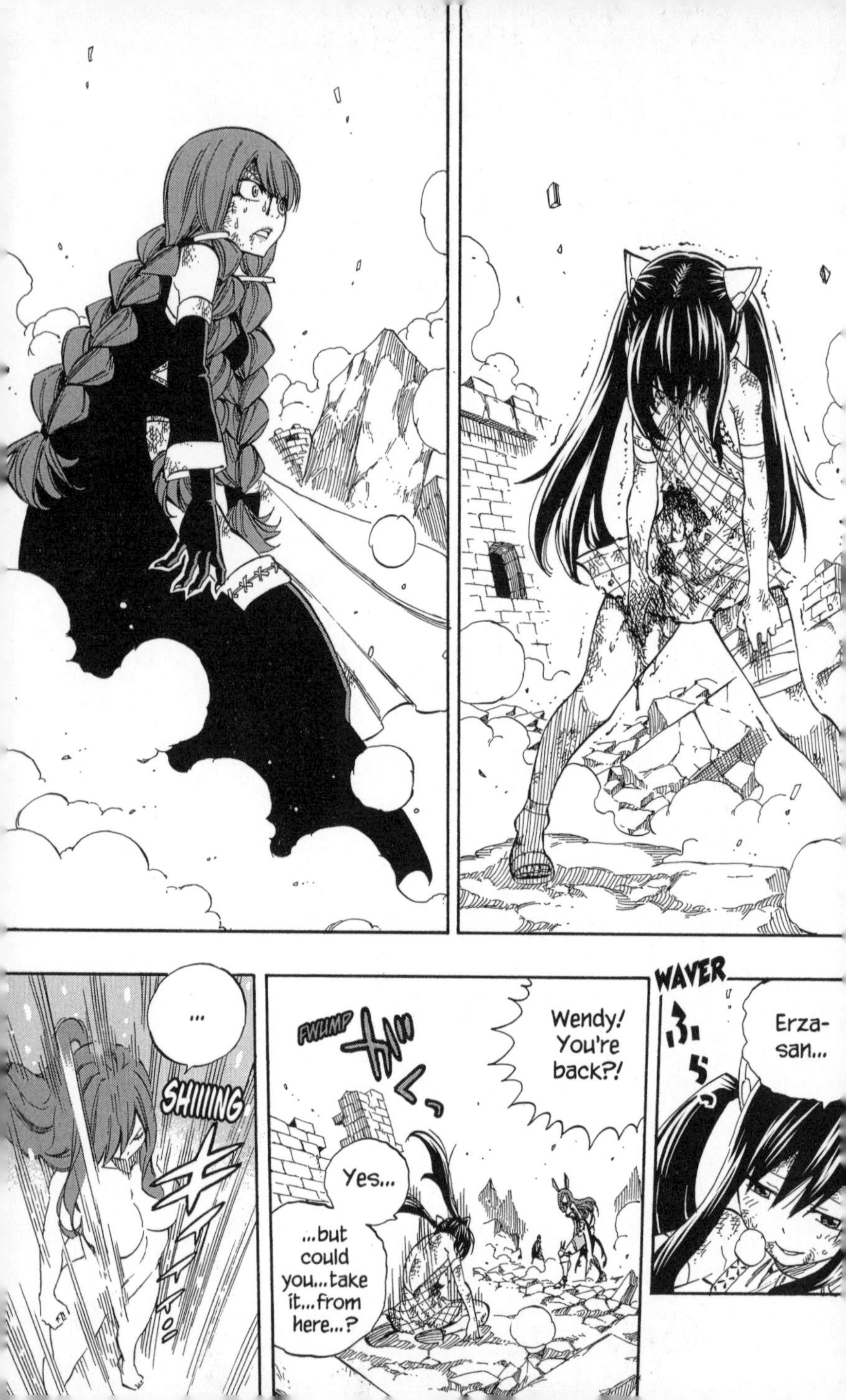
WAVER
Erza-san...
Wendy! You're back?!
FWUMP
Yes...
...but could you...take it...from here...?
...
SHIIIING

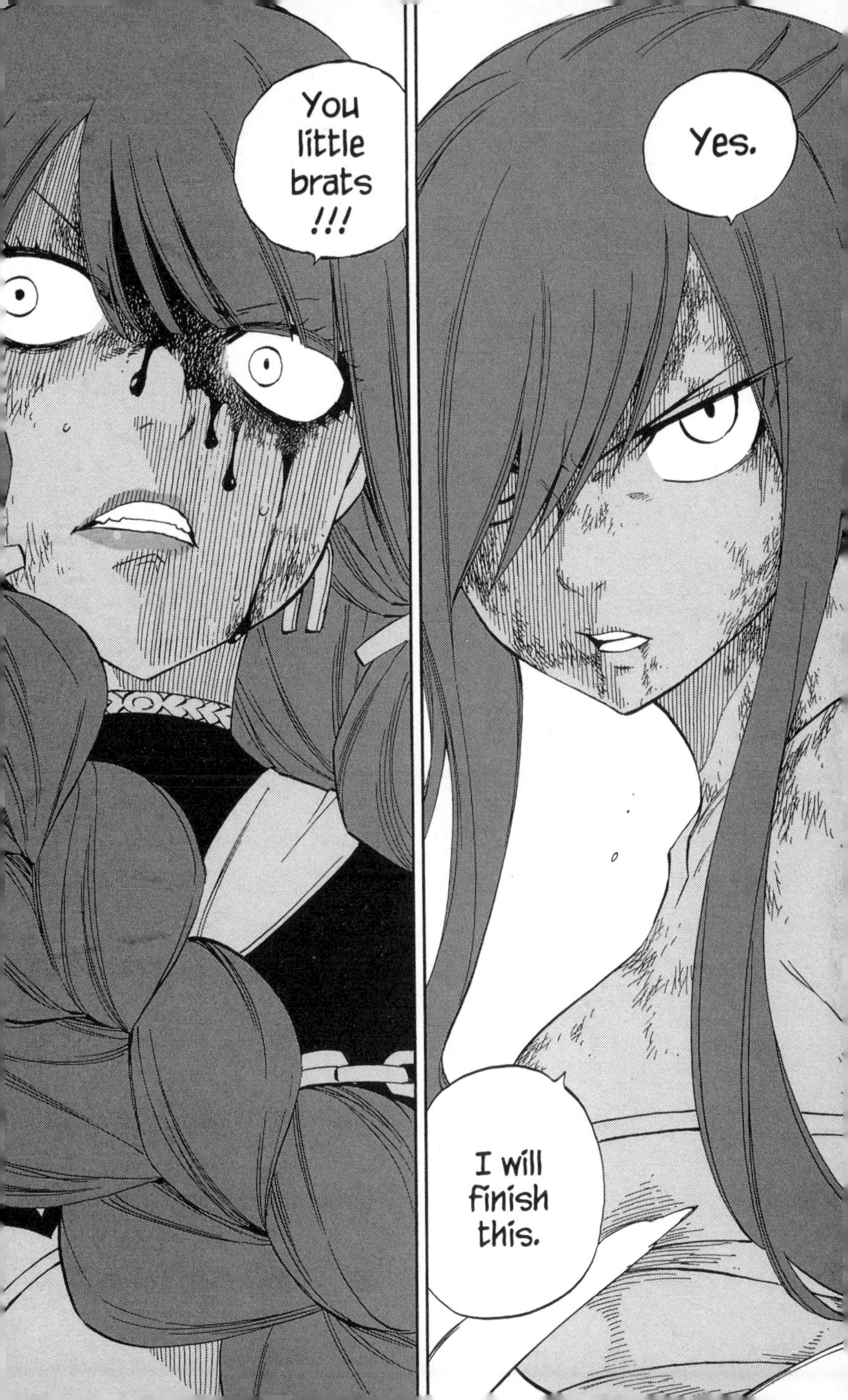
Yes.
I will finish this.
You little brats!!!

FAIRY TAIL

フェアリーテイル

Chapter 518: Master Enchant

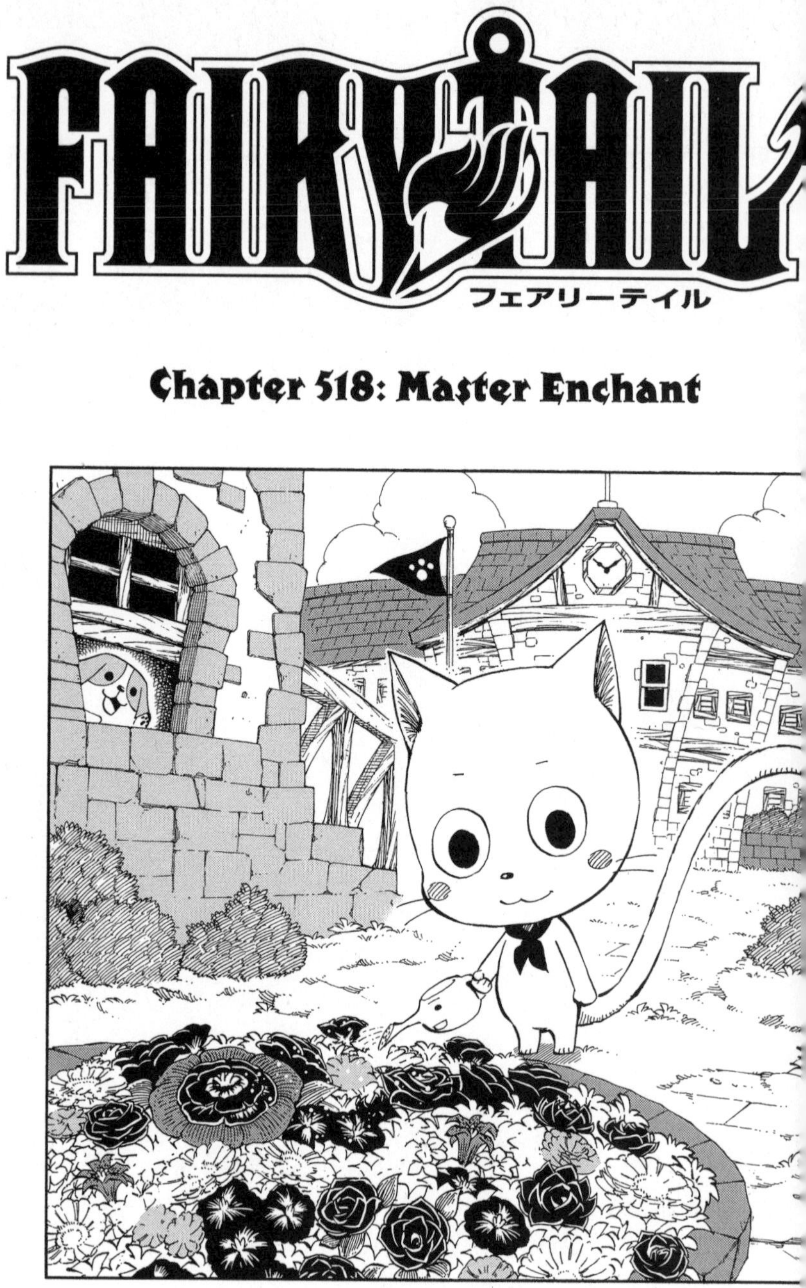

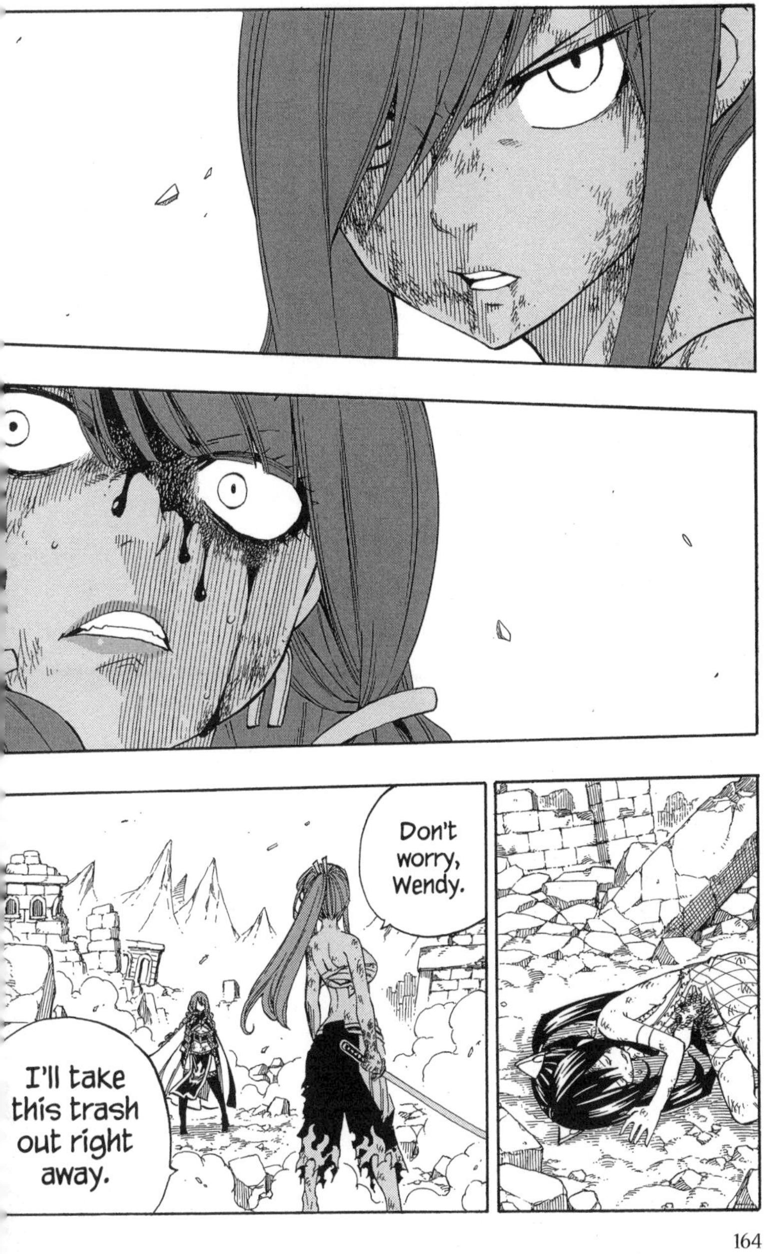
Don't worry, Wendy.
I'll take this trash out right away.

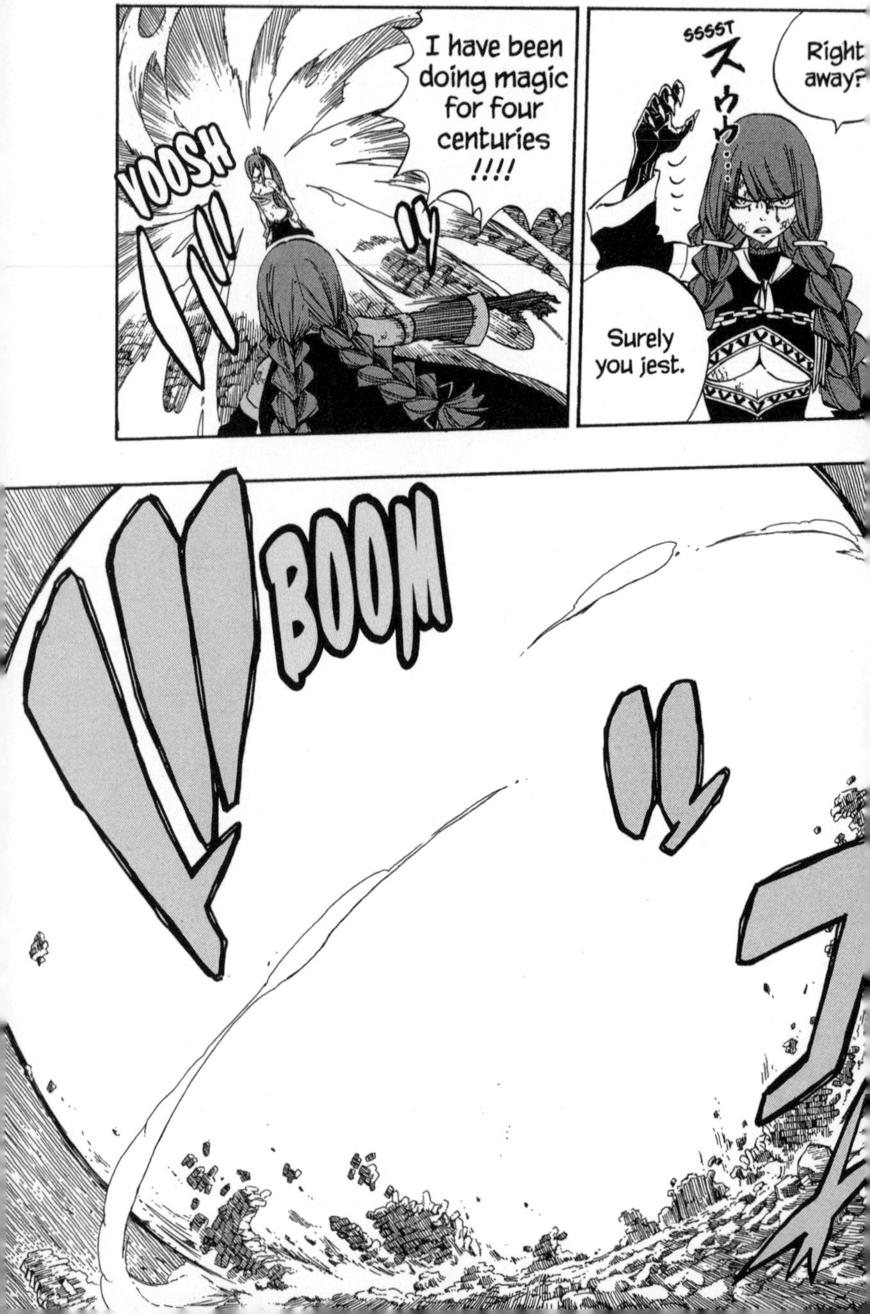
SSSST
Right away?
Surely you jest.
I have been doing magic for four centuries !!!!
VOOSH
BOOM

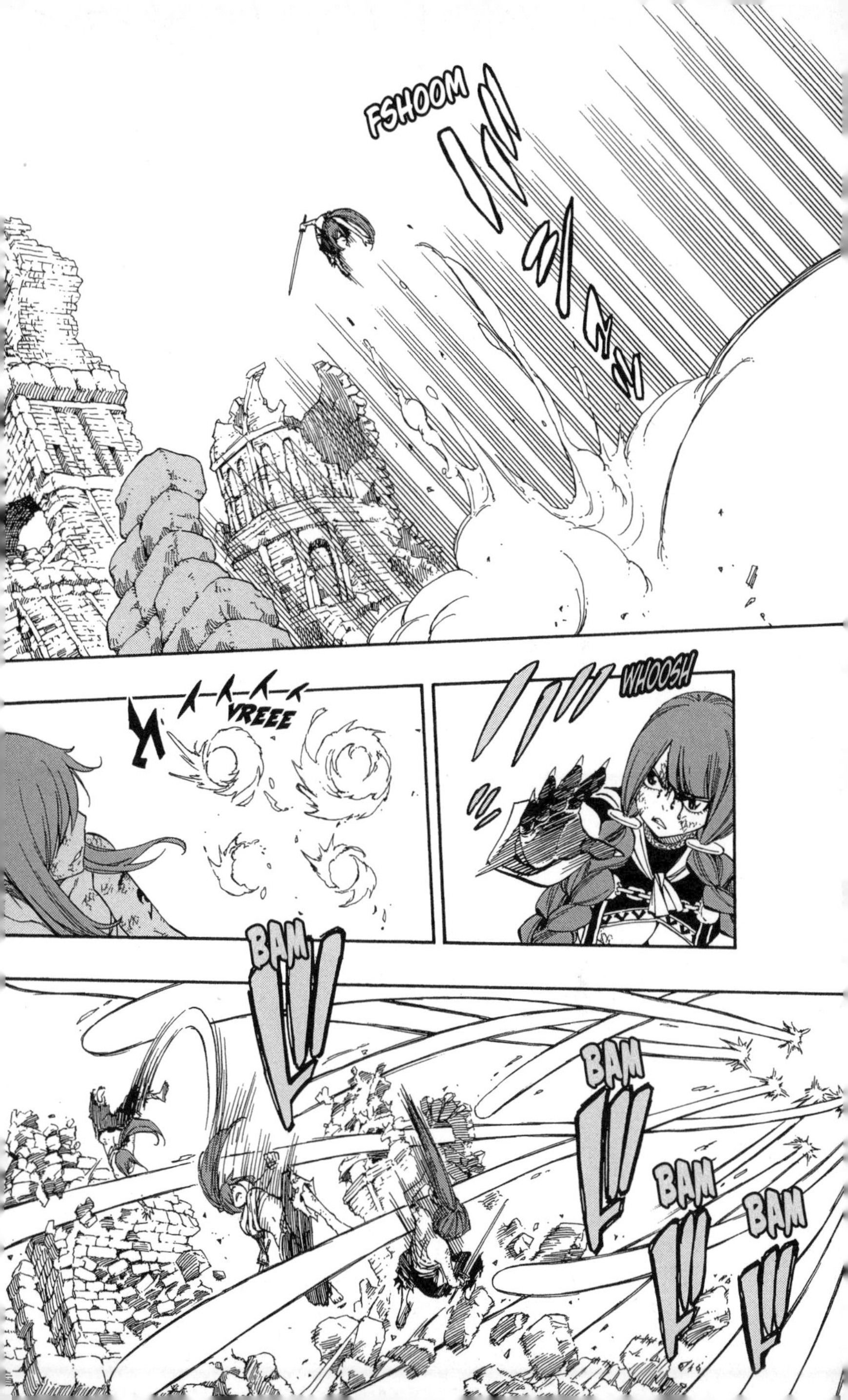
FSHOOM
WHOOSH
VREEE
BAM
BAM
BAM
BAM

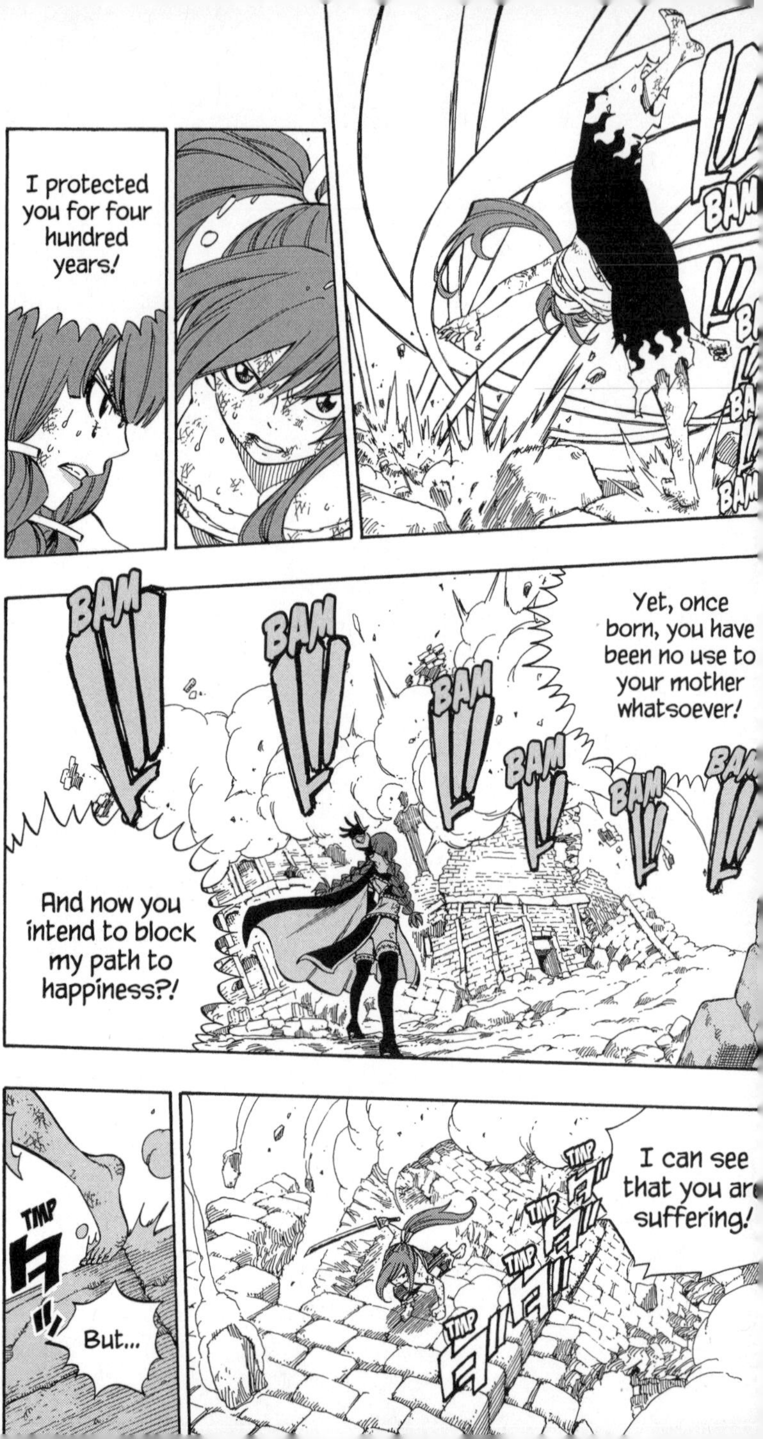
BAM
BAM
BAM
I protected you for four hundred years!
Yet, once born, you have been no use to your mother whatsoever!
BAM
BAM
BAM
BAM
BAM
BAM
And now you intend to block my path to happiness?!
I can see that you ar
suffering!
TMP
TMP
TMP
TMP
TMP
But...

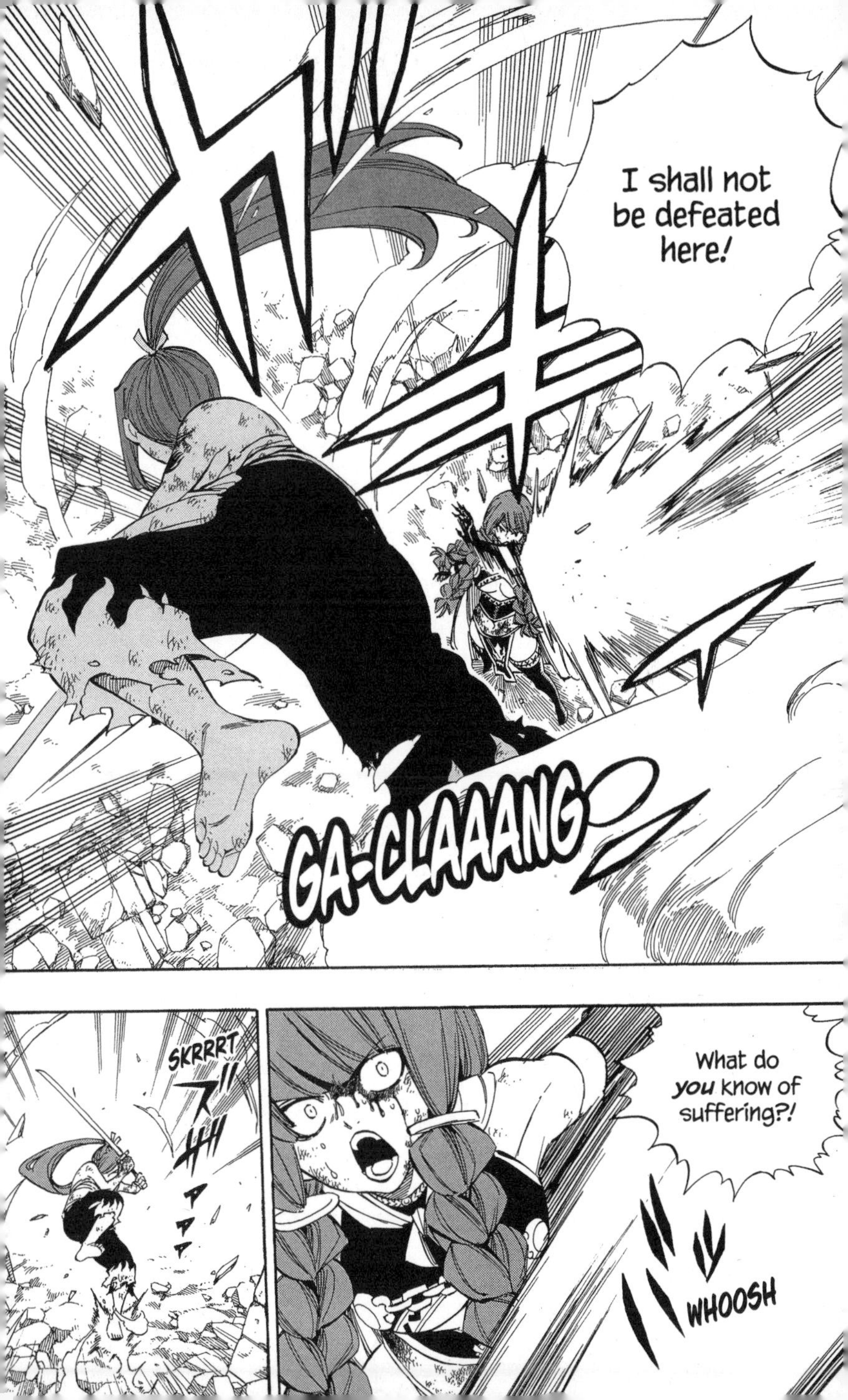
I shall not be defeated here!
GA-CLAAANG
What do *you* know of suffering?!
WHOOSH
SKRRRT

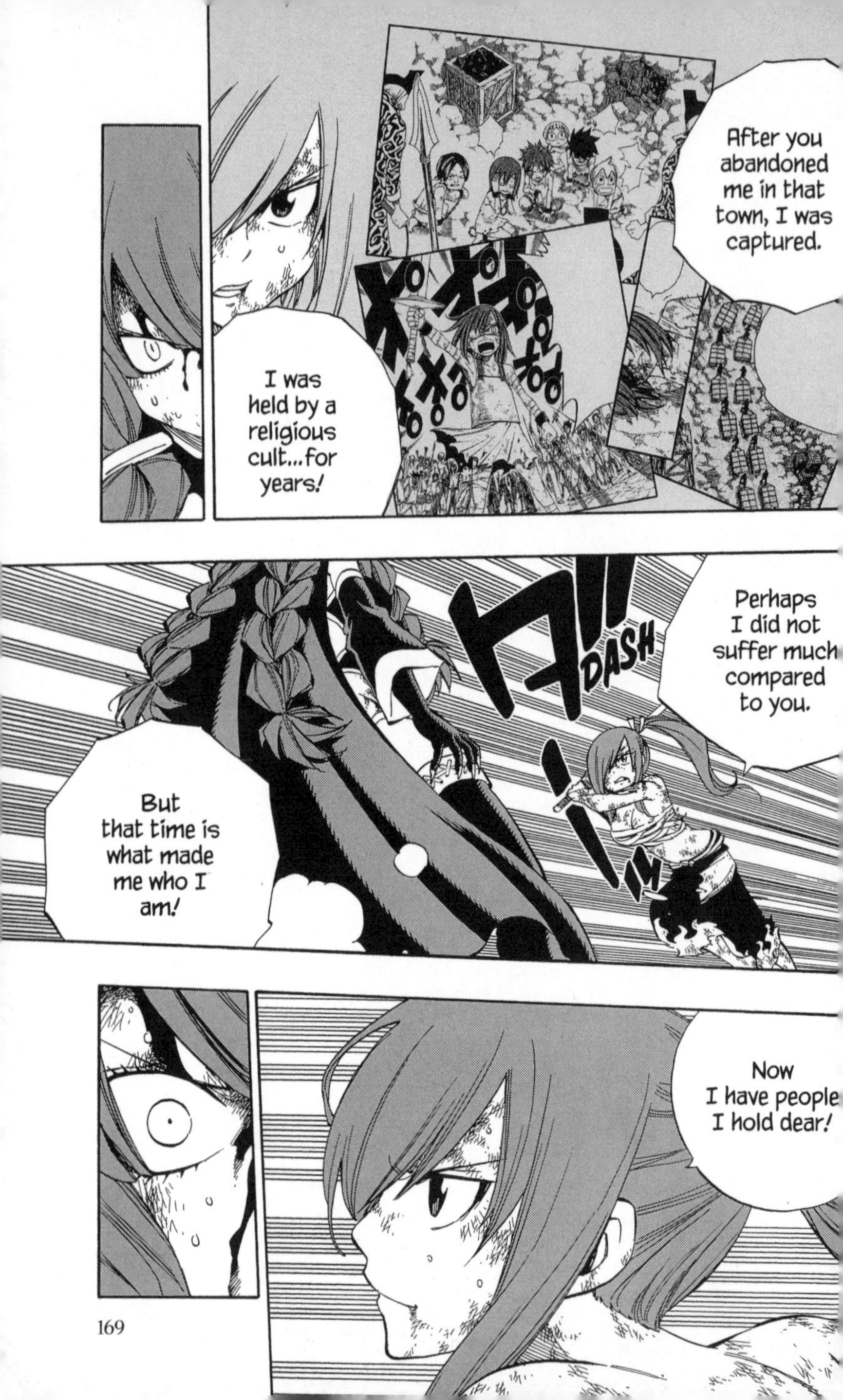
After you abandoned me in that town, I was captured.
I was held by a religious cult...for years!
Perhaps I did not suffer much compared to you.
DASH
But that time is what made me who I am!
Now I have people I hold dear!

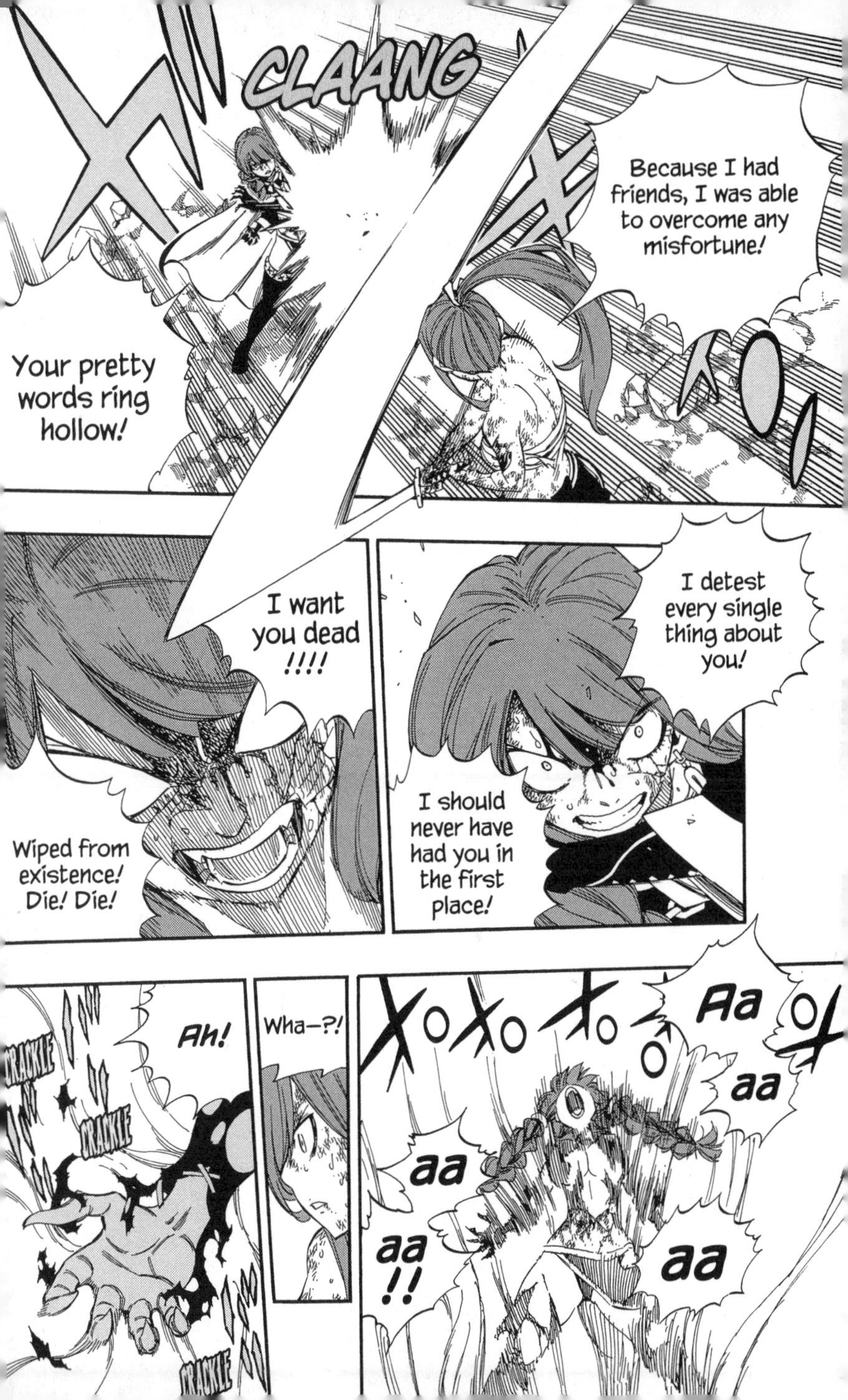
Because I had friends, I was able to overcome any misfortune!
CLAANG
Your pretty words ring hollow!
I detest every single thing about you!
I should never have had you in the first place!
I want you dead !!!!
Wiped from existence! Die! Die!
Aa aa
aa
aa !!
aa
Wha—?!
Ah!
CRACKLE
CRACKLE
CRACKLE

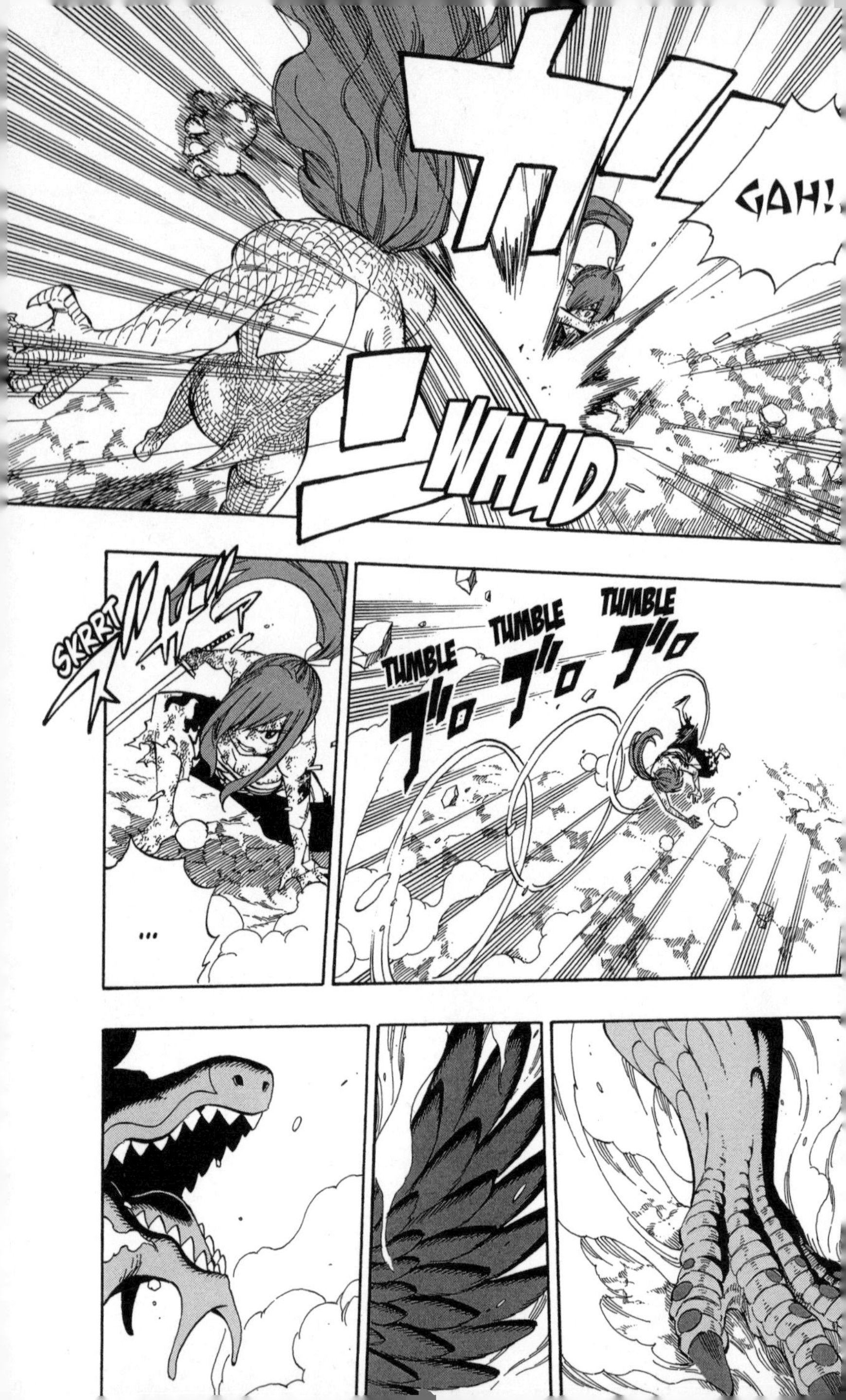
GAH!!
WHUD
TUMBLE
TUMBLE
TUMBLE
SKRRT
...

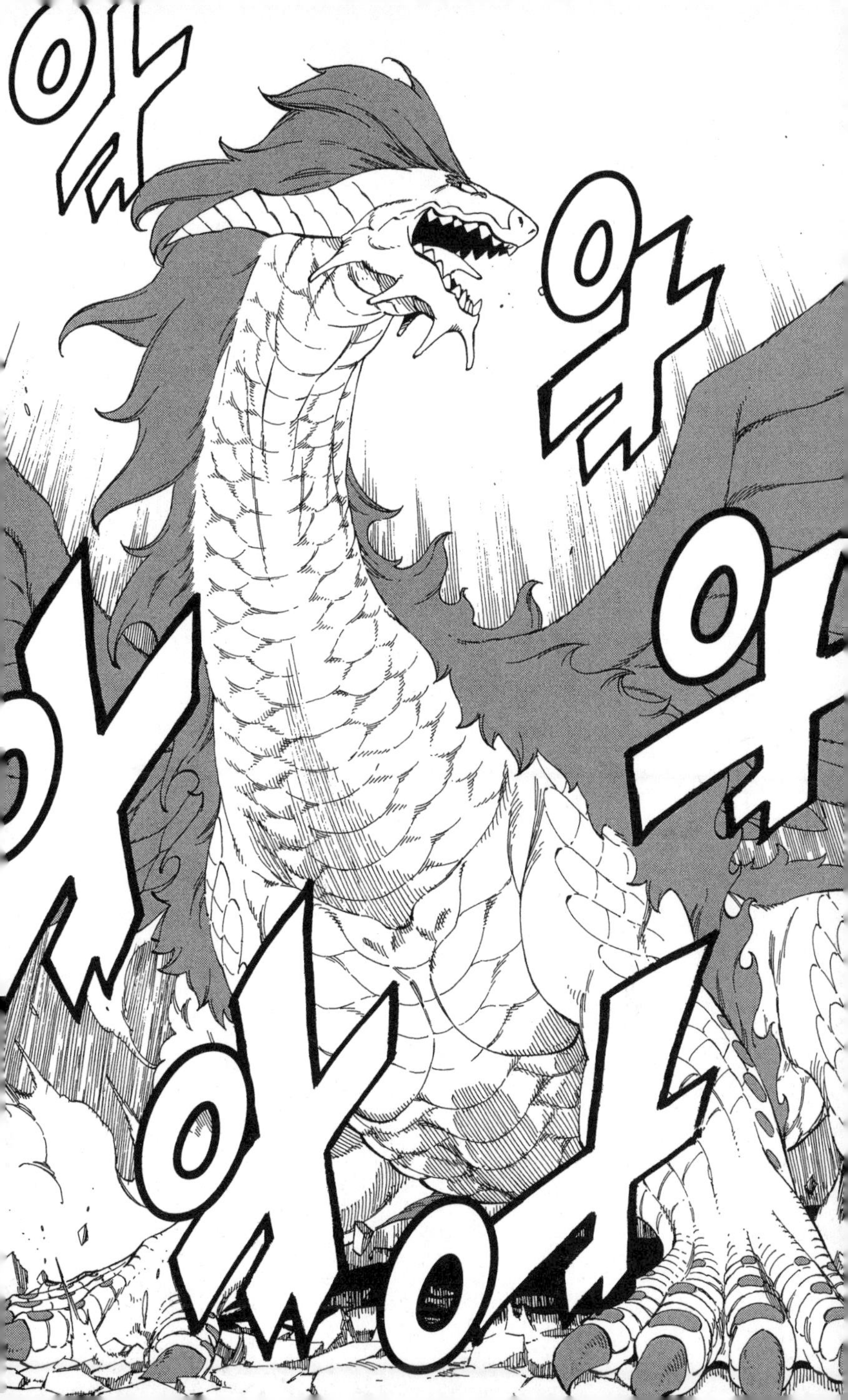

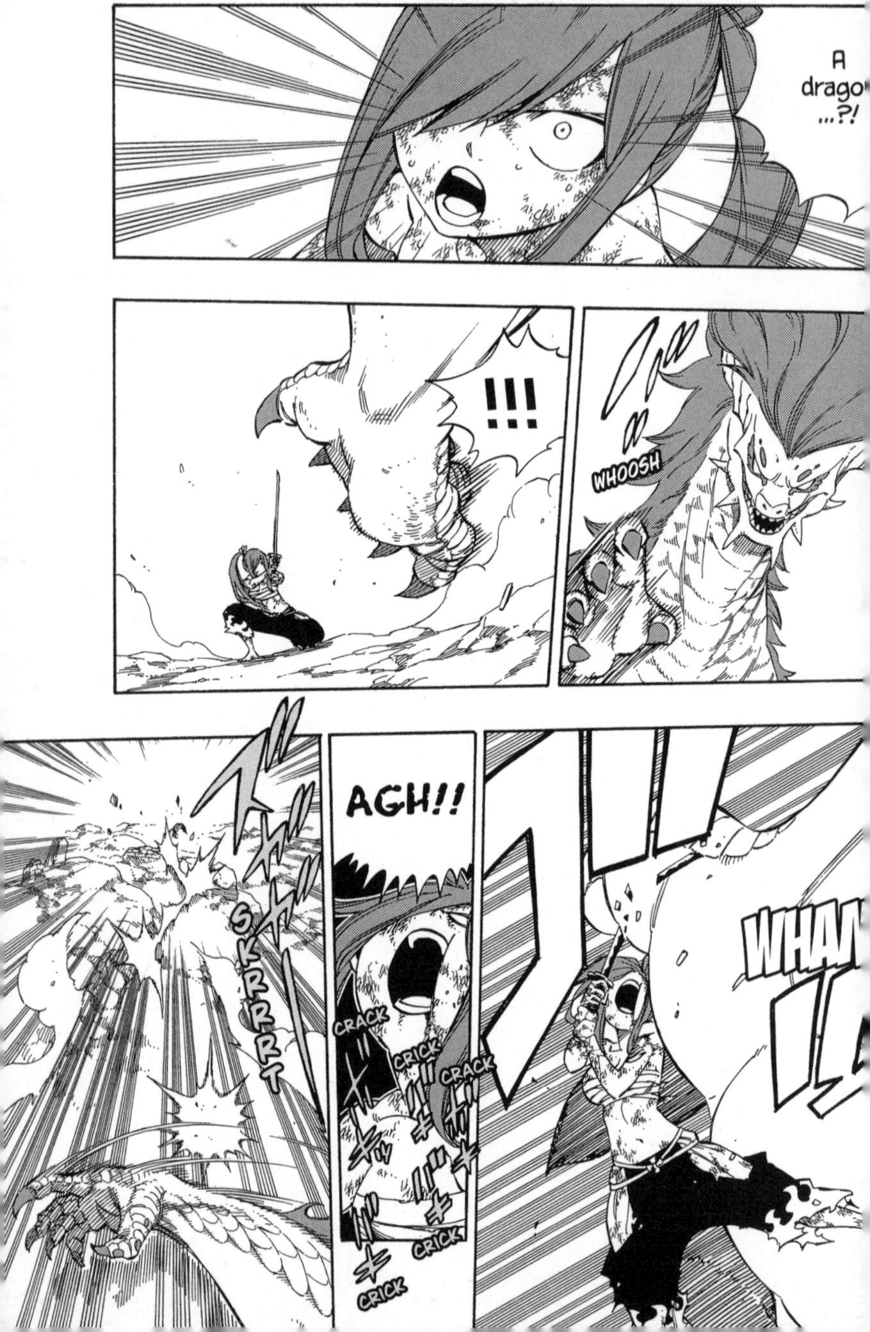

A drago
...?!
WHOOSH
!!!
WHAM
AGH!!
CRACK
CRICK
CRACK
CRICK
CRICK
SKRRRT

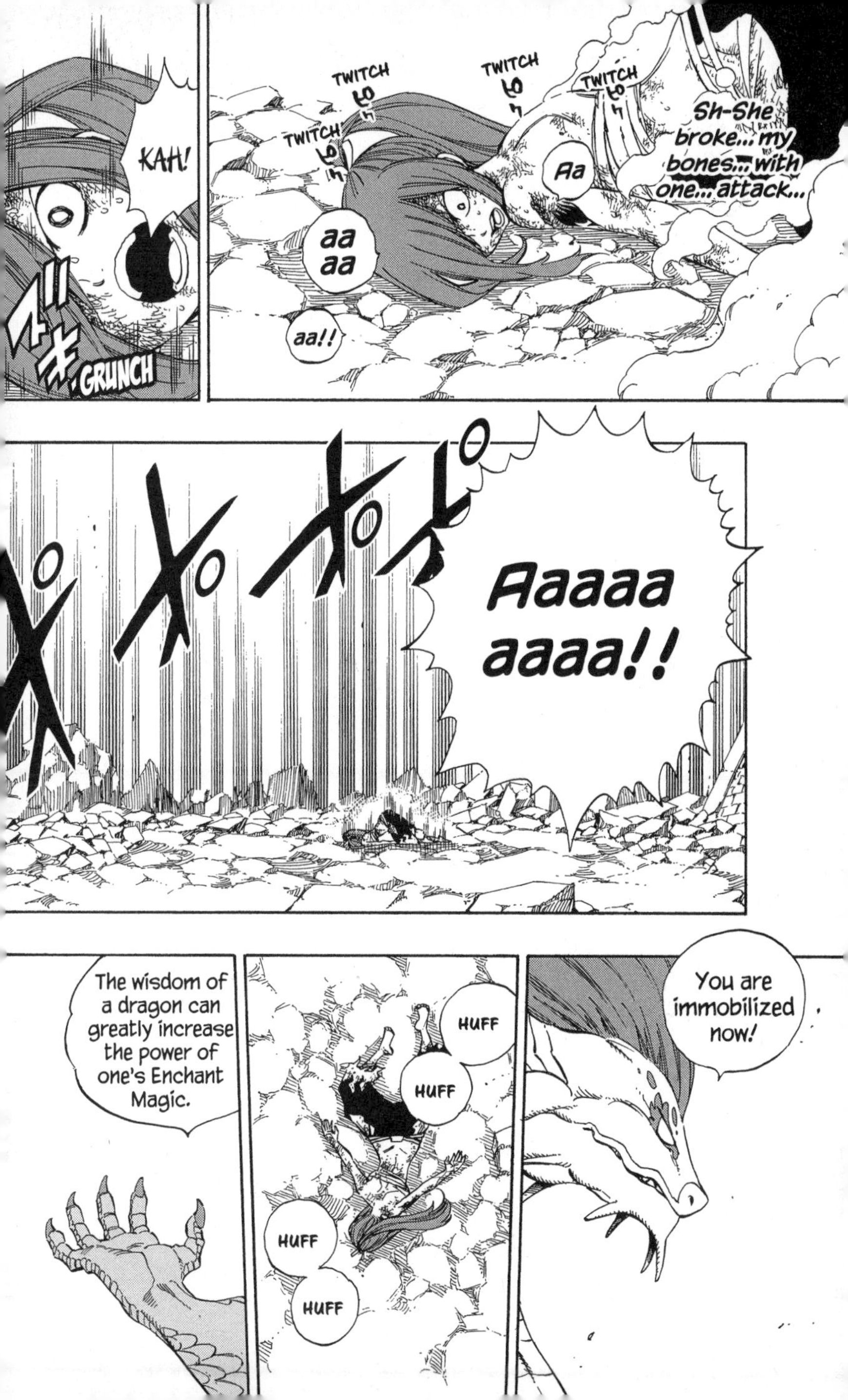
TWITCH
TWITCH
TWITCH
TWITCH
Sh-She broke... my bones... with one... attack...
Aa
aa aa
aa!!
KAH!
GRUNCH
Aaaaa aaaa!!
You are immobilized now!
HUFF
HUFF
HUFF
HUFF
The wisdom of a dragon can greatly increase the power of one's Enchant Magic.

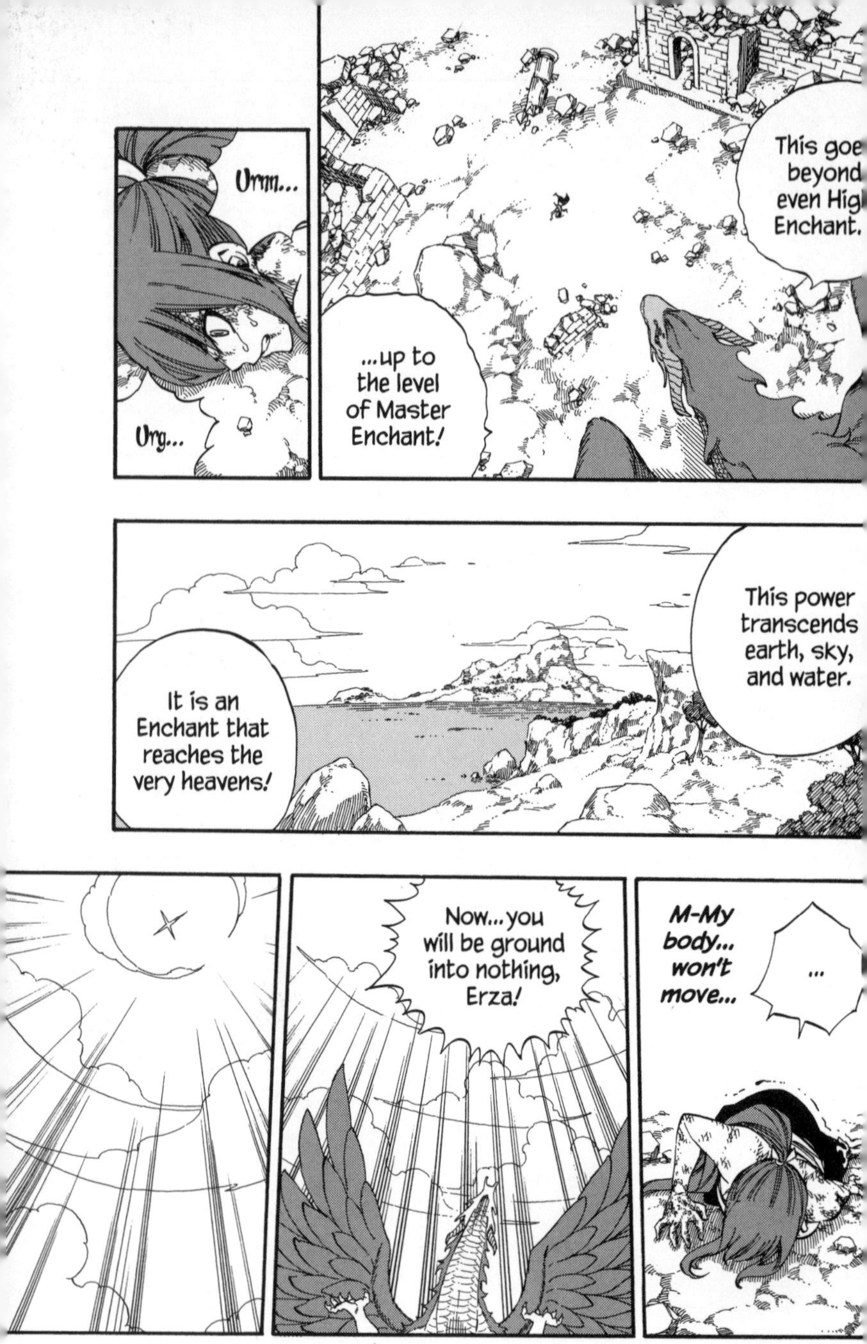
This goe
beyond
even Hig
Enchant.
...up to the level of Master Enchant!
Urrn...
Urg...
This power transcends earth, sky, and water.
It is an Enchant that reaches the very heavens!
...
M-My body... won't move...
Now...you will be ground into nothing, Erza!

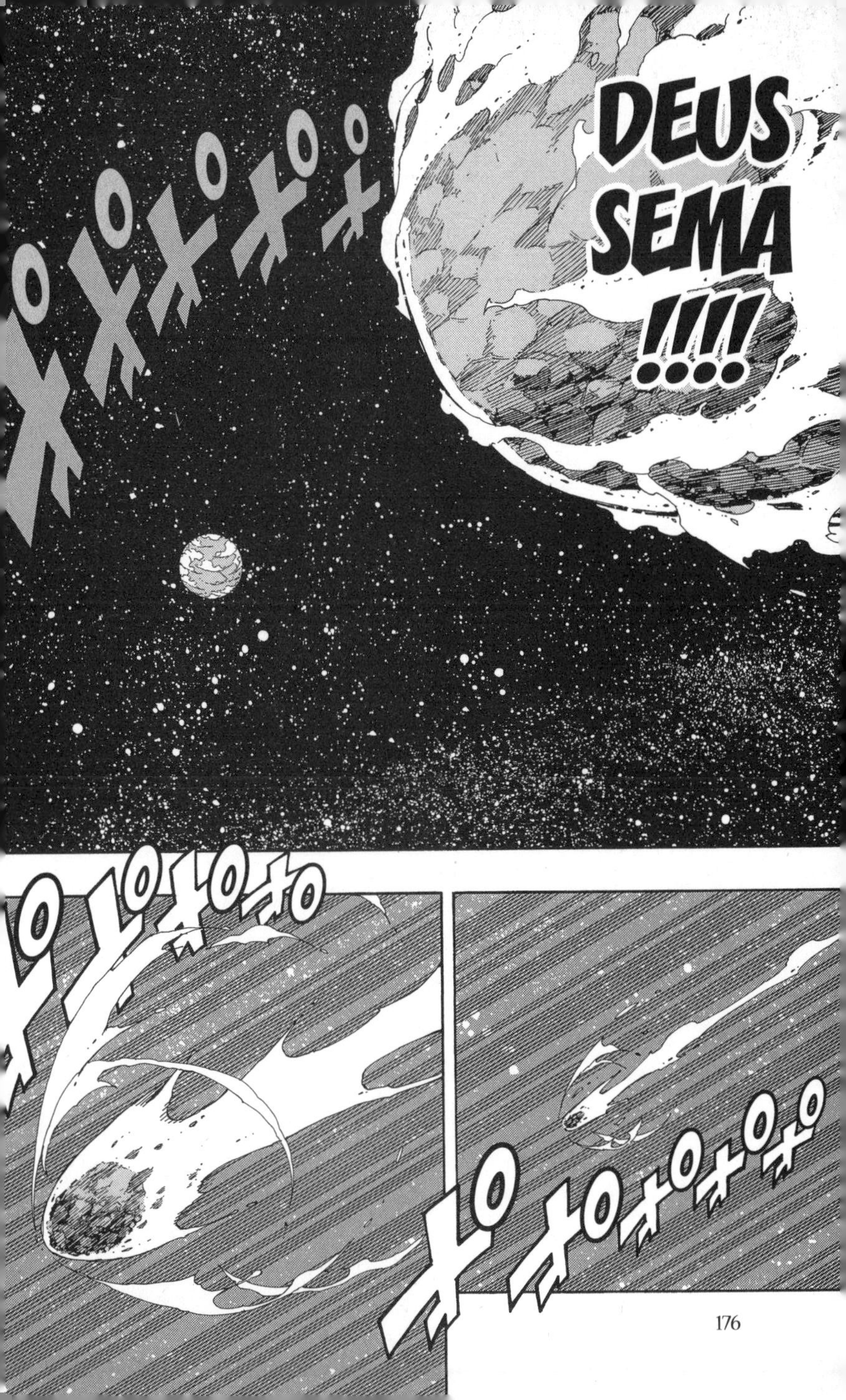
DEUS SEMA !!!!

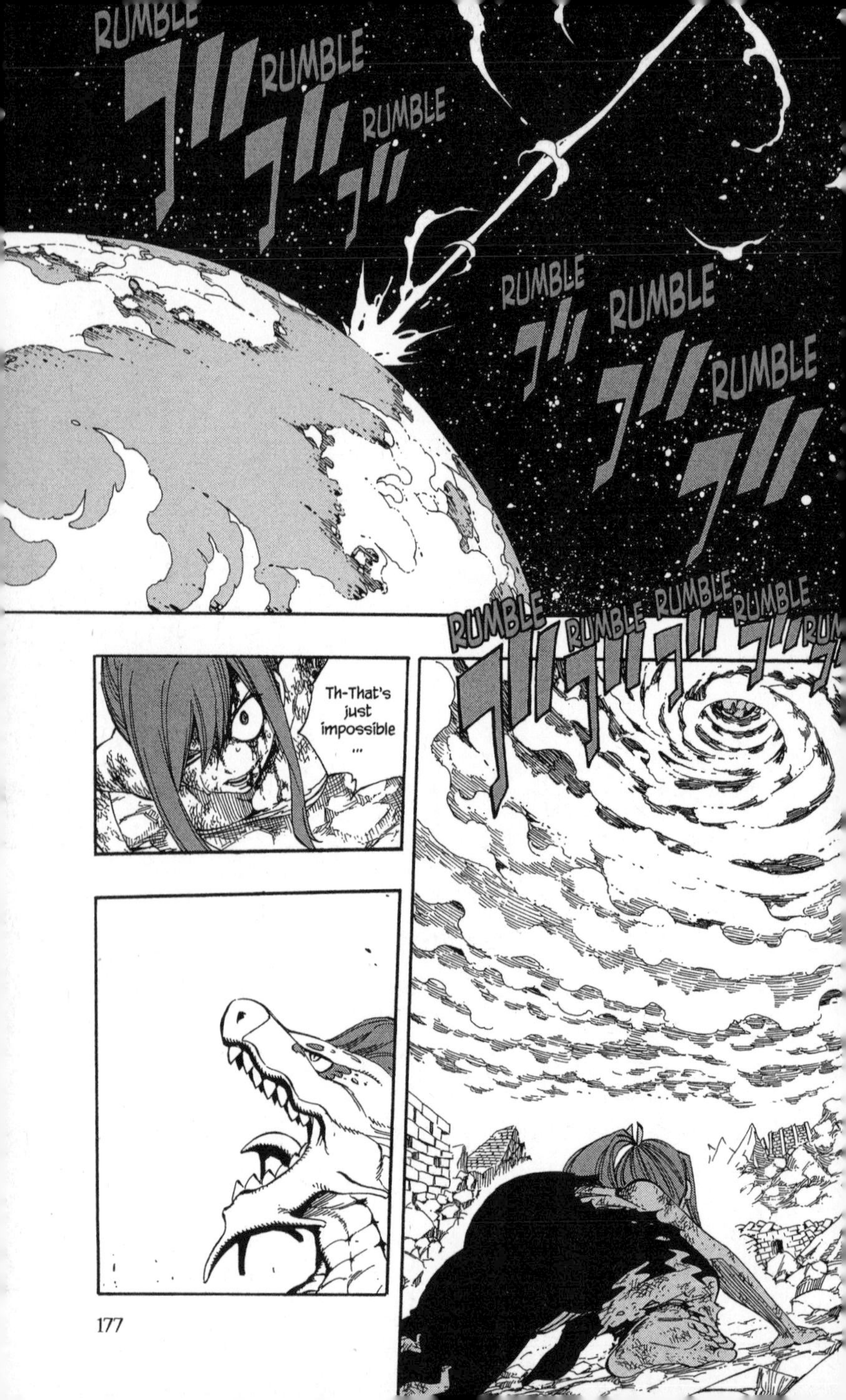
RUMBLE
RUMBLE
RUMBLE
RUMBLE
RUMBLE
RUMBLE
RUMBLE
RUMBLE
RUMBLE
RUMBLE
Th-That's just impossible ...

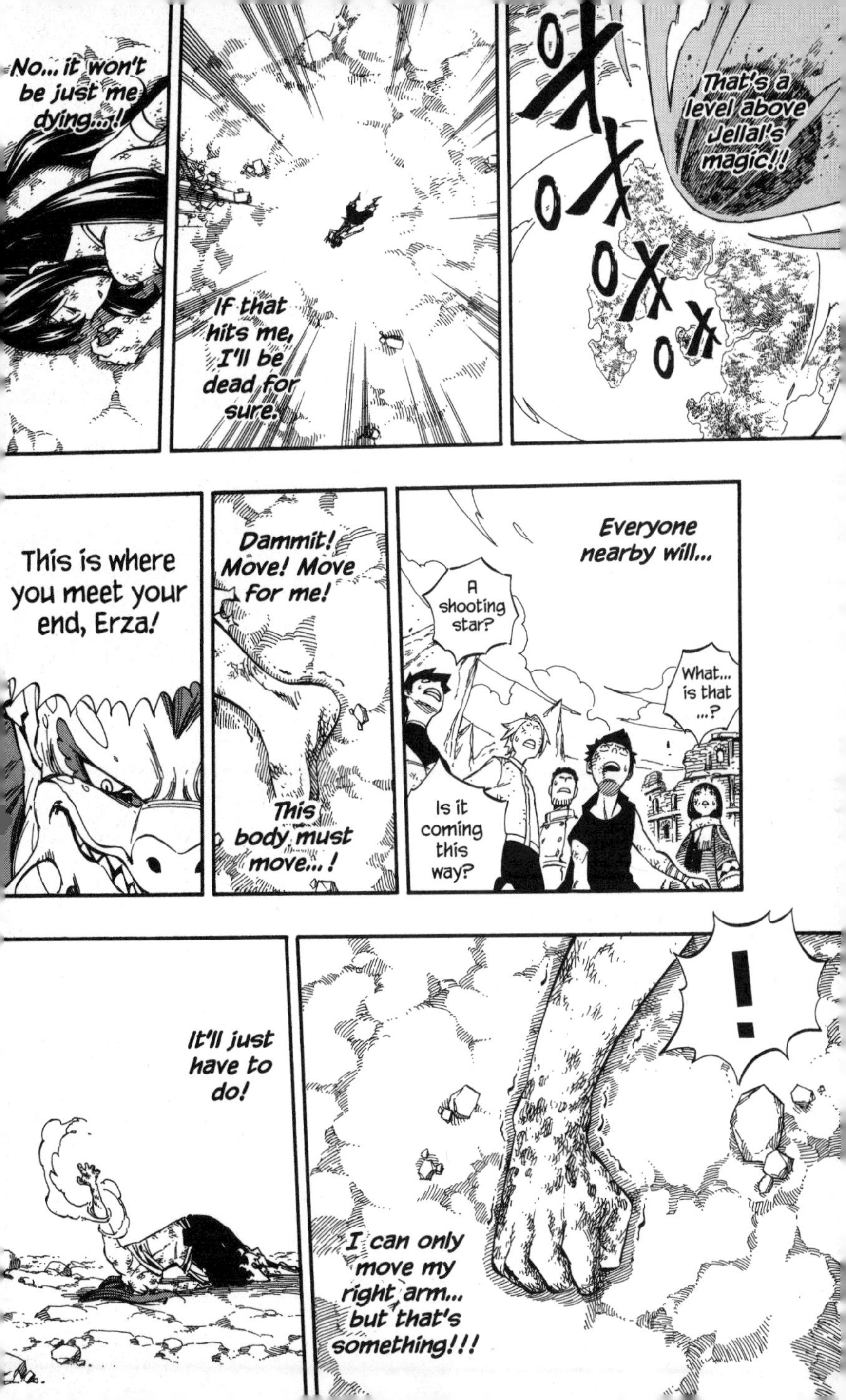
That's a level above Jellal's magic!!
If that hits me, I'll be dead for sure.
No... it won't be just me dying...!
Everyone nearby will...
What... is that ...?
A shooting star?
Is it coming this way?
Dammit! Move! Move for me!
This body must move...!
This is where you meet your end, Erza!
!
I can only move my right arm... but that's something!!!
It'll just have to do!

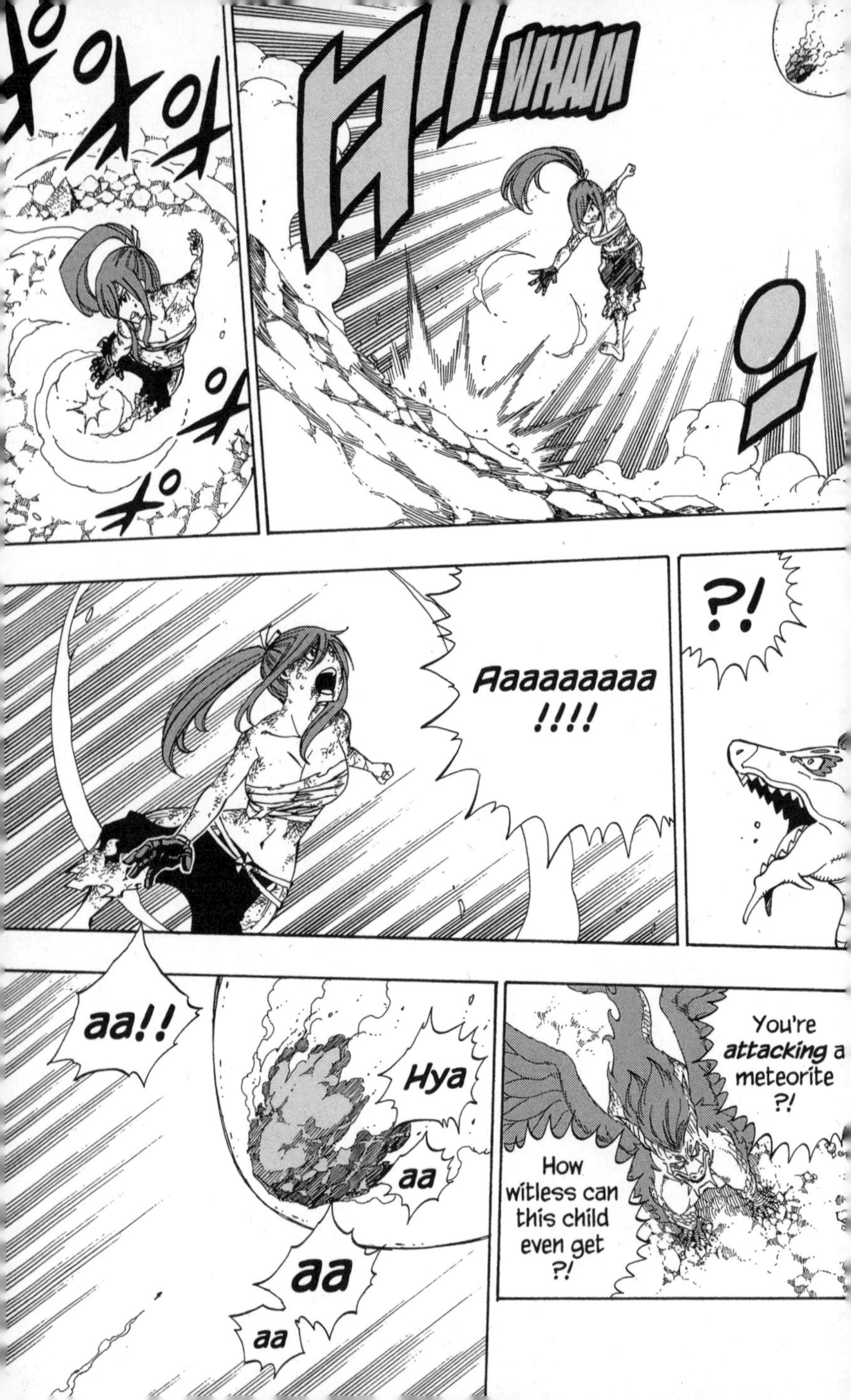
WHAM
?!
Aaaaaaaaa !!!!
You're *attacking* a meteorite ?!
How witless can this child even get ?!
Hya
aa
aa
aa
aa!!

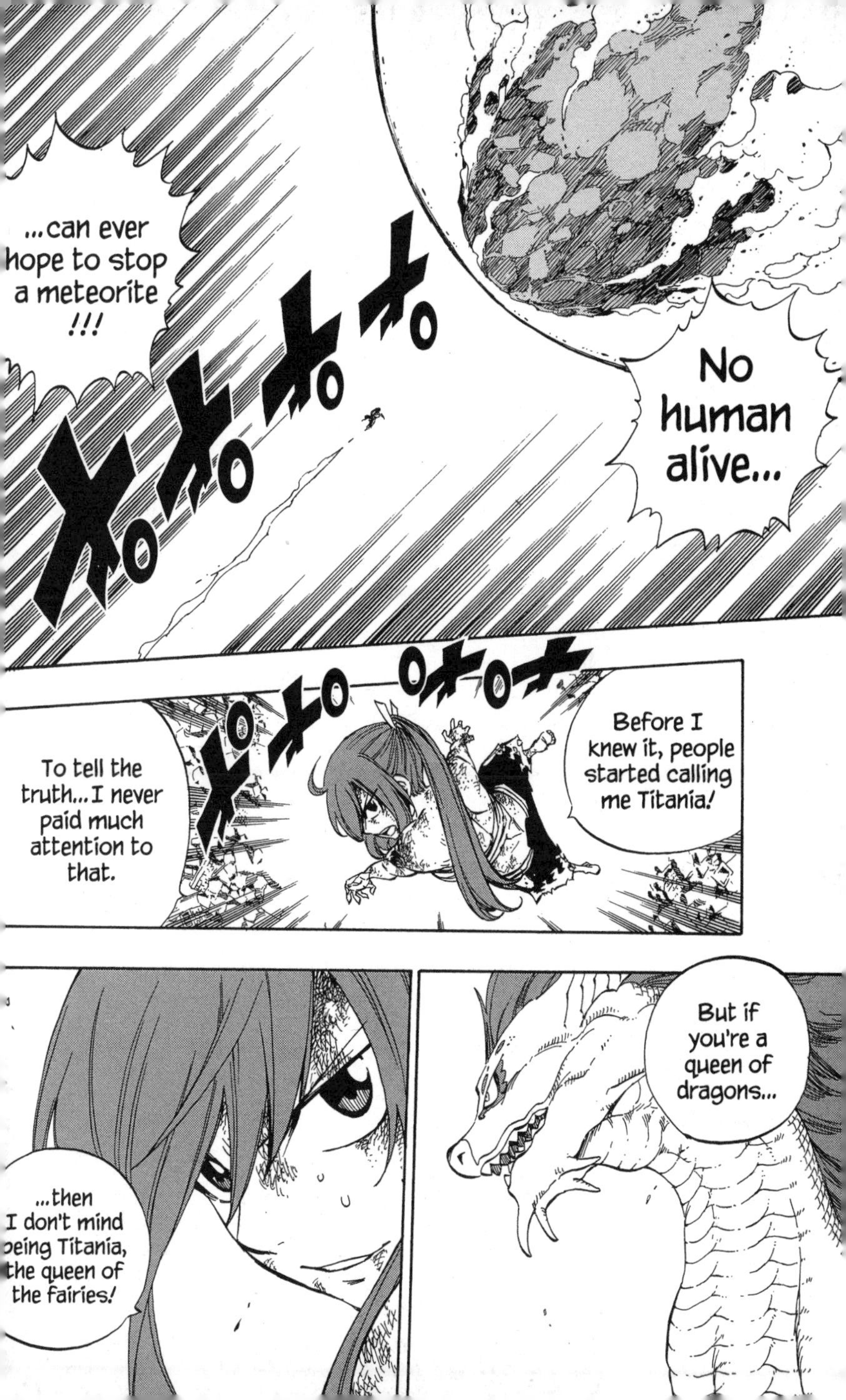
No human alive...
...can ever hope to stop a meteorite!!!
Before I knew it, people started calling me Titania!
To tell the truth...I never paid much attention to that.
But if you're a queen of dragons...
...then I don't mind being Titania, the queen of the fairies!

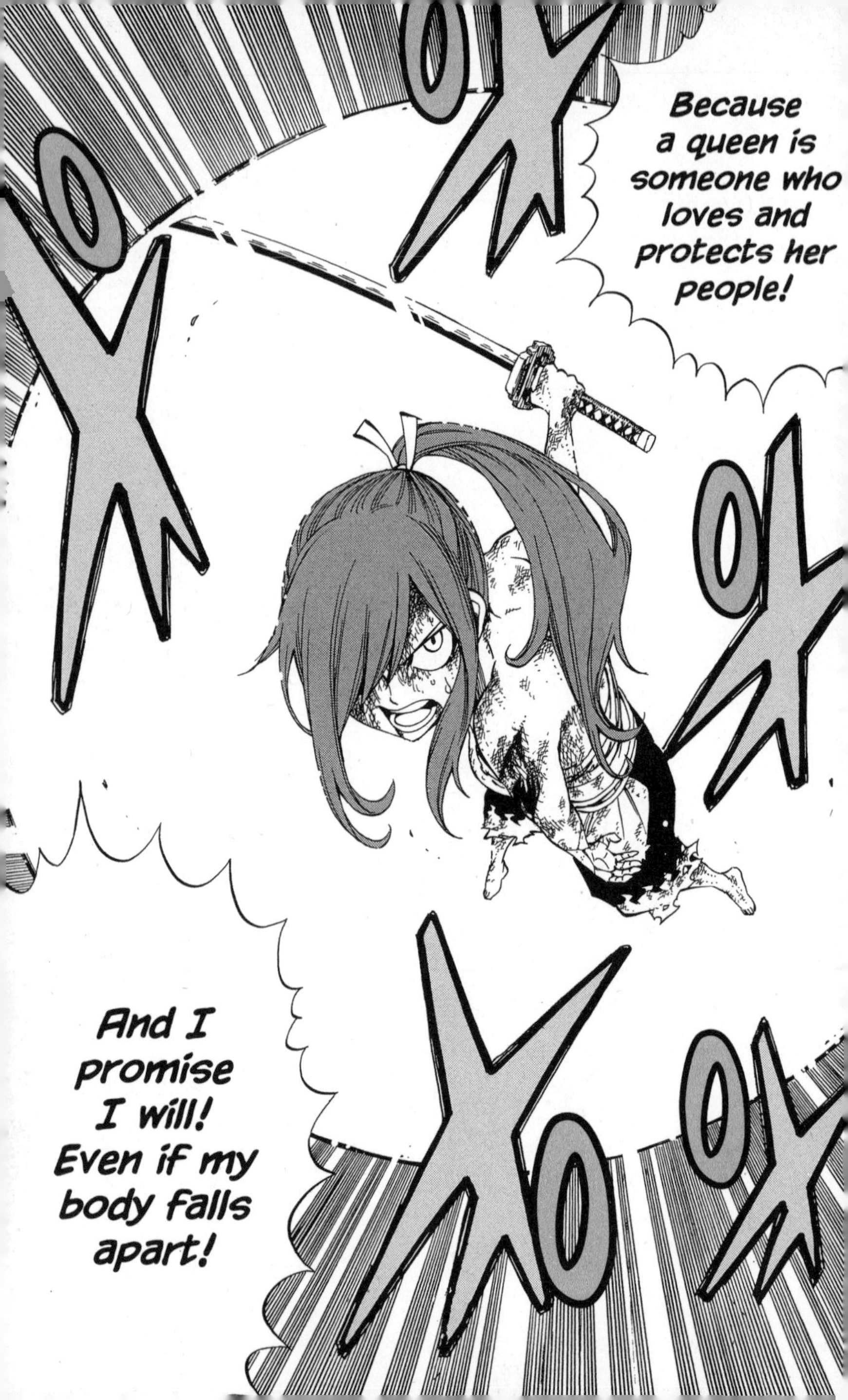
Because a queen is someone who loves and protects her people!
And I promise I will! Even if my body falls apart!

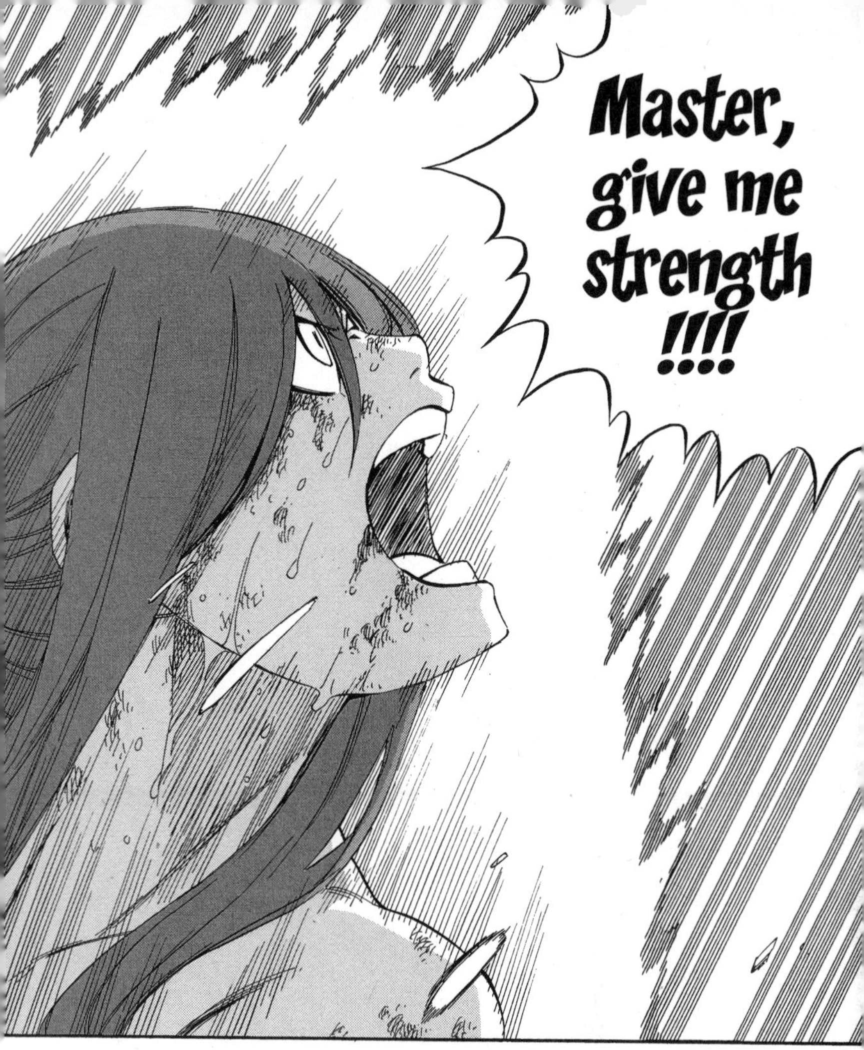
Master, give me strength!!!!

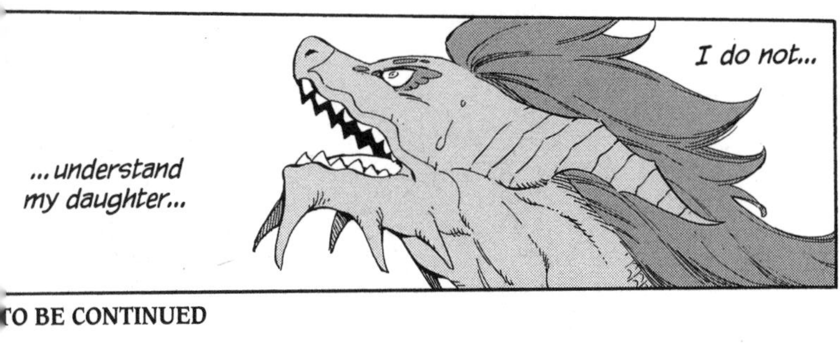
I do not...
...understand my daughter...

TO BE CONTINUED

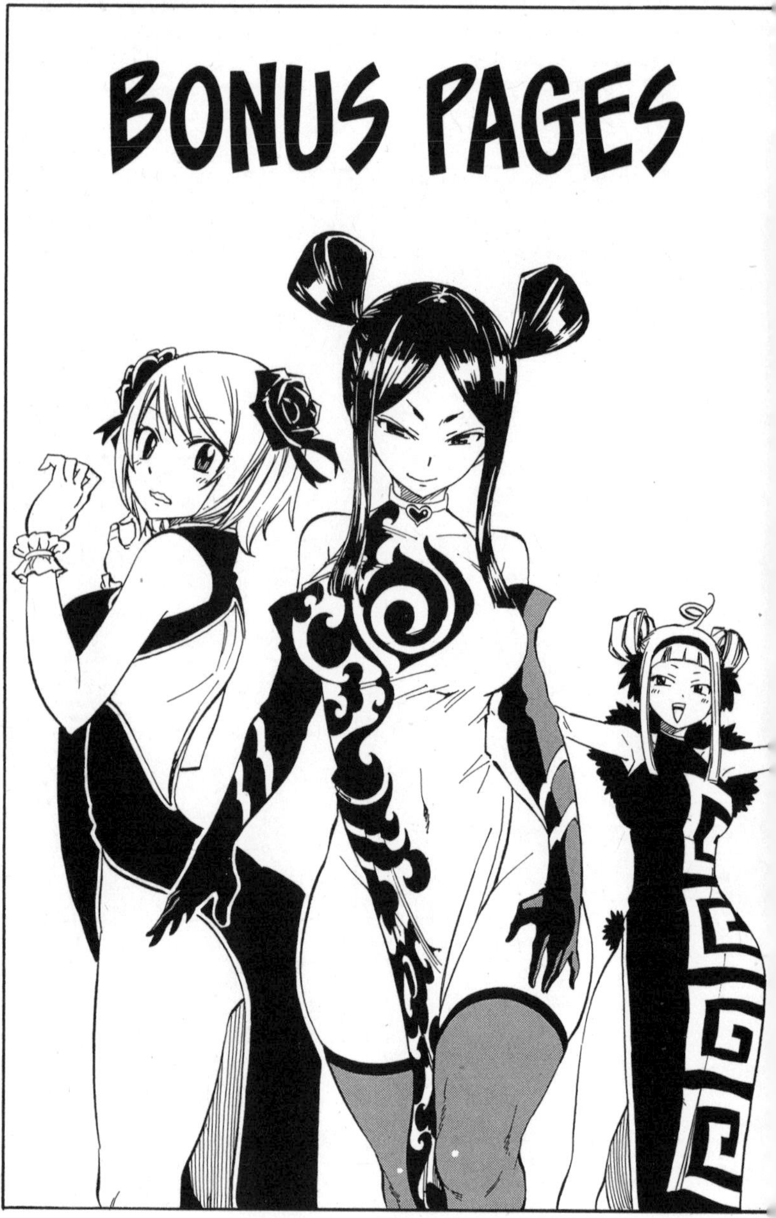
BONUS PAGES

Continued from the left-hand page. ⬇

Mira: Next question!

In Chapter 503, during DiMaria's stopped time, what really went down?

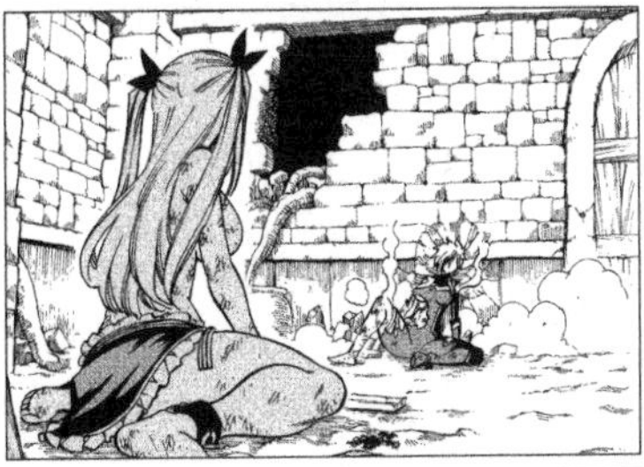

Lucy: O-Oh, that. Well that whole thing saved me, but Natsu went a little weird...

Mira: Considering how scared DiMaria got, it had to be something well out of the ordinary.

Lucy: Meaning that Natsu was able to move within stopped time?

Mira: How about we consider the order of events?

① DiMaria stopped time.

② When Lucy wakes up, DiMaria is out cold!

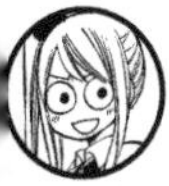
: Hold on a minute! How could he have moved in stopped time?

Mira: Maybe it's a power he got for being E.N.D. or something like that?

Lucy: Natsu was tied up, too, wasn't he?

Mira: He just went, "BOOM!" and used his E.N.D. power!

Lucy: He had those magic-power blocking handcuffs on, too.

Mira: **E.N.D. Power!!**

Lucy: That's a really useful power.

Mira: Then, right after that...
③ Natsu notices Lucy (and stares at her chest).

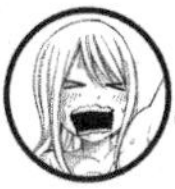
: Don't you dare stare, Natsu!!!

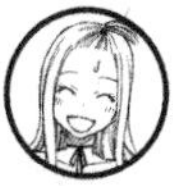
: But her words come too late.
④ Anyway, Natsu removes the ropes from Lucy (and in doing so, takes another long gander at her chest).

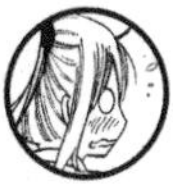
: Too much gandering!!!!

Mira: See, Natsu's a hot-blooded male...
⑤ Natsu sees an unmoving Lucy and mistakes her for dead.
⑥ The power of E.N.D. awakens!
⑦ He gives DiMaria one last punch, and...
⑧ Heads out to find Zeref.

Lucy: That's pretty much what happened, huh?

Mira: 'Cause, y'know, he's a hot-blooded male.

Lucy: Can we drop the subject already?

When are we going to see the Capricorn form of Lucy's Star Dress?

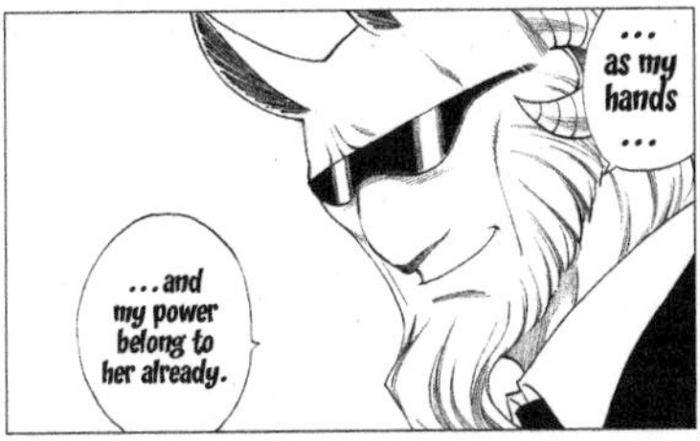

...as my hands...
...and my power belong to her already.

Lucy: Well, it's just possible that it may appear in the **Second Theatrical Film** release, or maybe not.

Mira: Huh? Well, is it or isn't it?!

Lucy: I can't say yet!

Mira: Purupurupu, pipiiin!

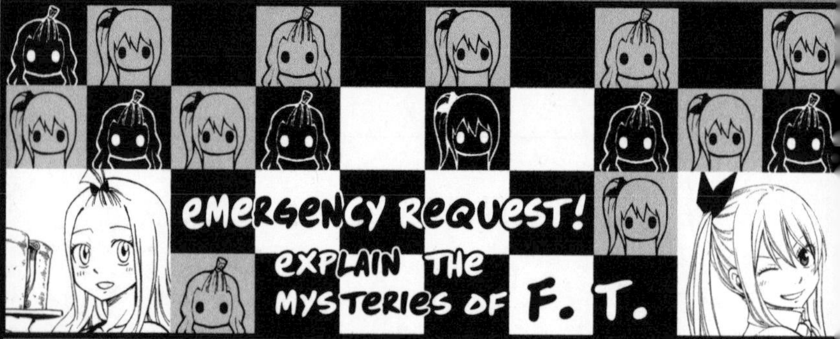
EMERGENCY REQUEST!
EXPLAIN THE MYSTERIES OF F.T.

At a café in Magnolia...

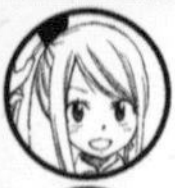
: Hi there, everybody!!

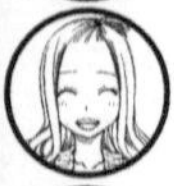
: Purupurupu, pipiiin!♪

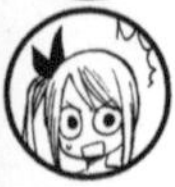
: Huh?! What's that about?!

Mira: You know! I was doing an impression of your Celestial Spirit, Plue!

Lucy: Nope! That was nothing like him!

Mira: Anyway, let's give this section our all once more!

Lucy: O-Okay... Then, let's dive into the first question.

I really love Brandish-chan, so give her a happy ending!

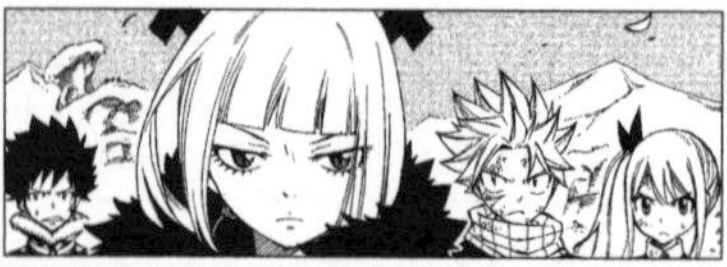

Mira: I think Brandish may be the most popular of The 12.

Lucy: Although Irene and DiMaria (who really put me through the ringer) are also really well loved.

Mira: Well, the ladies of The 12 are popular.

Lucy: In regards to the men, we've got **God Selena!**

Mira: Huh? But he's just...you know...

Lucy: Kind of cute in a "too bad" sort of way...?

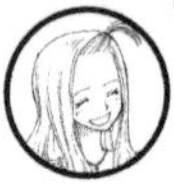
: The author is leaning towards Jacob.

Lucy: Come to think of it, you're right in the middle of battling him, right? Good luck with that!

Mira: I am. But for some reason, he's keeping his eyes shut for the whole match.

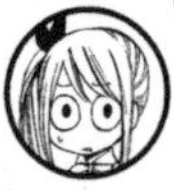
: What?

Mira: I'm sure he's an extremely powerful wizard, but thanks to that, we're pretty evenly matched.

Lucy: Mira-san, that couldn't be because you're wearing something **really revealing**, is it?

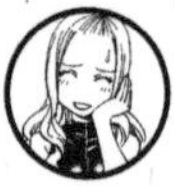
: Oh, dear! I can't seem to stay ladylike!

Lucy: Going back...to the subject at hand... I really want Brandish to have a happy ending, too!

Mira: That would be nice... Well, the best would be for everyone to have a happy ending.

Lucy: But the latest plot developments make me wonder if they will...

Continued on the right-hand page.

The Fairy Tail Guild is looking for illustrations! Please send in your art on a post card or at post-card size, and do it in black pen, okay? Those chosen to be published will get a signed mini poster! ♪ Make sure you write your real name and address on the back of your illustration!

TAIL
d' ART

Hokkaido, Melon Pan

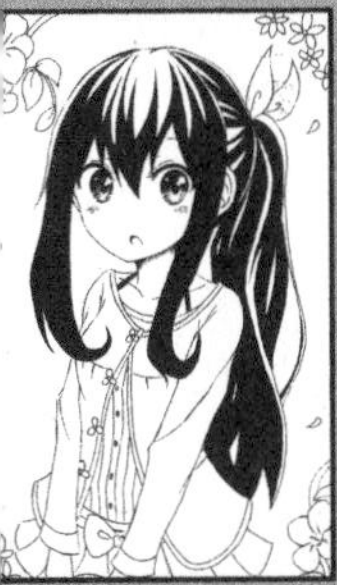

Really good!! And cute!! anks so much for the eat Wendy!

▼ That's Natsu's scarf, right?

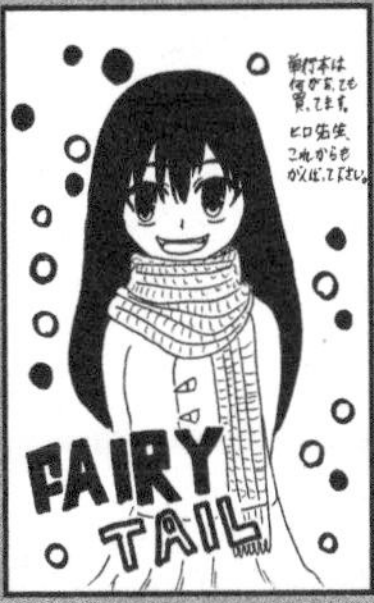
FAIRY
TAIL

Shizuoka Prefecture, Daiki Fujita

Tokyo, Yoshiyu Kurioka

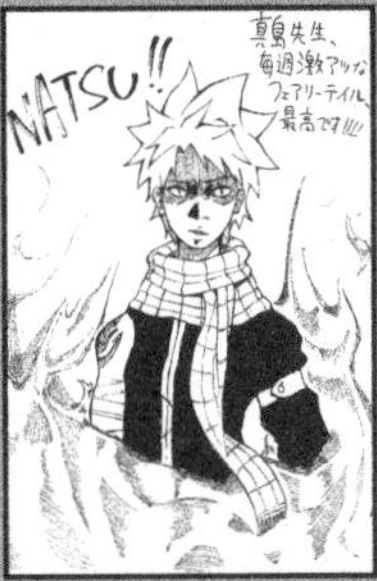
NATSU!!
真島先生、毎週激アツなフェアリーテイル最高です!!!!

▲ Wow! Fired-up Natsu is really cool!

▼ Oh! This is cute! And the plunging neckline is so sexy!

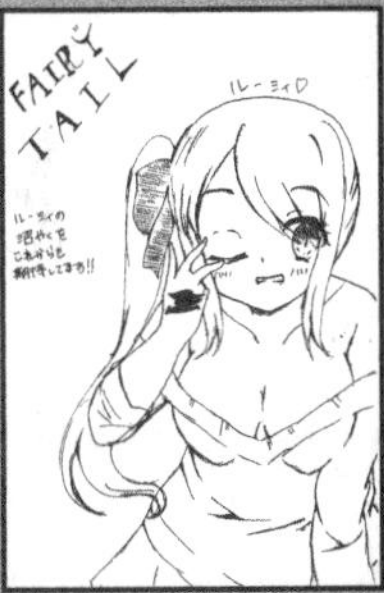
FAIRY TAIL
ルーシィ♡

Gunma Prefecture, Manami Yamamoto

That's ▶ kind of cute. It's weird how cute it is.

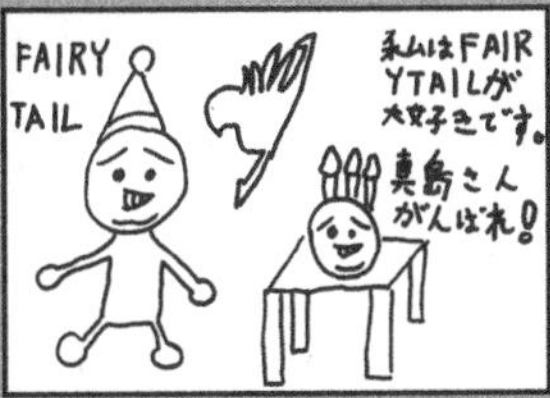
FAIRY TAIL
私はFAIRYTAILが大好きです。
真島さんがんばれ!

Hyogo Prefecture, Yūki Takezawa

I'll bet ▶ the artist put a lot of thought into the Chinese characters for each name!

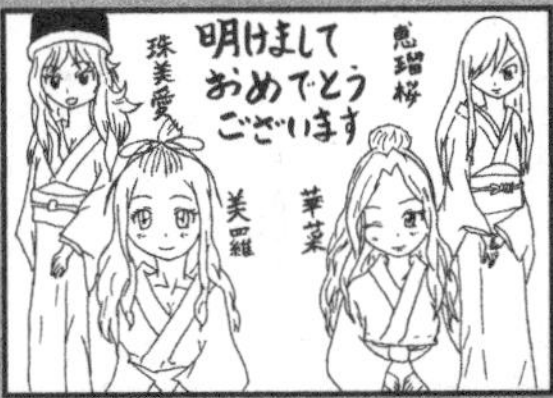
明けましておめでとうございます

Fukuoka Prefecture, Manami Asada

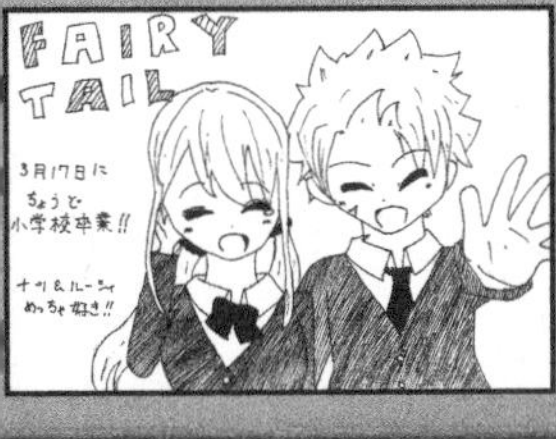
FAIRY TAIL
3月17日にちょうど小学校卒業!!
ナツ&ルーシィめっちゃ好き!!

◀ You graduated! Congratulations! Hope you have fun in Jr. High!

Osaka, Tamaki

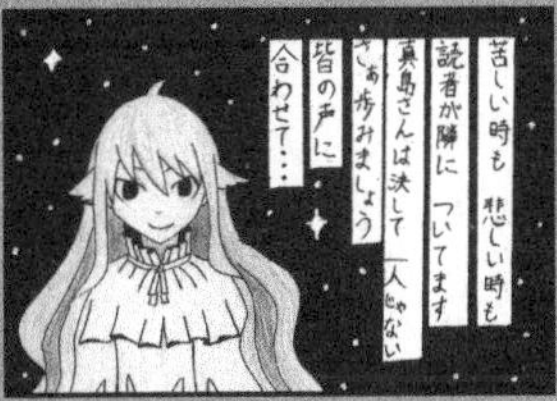
苦しい時も 悲しい時も
読者が隣についてます
真島さんは決して一人じゃない
さぁ歩みましょう
皆の声に
合わせて…

◀ Thank you...uu... It gave me a lot of courage!

Send to Hiro Mashima, Kodansha Comics
451 Park Ave. South, 7th Floor New York, NY 10016

FAIRY GUILD

Hokkaido, Sakura-mochi

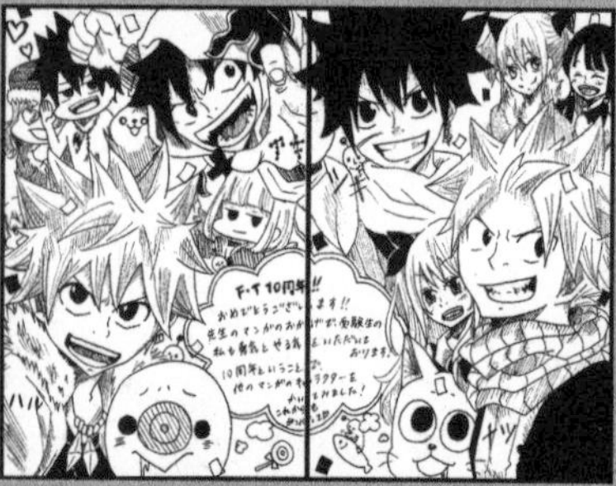

▲ Wooow... Lots of characters! Even ones from my past stories. Thank you!

▼ This Wendy is so cute! It just makes me feel better!

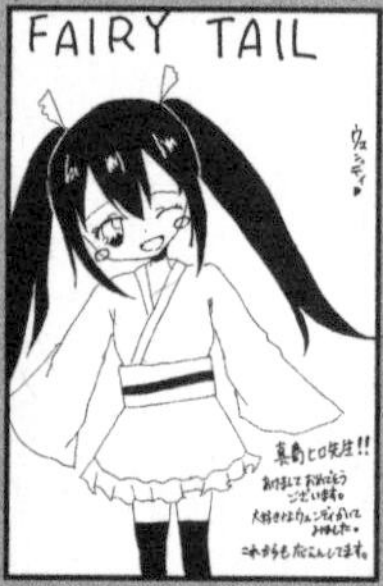
FAIRY TAIL

Tochigi Prefecture, NaaaMero-tan

Miyazaki Prefecture, Yûdai Iwamo

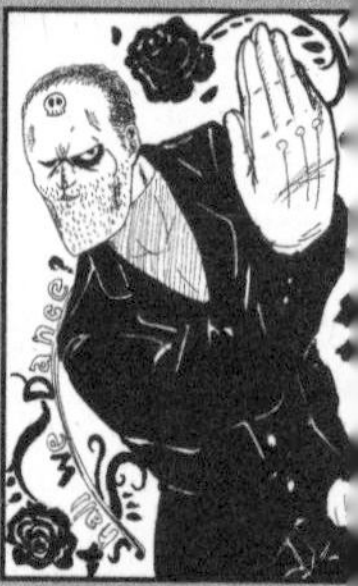

▲ Yaaay! A Jacob!! Huh? He wants to dance? With you?

REJECTION CORNER

Osaka, Harukaze Gokijetto

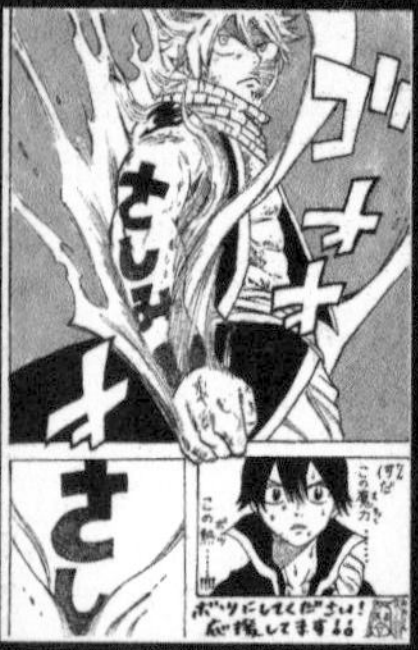

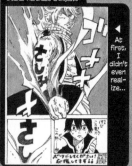

◀ At first, I didn't even realize...

▼ That way he's eating it makes it look so delicious! I'd like to eat it myself! Aye!

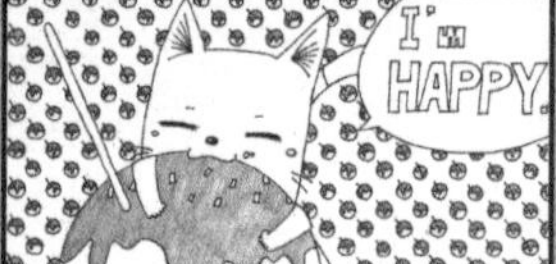
I'm
HAPPY

Nara Prefecture, Takumi Sakaki

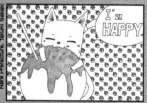

Any letters and post cards you send means that your personal information such as your name, address, postal code, and other information you include will be handed over, as is, to the author. When you send mail, please keep that in mind.

Okayama Prefecture, mei

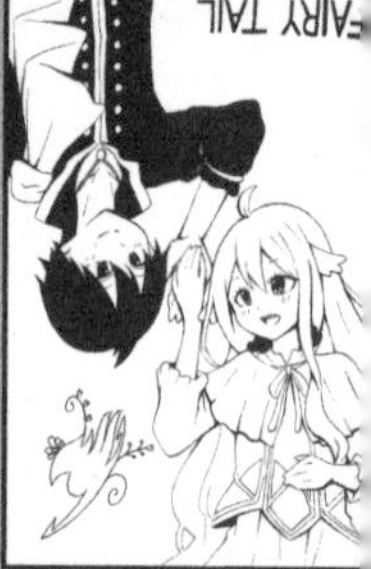

▲ I'm going to do the story of these two very soon. Really!

Spot the difference!

This image and the image on the title page of Chapter 517 on page 143 look exactly alike! But when you look closer, there's something a bit peculiar... There are a total of ten differences. Can you spot them all?

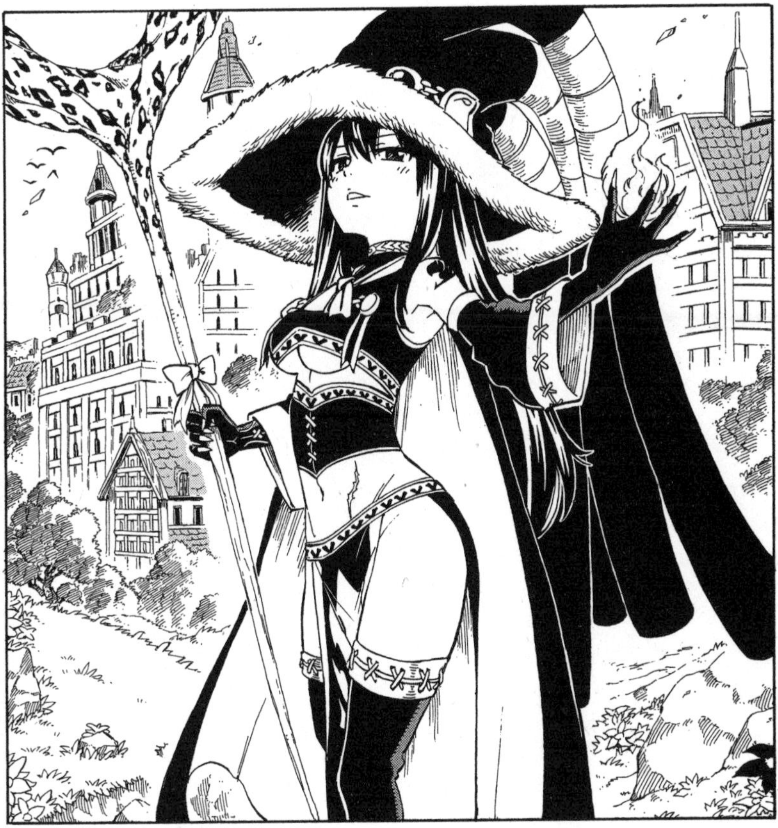

Afterword

There's a chapter this time where I give away some vital secrets regarding the dragon slayers. What did you think of it? Some people said, "How amazing that you planned this from the beginning!" and others said, "That's an awful thing to just tack on as an after thought!" but the thing I heard the most was, "Hmmm…" Well, I can't deny that I came up with it later, but most of the story's setup was thought up after Chapter 1. There was once an editor who said, "A story is a living thing." It has a tendency to grow and many aspects get added. You know, I didn't have everything set in stone from the very start, so as the story progressed, I thoughtfully added little by little to match it.

So, about Irene's setup. From well before she arrived, I had decided that she would be the mother of dragon slayers. But it may surprise you to learn that her relationship to Erza hadn't been decided then. That's why when she faced off against Acnologia earlier, I wasn't able to have the two talk about dragon slayer magic too much. Yup, it's because I still hadn't decided on her relationship to Erza. I should have been a bit more careful about what I did there.

Speaking of things that I thought up afterwards, I think I've written about this before, but nearly all of Erza's setup as a character was thought up after her introduction.

Back when she first showed up, I had decided on her magic and her relationship with Jellal (Siegrain). But I hadn't decided on how she would become mixed up with the various things that Natsu was up to. Things just started rolling along without perfect planning, but as if trying to prove that "a story is a living thing," Erza grew and became one of the most popular characters in Fairy Tail.

As long as it's a weekly manga series, there will always be a part that is "thought up after the fact." But still, not letting the reader see through that is one of the jobs of a professional, I suppose!

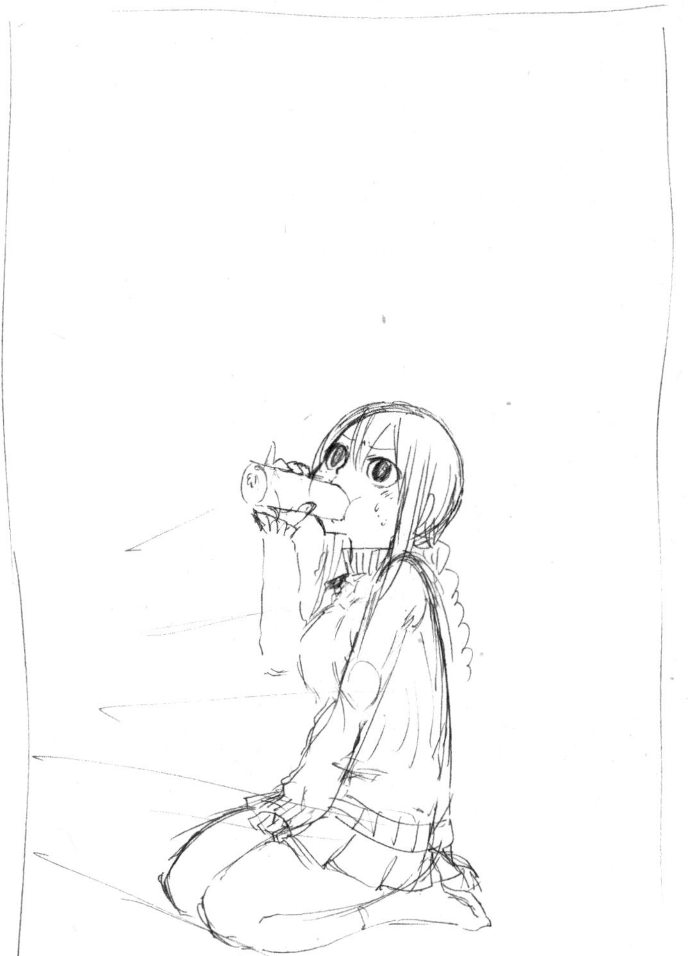

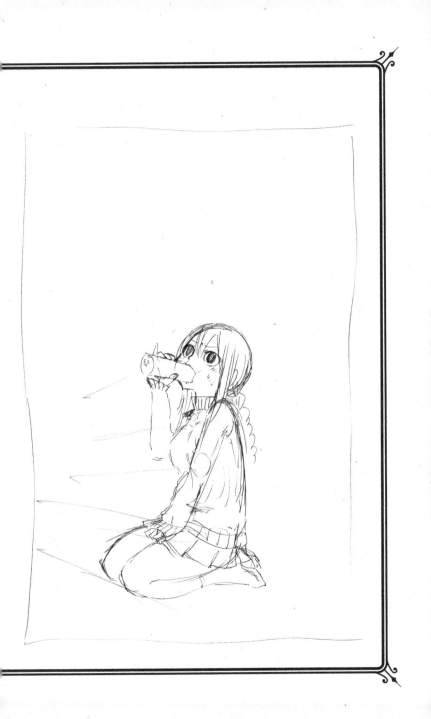

FAIRY TAIL

フェアリーテイル

60

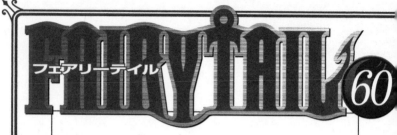

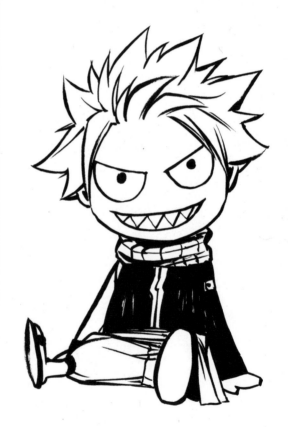

真島ヒロ

FROM  HIRO MASHIMA

I feel like I was just clamoring about the 50th volume, and now we're already at Volume 60!!
It's surprising how quickly it all goes by, isn't it?
Well, I'm sure some of you have begun to sense this, but this arc is Fairy Tail's final story.
I'm going to continue drawing, and charge to the end with all my might.
Your support from here on out would mean a lot to me.
Thank you very much.

Original Jacket Design: Hisao Ogawa

Translation Notes:

Japanese is a difficult language, and translation is often more art than science. For your edification and reading pleasure, here are notes on some of the places where we could have gone in a different direction with our translation of the work, or where a Japanese cultural reference is used.

Page 28, Akujiki no Kon

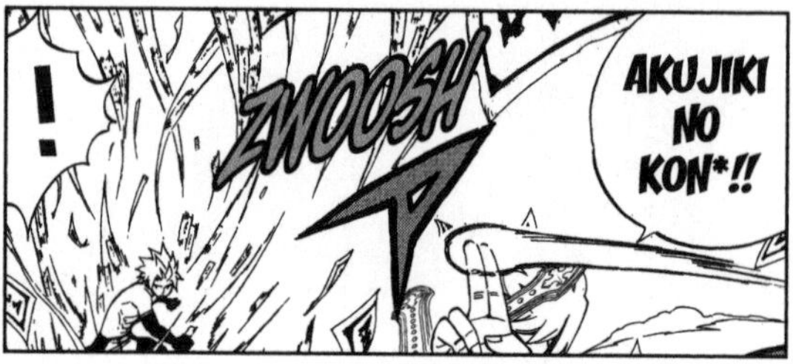
ZWOOSH
AKUJIKI NO KON*!!

The term, *akujiki* can mean a person who sometimes eats bizarre things, or a person who eats nothing but things that humans don't normally eat. In any case, it refers to eating unusual items. *Kon* uses the *kanji* for "soul."

Page 44, Fuda

The paper strips with writing that appear here are very common in Japan. The normal household *fuda* can be obtained at shrines and temples, and usually call on some supernatural power to protect the home from things such as fire or flood. However, *fuda* are often found in manga as indicating the boundaries of a magical ward or flying toward an opponent as part of a magical attack.

Page 52, Ashiginu

As mentioned in the notes of Volume 48, *ashiginu* is a coarse and thick variety of silk for cheap silk garments.

Page 75, Hanamaru

In some western elementary schools, a teacher may give the student a gold-star sticker for good work. In Japan, it tends to be a flower symbol called the *hanamaru*. It's usually drawn by hand in pen or pencil, and it marks correct answers or a "good effort" by the student.

Page 138, Deus Equis

Wendy has used this Enchant spell before during her fight with the Tartaros demon, Ezel. Although the Latin Equis is means "horse," in Japanese, it's written with the *kanji* for "knight."

Page 155, Deus Corona

With Equis and Corona, you'd think that Enchant magic is an advertisement for beer brands, but it's just Latin. In this case, Corona means "crown," and in the original Japanese manga, the *kanji* next to the pronunciation guide expresses that.

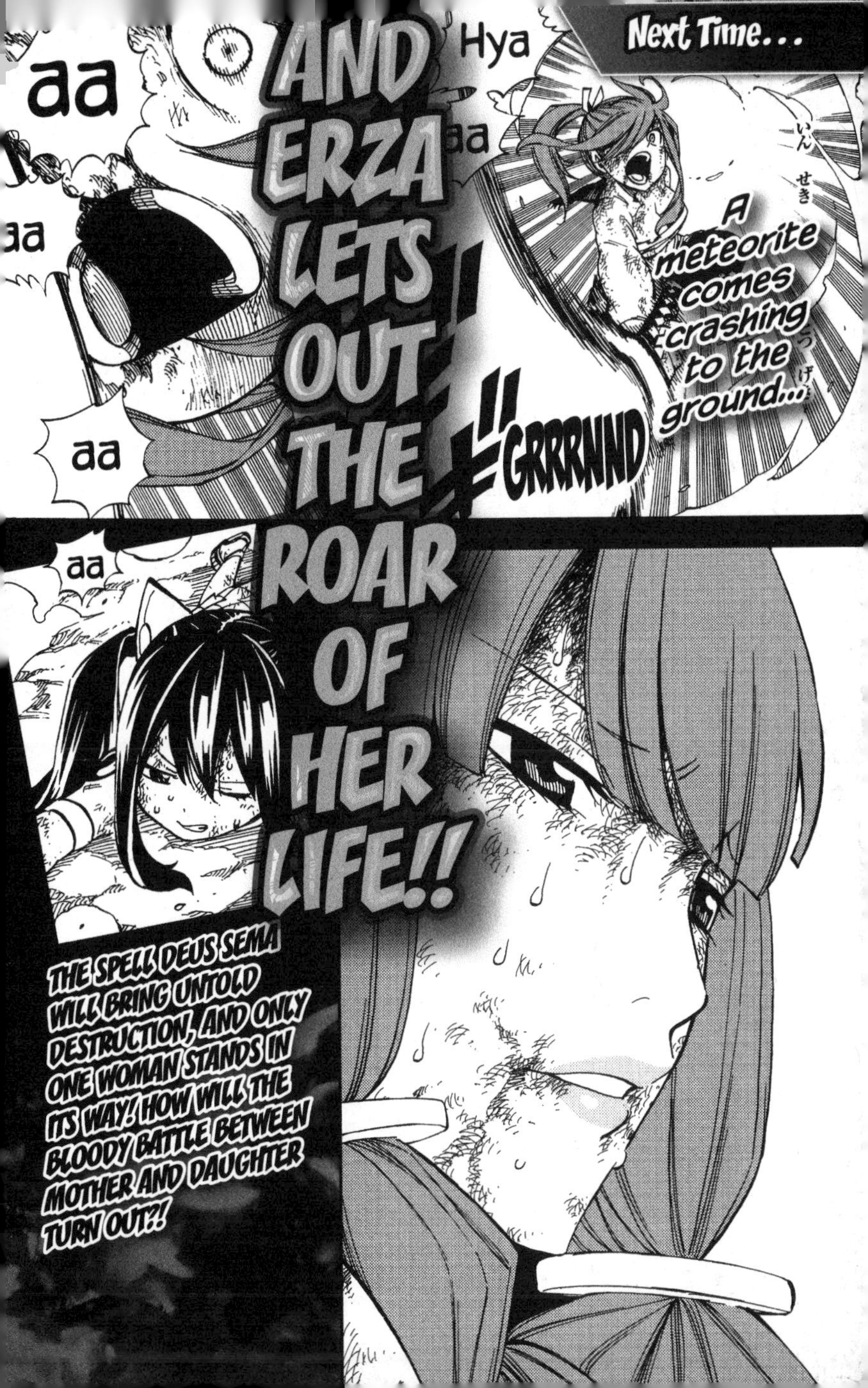
Next Time...
Hya
aa
A meteorite comes crashing to the ground...
GRRRNND
aa
aa
aa
aa
AND ERZA LETS OUT THE ROAR OF HER LIFE!!
aa
THE SPELL DEUS SEMA WILL BRING UNTOLD DESTRUCTION, AND ONLY ONE WOMAN STANDS IN ITS WAY! HOW WILL THE BLOODY BATTLE BETWEEN MOTHER AND DAUGHTER TURN OUT?!

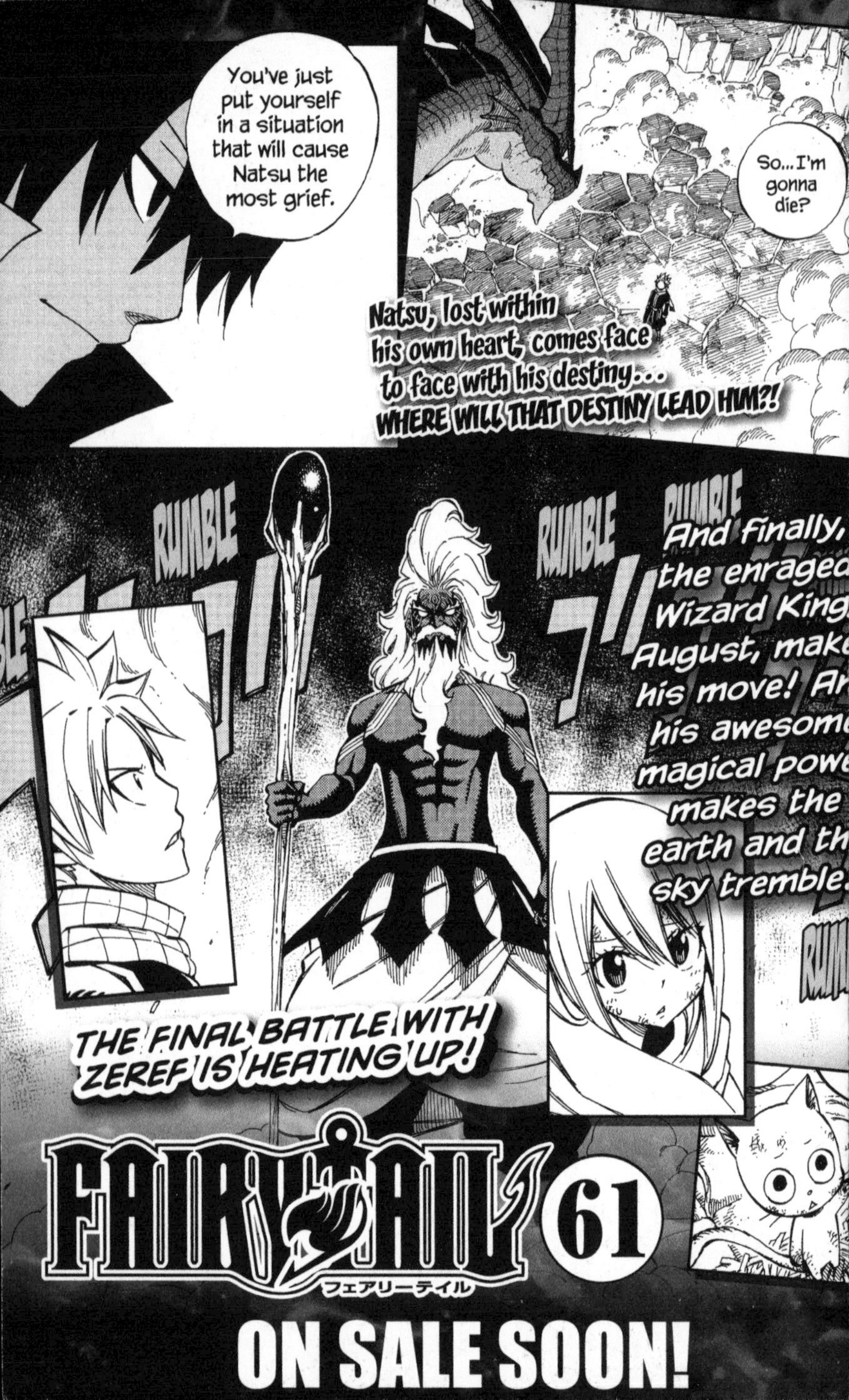
So...I'm gonna die?
Natsu, lost within his own heart, comes face to face with his destiny... WHERE WILL THAT DESTINY LEAD HIM?!
You've just put yourself in a situation that will cause Natsu the most grief.
RUMBLE
RUMBLE
And finally, the enraged Wizard King, August, make his move! An his awesome magical powe makes the earth and th sky tremble.
RUMBLE
THE FINAL BATTLE WITH ZEREF IS HEATING UP!
FAIRY TAIL 61
フェアリーテイル
ON SALE SOON!

Maria
THE VIRGIN WITCH

"Maria's brand of righteous justice, passion and plain talking make for one of the freshest manga series of 2015. I dare any other book to top it."
—UK Anime Network

PURITY AND POWER

As a war to determine the rightful ruler of medieval France ravages the land, the witch Maria decides she will not stand idly by as men kill each other in the name of God and glory. Using her powerful magic, she summons various beasts and demons —even going as far as using a succubus to seduce soldiers into submission under the veil of night— all to stop the needless slaughter. However, after the Archangel Michael puts an end to her meddling, he curses her to lose her powers if she ever gives up her virginity. Will she forgo the forbidden fruit of adulthood in order to bring an end to the merciless machine of war?
Available now in print and digitally!

KODANSHA COMICS

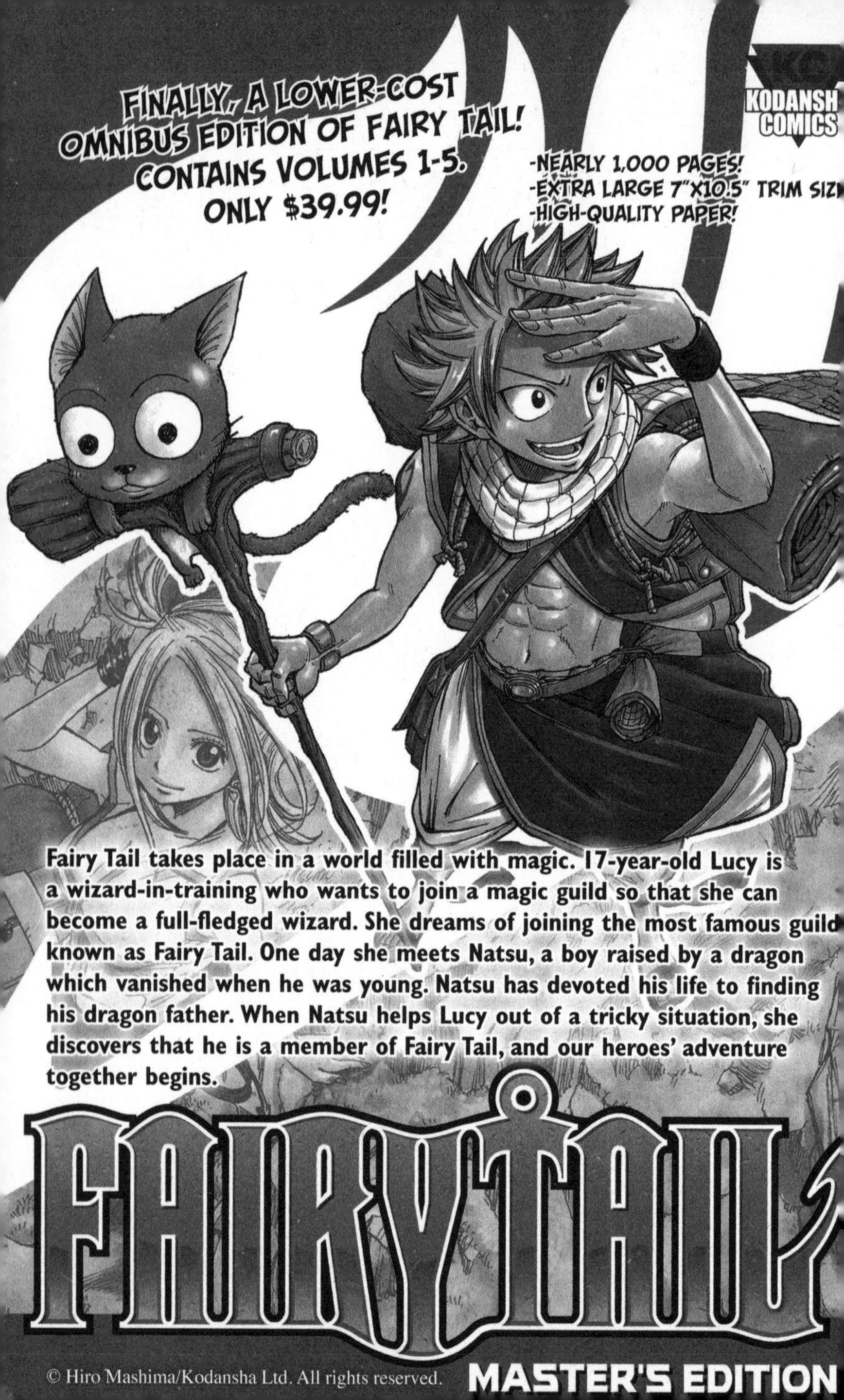
KODANSH COMICS
FINALLY, A LOWER-COST OMNIBUS EDITION OF FAIRY TAIL! CONTAINS VOLUMES 1-5. ONLY $39.99!
-NEARLY 1,000 PAGES!
-EXTRA LARGE 7"X10.5" TRIM SIZ
-HIGH-QUALITY PAPER!
Fairy Tail takes place in a world filled with magic. 17-year-old Lucy is a wizard-in-training who wants to join a magic guild so that she can become a full-fledged wizard. She dreams of joining the most famous guild known as Fairy Tail. One day she meets Natsu, a boy raised by a dragon which vanished when he was young. Natsu has devoted his life to finding his dragon father. When Natsu helps Lucy out of a tricky situation, she discovers that he is a member of Fairy Tail, and our heroes' adventure together begins.
FAIRY TAIL
MASTER'S EDITION
© Hiro Mashima/Kodansha Ltd. All rights reserved.

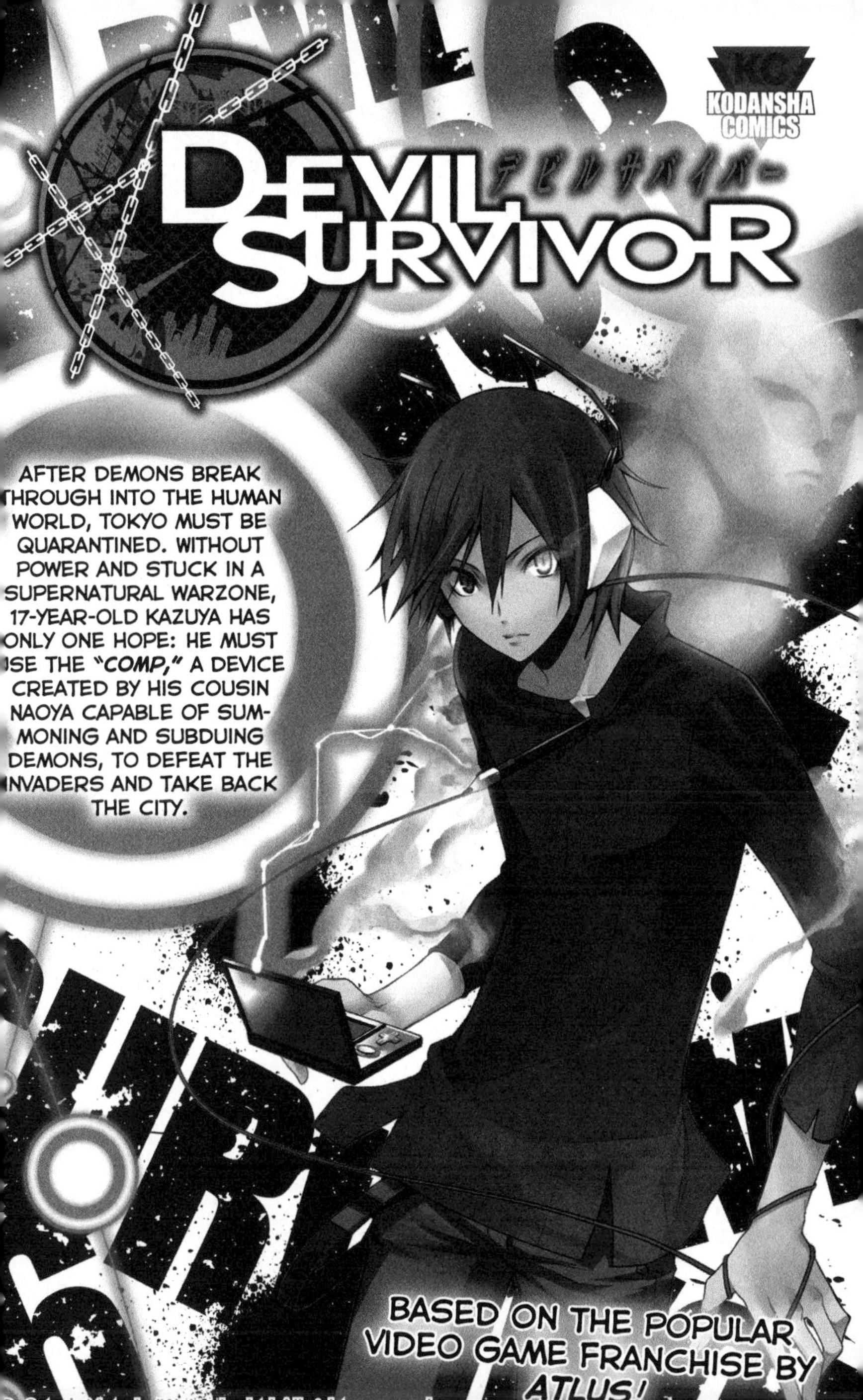
KODANSHA COMICS
DEVIL SURVIVOR
AFTER DEMONS BREAK THROUGH INTO THE HUMAN WORLD, TOKYO MUST BE QUARANTINED. WITHOUT POWER AND STUCK IN A SUPERNATURAL WARZONE, 17-YEAR-OLD KAZUYA HAS ONLY ONE HOPE: HE MUST USE THE *"COMP,"* A DEVICE CREATED BY HIS COUSIN NAOYA CAPABLE OF SUMMONING AND SUBDUING DEMONS, TO DEFEAT THE INVADERS AND TAKE BACK THE CITY.
BASED ON THE POPULAR VIDEO GAME FRANCHISE BY *ATLUS!*

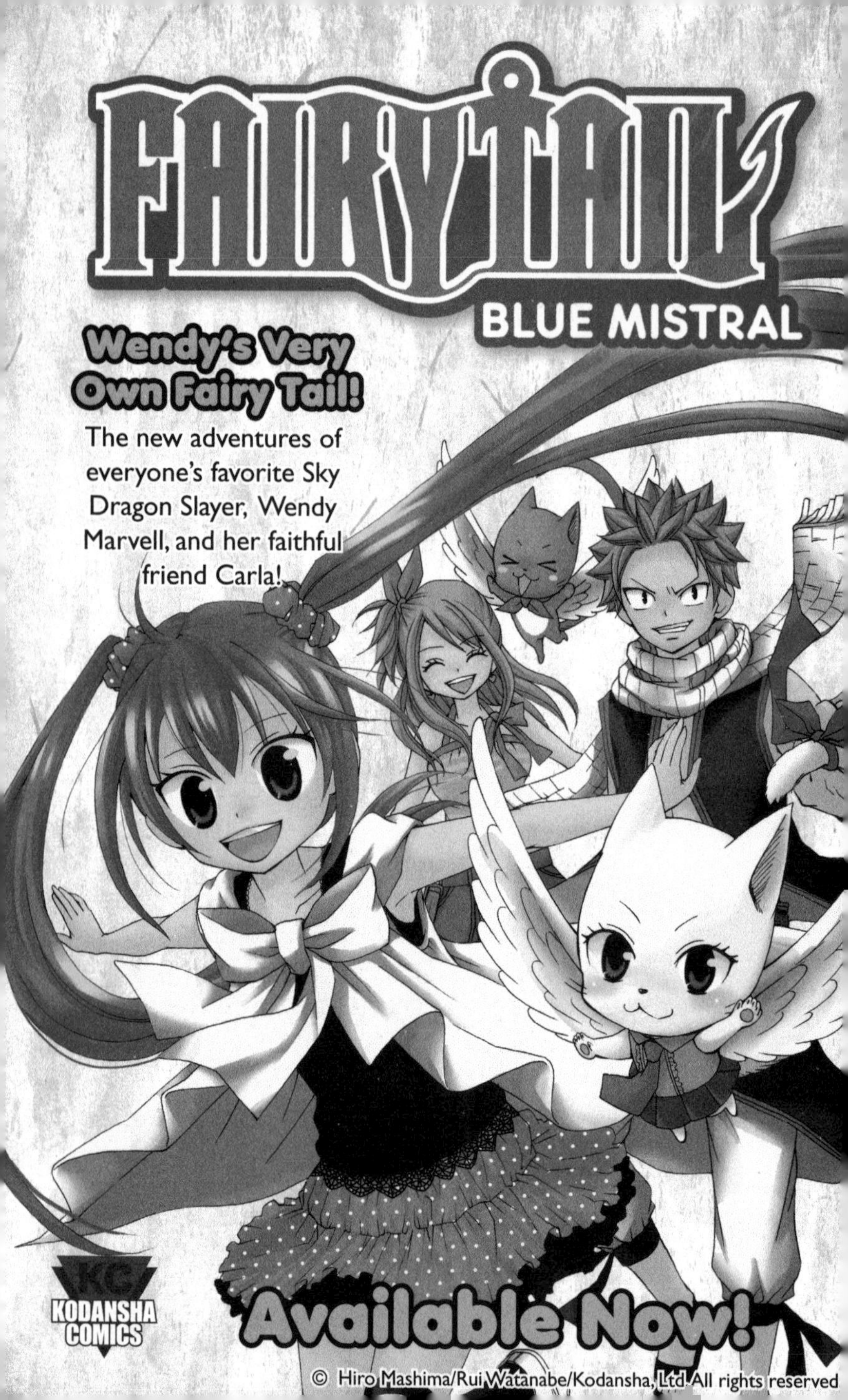

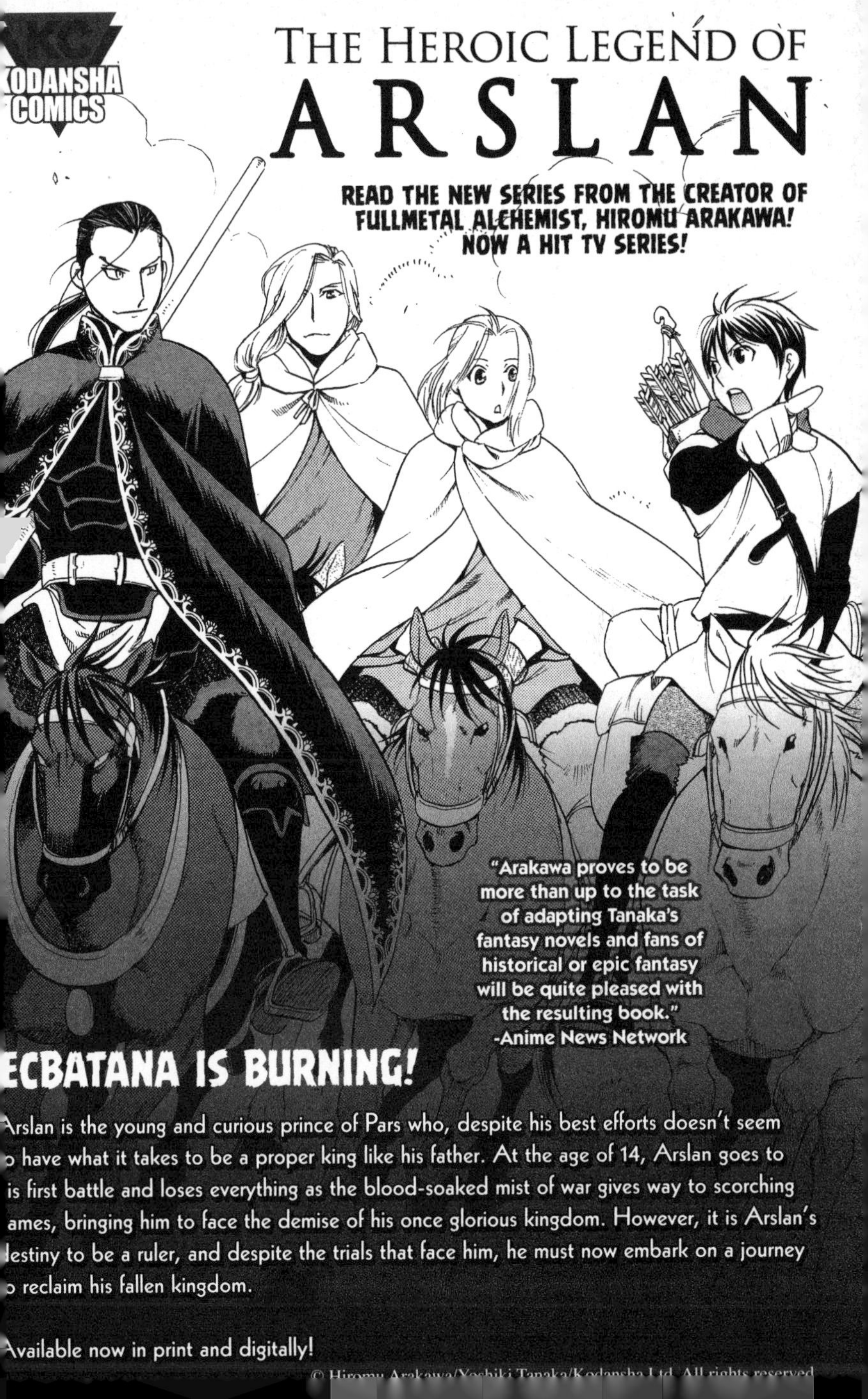
KODANSHA COMICS
THE HEROIC LEGEND OF
ARSLAN
READ THE NEW SERIES FROM THE CREATOR OF FULLMETAL ALCHEMIST, HIROMU ARAKAWA! NOW A HIT TV SERIES!
"Arakawa proves to be more than up to the task of adapting Tanaka's fantasy novels and fans of historical or epic fantasy will be quite pleased with the resulting book." -Anime News Network
ECBATANA IS BURNING!
Arslan is the young and curious prince of Pars who, despite his best efforts doesn't seem o have what it takes to be a proper king like his father. At the age of 14, Arslan goes to is first battle and loses everything as the blood-soaked mist of war gives way to scorching ames, bringing him to face the demise of his once glorious kingdom. However, it is Arslan's lestiny to be a ruler, and despite the trials that face him, he must now embark on a journey o reclaim his fallen kingdom.
Available now in print and digitally!
© Hiromu Arakawa/Yoshiki Tanaka/Kodansha Ltd. All rights reserved.

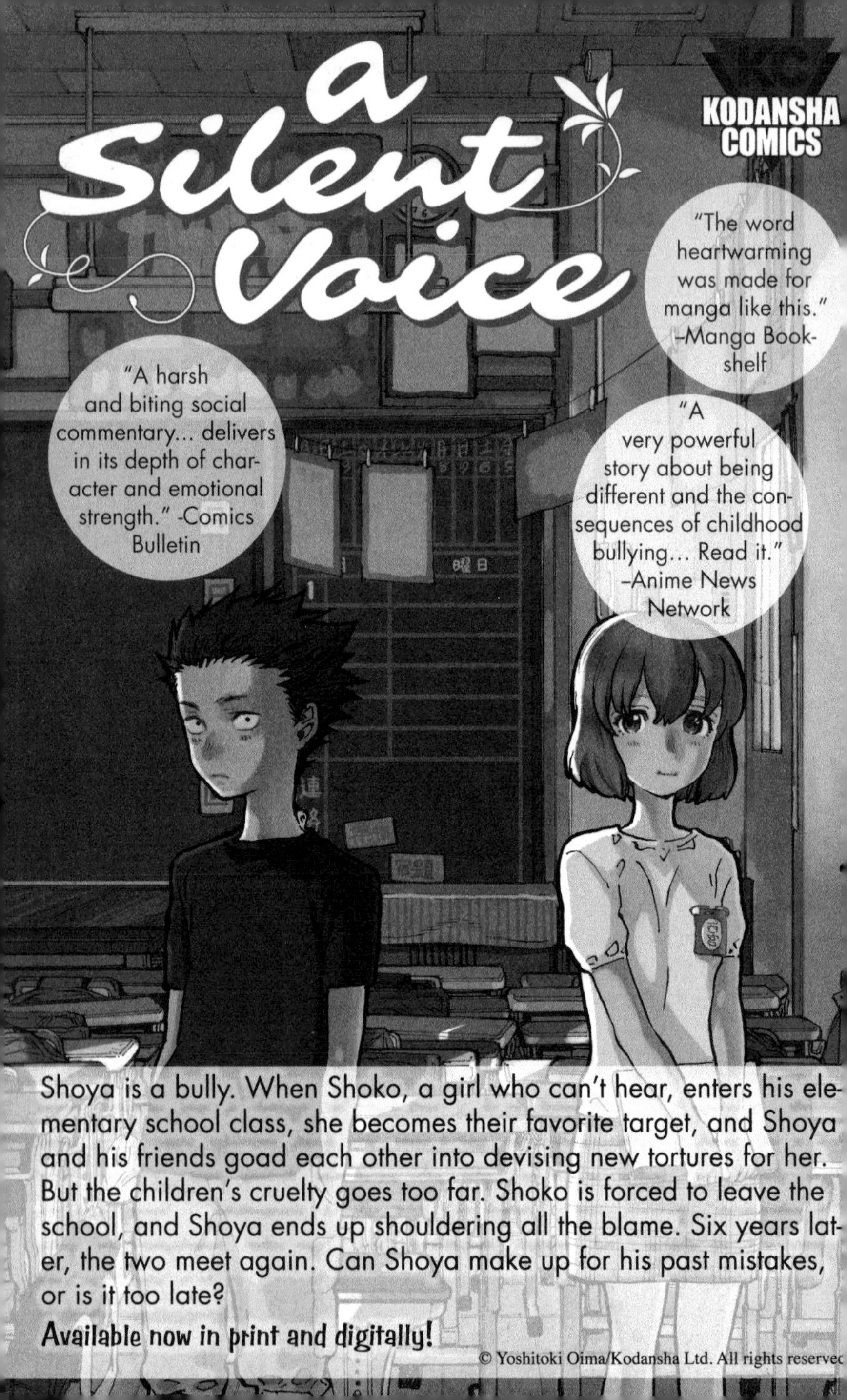
KODANSHA COMICS
a Silent Voice
"The word heartwarming was made for manga like this." –Manga Bookshelf
"A harsh and biting social commentary... delivers in its depth of character and emotional strength." -Comics Bulletin
"A very powerful story about being different and the consequences of childhood bullying… Read it." –Anime News Network
Shoya is a bully. When Shoko, a girl who can't hear, enters his elementary school class, she becomes their favorite target, and Shoya and his friends goad each other into devising new tortures for her. But the children's cruelty goes too far. Shoko is forced to leave the school, and Shoya ends up shouldering all the blame. Six years later, the two meet again. Can Shoya make up for his past mistakes, or is it too late?
Available now in print and digitally!
© Yoshitoki Oima/Kodansha Ltd. All rights reserved

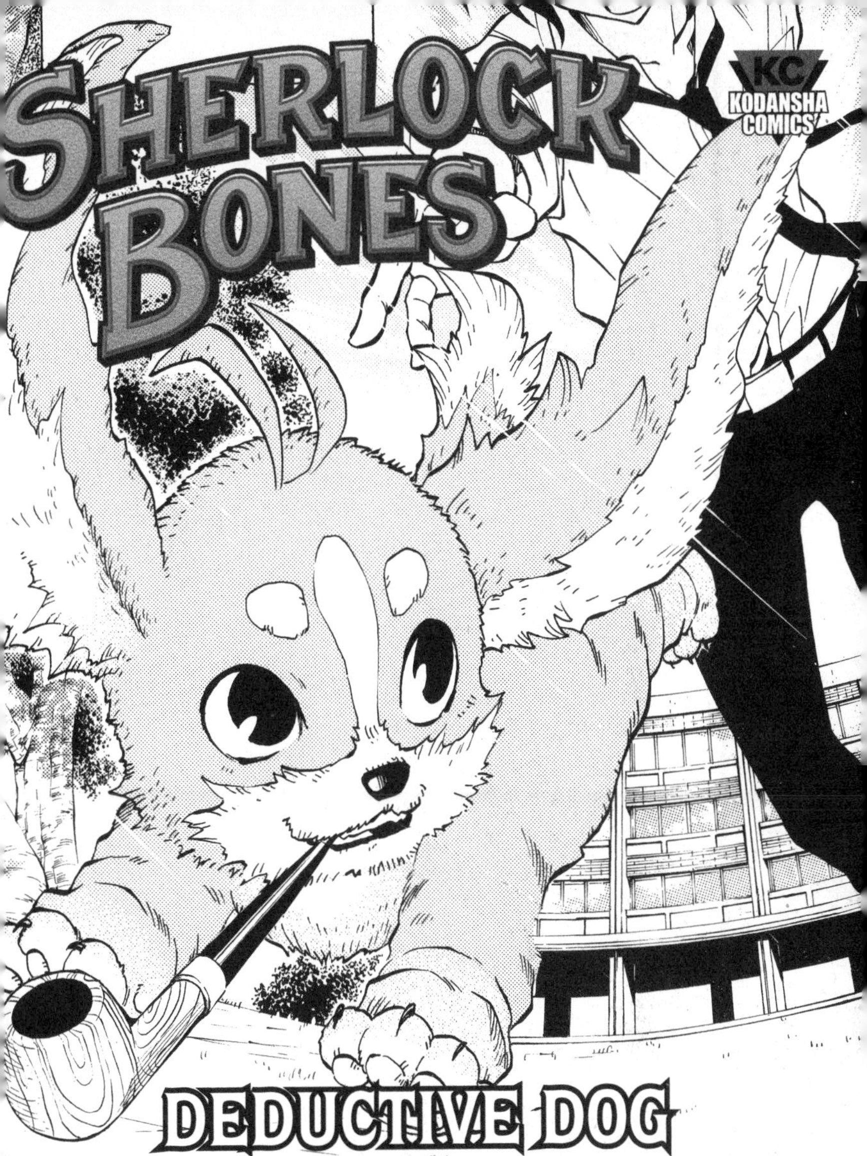
KC
KODANSHA COMICS
SHERLOCK BONES

DEDUCTIVE DOG DETECTIVE

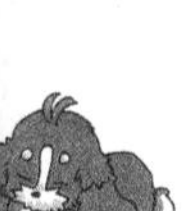

When Takeru adopts a new pet, he's in for a surprise—the dog is none other than the reincarnation of Sherlock Holmes. With no one else able to communicate with Holmes, Takeru is roped into becoming Sherdog's assistant, John Watson. Using his sleuthing skills, Holmes uncovers clues to solve the trickiest crimes.

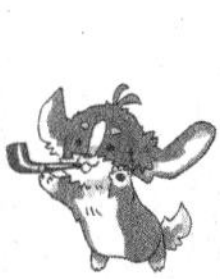

SAY I LOVE YOU.

KC
KODANSHA
COMICS

Mei Tachibana has no friends — and says she doesn't need them!
But everything changes when she accidentally roundhouse kicks the most popular boy in school! However, Yamato Kurosawa isn't angry in the slightest— in fact, he thinks his ordinary life could use an unusual girl like Mei. But winning Mei's trust will be a tough task. How long will she refuse to say, "I love you"?

SANKAREA

undying love

"I ONLY LIKE ZOMBIE GIRLS."

Chihiro has an unusual connection to zombie movies. He doesn't feel bad for the survivors – he wants to comfort the undead girls they slaughter! When his pet passes away, he brews a resurrection potion. He's discovered by local heiress Sanka Rea, and she serves as his first test subject!

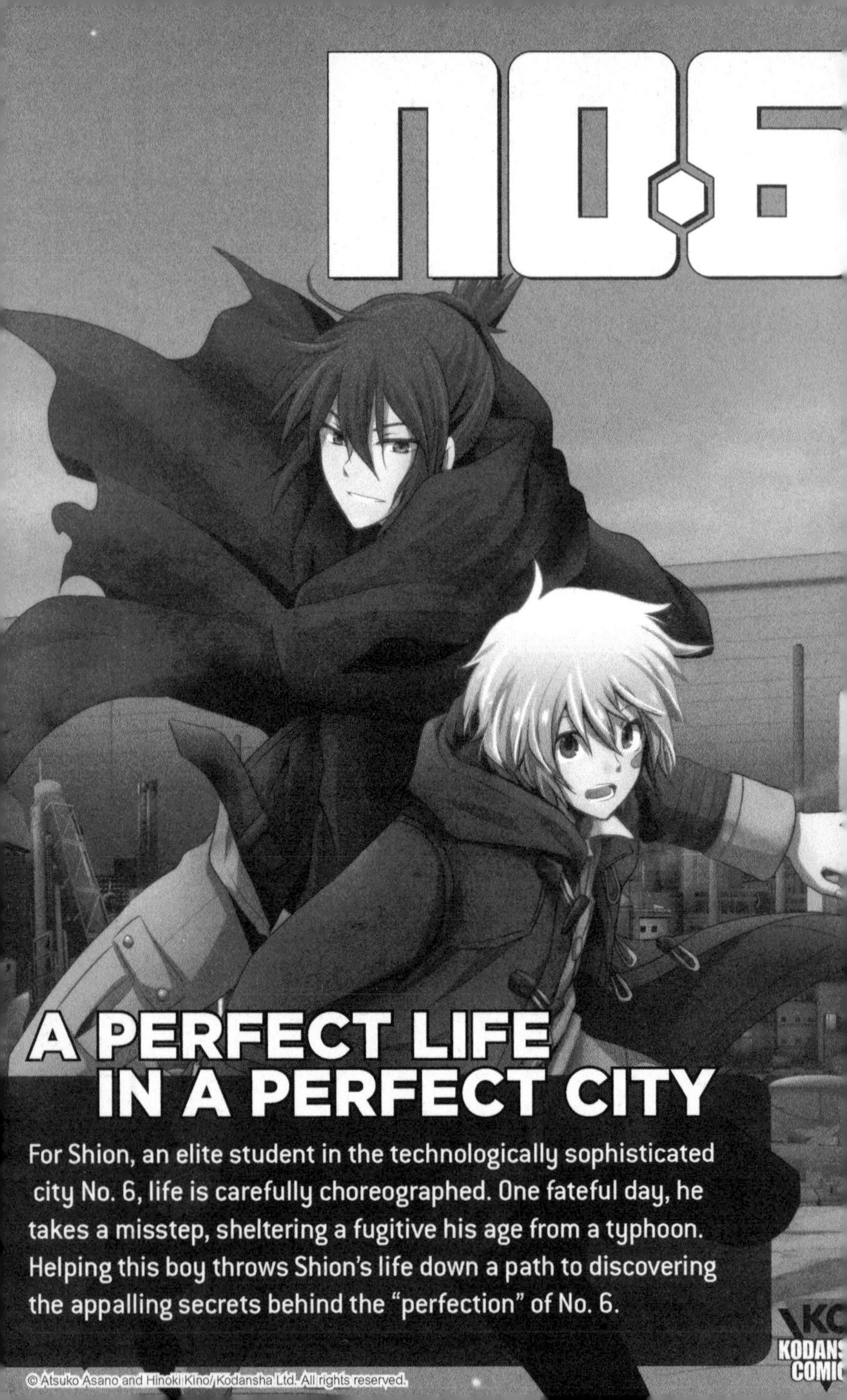
NO.6
A PERFECT LIFE
IN A PERFECT CITY
For Shion, an elite student in the technologically sophisticated city No. 6, life is carefully choreographed. One fateful day, he takes a misstep, sheltering a fugitive his age from a typhoon. Helping this boy throws Shion's life down a path to discovering the appalling secrets behind the "perfection" of No. 6.
KODANSHA COMICS
© Atsuko Asano and Hinoki Kino/Kodansha Ltd. All rights reserved.

A Kodansha Comics Trade Paperback Original.

Fairy Tail volume 60 copyright © 2017 Hiro Mashima
English translation copyright © 2017 Hiro Mashima

Published in the United States by Kodansha Comics, an imprint of Kodansha
USA Publishing, LLC, New York.

Publication rights for this English edition arranged through Kodansha Ltd.,
Tokyo.

First published in Japan in 2017 by Kodansha Ltd., Tokyo
ISBN 978-1-63236-336-7

Printed in the United States of America.

www.kodanshacomics.com

9 8 7 6 5 4 3 2 1

Translation: William Flanagan
Lettering: AndWorld Design
Editing: Haruko Hashimoto
Kodansha Comics edition cover design by Phil Balsman

TOMARE!

[STOP!]

You're going the wrong way!

Manga is a completely different type of reading experience.

To start at the *beginning,* go to the *end!*

at's right! Authentic manga is read the traditional Japanese way—om right to left, exactly the opposite of how American books are ad. It's easy to follow: Just go to the other end of the book and read ch page—and each panel—from right side to left side, starting at e top right. Now you're experiencing manga as it was meant to be!